U.S. Presidents and Latin American Interventions

ATLANTIC
OCEAN

Cuba

Dominican
Republic

Mexico

Honduras

Haiti

Dominica

St. Lucia

Barbados

Guatemala

Nicaragua

Grenada

El Salvador

Costa Rica

Venezuela

British
Guiana

Panama

Colombia

Peru

Brazil

Bolivia

Paraguay

PACIFIC
OCEAN

Chile

Argentina

Uruguay

0   500 mi

0   800 km

U.S. Presidents and Latin American Interventions

Pursuing Regime Change in the Cold War

Michael Grow

University Press of Kansas

Published by the University Press of Kansas (Lawrence, Kansas 66045), which was
organized by the Kansas Board of Regents and is operated and funded by Emporia
State University, Fort Hays State University, Kansas State University, Pittsburg State
University, the University of Kansas, and Wichita State University

Library of Congress Cataloging-in-Publication Data

Grow, Michael.
  U.S. presidents and Latin American interventions : pursuing regime change in the
Cold War / Michael Grow.
     p. cm.
  Includes bibliographical references and index.
  ISBN 978-0-7006-1586-5 (cloth : alk. paper)
  1. United States—Foreign relations—Latin America. 2. Latin America—Foreign
relations—United States. 3. United States—Foreign relations—1945–1989—Case
studies. 4. Presidents—United States—Decision making—Case studies.
5. Intervention (International law)—History—20th century—Case studies.
6. Regime change—Latin America—History—20th century—Case studies. I. Title.
II. Title: US presidents and Latin American interventions.
  F1418.G83 2008
  327.73080090'45—dc22   2008007364

British Library Cataloguing-in-Publication Data is available.

Printed in the United States of America

10 9 8 7 6 5 4 3 2 1

The paper used in this publication is recycled and contains 50 percent postconsumer
waste. It is acid free and meets the minimum requirements of the American National
Standard for Permanence of Paper for Printed Library Materials Z39.48–1992.

To Catherine and Nathaniel

Contents

Preface

David Atlee Phillips faced a moral dilemma. It was March 1954, and the young American newspaper editor was being recruited by the Central Intelligence Agency to assist in the overthrow of Guatemala's government. The assignment, an agency official indicated, was to conduct psychological-warfare operations for a U.S. proxy army of Guatemalan dissidents that was about to launch a revolution against President Jacobo Arbenz. "But Arbenz became President in a free election," Phillips protested. "What right do we have to help someone to topple his government and throw him out of office?" The problem, his CIA contacts explained, was that Arbenz was "drifting more and more to the left" and "responding more and more to overtures from Moscow"; in the agency's view, it was simply "unacceptable to have a Commie running Guatemala." Phillips remained ambivalent. "I'm still not sure that gives us the right to intervene," he responded.[1]

Despite lingering misgivings, Phillips eventually decided to lend his services to what he regarded as the CIA's "brazen intervention" in Guatemala. Even after the operation had succeeded in ousting Arbenz, however, he continued to ponder the morality of his involvement, wondering—as he put it—"whether I was pleased with myself or not." In the end, Phillips was able to persuade himself that the intervention had been "a justifiable act of American foreign policy," and he took comfort in the knowledge that President Eisenhower had not had "any moral qualms about sponsoring it."[2]

Eisenhower's overthrow of the Guatemalan government in 1954 was the first in a long series of U.S. interventions in Latin America and the Caribbean during the Cold War. In 1961, the Kennedy administration sponsored an unsuccessful invasion of Fidel Castro's Cuba. In 1963, Kennedy carried out a covert operation that undermined the government of Cheddi Jagan in British Guiana. In 1964, Lyndon Johnson deployed U.S. forces in support of a Brazilian military coup that overthrew the government of President João Goulart. A year later, Johnson carried out a full-scale U.S. military invasion of the Dominican Republic. In 1970, the Nixon administration secretly intervened in Chile in an attempt to block Salvador Allende's inauguration as president. In 1981, Ronald Reagan launched a campaign of U.S.-sponsored covert warfare against Nicaragua's Sandinista government. Two years later, in 1983, Reagan ordered a major U.S. military assault on the Caribbean microstate of Grenada. And in 1989, the Bush administration conducted a massive U.S. military invasion of Panama that toppled dictator Manuel Noriega. All told, six of the nine U.S. presidents who occupied the White House during the Cold War carried out at least one major intervention against a perceived enemy in the Western Hemisphere during their terms in office.

For students of contemporary history, the obvious and challenging question is, Why? Why did so many of our recent presidents opt to deploy the military might and subversive power at their disposal to overthrow the governments of their neighbors? Why did interventionism in Latin America and the Caribbean become such a regularly recurring feature of U.S. foreign policy during the Cold War?

The standard scholarly explanations—reflected in a vast body of case-specific literature on individual interventions—emphasize two traditional factors: U.S. national-security concerns and U.S. economic interests. There is, without question, ample evidence to document the presence of each of those factors in every episode of U.S. intervention.

Throughout the Cold War, U.S. presidents tended to view Marxist elements in Latin America and the Caribbean as agents of Soviet imperialism and hence as threats to U.S. national security. Eisenhower intervened in Guatemala in part out of concern that communist functionaries in Arbenz's reformist government were exercising a degree of influence that would soon produce an initial beachhead for Soviet imperialism in the Western Hemisphere. Kennedy's efforts to rid Cuba of Castro stemmed from U.S. perceptions that Fidel was allowing Cuba's communists to subvert his revolution and that in the process the Soviets were acquiring a strategic ally 90 miles from the U.S. mainland. Kennedy authorized a covert CIA intervention in British Guiana partly out of concern that the Marxist Jagan government intended to align the soon-to-be-independent British colony with Cuba and the Soviet Union. Johnson supported the 1964 Brazilian military coup in the belief that the increasingly radical tone of Goulart's populist rhetoric was leading to intensified polarization and potential class warfare that might end in a communist takeover of Latin America's largest nation. Johnson injected U.S. military power into a 1965 civil war in the Dominican Republic in response to the reported presence of "Castroite Communists" among the rebel leadership, and he used the occasion to proclaim his Johnson Doctrine: that henceforth the United States would exercise the right of unilateral military intervention to prevent any communist government from coming to power in the Western Hemisphere. Richard Nixon attempted to subvert Chilean politics, among other reasons, in order to prevent Allende's Marxist regime from serving as the stimulus for a domino-like series of communist victories in the Andes. Reagan conducted military interventions in Central America and the Caribbean to prevent local Marxist forces thought to be linked to a "Moscow-Havana Axis" from expanding the communist bloc's geopolitical influence and military power in a region deemed vital to U.S. security. As the Cold War wound down, George H. W. Bush justified his invasion of Panama as a critical step in the U.S. "war on drugs" at a time when Americans were beginning to regard international narcotics trafficking as a greater threat to their national security than international communism.

Each U.S. intervention also occurred in a hemispheric nation where U.S. economic interests were perceived to be at risk. Shortly before his U.S.-sponsored overthrow, Arbenz had expropriated a majority of the U.S.-owned United Fruit Company's properties in Guatemala. Castro was preparing to nationalize nearly $1 billion in private U.S. investment capital in Cuba at the time of the Bay of Pigs invasion. Jagan had threatened to nationalize British Guiana's foreign-owned bauxite deposits (a valuable resource for the North American aluminum industry) prior to Kennedy's decision to intervene. Goulart was advocating a broad range of nationalistic economic reforms—including legislation to limit the profit remittances of U.S. corporations in Brazil—prior to his overthrow by pro-U.S. military forces. Juan Bosch and his rebel forces in the Dominican Republic had alienated U.S. officials with proposals to curtail foreign ownership of their country's land and sugar resources prior to the 1965 U.S. invasion. Allende was preparing to carry out a sweeping nationalization of U.S. capital in Chile, including the holdings of the International Telephone & Telegraph Company and the major U.S. copper companies, when Nixon ordered the CIA to block his inauguration. Reagan administration officials regularly warned that if Nicaragua's Sandinistas were allowed to export their Marxist revolution to neighboring countries, the result would be a torrent of Central American political refugees into the United States, overloading the nation's welfare system and further straining its already deficit-ridden domestic economy. Marxist Grenada was viewed by the Reagan administration as a serious threat to U.S. control of vital Caribbean sea-lanes, through which—according to Reagan's estimate— nearly half of U.S. trade, two-thirds of the nation's oil imports, and a majority of its imported strategic materials passed. Bush's invasion of Panama took place days before managerial control of the commercially significant Panama Canal was scheduled to be transferred to Manuel Noriega's increasingly nationalistic dictatorship.

As originally conceived, this book was to be an inquiry into the relative influence of economic and security factors on this long list of hemispheric interventions. From the start, research proceeded from the assumption that the key to identifying interventionist causation was to focus on the highest level of U.S. decision-making authority: the White House. In examining the concerns that led Cold War presidents and their Oval Office advisers to unleash the CIA or 82nd Airborne on perceived enemies in neighboring countries, however, it soon became apparent that the factors of national security and economic self-interest provided an inadequate analytical framework for explaining U.S. interventionism. Instead, it became increasingly evident that three entirely different factors—U.S. international credibility, U.S. domestic politics, and lobbying by Latin American and Caribbean political actors—consistently combined to exert decisive influence on presidential decisions to intervene.

The internal record of White House deliberations in the lead-up to each intervention reveals, first, that the incumbent administration's top leaders opted for intervention in the belief that the international image of the United States would be weakened if they failed to take aggressive action—and that by moving forcefully against an unfriendly regime in the U.S. sphere of influence they would increase respect for U.S. power in the eyes of the international community. Every intervention was in that sense a deliberate demonstration to other nations—Eastern bloc adversaries, Western allies, and fence-sitting neutrals alike—that the United States remained a strong, resolute, "credible" global superpower fully capable of projecting its power in defense of its interests—a signal to the rest of the world that, in the parlance of the period, the United States was no paper tiger or helpless giant.

The record also reveals that every intervention was to some extent a conscious attempt on the part of the White House to advance the domestic political interests of the president. To suggest that Cold War presidents factored calculations of political self-interest into their foreign-policy decisions may strike some readers as an overcynical interpretation reminiscent of the 1997 motion picture *Wag the Dog*, in which a fictional U.S. president declares war on Albania to divert public attention from a sex scandal at home. As the following chapters make clear, however, domestic political considerations of one form or another—pressure to live up to militant campaign promises, the need to project an image of bold, assertive presidential leadership to domestic political constituencies, a desire to protect the president from partisan accusations that he "lost one on his watch," thereby denying his political enemies a potentially damaging issue on which to attack his administration or party in future election campaigns—*did* factor into every presidential determination to launch an intervention.

But it also became evident as research progressed that to focus exclusively on White House–centered, Washington, D.C.–based decision making risked overlooking another significant element of interventionist causation: the influence of Latin American and Caribbean political actors. The suggestion that citizens of Latin America and the Caribbean played vital roles in instigating U.S. interventions in their countries seems, on the surface, to fly in the face of logic—what influence, after all, can the weak exert over the strong? And yet there is abundant evidence that in every episode of U.S. intervention members of the local elites—Guatemalan conservatives, Cuban exiles, Dominican military officers, wealthy Chilean businessmen, opposition Guianese and Panamanian politicians, the conservative leaders of Nicaragua's and Grenada's regional neighbors—were actively at work promoting intervention in their own self-interest, helping to shape White House perceptions and U.S. strategies in the process. Every intervention unfolded against a contextual backdrop in which local elements were providing U.S. officials with an alarmist (and frequently exaggerated, if not distorted) picture of threats to U.S. interests in their country, inviting the United States to intervene, offering their services as instruments of U.S. intervention, and/or presenting themselves as viable alternatives to the anti-American forces that they were urging the United States to overthrow. In every case, local political actors played an influential, and in some cases decisive, role in the U.S. decision to intervene.

It is this multicausal structure—emphasizing credibility concerns, domestic politics, and (to paraphrase historian Geir Lundestad) "intervention by invitation"[3]—that provides the interpretive framework for the case studies that follow.

It may be helpful at the outset to define more specifically what this book is and what it is not. What it *is* is a fresh interpretation of the root causes of U.S. interventionism in the Western Hemisphere during the Cold War—a reconceptualization that seeks to move the historiography of hemispheric interventionism beyond old orthodoxies of "security versus economics" by incorporating previously underemphasized factors of politics, credibility, and Latin American/Caribbean agency into the equation. It is *not* a descriptive history of the interventions themselves. Readers seeking detailed accounts of the operational aspects of the various interventions will be disappointed and should refer to the Essential Sources for relevant sources. Nor is this book an assessment of the *consequences* of U.S. interventionism. Several of the interventions under discussion (Guatemala, Chile, Nicaragua) were immediately followed by long, tragic interludes of political bloodshed and (in the Guatemalan and Chilean cases) authoritarian brutality. Others (the Dominican Republic, Grenada, Panama) led to the installation (or reinstallation) of conservative, pro-U.S. democratic governments. One of the interventions (British Guiana) opened the way for the establishment of a corrupt, personalistic, quasi-socialist dictatorship, while another (Cuba) inadvertently helped the incumbent revolutionaries strengthen their totalitarian grip on power. These diverse outcomes—and moral judgments about them—are not the focus of this project, and readers interested in such issues have an extensive literature available to them, some of it cited in the Essential Sources. This book also does not examine Latin American/Caribbean reactions to the interventions or the impact that U.S. interventionism had on Cold War Latin American/Caribbean attitudes toward the United States, consequences that again lie beyond the project's purview. Instead, I focus on the interventionist decision-making process and the factors that prompted U.S. leaders to pursue regime change in neighboring countries. It is, in short, about causation and causation alone.

In a fundamental sense, *U.S. Presidents and Latin American Interventions* would not have been written without the friendship and support that I have received over the years from a long list of professional colleagues, among them Peter Klarén, Abraham Lowenthal, Howard Wiarda, John Gaddis, Alonzo Hamby, and Steven

Miner. The book benefited immeasurably from the interpretive insights and research efforts of many of my graduate students in the Contemporary History Institute and Latin American Studies Program at Ohio University, including Michael Hall, Gil Hallows, Michael Ruhl, Ariel Armony, Mirna Kolbowski, Richard "D. J." Clinton, James Anderson, Victor "Scott" Kaufman, Steve Taaffe, Carlos Guevara Mann, Federico Veírave, Angela Young, Scott Miller, Janet Westrick, Christopher Lapos, George Kourous, Bryan Whitford, John Ruedisueli, Ricardo Gonzalez, Brian Straight, Lazarus O'Sako, Dewan Chowdhury, Jesus Sanchez Meleán, Philippe Girard, and Steven George. I owe a particular debt of gratitude to Michael Briggs, editor in chief of the University Press of Kansas, for his remarkable patience and steadfast support. Constructive critiques by the two distinguished scholars who reviewed the manuscript for the University Press of Kansas, Mark Gilderhus and John Prados, helped to make the final product a better book. Finally, Kara Dunfee, the administrative associate at Ohio University's Contemporary History Institute, cheerfully provided invaluable technical assistance throughout the manuscript-preparation process. To all of the aforementioned: thank you.

CHAPTER ONE
Guatemala, 1954

President Eisenhower was "immensely pleased." Secretary of State John Foster Dulles was "exultant." CIA Director Allen Dulles felt "giddy" and "exuberant." It was early July 1954, and the Eisenhower administration was secretly celebrating an important international victory. A few days earlier, an improbable CIA experiment in covert intervention had succeeded in forcing the government of Jacobo Arbenz from power in Guatemala.[1]

The Guatemalan operation, code-named "PBSUCCESS," was a masterpiece of psychological warfare and bluff.[2] Throughout May 1954, CIA "black propaganda," clandestine radio warfare, and sabotage operations concocted the impression that a powerful "liberation army" of Guatemalan exiles was about to overthrow the Arbenz regime. Then, with anxiety spreading throughout the country and the government's nerves wearing thin—with the target softened up—the operation's endgame commenced. On June 17, a minuscule paramilitary force of 480 CIA-trained Guatemalan insurgents and foreign mercenaries, commanded by the former Guatemalan army colonel Carlos Castillo Armas, began moving into Guatemala. The CIA proxy army's "armed invasion" was designed to traumatize the Arbenz regime and its support base within the Guatemalan armed forces by conveying the distorted impression that "very substantial military strength" was moving to destroy them.[3]

From its conception, the Guatemalan intervention had been predicated on the assumption that psychological intimidation and a skillfully conducted war of nerves would cause the Guatemalan armed forces to abandon Arbenz and force his resignation. For months the U.S. embassy and U.S. military missions in Guatemala had put enormous pressure on Guatemalan officers to oust Arbenz, hinting that if they failed to act the Eisenhower administration might be forced to resort to direct U.S. military intervention. Castillo Armas' June invasion consequently had a profoundly demoralizing impact on the Guatemalan armed forces, as intended. Guatemalan military commanders feared that Castillo Armas' tiny "Army of Liberation" was "part of a larger US plan to create a pretext for direct intervention" and that if they defeated Castillo Armas militarily—a relatively easy assignment for Guatemala's 6,000-man army—they would face devastating U.S. retribution in the form of a military invasion. Overwhelmed by the "gnawing fear" of a prospective "head-on collision" with U.S. military forces, the Guatemalan Army refused to fight Castillo Armas and instead informed Arbenz that he must resign the presidency or face removal by the military. Arbenz, lacking an armed counterweight to the defecting army, stepped down on June 27th—in effect de-

1

posed in a military coup produced by U.S. intimidation and deception. Even the operation's CIA planners found the denouement "curious and magical."[4]

Why did Eisenhower overthrow Arbenz? Published histories of the intervention have offered a variety of answers ranging from anticommunist paranoia, to protection of U.S. investors, to "imperial hubris."[5] More than a half century after the event, however, a definitive explanation of Eisenhower's motives remains elusive. The key undoubtedly lies in the president's "threat perceptions" during his early months in office, when the intervention was conceived and planned. Eisenhower entered office with a powerful and widely shared perception that Soviet-directed international communism was engaged in a relentless pursuit of world domination. By the time of his inauguration in January 1953, Eastern Europe had been absorbed into the Soviet sphere of influence, Berlin had been subjected to a yearlong Soviet blockade, and a newly acquired Soviet nuclear capability had added a terrifying dimension to the communist state's already formidable military arsenal. In Asia, China had fallen, and communist armies were fighting to seize control of Korea and Indochina. In the Middle East and Latin America, where communist parties and front organizations were collaborating with the regions' nationalist reform movements, Eisenhower identified two flash points of imminent danger as he entered office: Iran, which in the president's words was "almost ready to fall into Communist hands," and Guatemala, where "Communism was striving to establish its first beachhead in the Americas."[6]

The origin of the Guatemalan "threat" was a 1944 revolution in which a coalition of middle-class reformers—predominantly university students, teachers, and junior army officers—ended a seventy-year era of corrupt, repressive oligarchical rule. Guatemala's statistical profile at the time of the 1944 revolution reflected the classic patterns of Latin American underdevelopment in their purest forms. Some 300 upper-class families and a handful of U.S. companies controlled the country's economy—a classic monocultural economy overwhelmingly dependent on coffee and fruit exports to U.S. markets. Roughly 2 percent of Guatemala's 2.5 million population owned 72 percent of the land, most of which remained uncultivated and inaccessible to the country's peasants. Wages for agricultural workers ranged between five and twenty-five cents a day, and Mayan Indians (who constituted two-thirds of Guatemala's population) were still subject to a variety of forced labor requirements. Over 70 percent of the population was illiterate (the second highest figure in Latin America at the time), while in Indian communities illiteracy rates surpassed 90 percent. Life expectancy was less than forty years; the infant-mortality rate more than 50 percent. Annual per capita income averaged $180, with two-thirds of the population earning approximately $70 per year.[7] It was this neofeudal national reality of elite domination, poverty, and dependency that Guatemala's middle-class revolutionaries of 1944 proposed to transform.

In many respects, the Guatemalan revolution was a rather typical example of prevailing political trends in Latin America during the 1940s. Throughout the region, nationalist revolutionary movements were mobilizing to attack the entrenched upper-class oligarchies that had dominated their countries' power structures for a century or more. Invariably, the revolutionary forces were multiclass in composition, with middle-class leaders and lower-class power bases. Ideologically, they ranged across a remarkably diverse spectrum: from the populist authoritarianism of Argentina's Peronistas, Peru's Apristas, and the Bolivian Movimiento Nacionalista Revolucionario, to the centrist democratic reformism of Venezuela's Acción Democrática, Costa Rica's Figueristas, and the Caribbean Legion, to the Marxist models of the radical leftists who were usually prominent among the revolutionary coalitions' labor supporters. Despite their ideological and class heterogeneity, however, the revolutionary movements of the period shared a nationalistic outrage at their nations' underdevelopment and a commitment to progressive structural reforms. And above all, they had a common perception that the *cause* of Latin America's underdevelopment was systemic and international—that poverty and backwardness were the products of an exploitative transnational alliance between their traditional neofeudal elites and U.S. imperialism.

For decades, nationalists charged, Latin America's *vendepatria* ("country-selling") oligarchies had been willfully alienating their nations' sovereignty to U.S. domination in exchange for personal profit and political gain. In that crass transaction, according to nationalists, U.S. capitalists received open, minimally regulated, highly profitable access to Latin America's natural resources, consumer markets, and low-wage labor forces, while the U.S. government received unwavering support for its foreign-policy initiatives from Latin America's slavishly acquiescent elite-controlled governments. In return, the Latin American elites obtained foreign investment capital, foreign-owned infrastructure, and jobs on the staffs of foreign corporations, along with a precarious form of economic growth tied exclusively to U.S. demand for Latin America's export commodities. Meanwhile, as payment for subordinating themselves to U.S. hegemony, the region's elite-controlled governments secured the U.S. military assistance and political backing that strengthened their hold on power, enabling them to preserve traditional class hierarchies in their neofeudal societies. The victims, nationalists argued, were Latin America's impoverished masses, who in the process were condemned to subsistence wages and a marginalized standard of living as their nations' wealth flowed into the bank accounts of the local elites and their U.S. business partners. To the nationalist revolutionary movements that were emerging as the vanguard of political change in Latin America in the 1940s, the essential prerequisite to meaningful reform and national progress was the destruction of an oppressive "system of domination"—an inextricably interconnected system of internal and external domination in which a "symbiotic alliance" of "antinational" oligarchs and their imperialistic U.S. patrons was ruthlessly exploiting the nation and its people. "Nationalist revolution," as they defined it, was first and foremost a struggle between neocolonialism and national self-determination. To be a revolutionary in Latin America in the 1940s (and well beyond) was to be an anti-imperialist as well.[8]

Guatemala fit the model. Although the 1944 revolution broke the oligarchy's hold on political power, a tiny minority of property owners, native and foreign, still dominated the economy. In the countryside, a small upper-class elite of coffee-estate owners continued to impose medieval working conditions on their Indian labor force. Guatemala's internal infrastructure, meanwhile, was virtually owned by U.S. companies. In return for political support, jobs, and bribes, previous Guatemalan government officials had granted U.S. investors immense privileges, including profitable concessions and charters, tax exemptions, and freedom from regulation. By 1944, U.S. investment capital in Guatemala totaled $93 million, and three U.S. corporations had a powerful stranglehold on the country's economic life. The Boston-based United Fruit Company (UFCO), the world's leading producer and exporter of bananas, was Guatemala's largest private landowner and largest employer. With some 566,000 acres of banana plantations and other landholdings and a labor force of more than 15,000 workers, the fruit company dwarfed all other economic enterprises in the country and wielded enormous economic and political power. Allowed to operate as "a private fiefdom" by Guatemala's cooperative oligarchy, UFCO paid minimal taxes, remitted huge profits back to its U.S. headquarters, and controlled its labor force with a racist-tinged ruthlessness. Most Guatemalans of the 1940s viewed the company as a vast imperial enclave. Guatemala's second largest employer was the U.S.-owned International Railways of Central America (IRCA), an UFCO subsidiary that monopolized Guatemala's commercial transportation and port facilities. While UFCO cargoes received priority treatment and discounted freight rates of $75 per railroad car from IRCA, the company's Guatemalan customers paid $575 per car (reportedly the highest rail rate in the world at the time) and suffered "excessive and discriminatory" port fees. Empresa Eléctrica, a subsidiary of U.S.-based Electric Bond and Share, monopolized the supply of electric power in the country and was notorious for its high rates and poor service. Meanwhile, Guatemala's pre-1944 political leaders had missed few opportunities to demonstrate their loyal friendship to the U.S. government. Jorge Ubico, the military caudillo ousted in the 1944 revolution, was an obsequious cultivator of U.S. favors who declared war on Japan one day after Pearl Harbor and permitted U.S. troops to be stationed in Guatemala during World War II. Under Ubico, a U.S. officer served as director of Guatemala's national military academy.[9]

The heavy U.S. contributions to Guatemala's status quo fostered inevitable stirrings of anti-American nationalism among the revolutionaries who ousted Ubico in 1944. From the start, the revolution's leaders spoke of their determination to transform Guatemala's neocolonial and neofeudal structures. The revolutionary government's first president, Juan José Arévalo (1945–1951), publicly attributed the nation's maladies to the oligarchy's "systematized servility" and "submission to foreigners," and pledged to liberate Guatemala's material riches from misuse by "creole feudalism" and "the powerful foreign companies *de tipo colonial.*" The enemies of the Guatemalan people, Arévalo told the nation in 1947, were "those who always defended the imperialist interests." Arévalo's revolutionary coalition was a congeries of competing ideological factions ranging from centrists to liberal "welfare capitalists" to socialists of varying hues to communists; the common objective that united them, one of Arévalo's supporters said, was their nationalistic determination to wage a "fight against feudal backwardness and against imperialism."[10]

Given the power of the entrenched interests arrayed against him, however, Arévalo proceeded cautiously. Rather than launch a redistributive frontal assault on the traditional land-tenure system that he believed was the basis of Guatemala's underdevelopment, Arévalo studiously avoided agrarian reform and instead chipped away with moderate social-reform initiatives: a literacy campaign, the country's first social-security program, and—the centerpiece of his reform program—the first labor legislation in Guatemalan history designed "to *protect*, rather than to further exploit," workers. His 1947 Labor Code granted Guatemala's workers the right to unionize and to strike and made collective bargaining and labor-management contracts compulsory—in effect giving workers their first legal power to redress grievances and demand wage increases from their employers. Yet even Arévalo's progressive labor legislation avoided a direct class confrontation with the country's powerful rural estate owners. The rights bestowed upon organized labor were limited for the most part to workers in Guatemala's few industrial enterprises and the handful of agricultural estates that employed more than 500 permanent (as opposed to seasonal) workers. Peasant unions on smaller estates were eligible for the Labor Code's protections and benefits only if two-thirds of their membership was literate—a virtually impossible prerequisite in rural Guatemala of the 1940s.[11]

Nor did Arévalo's nationalism embolden him to launch any radical attacks on U.S. interests in Guatemala. Rather than expropriate foreign-owned properties, he left them intact and instead tried only to regulate their operations "in accordance with national interests." Limits were imposed on Empresa Eléctrica's electricity rates. International Railways was made to accept a collective pact with its railroad workers. And, in a regulatory initiative that was to have fateful (and ultimately fatal) consequences for the Guatemalan revolution, Arévalo attempted to force the United Fruit Company, the country's largest and wealthiest employer, to comply with the provisions of the government's new Labor Code. From 1946 onward, UFCO banana workers engaged in nearly continuous strike actions against their employer, demanding wage increases (to $1.50 a day) and increased benefits, including expanded medical benefits for a work force routinely exposed to the carcinogenic insecticides and other toxins used on UFCO plantations. When UFCO responded by firing striking workers and threatening to suspend operations in the country, the government's labor courts intervened on behalf of the banana workers, enforcing the Labor Code's protections against arbitrary dismissal of workers, forcing UFCO to arbitrate, and settling the labor disputes by granting the workers some of their demands. On at least one occasion, Arévalo's courts threatened to confiscate UFCO property if the company failed to adhere to the country's new labor laws. Nevertheless, "beyond offering some legal protection to the company's workers, Arévalo did not disturb UFCO's privileges." Between mid-1947 and early 1949, government labor inspectors "repeatedly found UFCO guilty of violations of the Labor Code, yet the total amount of the fines levied against the company was $690."[12]

Other government initiatives reflected the revolution's inherent nationalism. A new foreign investment law of 1949 reserved future exploitation of Guatemalan resources, especially oil, to "the state," Guatemalan companies "whose capital is predominantly national," or foreign contractors working under government direction. In addition, Guatemalan foreign policy under Arévalo took its first cautious steps toward an international alignment independent of U.S. influence. From 1946 through 1949, despite repeated U.S. objections, Arévalo fervently supported the Caribbean Legion in its filibustering crusade to overthrow pro-U.S. dictators throughout the Caribbean basin. Guatemala delayed for three years (longer than any other Latin American republic) before agreeing to ratify the 1947 Rio Pact that committed the country to a Cold War mutual-security arrangement with the United States. And at the 1950 Central American and Caribbean Games held in Guatemala City, Arévalo's government tweaked U.S. "colonialism" by tacitly endorsing Puerto Rican independence: "Puerto Rican athletes were honored with a white flag bearing the Puerto Rican shield rather than the Stars and Stripes, and a military band played 'La Borinqueña' instead of the 'Star Spangled Banner.'"[13]

For the most part, however, Arévalo remained moderate and restrained in his relations with the United States. Like most of the revolution's leadership, he personally revered Franklin D. Roosevelt and frequently credited FDR's New Deal/Four Freedoms idealism as the inspiration for Guatemala's 1944 revolution. Arévalo also respected U.S. power, and he was sufficiently pragmatic "to accept the geopolitical reality that Guatemala was in the U.S. sphere of influence." On important global issues, he and his government officials generally "proclaimed their solidarity with the United States." During the Korean War, after some initial equivocation, Arévalo placed his country's military bases and troops at the United States' disposal. His government also renewed the contracts of U.S. military missions in Guatemala. In general, Arévalo's displays of anti-American nationalism were limited to regulatory attacks on U.S. investment capital and occasional gestures of independence from U.S. foreign policy—initiatives that, from his perspective, represented nothing more than fundamental expressions of Guatemalan sovereignty and national independence. Beyond that, he "hoped to maintain cordial relations with Washington."[14]

Arévalo admired Roosevelt, but if he had a role model it was probably Lázaro Cárdenas, the populist president whose state-directed reform programs and nationalistic attacks on foreign oil companies had helped to institutionalize a monolithic, "revolutionary," one-party state in neighboring Mexico between 1934 and 1940. Arévalo lauded Cárdenas' programs as models worthy of emulation. And his principal initiatives as Guatemala's president—the rhetorical attacks on feudalism, reforms on behalf of blue- and white-collar workers, cultivation of the banana- and railroad-workers' unions, the nationalistic assertions of Guatemalan sovereignty directed at U.S. interests—all seemed pointed toward the mobilization of a populist multiclass alliance as a power base for an eventual one-party "revolutionary" state modeled on Cárdenas' Partido Revolucionario Institucional.[15] Arévalo's political plans, however, eventually fell victim to the internal disunity that plagued his regime. After 1944, the idealism of many of Guatemala's revolutionaries quickly gave way to opportunism and personal ambition. The coalition of revolutionary political parties that supported Arévalo fragmented into a series of squabbling factions that "clashed over the scope and speed of social reforms and over the division of the spoils of political power." Revolutionary politicians devoted most of their energy to "personal aggrandizement" and the quest for "soft desk jobs and perks." Corruption became rampant, and graft "the order of the day at high levels." By the end of Arévalo's term in office in March 1951, many provisions of his reform laws remained unimplemented, and his administration had become engulfed in a "morass of corruption, nepotism, and incompetence."[16]

Under Arévalo's successor, Jacobo Arbenz (1951–1954), the Guatemalan revolution veered leftward. A middle-class army officer, hero of the 1944 revolution, and minister of defense under Arévalo, Arbenz evolved over the course of the revolution into that rarest of Latin American species: a Marxist military officer. In a search for solutions to his country's wretched condition, Arbenz spent the Arévalo years reading books on Marxist theory, the Russian Revolution, and Soviet history. He also formed warm friendships with the leaders of Guatemala's nascent communist party, the Guatemalan Labor Party (Partido Guatemalteco del Trabajo or PGT), a Marxist-Leninist "'vanguard' party of the proletariat" organized by José Manuel Fortuny and a few other radical young dissidents from the revolutionary parties in 1949–1950. Arévalo, like Cárdenas, Argentina's Juan Perón, Getúlio Vargas in Brazil, and other populist leaders of the era, had publicly declared the communist party illegal while quietly ceding communist organizers considerable influence in state-sanctioned trade unions—a strategy designed to co-opt the communists while at the same time verifying the populist government's progressive credentials among organized labor. To Arbenz, however, the communists' honesty, dedication, and commitment to hard work stood them in marked contrast to the rest of the venal, self-indulgent revolutionary politicians who surrounded Arévalo. Like Arbenz, the communists were fierce nationalists with "an ardent desire to improve the lot of the Guatemalan people." Unlike the other revolutionary politicians, they offered a comprehensive program for Guatemala's development. Over time, Arbenz and PGT founder Fortuny developed a close friendship and spent long hours together exchanging ideas and discussing strategies for their country's salvation. When Arbenz ran for the presidency in 1950, it was Fortuny who wrote his campaign speeches, carefully putting "a moderate spin" on Arbenz's statements to hide any impression of communist inspiration. Arbenz's conversion to Marxism was completed early in his presidency. By 1952, his wife later recalled, "Jacobo was convinced that the triumph of Communism in the world was inevitable and desirable. The march of history was toward Communism. Capitalism was doomed." During the last two years of his administration, scholar Piero Gleijeses concludes, Arbenz "considered himself a communist, and with his few confidants, he spoke like one."[17]

As president, Arbenz relied heavily on the PGT as one of his "strongest cornerstones" in "the fight against imperialism and the landowning national reaction." Inside his administration, "the communists gained influence far beyond their numbers. The PGT leaders—Fortuny foremost—were Arbenz's closest advisers and constituted his kitchen cabinet, which discussed all major decisions." By late 1952, Arbenz's "closest political friend was the PGT, and his closest personal friends were its leaders." Presidential friendship produced important political gains for the communists. Arbenz granted the PGT legal status in 1952. He was instrumental in consolidating Guatemala's two principal labor confederations into the communist-led Confederación General de Trabajadores de Guatemala a year earlier. And in 1954 he helped the communists win control of the railway union, "the only important urban labor union that still opposed them." Guatemala, meanwhile, became a safe haven for persecuted Marxists and other leftists from throughout Central America and the Caribbean.[18] In retrospect, U.S. ambassador John Peurifoy's oft-quoted 1953 observation that if Arbenz "is not a Communist he will certainly do until one comes along"[19] seems reasonably apt.

Despite their ideological convictions, however, Arbenz and his PGT advisers did not believe that Guatemala was ready for communism in the early 1950s. In their view, the country's semifeudal structures and geographic proximity to the United States made it highly unlikely "that a communist state, however desirable, could be established in Guatemala in the near future." Instead, adhering to Leninist prescriptions, they set out to lead Guatemala through an intermediate capitalist stage of development, during which the requisite "material conditions for socialism" could be created. They were uncertain about the length of time that would be required to prepare the country for the eventual transition to socialism, but Fortuny, extrapolating from the experiences of China and the "peoples' democracies" of Eastern Europe, believed that the capitalist stage could be relatively short if a communist-led proletariat emerged to "head . . . the struggle against feudalism and imperialism."[20]

Consequently, in his 1951 inauguration speech, Arbenz pledged "to transform

Guatemala from a backward country with a semi-feudal economy into a modern capitalist country." His subsequent development projects were consistently market oriented; many, in fact, were based on World Bank recommendations and blueprints. Plans were initiated for the construction of new nationally owned power installations, port facilities, and highways that would break foreign capital's monopolistic grip on the Guatemalan economic infrastructure. New state-supported industries were envisioned. And in June 1952 a comprehensive agrarian reform program was introduced. On the surface, the agrarian reform was "far more moderate than either the Mexican reform which preceded it or the Cuban measures which would come a few years later." Under its provisions, the Guatemalan government was authorized to expropriate land on estates larger than 223 acres and redistribute the seized property to landless peasants. Only uncultivated land was eligible for confiscation, and estate owners were to be compensated with twenty-five-year government bonds yielding 3 percent interest, with the amount of compensation determined by the land values declared by the estate owners on their most recent tax returns. According to the government, the agrarian reform was designed "to liquidate feudal property . . . in order to develop capitalist methods of production in agriculture." By putting land in the hands of the landless rural masses, the government said, the reform would increase mass purchasing power, expand the domestic market, and eventually "prepare the path for Guatemala's industrialization." Even the U.S. embassy concluded that the program was "relatively moderate in form."[21]

For Arbenz and his communist advisers, however, agrarian reform was essentially a political weapon in their strategy to radicalize the revolution. By breaking up large estates, they would destroy the power of their entrenched enemies: the landed elites and foreign enclaves that still controlled the country's resource base and preserved the "semi-feudal and semi-colonial economic structure" that Arévalo had failed to transform. By redistributing the expropriated land to Guatemala's peasants, they would mobilize the mass support base on which a Marxist revolutionary state could eventually be constructed. Fortuny predicted that agrarian reform would "lay the groundwork for the eventual radicalization of the peasantry" and sow "the seeds of a more collective society." Large-scale land redistribution, he believed, would create the "powerful force of rural workers and peasants" that under communist direction would provide the power base for a Marxist revolution.[22]

The strategy proved strikingly effective in practice. In less than two years, Arbenz expropriated over 1.4 million acres of land and redistributed it to approximately 500,000 landless peasants in plots of between 8.5 and 33 acres. Upper-class absentee landowners and the United Fruit Company bore the brunt of the reform; UFCO alone lost more than 400,000 of its 566,000 acres, approximately one-seventh of Guatemala's arable land. Arbenz's communist supporters assumed important leadership roles in the National Agrarian Department, the government agency that administered the agrarian reform, while communist union leaders and their allies dominated the local agrarian committees that selected properties for expropriation. The communists quickly used these positions of influence to begin "penetrating the countryside" politically. By 1954, according to Gleijeses, "the PGT had over five thousand members—a not insignificant number in a country of 3 million inhabitants and for a party that three years earlier had claimed less than a hundred." Many of the new members were agricultural workers who had received land under the agrarian reform. On the eve of the U.S. intervention, the PGT was anticipating major gains in future congressional elections, as agrarian reform continued to gain momentum.[23] And if Arbenz succeeded in mobilizing Guatemala's grateful peasants within the ranks of his government-subsidized national peasant confederation (Confederación Nacional Campesina de Guatemala), as seemed likely, he and the communists would have at their command a potent source of organized mass power to use against any groups—including Guatemala's armed forces—that might oppose future moves toward radicalization.

Where was the revolution heading internationally under Arbenz? The answer, clearly, was, out of the U.S. sphere of influence, and—perhaps less clearly—toward eventual alignment with the Soviet bloc. Officially, Arbenz's foreign ministry maintained a posture of neutral nonalignment in international affairs. In practice, however, Guatemalan foreign policy exuded a strident anti-American nationalism that on several occasions found Guatemala positioned alongside the Soviet Union in international politics. As president, Arbenz publicly rescinded Arévalo's offer to make Guatemalan troops available for service in the Korean War, and his official government newspaper, *Diario de Centro América*, harshly criticized the U.S. military presence in Korea. Unable to disguise "its preference for the Soviet bloc," the *Diario de Centro América* regularly singled out Czechoslovakia for praise as a socialist workers' paradise. During the Sixth Session of the United Nations' General Assembly in 1952, Guatemala was the only Latin American nation to support a Soviet resolution on behalf of Communist China's admission. In March 1953, the Guatemalan Congress observed a moment of silence "to honor the memory of the great statesman and leader of the Soviet Union, Joseph Vissarionovich Stalin, whose passing is mourned by all progressive men." It was the only Latin American government body to do so.[24]

Although Arbenz was "generally cautious in his public statements," his pro-Soviet sympathies were "unmistakable." According to one of his PGT supporters, "three basic facts" attracted Arbenz to the Soviet Union: "It was governed by a class which had been ruthlessly exploited; it had defeated illiteracy and raised the standard of living in a very short time"; and unlike the United States, "it had never harmed Guatemala." For its part, the PGT "proudly" proclaimed its connection with the international communist movement and applauded the Soviets and their policies "with genuine enthusiasm." The party had only minimal and indirect links to Moscow, and the Soviets showed no interest in aiding communism in

Guatemala, but the PGT apparently hoped to cultivate future Soviet support. "We were knocking on the Soviets' door," PGT cofounder Carlos Manuel Pellecer later admitted, "but they did not answer."[25]

Why did Arbenz and his communist advisers assume that the United States would tolerate a nationalistic, *yanqui*-phobic, proto-Marxist state deep in the heart of the U.S. sphere of influence? Because, according to Gleijeses, a "false sense of security" led them to "underestimate . . . the American threat." The United States, after all, had not intervened in Latin America in two decades, and the Roosevelt and Truman administrations had seemingly institutionalized nonintervention as a basic principle of U.S. policy toward Latin America. In addition, from the perspective of Arbenz and the PGT, communism appeared to be the inevitable wave of the future in world politics. If Guatemala's revolutionaries remained patient and careful and continued to devote themselves to progressive, nationalistic reforms and the construction of a proletarian power base, surely the correlation of forces both domestically and internationally would shift increasingly in their favor. In the end, Arbenz and his supporters "believed that the United States might holler, threaten, and even impose limited sanctions on Guatemala. They did not believe, however, that the United States would overthrow" them.[26] They miscalculated badly.

The seeds of U.S. intervention in Guatemala were planted in 1947, and it was the revolution's enemies who planted them. By mid-1947, the United Fruit Company, the Guatemalan upper classes, and the ruling elites of Guatemala's Central American neighbors were all actively lobbying the U.S. government to assist them in their efforts to block Arévalo's reform programs. And significantly, to enlist U.S. power on their behalf, the antirevolutionary actors deliberately played on U.S. officials' Cold War national-security anxieties by charging that Arévalo's reforms were communist inspired.

"It was United Fruit that first raised the spectre of serious communist infiltration in Guatemala," Gleijeses writes, and it was Arévalo's May 1947 Labor Code "that provoked it to do so." United Fruit officials regarded the Labor Code as a direct attack on their company and complained that several of its provisions were blatantly discriminatory—particularly ones that gave workers on large agricultural estates collective-bargaining rights, the right to strike during harvesttime, and other rights and benefits that were denied to workers on smaller estates.[27] United Fruit's charges of discrimination were not without foundation. Arévalo designed his Labor Code not only as a progressive reform mechanism that would help him build a populist power base among organized labor but as a weapon in the nationalist revolution's campaign to curb the power of foreign capital. He openly admitted to U.S. officials that several articles of the Labor Code were in fact "directly discriminatory against the United Fruit Company and that they were a virtual 'machine gun' held against the head of the Company."[28] In a series of bitter labor disputes that disrupted UFCO plantations between 1947 and 1949, Arévalo's government vigorously supported the company's banana workers. Unaccustomed to governmental interference in its Guatemalan operations, UFCO arrogantly refused to comply with the country's new labor laws. Instead the company turned to the U.S. government for protection. From 1947 onward, UFCO representatives exerted constant pressure on the State Department to intervene on the company's behalf. And to ensure a forceful response from Washington, UFCO shrewdly linked its local labor problems to broader U.S. security concerns by ominously warning the State Department that Arévalo's reform programs were being orchestrated by "communistic influences emanating from outside Guatemala."[29]

Guatemala's upper classes reinforced UFCO's warnings of communist penetration. Outraged by Arévalo's labor reforms, and long accustomed to labeling all reformers "communists," the old elites "brandish[ed] charges of communist infiltration with even greater gusto" than UFCO. They also conspired to overthrow Arévalo's government in a series of unsuccessful coup attempts and relentlessly sought U.S. support for their conspiracies. Beginning in 1947, a steady stream of right-wing plotters visited U.S. embassies throughout Central America and State Department offices in Washington, warning U.S. officials that Guatemala's government had fallen into the hands of communists and soliciting U.S. financial and military backing for "anticommunist" counterrevolutions. In September 1947, four months after his Labor Code went into effect, Arévalo informed his countrymen in a nationwide radio address that "Guatemalan reaction . . . has been knocking at the doors of the Department of State in Washington in order to convince the government [of the United States] that the present Government of Guatemala is a danger to the unity of the Continent and to the peace of the world." The counterrevolutionaries' lobbying efforts continued without letup for the next seven years. As late as June 1954, the conservative archbishop of Guatemala's Catholic Church was appealing for "direct U.S. intervention" as the only way to protect "anti-communists and Christians" in Guatemala.[30]

The authoritarian oligarchies of neighboring Central American nations also "tirelessly condemned" Arévalo's government as communist. Fearful that reforms in Guatemala would lead to demands for change in their societies, the governing elites of El Salvador, Honduras, and Nicaragua bombarded U.S. officials with "disquieting reports" of Arévalo's extremism. No Central American leader was more vociferous in his antipathy to the Guatemalan revolution than Nicaragua's Anastasio Somoza Sr. Throughout the course of the revolution, Somoza actively networked with Guatemalan counterrevolutionaries and solicited U.S. support for plots to overthrow the revolutionary governments. For their part, the regimes of Juan Manuel Gálvez in Honduras and Oscar Osorio in El Salvador regularly vented their concern to U.S. officials that "communist subversion" from Guatemala was infiltrating their societies. In the end, Guatemala's Central American neighbors played a pivotal role in convincing the United States that the Guatemalan revolution was a security threat that "had to be removed."[31]

The alarmist allegations of the revolution's enemies focused the Truman administration's attention on Guatemala and helped to prejudice it against Arévalo. Throughout the late 1940s, U.S. embassy analysts relied heavily on U.S. businessmen and the local upper classes as sources of information on Guatemalan political conditions, and UFCO, more than any other source, served as the State Department's "interpreter of matters Guatemalan."[32] Consequently, by 1948 U.S. officials viewed Guatemala as "a nightmarish world" of Marxist infestation, a place where "infiltration of indoctrinated communists, fellow-travelers, and Marxist ideas" had "unquestionably reached dangerous proportions." Arévalo's Labor Code, a 1948 U.S. embassy study reported, was a "drastic document which, if enforced literally, would greatly facilitate the communist objective of state or worker control of industry," while his social policies were "motivated in part by a calculated effort to further class warfare." By 1950, State Department analysts had concluded that, although Arévalo was "an extreme leftist rather than a communist," he had "collaborated openly with communist elements in Guatemala who, with the acquiescence if not the active support of the Government, have succeeded in gaining complete control of organized labor and in placing their partisans in Government positions." It was Guatemalan communists, the State Department informed Truman in September 1950, who "have prevented ratification of the Rio Treaty . . . influenced the Government to support the so-called 'Caribbean Legion' . . . [and] caused the Government to adopt a hostile and nationalistic attitude towards American capital." Arévalo's collaboration with communists, the CIA warned bluntly in July 1950, "is a potential threat to U.S. security interests."[33]

To be sure, the Truman administration's "distorted assessment" of Arévalo was based on "a grain of truth." A few Marxists were in fact to be found among Arévalo's revolutionary parties. Communists were also visible in Guatemala's nascent labor movement, none more so than Victor Manuel Gutiérrez, the secretary general of the Confederation of Guatemalan Workers, whose fiery anti-American speeches did little to calm U.S. security fears. ("Are we with imperialism and against the Soviet Union, or are we fighting for peace and against imperialism?" Gutiérrez asked his union followers in 1949. "From today onward," he answered, "all should know that when the hour of a new war arrives, we of the proletariat, here as well as in all Latin America, should be the first saboteurs of that war and fight against imperialism.") Nevertheless, U.S. officials grossly exaggerated the communist threat. Not only did they fail to discern the populist motives and Mexican models that explained Arévalo's tolerance of Marxist labor organizers, they also badly overestimated the communists' strength and influence. A communist party did not even exist in Guatemala until late 1949, and by the end of Arévalo's presidency it numbered fewer than 100 members, only a handful of whom had even a rudimentary knowledge of Marxist doctrine.[34]

The Truman administration, however, responded to the perceived security threat by applying diplomatic and economic pressure to curb Arévalo's "extremist" tendencies. U.S. ambassador Richard Patterson—who was frequently seen in the company of UFCO officials and Guatemalan counterrevolutionaries—warned Arévalo in 1949 that "American interests in Guatemala . . . had been persecuted, prosecuted, and kicked around over the past two years and that personally I was fed up and the patience of my government nearly exhausted." A few months later, Patterson demanded that Arévalo "dismiss from his government" seventeen officials whom the ambassador accused of being communists, warning that the Truman administration would deny Guatemala any further U.S. aid if Arévalo refused. Arévalo calmly responded to Patterson's browbeating by reminding him that "the world cannot be ruled as it was in 1920, because times have changed" and promptly secured Patterson's recall as ambassador.[35] A policy of withholding U.S. favors had already begun, however. In 1949, the Truman administration imposed an embargo on the sale of U.S. military equipment to Guatemala as a message to the Guatemalan armed forces that the United States was displeased with Arévalo. The following year, U.S. officials excluded Guatemala from their new Point Four technical-assistance program and quietly blocked a "much-needed" World Bank development loan that Arévalo had requested.[36]

The Truman administration applied pressure on Arévalo, but it did not seek to overthrow him. Truman's State Department based its approach to hemispheric relations on Franklin D. Roosevelt's Good Neighbor policy, a centerpiece of which was the formal renunciation of U.S. intervention in Latin America's domestic politics. In particular, the Department's Bureau of Inter-American Affairs—which had primary control over information flows and policy implementation—remained committed to nonintervention as "an almost sacrosanct principle" and adamantly opposed any proposals to intervene in Guatemala. When, in May 1950, an UFCO representative tried to interest the State Department in a project "to bring moderate elements into power in Guatemala" by "bringing about the election of a middle-of-the-road candidate" in the forthcoming 1950 presidential election, Thomas Mann, director of the Bureau's Office of Middle American Affairs, rebuffed the overture, responding that any such attempt to intervene in Guatemala's domestic politics would inevitably become public and produce a backlash against the United States throughout Latin America.[37] Furthermore, since U.S. intelligence reports indicated that the likely winner of the 1950 election, Jacobo Arbenz, was a military opportunist who could be expected to move the revolution rightward, the Truman administration could afford to remain patient and noninterventionist.[38]

Once he assumed office, Arbenz's leftist proclivities surprised and dismayed U.S. officials. Three months into his presidency, the State Department glumly reported that "the ascending curve of communist influence has . . . continued upward on an accelerated incline." Central Intelligence Agency officials were even "more apprehensive about Guatemala than their counterparts at State." Agency analysts were skeptical that State Department pressure would have any constructive effect on Arbenz and "saw direct, covert action as the only remedy" to an eventual communist takeover of Guatemala. Accordingly, in early 1952, CIA director Walter Bedell Smith tasked the agency's Western Hemisphere Division "to find out whether Guatemalan dissidents with help from Central American dictators could overthrow the Arbenz regime." Suddenly, the revolution's enemies had a potential ally within the Truman administration, one that could assist them in circumventing the State Department's opposition to U.S. intervention.[39]

They were quick to exploit the opportunity. Shortly after arriving in Washington for a state visit in April 1952, Nicaraguan president Anastasio Somoza told Truman and other White House officials that, if they provided arms, he and his Guatemalan protégé Castillo Armas would "clean up Guatemala for you in no time." (The proposal, Somoza's son later revealed, had originally been conceived by Somoza and UFCO representatives in Nicaragua.) Truman found the proposal interesting, and—without consulting the Bureau of Inter-American Affairs—instructed the CIA to follow up. By mid-June, a CIA agent was in Guatemala establishing contact with Castillo Armas' counterrevolutionary forces and coordinating plans for a covert intervention. The operation, code-named "PBFORTUNE," received official White House authorization in September 1952. It called for a CIA-armed and -financed invasion of Guatemala by Castillo Armas (from bases in Honduras, El Salvador, and Mexico) as the prelude to a revolt by "important officers of the Guatemalan army." United Fruit assisted the CIA in the delivery of U.S. arms, while the dictatorships of Rafael Trujillo in the Dominican Republic and Marcos Pérez Jiménez in Venezuela contributed additional funds. As preparations were being finalized, however, Somoza leaked word of the CIA's involvement to other Central American government officials. Learning that the operation's cover had been blown, the State Department warned Truman that public exposure of an attempted U.S. intervention would destroy the Good Neighbor policy and jeopardize Latin American support for U.S. hemispheric leadership, and Secretary of State Dean Acheson persuaded the president to call off the operation in early October. Disappointed, CIA officials subsequently continued to provide Castillo Armas with money and supplies in the hope that the incoming Eisenhower administration "would breathe new life into the project."[40] Their hopes were soon fulfilled.

From the start, Eisenhower and his advisers interpreted the Guatemalan situation as a national-security problem. The United Fruit Company—and economic considerations in general—played a secondary role at best in Eisenhower's decision to overthrow Arbenz. Much has been made of the many personal ties linking influential Eisenhower administration figures to United Fruit.[41] The fruit company undoubtedly exploited those connections to lobby for U.S. intervention. Nevertheless, no hard evidence has yet come to light that any U.S. officials made policy on the basis of UFCO's interests. It appears, in fact, that rather than being the tool of UFCO, Eisenhower sought to "use" the company to contain communism in Central America. In June 1953, the administration postponed a long-pending Justice Department antitrust suit against United Fruit because such action would have "terrible repercussions" for the U.S. "strategic position" in Central America. To accuse UFCO of illegal practices, Eisenhower's National Security Council concluded, "would appear to justify" the Guatemalan revolutionaries' accusations against the company and "consolidate the position of the Communist-dominated Arbenz government"; it would also "greatly stimulate movements to nationalize [UFCO] properties" elsewhere in Central America, resulting in the loss of U.S. control over "the largest communications and transport network in the area, represented by the United Fruit Company's freight and passenger ships . . . ports, docking facilities and warehouses . . . railroad system . . . wireless [radio] communication service" and other "essential services" that "in friendly American hands, constitute a strategic interest in time of war." Eisenhower thought it best to delay legal proceedings until the United States strengthened its position in Central America, and the antitrust suit was not filed until July 2, 1954, a week after Arbenz's ouster.[42] The State Department defended UFCO vociferously in the company's bitter dispute with Arbenz over land expropriation, but in the Eisenhower administration's view, "the threat to American business" in Guatemala "was a minor part of a larger danger to the United States' overall security." That assessment was acknowledged by influential protagonists on both sides of the U.S.-Guatemalan confrontation. "If the United Fruit matter were settled," Secretary of State John Foster Dulles told reporters a few days before the intervention, "if they gave a gold piece for every banana, the problem would remain just as it is today as far as the presence of communist infiltration of Guatemala is concerned. That is the problem, not United Fruit." The PGT's Fortuny concurred. "They would have overthrown us," he later recalled, "even if we had grown no bananas."[43]

From Eisenhower's inauguration in January 1953 until his August 1953 decision to intervene, the White House was subjected to a steady barrage of intelligence warnings that Guatemala was a potential security threat. At a February 18 NSC meeting, during the administration's first substantive discussion of Latin American affairs, CIA director Allen Dulles told the president that Guatemala's "Communist infection" was "such as to mark an approaching crisis." In April, Assistant Secretary of State for Inter-American Affairs John Moors Cabot returned from a visit to Guatemala and reported that "President Arbenz had the pale, cold-lipped look of the ideologue and showed no interest in my suggestions for a change of course in his government's direction. He had obviously sold out to the Communists and that was that." A May 19 National Intelligence Estimate (NIE) by the U.S. intelligence community warned that Arbenz had formed "an effective working alliance" with the communists, who "exercise a political influence far out of proportion to their small numerical strength" and whose "influence will probably continue to grow as long as President Arbenz remains in power." Arbenz's agrarian reform program, the NIE continued, was politically motivated and would be used by the communists "to extend their influence by organizing the peasantry as they have organized other workers." "The current political situation in Guatemala," it concluded, "is adverse to U.S. interests." That message was reinforced more personally in late July when Eisenhower's brother and trusted adviser Milton returned from a Latin American fact-finding mission for the White House and reported that Guatemala had "succumbed to Communist infiltration." Then, in August, a bleak NSC assessment warned the administration that "our present position in Guatemala is progressively deteriorating. Politically, Communist strength grows, while opposition forces are disintegrating. . . . Ultimate Communist control of the country and elimination of American economic interests is the logical outcome, and unless the trend is reversed, is merely a question of time." "A policy of [U.S.] inaction," the study concluded, "would be suicidal."[44] CIA planning for covert action against Arbenz commenced around Labor Day.[45]

Why did U.S. officials regard the eventuality of a communist-controlled Guatemala as a threat to U.S. national security? Because, they believed, a communist Guatemala would be "a potential Soviet beachhead in the Western Hemisphere." Administration analysts were convinced that "communists the world over were agents of Soviet imperialism and constituted a mortal threat to our own national existence." It naturally followed, therefore, that Guatemala's communists were "servants of Moscow" and "disciplined agents" of a Soviet-directed international communist conspiracy against the United States. Evidence of a link between the PGT and the Soviet Union proved frustratingly elusive, but U.S. officials believed intuitively that "such a tie must exist." "Evidence that the Communist program in Guatemala has been organized and directed in the world capitals of Communism" was "largely circumstantial," the State Department admitted, but "it is abundantly clear that what has happened in Guatemala is a part of Moscow's global strategy. . . . We must recognize that the political institutions of that American State are now dominated and controlled by the international Communist organization."[46]

But how, specifically, would a Soviet-controlled Guatemala imperil the U.S. national existence? The country's strategic significance was slight, administration analysts acknowledged. It was of negligible importance to the United States as a source of strategic materials. More importantly, it was virtually defenseless against U.S. military power. Even if Guatemala's government assumed "a hostile attitude" toward the United States and permitted "an enemy power" to use "its airfields, ports and other facilities and resources," an August 1953 NSC study reported, U.S. military forces could secure the country's "strategic points . . . with a battalion or two of well-trained troops." If a future emergency should necessitate "direct unilateral action," the report concluded, "the Arbenz regime could easily and quickly be overthrown."[47] U.S. officials fretted over Guatemala's relative proximity to the Panama Canal. They occasionally speculated that Guatemala's "Communist infection" "might spill over into neighboring states." And they suspected that the Soviets would use Guatemala "to create a diversion in the US backyard" and thereby weaken U.S. defense forces elsewhere in the world. Yet, by August 1953, there were no Soviet troops, advisers, aircraft, or weapons in Guatemala—or any Soviet diplomats, for that matter, since Arbenz had not even established diplomatic relations with the Soviet Union. As late as May 1954, less than three weeks before the intervention began, U.S. military intelligence analysts and members of the State Department's Policy Planning Staff were reporting that the Guatemalan situation posed "no immediate military threat to the safety of [the] US" and could even "safely get worse."[48]

What, then, *was* the security threat? Above all, Eisenhower administration officials regarded communist influence in Guatemala as a dangerous challenge to the credibility of U.S. international leadership in the Cold War. The successful consolidation of communist power in Guatemala—in the very heart of the traditional U.S. sphere of influence in Latin America—would, U.S. officials feared, create a powerful perception of U.S. weakness in the eyes of foreign adversaries and allies. A weak or ineffectual U.S. response to that challenge, they believed, would encourage further Soviet adventurism and cause nervous U.S. allies to doubt the reliability of U.S. power, resulting in dangerous shifts in the global balance of power.

The most immediate U.S. fear was that Guatemala's communists would damage the United States' carefully constructed Cold War security alliance with Latin America. U.S. leaders consistently regarded a unified bloc of Latin American allies as an essential component of the U.S.-led Western alliance against the Soviet bloc. Eisenhower administration officials placed a high value on Latin America's collaboration in two U.S.-created Cold War hemispheric organizations: the Rio Pact, the mutual-defense agreement formalized in 1947, and the Organization of American States, the regional peace-keeping body established in 1948. They also counted heavily on a reliable bloc of Latin American votes in the United Nations, where Latin American member states constituted some 20 percent of the General Assembly. For U.S. policy makers, "inter-American solidarity" was a primary cornerstone of U.S. national security. As Eisenhower told the National Security Council early in his presidency, the great challenge for the United States in Latin America was to design policies that would continue to "secure the allegiance of these republics to our camp in the cold war." The top U.S. objective in Latin America, a March 1953 NSC policy statement affirmed, was "hemispheric solidarity in support of our world policies, particularly in the UN and other international organizations."[49] It was in this context that the Eisenhower administration defined Arbenz's Guatemala as a threat to U.S. national security.

In the State Department's view, "Communist success in Guatemala thus far does not constitute a direct military or economic threat to the United States. . . . The Communists are not seeking open and direct control of the Guatemalan Government, at the present time." Instead, "the underlying Communist objectives in Guatemala are to prevent collaboration of that country with the United States in [the] event of [a] future international crisis, and to disrupt hemispheric solidarity and weaken the United States position." The CIA concurred; what was really occurring in Guatemala, the agency believed, was "a determined Communist effort to neutralize Guatemala and remove it from the Western camp." A May 1953 National Intelligence Estimate expressed the U.S. intelligence community's conclusion that the PGT's "immediate objective is not a 'People's Democracy' under open and direct Communist control, but rather to neutralize Guatemala as an ally of the United States and to convert the Government into an effective, though indirectly controlled, instrument of Communism." The Guatemalan government, the NIE added, "has frequently taken occasion to demonstrate its independence of U.S. leadership and in general has been less cooperative than could be desired, particularly in Hemispheric affairs." Arbenz was already "reluctant to take a positive stand against Communism and the USSR," the State Department warned, and displayed "an unwillingness to implement the measures designed to protect the West against subversion and other forms of Communist attack." The continued drift of a "neutralized" Guatemala "out of the western camp" would be a conspicuous indication that hemispheric solidarity was unraveling. And if Guatemala's communists should spread their "infection . . . through the example of independence of the U.S. that Guatemala might offer to nationalists throughout Latin America," other Latin American nations might abandon their international alignment with the United States, destroying the hemispheric alliance system that was considered the cornerstone of U.S. security. "Continuation of the present trend in Guatemala," the NSC concluded in August 1953, "would ultimately endanger the unity of the Western Hemisphere against Soviet aggression."[50]

Much to the chagrin of U.S. strategists, however, most of the available policy options ran the risk of further damaging U.S. credibility in the eyes of the country's Latin American allies. Overt U.S. military intervention in Guatemala, the State Department warned, "would violate solemn United States commitments and . . . endanger the entire fund of good will the United States has built up in the other American Republics through its policies of non-intervention. . . . Loss of this good will would be a disaster to the United States far outweighing the advantage of any success gained in Guatemala." Alarmist U.S. appeals for "collective action" by "the inter-American community" against "little Guatemala" would only encourage "the Latin Americans to look upon the whole business as a David-Goliath contest in which they identify themselves naturally with David." "The spectacle of the elephant shaking with alarm before the mouse," the State Department's Policy Planning Staff noted, would greatly enhance "the prestige of underdog Guatemala . . . throughout Latin America . . . , and Latin American bosoms will (secretly or otherwise) swell with pride at the spectacle of one of the least among them actually arousing us to alarm for our own safety. Our own prestige and influence will be correspondingly diminished." On the other hand, if the Eisenhower administration responded to the communist threat in Guatemala with a policy of inaction and "watchful waiting," other nations in the hemisphere would question the U.S. resolve to combat communist expansionism, and "the Latin Americans would begin to ask whether the U.S. could be counted on to defend them against this growing menace."[51]

The danger extended far beyond the Western Hemisphere, however. Communist success in Guatemala, U.S. officials believed, would give international communism a powerful psychological advantage in the Cold War and dishearten U.S. allies in Europe and Asia. Secretary of State Dulles was convinced that if the Soviets were allowed to "establish a puppet state in this hemisphere" without the support or "threat of the Red Army," it would be "a tremendous propaganda victory" for communism. Such a victory would weaken U.S. "assurances to states in Asia and in Europe that we would support them in their efforts to eliminate communism . . . because of our demonstrated inability to prevent the establishment of a communist puppet state in our own hemisphere."[52] Assistant Secretary of State for Inter-American Affairs Henry Holland reinforced Dulles' analysis. "From time to time around the world," he wrote,

> frontal tests of strength between the force of the free nations and that of the Communist organization arise. One occurred in Korea. Another is in progress in Indochina. A less publicized collision is now reaching its crisis in Guatemala.
>
> In this last situation the test is whether the world Communist organization has the strength to establish a satellite nation in this hemisphere and, conversely, whether the free nations have the power to resist that attempt. . . .
>
> This contest is of crucial importance in the global struggle between free nations and the Communist forces. . . . It has been asserted that Moscow cannot establish a satellite state save where the weight of the Red Army can be brought to bear directly or indirectly. Obviously, Russia recognizes, therefore, that establishment of a satellite state in this hemisphere would mark a victory which would strengthen the power of Communist forces in every free nation of the world. Establishment of a Communist state in this hemisphere, and particularly so close to the United States, would enable Russia to claim throughout the world that the power of Communism lies in its appeal to men's minds and not in fear or force.[53]

From Washington's perspective, then, Guatemala represented nothing less than a "crucial test" of superpower strength in the Cold War. Forces on both sides of the Iron Curtain were watching the confrontation closely, U.S. officials believed, and would draw important inferences about U.S. power from Eisenhower's response to the situation. The international balance of power and the fate of the "free world" were ultimately at stake.

Amidst danger, however, lay opportunity. "In the world chess game," Secretary of State Dulles told Eisenhower in May 1953, "the Reds today have the better position. . . . Practically everywhere one looks, there is no strong holding point and danger everywhere of Communist penetration." The United States was losing the free world "bit by bit," he warned, and Western civilization would only survive if the Eisenhower administration accepted its "duty to take leadership at a fast and vigorous pace." Dulles urged Eisenhower "to attempt to restore the prestige of the West by winning in one or more areas a success or successes." The "Communists have won victory after victory in the post-war years," he said; a "success for the free world is badly needed." According to Dulles, by pursuing a policy of "boldness," Eisenhower could deter further Soviet advances and revive the morale of the Western alliance.[54] A few weeks later, a secret White House task force on national security reiterated Dulles' recommendations by advising Eisenhower that immediate "tactical victories" were needed to create a "climate of victory" in the West and reverse the tide of the Cold War.[55] Guatemala offered an auspicious opportunity for a quick, morale-boosting tactical victory. The successful overthrow of Arbenz's government would convey an image of U.S. strength and demonstrate to a watchful world that, under the Eisenhower administration, the United States could effectively stanch the tide of international communist expansionism.

Another factor, however, was also simultaneously leading the administration toward intervention. A potential national-security threat in Guatemala held important political implications for Eisenhower's presidency. From Eisenhower's perspective, Guatemala was a test of his ability to provide the strong presidential leadership that he had promised the nation in his 1952 election campaign.

Eisenhower won the presidency in 1952 by promising to manage U.S. global interests more effectively, aggressively, and inexpensively than his Democratic predecessor. Throughout the 1952 campaign, the Republicans had castigated the Truman administration for inadequate foreign-policy leadership and mismanagement of the country's security interests. According to Republican partisans, Truman and the Democrats were soft on communism—they had abandoned the peoples of Eastern Europe to communist rule; their mishandling of the Far East had resulted in the loss of China and a bloody military stalemate in Korea; and in Latin America, their "poor neighbor policy" of "drift and neglect" was allowing popular unrest to be "skillfully exploited by Communist agents." Truman's strategy of containing communism's expansionist thrusts with U.S. military counterforce was too reactive and defensive, the GOP charged; moreover, the spiraling defense expenditures and budget deficits that resulted were sapping the nation's economic strength. By contrast, the Republicans promised, an Eisenhower administration would give the nation the "leadership of wisdom and courage" that Truman and the Democrats had failed to provide. Under Eisenhower's leadership, party spokesmen assured voters, the United States would retake the initiative in the Cold War, "roll back" Soviet power, and "liberate captive peoples." Eisenhower underscored that Republican campaign theme by suggesting that the nation should not "rest content until the tidal mud of aggressive Communism has receded within its own borders." His administration, he vowed, would devise a bold, dynamic, and cost-effective new national-security strategy that would deal firmly with communist threats in both "core and peripheral regions of the globe" without overburdening the economy. With his "firm" and experienced "hand at the tiller," he said, the American people would enjoy "security with solvency." Consequently, by the time of Eisenhower's landslide electoral victory in November, Republican campaign rhetoric had created a widespread expectation in U.S. public opinion that the incoming administration would give the nation strong, aggressive, effective foreign-policy leadership. From Eisenhower's perspective, the magnitude of the landslide—55 percent of the vote and a 442–89 electoral-college majority—imposed nothing less than a mandate on him to do so.[56]

The Republican victory presented the United Fruit Company with an auspicious opportunity to exploit the domestic political environment for its own purposes. Eisenhower did not overthrow Arbenz on UFCO's behalf, but the fruit company influenced his decision to intervene in one important respect: during 1953, a smoothly orchestrated UFCO publicity campaign succeeded in focusing U.S. public attention on the issue of Guatemalan communism, generating political pressure on Eisenhower to honor his campaign commitments and take strong action against a communist challenge in the hemisphere.[57]

For several years, UFCO public-relations consultant Edward Bernays had been urging the company to increase the visibility of its Guatemalan problems by placing articles about the country's growing "communist menace" in the U.S. media; UFCO could then "count on public opinion in this country to express itself," Bernays advised. The company's directors eventually put Bernays' media program into high gear in 1952, when Arbenz began expropriating UFCO's land. The campaign was then stepped up in January 1953 "to coincide with the change of administrations" in Washington. Under Bernays' direction, UFCO invited influential U.S. publishers and editors to be the company's guests on all-expenses-paid "fact-finding" junkets to Guatemala, where the journalists "were shepherded on elaborately choreographed tours of Fruit Company facilities, and talked to local politicians who were sympathetic to the company's plight (and, not infrequently, were on the company payroll)." The press junkets, Bernays later recalled, "produced a flood of news of worsening conditions in Guatemala." By the time of Eisenhower's inauguration, U.S. newspapers and magazines were portraying Guatemala as a communist-dominated "Soviet pawn" whose airfields were within easy striking distance of the Panama Canal and Texas' oil fields. "After [the journalists'] return," Bernays noted with satisfaction, "as I had anticipated, public interest in the Caribbean skyrocketed in this country."[58]

By 1953, UFCO was also distributing a Guatemala newsletter and other anti-Arbenz "information reports" to influential opinion molders throughout the

United States. The explicit message in the company's mailings was that the Guatemalan government's attacks on UFCO were the work of international communism. In addition, the company hired prominent spokesmen like Spruille Braden, the outspoken former assistant secretary of state for inter-American affairs under Truman, to take UFCO's case "directly to the United States public." From late 1952 to early 1953, while on UFCO retainer, Braden chaired a series of study groups organized by the prestigious Council on Foreign Relations to "formulate a new policy on Latin America to be recommended to the incoming administration." Under Braden's direction, the project concluded that in Guatemala the Eisenhower administration should have "no hesitation in . . . backing a political tide which will force the Guatemalan government either to exclude its Communists or to change." "Perhaps," Braden told the forum, "we are getting to the point where actual armed intervention is the only solution." Shortly thereafter, in a widely reported public address at Dartmouth College, Braden challenged Eisenhower to live up to the Republicans' campaign promises by intervening in Guatemala to stop a communist takeover. It was necessary, Braden said, "to fight fire with fire. . . . I pray that the new Administration will attack this danger rapidly, intelligently and energetically." By the end of Eisenhower's first year in office, UFCO's multifaceted media blitz had helped to create "an atmosphere of deep suspicion and fear in the United States about the nature and intentions of the Guatemalan government."[59] Eisenhower's ambassador in Guatemala, John Peurifoy, indirectly acknowledged the impact of UFCO's public pressure tactics in January 1954 when he confided to reporters that "public opinion in the United States may force us to take some measures to prevent Guatemala from falling into the lap of international Communism."[60]

A final weapon in UFCO's arsenal was the platoon of high-powered lobbyists that the company unleashed on Washington's corridors of power. During the Truman years, UFCO hired well-placed liberals to lobby the executive and legislative branches of government; their ranks included former FDR brain-truster Thomas Corcoran, a "consummate Washington power broker" and "purveyor of concentrated influence," as well as Robert La Follette Jr., the progressive four-term Wisconsin senator defeated by Joseph McCarthy in 1947. Corcoran in particular enjoyed easy access to high-level officials at the State Department and CIA and served as UFCO's liaison to the CIA during the aborted 1952 Operation PBFORTUNE. In 1952, with the likelihood of a Republican administration looming on the political horizon, lobbyists with prominent conservative connections were enlisted—most notably John Clements, a right-wing journalist and public relations man closely associated with the McCarthyite end of the U.S. political spectrum. Clements concentrated his efforts on Capitol Hill, disseminating anti-Arbenz "research reports" and other UFCO propaganda to members of Congress in a campaign to generate congressional pressure on Eisenhower to intervene.[61] According to E. Howard Hunt, a longtime CIA field operative who played a central role in the

1954 intervention, the fruit company was instrumental in prompting the Eisenhower administration to authorize Operation PBSUCCESS. When Hunt was assigned to the operation in the latter part of 1953, he asked his agency superiors "why . . . the climate was suddenly right for a political-action effort in Guatemala" when a Hunt recommendation for covert CIA intervention against Arbenz a year and a half earlier had gone nowhere. "The difference," Hunt was told, "had to do with domestic politics" and UFCO's energetic lobbying efforts. In response to Arbenz's agrarian-reform program, Hunt learned, Corcoran "had begun lobbying in behalf of United Fruit and against Arbenz. Following this special impetus our project had been approved by the National Security Council."[62]

But Eisenhower was facing political pressures independent of UFCO instigation. Throughout 1953 and 1954, the powerful right wing of his own Republican Party was openly criticizing his performance as president. Eisenhower's relationship with the Republican Right had been fragile since the 1952 party convention, when Eisenhower and Republican moderates had defeated Senator Robert Taft, the leader of the GOP's conservative Old Guard, in a bitter battle for the party's presidential nomination. During the ensuing 1952 campaign, the bellicose rhetoric of "liberation" and "rollback" that colored the public statements of Eisenhower's spokesmen was designed in part to placate party conservatives and restore party unity. But when, as president, Eisenhower's policies failed to match the campaign rhetoric, the Old Guard lashed out at him. In Congress—where right-wing Republicans held a majority of the party's seats and controlled most of the key committee chairmanships—GOP conservatives attacked Eisenhower for his failure to dismantle the liberal welfare state erected by Roosevelt and Truman. They opposed his nominations of Republican moderates and Truman appointees to a number of foreign-policy posts. They attempted to pass a constitutional amendment (the Bricker Amendment) that would have limited his executive authority in foreign policy. They criticized his July 1953 Korean War armistice agreement as appeasement of communist aggression. And they impatiently called on him to "sterilize" the "Red infection" in Guatemala.

Eisenhower was not a weak leader likely to cave in to the conservatives' pressure. And yet, with razor-thin Republican majorities in both houses of Congress (221–214 in the House, 49–47 in the Senate), he needed their cooperation if he was to pass the legislative programs—deficit limitation, reduced defense spending, expanded Social Security and Mutual Security Program funding, and so forth—that he believed were necessary if the Republicans were to build the creditable record that would enable them to keep control of Congress in the 1954 elections. Consequently, by the middle months of 1953, dissension within his own party had driven him "almost to despair of being able to succeed in the Presidency." By August—when the decision was made to overthrow Arbenz—party disunity was generating increased pressure on the White House for a foreign-policy victory that would win the respect of disgruntled Republican conservatives.[63]

Eisenhower ran for the presidency in 1952 because he was convinced that neither the Democrats nor the Taft Republicans possessed the strategic vision required to protect the United States from eventual communist encirclement in the Cold War. During the election campaign, he confidently put himself forward as the leader who could provide that vision and reverse the tide of Soviet expansionism. His early months in office were devoted to the formulation of his New Look national security strategy, which emphasized air power, nuclear deterrence, and collective security arrangements, combined with defense spending reductions and increased reliance on covert operations.[64] During those same months, Guatemala was becoming an increasingly visible issue in U.S. public opinion and U.S. domestic politics. To the Eisenhower administration, Guatemala represented not only a potential threat to U.S. international credibility but a situation that tested the new administration's leadership capabilities and its commitment to recent campaign promises. According to a recently declassified CIA internal history of the Guatemalan intervention, "In Eisenhower's mind, finding creative responses to Communist penetration of peripheral areas like Guatemala posed one of the critical tests of his ability as a leader." "Guatemala," the CIA history concludes, "put the new administration on trial."[65] From Eisenhower's perspective, a successful intervention in Guatemala would achieve multiple benefits: it would eliminate a potential Soviet beachhead in Latin America; it would demonstrate to disheartened free-world allies, communist-bloc adversaries, and world opinion generally that the U.S.-led forces of Western anticommunism had the power, and the will, to defeat Soviet-backed subversion; and at home it would demonstrate that the Eisenhower administration could carry out the successful (and inexpensive) "rollback" of communism that the Republican Right demanded and that U.S. public opinion had been led to expect.[66] From Eisenhower's standpoint, U.S. international credibility, effective presidential leadership, and ultimately his prospects for a successful presidency all required that his administration—early in its first term in office and "on trial" politically—remove Jacobo Arbenz from power.

Preparations for the intervention began in mid-August, and subsequent developments in Guatemala only intensified Eisenhower's determination to proceed. In December, after a tense, six-hour dinner conversation during which Arbenz and his wife gave "lame" and transparently duplicitous responses to U.S. ambassador Peurifoy's accusations of communist influence in the Guatemalan government, Peurifoy strongly reaffirmed Washington's conviction that Arbenz was a Marxist and that "normal approaches will not work in Guatemala."[67] Four months later, in April 1954, U.S. intelligence discovered a secret shipment of Soviet-bloc military equipment headed for Guatemala. The armaments—which Arbenz and the PGT intended to use to create "workers' militias"—were eventually seized by the Guatemalan Army, but the incident produced a wave of anti-Guatemala hysteria in the U.S. Congress and news media and provided Eisenhower with a final justification for intervention.[68]

Following Arbenz's ouster, the president and his key advisers moved quickly to exploit their victory. Secretary of State Dulles was particularly eager to publicize what he regarded as "the biggest success in the last five years against Communism" and "made sure the administration . . . derive[d] the maximum political capital from it." In a nationwide radio and television address three days after Arbenz stepped down, Dulles portrayed Castillo Armas' counterrevolution as a dramatic Cold War victory for the West. Without openly acknowledging U.S. involvement, he praised the Guatemalan people for having "cured" their country of "an alien despotism which sought to use Guatemala for its own evil ends," namely "to destroy . . . the inter-American system." "In the face of terrorism and violence and against what seemed insuperable odds," Dulles told the nation, "the loyal citizens of Guatemala . . . had the courage and the will to eliminate the traitorous tools of foreign despots." The example set by Castillo Armas' "patriots," he said, would make "ambitious and unscrupulous" elements in the Western Hemisphere "less prone to feel that communism is the wave of their future."[69] Privately, Dulles also viewed Arbenz's overthrow as the fulfillment of the Republicans' 1952 campaign pledge to liberate countries suffering under communist rule. According to former State Department official Cole Blasier, Dulles "regarded this 'victory' as one of the major constructive achievements of the Eisenhower administration and used it as a rallying cry in the 1954 and 1956 elections."[70]

Eisenhower, for his part, had been making political capital out of the intervention before it even occurred. From early 1954 onward, the White House tried to reassure the disgruntled Republican conservatives in Congress that Eisenhower was "in full control of the Guatemalan situation" by leaking indications to key Republican congressmen that "action was in the offing." Following Arbenz's overthrow, Eisenhower exploited the intervention to good effect in the fall congressional elections; in campaign speeches from coast to coast he deflected criticism of his foreign policy by emphasizing that under his administration Guatemala (and Iran) had been saved from communism. In January 1955, during his first televised press conference, Eisenhower "listed the elimination of the Arbenz regime as one of his proudest accomplishments," while in his memoirs he discussed the operation "in some detail and with great pride," citing it "as a reason why he deserved a second term as president."[71]

In addition, CIA director Allen Dulles used the intervention to bolster the CIA's public image and ward off a possible investigation of the agency by Senator Joseph McCarthy. In late October–early November 1954, Dulles fed a series of articles to the *Saturday Evening Post* publicizing the CIA's role in overthrowing Arbenz and heaping "lavish praise on the agency as the 'first line of defense'" in the United States' "underground war with Russia." The articles reported how "the CIA, working with Guatemalan 'freedom forces,'" had "met the Reds early enough to hand Russia its defeat in Guatemala." Under the Eisenhower administration, the authors assured their readers, the CIA was "hit[ting] the Russians where it hurts."[72]

For Eisenhower and his advisers, their exhilarating triumph in Guatemala was a strategically significant and politically beneficial demonstration that they were managing the nation's security interests effectively. Seven years later, their successors in office would attempt to achieve similar results in Cuba, at the Bay of Pigs.

CHAPTER TWO

Cuba, 1961

President Kennedy knew that, in his words, he had "fucked up" and was in "deep trouble." Less than three months into his presidency, a U.S.-sponsored invasion of Cuba by a CIA-trained proxy army of Cuban exiles had been routed by Fidel Castro's armed forces at the Bay of Pigs. Of the 1,511 Cubans that Kennedy had sent to overthrow Castro, 1,303 had been captured or killed. Kennedy's immediate reaction was one of "personal shock and political calculation"—the Cuban debacle would undoubtedly have a devastating impact on his administration's "domestic popularity and international reputation." Politically, he told White House assistant Theodore Sorensen, the Bay of Pigs disaster was "the worst defeat of his career"; he had "handed his critics a stick with which they would forever beat him." Internationally, U.S. prestige had been seriously damaged; Kennedy's failure to defeat the military forces of a small Caribbean island neighbor would inevitably create the impression in Latin America, in NATO, in the Kremlin, indeed everywhere, that Kennedy was a weak president and that under his administration the United States had become a paper tiger. The president's aides "had never seen him so distraught" or "as close to crying."[1]

Three days after the Bay of Pigs operation collapsed, Kennedy began the process of damage limitation. On April 20, 1961, in a speech on Cuba before the American Society of Newspaper Editors, the president was neither apologetic nor contrite; instead, he projected an image of strength and resolve reminiscent of Winston Churchill during the Battle of Britain. Although U.S. military forces had not participated in the Cuban invasion, Kennedy told his audience, "Let the record show that our restraint is not inexhaustible. Should it ever appear that the inter-American doctrine of non-interference merely conceals or excuses a policy of inaction—if the nations of this Hemisphere should fail to meet their commitments against outside Communist penetration—then I want it clearly understood that this Government will not hesitate in meeting its primary obligations which are to the security of our Nation!" He wanted to make clear that "as the President of the United States" he was "determined" to protect U.S. security interests "regardless of the cost and regardless of the peril!" The main purpose of the speech, Kennedy told an aide afterward, was "to make us appear tough and powerful."[2]

The target of Kennedy's interventionism, and the source of his discomfiture, was a Latin American nationalist revolution similar in many respects to the Guatemalan revolution. Fidel Castro's 26th of July Movement was another multiclass coalition dedicated to internal reforms and international independence. Like the Guatemalan revolution, it contained within itself a variety of ideological tendencies ranging from social democratic reformism to Marxism-Leninism. And, as in Guatemala, Marxist elements gradually gained ascendancy and eventually set the revolution's programmatic agenda. Cuba's revolutionaries had also learned crucial lessons from Arbenz's defeat, however—notably the importance of masking their Marxian proclivities and dismantling the prerevolutionary national armed forces—and they were accordingly better prepared to anticipate, and survive, eventual U.S. intervention.

Cuba was not Guatemala. Its economy was more highly developed. Its national income levels were substantially higher. Its upper class was neither as homogeneous nor as manorial as its Guatemalan counterpart; its middle class was larger and more experienced in politics; and its lower class had a longer tradition of labor activism. And yet Cuba, like Guatemala, was merely a variation on the theme of Latin American underdevelopment. Its monocrop economy was overwhelmingly dependent on the production and export of a single commodity—sugar—and the sugar-based economy condemned hundreds of thousands of Cuban workers to unemployment or underemployment and a precarious standard of living during the eight-month "dead time" that followed the annual sugarcane harvest. In the countryside, where 8 percent of the population owned 71 percent of the land, more than two-thirds of the population lived in dirt-floor thatched huts, without running water or electricity. Average income for Cuba's rural workers in the late 1950s was $90 a year, and their nutritional intake and access to health-care facilities were so inadequate that nutrition-related diseases were virtually endemic among the rural lower classes. The Cuban educational system was so inaccessible to the country's lower classes that in 1958 one-third of the population had received no schooling whatsoever while another third had no more than three years of primary education.[3]

If anything, the hegemonic presence of the United States weighed even more heavily on Cuba than on Guatemala. U.S. military intervention had freed the island from Spanish colonial rule in 1898, after which the Cubans gained a conditional form of national independence as a U.S. political protectorate and informal economic colony. By the late 1950s, Cuba had been molded into the centerpiece of the U.S. sphere of influence in the Caribbean. More U.S. capital (approximately $1 billion) was invested in the island than in any other Latin American nation with the exception of Venezuela. U.S.-owned sugar mills produced 40 percent of Cuba's sugar; U.S. companies controlled the island's public utilities, railroads, and oil refineries; and U.S.-owned cattle ranches, mines, banks, hotels, and casinos were influential players in the Cuban economy. A special instrument of U.S. hegemonic power was the U.S. sugar quota, an arrangement in which Cuba was allowed to supply an annual fixed percentage of U.S. sugar imports; the quota guaranteed Cuba a profitable market for its principal crop, but threats to reduce the quota gave U.S. officials powerful leverage over Cuban policy makers if they stepped out of line.[4]

There was seldom any need. For six decades, Cuba's political leaders complaintly accommodated themselves to U.S. power. They maintained close bonds of diplomatic and military collaboration with Washington; they permitted U.S. ambassadors to exercise proconsular influence over Cuban policy matters; and they accepted (in fact occasionally invited) periodic U.S. interventions that stabilized Cuba's fractious political system. They provided U.S. investors with open doors, lenient regulations and tax laws, guarantees against nationalization of property, and a stable cheap-labor force. And they stole the Cuban treasury blind. Official corruption in Cuba reached levels of such excess that a U.S. ambassador would later recall: "I know of no country among those committed to the Western ethic where the diversion of public treasure for private profit reached the proportions that it attained in the Cuban Republic." Cuba's long tradition of corrupt, servile government reached its nadir with the Fulgencio Batista dictatorship of 1952–1958. Batista, who eventually fled into exile with riches estimated at between $60 million and $300 million, served as one of the United States' most reliable Cold War allies in Latin America. He "faithfully backed" U.S. positions in international forums, outlawed Cuba's Communist Party, and rejected diplomatic relations with Eastern bloc nations, while his generous tax exemptions and "lightened controls on capital remittances" stimulated nearly a 50 percent increase in U.S. investments in Cuba during his tenure in office. As rewards, Cuba received nearly $40 million in U.S. Export-Import Bank loans, $16 million in U.S. armaments, and extensive U.S. military training programs for the repressive Cuban national-security forces that kept Batista's increasingly unpopular regime in power. To a generation of young Cubans reaching political maturity in the 1950s, Batista's symbiotic alliance with the United States was merely the latest proof that Cuba's struggle for genuine national independence remained "unfinished business."[5]

The most prominent figure to emerge from that generation, Fidel Castro, was a product of the same currents of revolutionary nationalism and anti-imperialism that inspired Arévalo and Arbenz. Like Guatemala's revolutionaries, Castro attributed his nation's underdevelopment to the elite classes' long tradition of exploitative collaboration with foreign imperialism. As a twenty-year-old student at the University of Havana in 1947, Castro publicly denounced Cuba's leaders as "puppets at the orders of foreigners." After Batista's 1952 seizure of power interrupted his budding career as a parliamentary politician, Castro labeled Batista "a faithful dog of imperialism" and launched a guerrilla insurrection against his dictatorship.[6] During a 1955 meeting with the leaders of competing opposition movements, Castro called on them to join him in "fighting against the past"; he went on to explain, according to an aide present at the meeting, that

> he was against the unscrupulous politicians, against the scoundrels in government, against the embezzlers, against the military . . . , against the rich, against the landowners, against the big foreign interests, against Yankee imperialism.

"*Con todo esto hay que acabar*" ("We have to do away with all this"). . . . Then he turned once again to his favorite, almost obsessive theme: a denunciation of the *viejos políticos* ["old politicians," for whom] he reserved his most scathing diatribes and epithets . . . : scoundrels, shameless thieves, spineless lackeys of Yankee imperialism.[7]

After forcing Batista from power on January 1, 1959, Castro regularly identified the "alliance" of "national and international oligarchies" as the principal enemy of structural change in Cuba, and he warned the Cuban people that Cuban reactionaries—"those who sold out to foreign interests"—would inevitably attempt a counterrevolution supported by "foreign aid" from the "international oligarchy."[8]

The principal international and foreign threat to which Castro alluded, of course, lay 90 miles to the north. Castro, like most Cubans of his generation, had a deep-seated resentment of U.S. domination. His bitterness toward the United States dated back to his student days at the University of Havana, where he was active in a variety of anti-imperialist organizations and promoted student militancy on behalf of Cuba's "true independence . . . economic liberation . . . [and] genuine emancipation." In 1948, he headed a delegation of Cuban students that traveled to Bogotá, Colombia, to participate in the formation of an anti-imperialist organization of Latin American students and to disrupt a conference of hemispheric foreign ministers that was convening in the Colombian capital to formalize the creation of the Organization of American States—a conference that, in Castro's words, had been "called by the United States to consolidate its system of domination here in Latin America." During the subsequent guerrilla war that he waged against the Batista dictatorship, Castro on several occasions characterized his insurrection as a struggle for national liberation. If anything, the military campaign against Batista's U.S.-trained and -supplied forces intensified his resentment of the U.S. presence in Cuba and persuaded him that, as he told a compatriot in 1958, his true destiny was to wage "a much longer and bigger war" against the Americans and "make them pay dearly for what they're doing" in Cuba once Batista had been defeated.[9]

After Batista's flight into exile, Castro's public statements bristled with defiant indications that U.S. hegemony in Cuba was now a thing of the past. "This time the Revolution will not be frustrated," he told cheering crowds in Santiago on January 2, 1959. "This time . . . it will not be like 1898 when the Americans came and made themselves masters of the country." "For the first time," he told a Havana audience two weeks later, Cuba had political and military leaders who were "not taking orders from abroad" and who "cannot be bribed or intimidated." In at least two January speeches, he declared that he was "not selling out to the Americans" and would not "receive orders from them." He was not going to be "another Yankee lackey," he told a Cuban journalist. "If the Americans don't like what is going on in Cuba," he said in angry response to U.S. criticism of his firing-squad executions of Batista henchmen, "they can land the Marines and then there will be 200,000 *gringos* dead." The United States had been "interfering in Cuban affairs for more than fifty years," he stated in February, and it was time for a change, time for Cuba to "solve its own problems."[10]

Meanwhile, Castro was announcing his plans for a revolutionary transformation of Cuba. The "Republic that we are building and the *Patria* that we are redeeming," he told a Havana mass audience in March, "will not be a paradise for vested interests, as it was in the past, but rather a home where humble people can find happiness." The "onerous concessions" that Batista's government had granted "to foreign monopolies" were "going to be reviewed and cancelled." Cuba would no longer be subject to the United States' "continual threats" to reduce the sugar quota and would, in the future, "sell sugar to anyone who has the money to buy it."[11] Castro also hinted that Cuba would be withdrawing from the U.S. sphere of influence and the Western bloc in favor of neutral nonalignment in the Cold War. In March, he defined Cuba's revolution as "a new doctrine which is between the two hegemonies struggling to control the world." "Why should Latin America be with either side?" he asked. He expressed open contempt for hemispheric solidarity and the U.S.-led inter-American system, calling the Organization of American States "a useless organization." In February, he rejected membership in the newly formed Inter-American Development Bank, and the following month announced that Cuba would no longer "accept actions taken under the Rio Treaty." By year's end, Cuba had withdrawn from the World Bank as well.[12]

Cuba's revolutionaries had studied the 1954 Guatemalan intervention closely, and they anticipated that their defiant gestures of anti-American nationalism would eventually provoke U.S. intervention. In January, Castro warned a mass rally in Havana that "the U.S. Government has not directly attacked us . . . but we know what the mechanics are in the United States. A certain campaign is begun; the interests that fear the revolution organize a campaign against the revolution; they shape public opinion, and then ask the U.S. Government to take action." Accordingly, from the moment of their arrival in Havana, Castro's forces were taking steps to reduce their vulnerability to U.S. aggression while they consolidated their revolutionary government in power. Batista's national army was quickly dissolved and replaced by a new institution commanded by "radical guerrilla chieftains." The U.S. military missions in Cuba were also asked to leave the country. As a result, historian Jules Benjamin writes, "one of the old channels of U.S. influence . . . rapidly dried up." Castro also attempted to secure alternative sources of economic assistance that would enable him to proceed with his plans to nationalize U.S. capital in Cuba without fear of U.S. economic retaliation. In late January, during a state visit to Venezuela, he told President-elect Rómulo Betancourt that he was thinking of "having a game with the gringos" and needed a $300 million loan from Venezuela "to free his government from dependence on the U.S. sugar-market quota, loans from U.S. banks, and international credit agencies."[13]

Castro's revolutionary ambitions did not confine themselves to Cuba, however. From the start, he felt that his ultimate destiny was to liberate all of Latin America from the chains of domination that the United States had forged in collaboration with Latin America's reactionary elites. As early as 1955, he was telling his revolutionary colleagues that "the struggle in Cuba was part of the continental struggle against the Yankees that Bolívar and Martí had already foreseen." Shortly after coming to power, he confided to a prominent supporter that "he hoped to do nothing less than free Latin America from U.S. economic domination as Simón Bolívar more than a century earlier had freed it from Spanish political control." "He saw himself as a liberator and as the potential spiritual leader of a great new Latin American revolutionary bloc," recalls former U.S. diplomat Wayne Smith, who observed Castro closely during the early days of the revolution. "The main enemy was U.S. economic imperialism, but as Castro assessed the power structure in most Latin American countries, most of the governments represented *vendepatria* (or sellout) classes whose interests were closely linked to those of the United States. Thus in the other countries, as in Cuba, the first step in driving out U.S. influence was the overthrow of the national governments themselves." Castro undoubtedly also calculated, of course, that as the leader of a Latin American alliance of nationalist revolutionary states his regime would be less isolated and consequently less vulnerable to U.S. intervention.[14]

Cuba's new leader lost little time in pursuing his "messianic vision" of hemispheric liberation. Throughout 1959, his revolutionary government attempted to ignite insurrectionary uprisings in neighboring countries. In April, Cuba sponsored an armed expedition against the Panamanian government. In June, Cuban-backed insurgents invaded the Dominican Republic. In August, a small Cuban invasion force attempted to land in Haiti. Although none of these early expeditions succeeded in establishing a guerrilla front, Castro remained convinced that Cuba's revolution would be the vanguard of a great anti-imperialist rebellion that would inevitably sweep through Latin America and liberate the region from the prevailing U.S.-controlled "system of domination."[15]

The first priority, however, was survival. Castro knew that he must avoid alarming the United States to the point where it would move to snuff out the revolution before he had had time to consolidate his power and strengthen his defenses. Accordingly, throughout the early months of 1959, he shrewdly balanced his outbursts of anti-American nationalism with a series of seemingly conciliatory gestures designed to keep U.S. officials off balance and uncertain of his real intentions. His initial revolutionary government was made up of internationally respected moderates known to favor democratic-capitalist development models for Cuba. Castro alternated his anti-U.S. comments (and in fact quickly apologized for his "200,000 dead *gringos*" remark) with public statements expressing his desire for good relations with Washington. He repeatedly asserted that Cuba would move toward a mixed economy in which foreign investment would play an important role; U.S. private capital and U.S. government aid, he said, were welcome in Cuba. During an April trip to the United States, Castro was the "guest who told everybody what they wanted to hear." In media appearances and meetings with U.S. officials, he affirmed his commitment to "real democracy," a free press, and "good relations" with the United States. He was opposed to communism and socialism, he informed U.S. audiences, and would side with the Western democracies in the Cold War. Nor, he said, would he expropriate U.S. property. According to Castro, his U.S. visit was designed "to win support . . . from American public opinion." Its real purpose, however, was to gain time.[16]

A month later, Castro announced the centerpiece of his planned structural revolution: the agrarian reform law of May 17, 1959. The law authorized the state to expropriate all properties larger than 1,000 acres, except for estates devoted to sugar, cattle, or rice production, where the limit was extended to 3,333 acres. Expropriated landowners were to be compensated with twenty-year bonds bearing 4.5 percent interest, with payments based—as in Arbenz's land reform—on the declared value of the land for tax purposes. Seemingly moderate on the surface, Castro's agrarian reform program was in actuality the foundation for a radical revolutionary transformation of Cuba. It was designed to abolish large-scale private landholdings—including the island's massive U.S.-owned properties, which ranged up to 480,000 acres in size—and to replace them with peasant cooperatives and, eventually, state farms. Again, as in Guatemala, the program was essentially viewed by its authors as a political instrument, "the decisive apparatus . . . for activating the country's masses." The government agency created to implement the program—the National Institute of Agrarian Reform (INRA)—immediately began mobilizing Cuba's peasantry in support of the government. Within two months, INRA had nationalized 400 of the largest U.S.- and Cuban-owned ranches—totaling nearly 2.5 million acres of land—and was moving quickly to create "its own armed 100,000-man militia units" to defend the revolution. A year later, INRA's executive director would describe the agency as "the bastion where the Revolution occurred in those initial months . . . the organism that dealt the real blow to [the] bourgeoisie and imperialism."[17]

The agrarian reform law was drafted in secret by a small circle of Castro's Marxist supporters.[18] Did this mean that Castro himself was a Marxist in early 1959? A vast number of books, polemical and scholarly, have addressed that question, and a good many more will be written before a definitive answer emerges. All that can be stated with any certainty is that by May 1959 Castro had cast his lot with the radical wing of his 26th of July Movement and that "unorthodox communists"—notably his younger brother Raúl and guerrilla comrade Ernesto "Che" Guevara—were serving as his closest advisers. Raúl Castro had close connections to Cuba's communist party, the Partido Socialista Popular (PSP), and was "a great admirer of the Soviet Union." He shared his older brother's conviction "that the struggle for power was to make a revolution on behalf of the people, and that this struggle was not only for Cuba, but for Latin America and against Yankee imperialism." Guevara was "a convinced Marxist" embarked on a personal mission to engage in "combat for the liberation of America from United States imperialism." Ideologically, Guevara said, he "belong[ed] to those who believe that the solution to the world's problems can be found behind the so-called iron curtain."[19] Raúl and Che were independent Marxist revolutionaries. Neither was under communist party discipline or Soviet direction. But they and the other 26th of July Movement radicals were convinced that genuine social revolutionary change in Cuba must inevitably lead to open confrontation with the United States and that if the revolution was going to survive U.S. hostility it would need the support of strong allies, including the Cuban communist party and the Soviet Union.[20] By the second half of 1959, Fidel Castro evidently shared that view.

Castro had long regarded the Partido Socialista Popular with disdain and distrust, owing to the party's failure to participate in armed struggle against Batista and its condemnation of Castro's rebels as a "movement of petit-bourgeois adventurers." By early 1959, however, he was conducting "discreet negotiations" with PSP leaders aimed at fusing the party (and its solid organizational base in the Cuban labor movement) with the radical wing of his 26th of July Movement in order to create a new mass-based revolutionary organization that he could use to institutionalize the revolution.[21] An early indication that the revolution was headed in a radical direction came in May with the naming of an "ardent Communist," Antonio Núñez Jiménez, to direct the government's new agrarian reform agency, INRA. During June and July, five moderate cabinet ministers were replaced by radicals, and Osvaldo Dorticós, a secret PSP member since 1953, replaced the moderate Manuel Urrutia as the country's figurehead president. By October, Raúl Castro had taken official command of Cuba's armed forces and intelligence services. During November, the last remaining moderates were forced to resign from the cabinet, communists secured influential positions in several government ministries and Cuba's principal labor confederation, and Che Guevara became president of Cuba's national bank. By the end of 1959, Castro's moderate supporters had been purged from nearly all positions of power, and the Cuban Communist Party was actively being integrated into Cuba's state structures under Castro's political control as the revolution's "Maximum Leader."[22]

Meanwhile, early feelers were being extended to Moscow. Castro had no particular love for the Soviet Union—as he informed his brother Raúl during the revolution's insurrectionary phase: "I hate Soviet imperialism as much as Yankee imperialism! I'm not breaking my neck fighting one dictatorship to fall into another." During 1959, however, as his early plans to construct a protective alliance of neighboring revolutionary states in Latin America proved unattainable in the short term, Castro—according to his first finance minister, Rufo López-Fresquet—became "interested in an alliance with Russia to counter intervention by the United States." In April, Raúl Castro asked the Soviets to supply a few military advisers from a group of Spanish communists trained in the Soviet military academy, "to help the Cuba army . . . on general matters and for the organization of intelligence work." The Soviet Presidium quickly approved the request. During June and July, Che Guevara led a Cuban trade mission to Africa and Asia, where he spent time with local Soviet and Eastern bloc diplomats, informing them that Moscow had a new Third World ally in Cuba and inviting Soviet economic aid and expanded commercial relations. In September, the Cubans requested permission to secretly purchase weapons from Poland. Again the Kremlin responded affirmatively. In October, the first Soviet KGB agent, Aleksandr Alekseev, arrived in Cuba and was quickly granted an audience with Castro, who enthusiastically suggested an increase in Cuban-Soviet trade relations and invited a touring Soviet cultural and technological exhibition to visit Cuba. In subsequent discussions with Alekseev, Castro confided that Cuba's dependent economy was vulnerable to U.S. economic strangulation and suggested that Soviet credits and a trade pact—one based, perhaps, on an exchange of Soviet oil for Cuban sugar—would reduce the revolution's vulnerability to U.S. aggression. And if done "very carefully," Castro indicated, an eventual Cuban alliance with the Soviet Union could probably be sold to the Cuban people.[23]

Castro's seduction of the Soviets was consummated in February 1960 with the signing of a major Soviet-Cuban commercial agreement. Under its terms, the Soviet Union extended Cuba a $100 million credit and agreed to buy 4.425 million tons of Cuban sugar over the next five years, "20 percent of which was to be paid for in hard currency and the remainder in Soviet goods, including 6 million barrels of oil per year." Economic agreements with East Germany and Poland soon followed. Consequently, by early 1960 Castro and his radical supporters were enjoying a growing sense of security. The foundation was nearly in place for the revolution's institutionalization at home, and bonds of alliance were rapidly being forged with a powerful foreign protector and patron. Now, Castro boasted confidently to Alekseev, "All U.S. attempts to intervene are condemned to failure."[24]

The Eisenhower administration had been watching Castro apprehensively since December 1956, when his revolutionary expedition landed in Cuba and launched its guerrilla war against Batista. From that point onward, Assistant Secretary of State for Inter-American Affairs Roy Rubottom recalled in 1960, the State Department had been trying "to pin a definite label on Castro in order to take stronger action against him." His 26th of July Movement was "composed of heterogeneous elements—most of them undesirable," the U.S. embassy in Havana reported as the insurrection gained momentum; "the political, economic and social policies which they would follow are too much of an unknown quantity." The CIA's assessment was more unequivocal. In Castro, the agency concluded in mid-1958, "the U.S. was up against an individual who could not be expected to be acceptable to

U.S. Government interests." Accordingly, the Eisenhower administration assumed an attitude of "malevolent neutrality" toward the rebels. During 1958, as Batista's position weakened, the United States withdrew its support from the dictator and embarked on a fruitless search for a "democratic third force" that could "block Castro's ascension to power." By late December, with Batista's collapse imminent, the State Department was working frantically "by all means short of outright intervention to bring about a political solution in Cuba which will keep the Castro movement from power." When Batista suddenly fled into exile, abandoning Cuba to Castro's forces, the administration realized it was left with no alternative but to "batten down the hatches" and prepare for "some real stormy weather."[25]

The early months of 1959 were, in Eisenhower's words, the "testing phase" of U.S. policy toward the revolution. The administration viewed the Castro brothers and Che Guevara with deep skepticism, but the presence of "Cubans of ability and moderation" in the new government gave U.S. officials reason to hope that the revolution's moderate faction might "check the extremists." Moreover, the president later recounted,

> the great popularity which Castro then enjoyed throughout this Hemisphere and the world gave us no alternative but to give him his chance.
>
> Our first actions, therefore, were directed to give Castro every chance to establish a reasonable relationship with us. . . . We sharply curbed all inclination to retort and strike back at his early diatribes against us, leaving the way open to him to climb off of this line and get down to the serious business of running the affairs of his country responsibly.
>
> Before the first six months had ended, it was clear Castro had failed this test.[26]

In June 1959, the State Department "reached the decision that it was not possible to achieve our objectives with Castro in power" and "that . . . we should devise means to help bring about his overthrow and replacement by a government friendly to the United States." Follow-up action was temporarily delayed when "important American interests" in Cuba reported a potential "change in the climate," but by late October U.S. officials were convinced that "definitive action against the Castro Government" was necessary. On November 5, Secretary of State Christian Herter formally recommended to Eisenhower that the United States give covert support to Cuban opposition elements in order to bring about "a reformed Castro regime or a successor to it" by "not later than the end of 1960." The goal, Herter indicated, was to see Castro's regime "checked or replaced." The president quickly approved Herter's recommendation. Four months later, on March 17, 1960, Eisenhower approved the CIA's proposed "Program for Covert Action Against the Castro Regime," the stated objective of which was "to bring about the replacement of the Castro regime with one more devoted to the true interests of the Cuban people and more acceptable to the U.S. in such a manner as to avoid any appearance of U.S. intervention." The program authorized the CIA to organize a viable Cuban opposition movement and train a paramilitary force of Cuban exiles "to be introduced into Cuba to organize, train and lead resistance groups." It was the framework for the Bay of Pigs invasion thirteen months later.[27]

But what specific aspects of the Cuban revolution had provoked Eisenhower's decision to overthrow it? One perception operative in Washington was that Castro posed a potential threat to U.S. national security. U.S. officials had been searching for signs of communist influence in the 26th of July Movement since the start of the insurrection against Batista. They were consistently wary of Raúl Castro and Che Guevara, whom they regarded as "staunch pro-Communists if not actual Communists." They were alarmed by the Cuban communist party's "infiltration" of Castro's guerrilla movement in 1958 and, beginning on New Year's Day 1959, its "penetration" of Cuba's government. And they feared that Castro's emerging entente with the Soviet Union in late 1959–early 1960 presented international communism with an opportunity to strengthen its position in the Caribbean.[28] But they could find no evidence that the revolution was communist led or even susceptible to communist control.

In late 1957, Secretary of State John Foster Dulles dismissed suggestions that Castro was "a procommunist . . . heavily influenced by Moscow" as "utter nonsense." A year later, as rebel forces advanced on Havana, the State Department concluded that although "the Communists are utilizing the Castro movement to some extent" and the 26th of July Movement's "nationalistic line is [a] horse which Communists know well how to ride," it would "not . . . be possible to pin a communist label on the Castro movement." Shortly after the rebels assumed power, CIA director Allen Dulles informed the Senate Foreign Relations Committee that Castro did not have "any Communist leanings." Nor could the U.S. embassy in Havana find any "serious evidence of effective Communist influence upon the new Cuban government either from the local Communist party or from abroad." After a three-hour private conversation with Castro during his April 1959 U.S. visit, Vice President Richard Nixon "guessed" that the Cuban leader was merely "incredibly naive about Communism" rather than "under Communist discipline." In early November, on the same day that Eisenhower approved Secretary of State Herter's recommendation for U.S. intervention, CIA deputy director C. P. Cabell told a Senate subcommittee that "Fidel Castro is not a Communist." "The Cuban Communists do not consider him a Communist Party member, or even a pro-Communist," Cabell testified; "they do not . . . control him or his government." The previous day, the State Department had again reported that there was "no evidence" of "Soviet activity" in Cuba. On March 17, 1960, the day Eisenhower authorized the CIA to undertake its program of covert action against Castro, Secretary of State Herter acknowledged that "our own latest National Intelligence Estimate [NIE] does not find Cuba to be under Communist control or domination, and we lack all of the hard evidence which would be required to convince skeptical Latin American Governments and the public opinion behind them." Five days later, as preparations for the intervention accelerated, a Special National Intelligence Estimate on "Communist Influence in Cuba" reported that Castro "almost certainly has no intention of sharing his power" with Cuba's communists and that he was "not disposed to accept . . . direction from any foreign source." "Fidel Castro and his government are not now demonstrably under the domination or control of the international Communist movement," the NIE concluded. "Moreover, we believe that they will not soon come under such demonstrable domination or control."[29]

Another aspect of the revolution that seriously disturbed U.S. officials was its nationalistic treatment of U.S. investment capital. Washington reacted to Castro's May 1959 agrarian reform law with indignation, charging that its compensation formula—twenty-year bonds based on tax valuations—failed to meet the traditional U.S. standard of "prompt" (immediate), "adequate" (full-value), and "effective" (in-cash) compensation for expropriated property. As land seizures commenced, frightened U.S. investors barraged the administration with requests for support.[30]

The chronology of U.S. policy responses to the revolution would seem to suggest that Castro's assault on U.S. investment capital played a decisive role in Eisenhower's decision to intervene. By the president's own admission, it was in June 1959—the same month the agrarian reform program went into effect—that the testing phase of U.S. policy ended and the administration decided that "a change in the Cuban Government" was needed. Initial planning for a covert operation was then temporarily put on hold when, according to Assistant Secretary of State Rubottom, "some U.S. companies reported to us . . . that they were making some progress in negotiations" with the Cuban government, "a factor which caused us to slow the implementation of our program." It was only after the hoped-for change in Cuba's nationalistic economic climate failed to materialize that Secretary of State Herter took his November 5 recommendation for intervention to Eisenhower. Four months later, on the same day that he authorized preparations for CIA action against Castro, Eisenhower acknowledged that "businessmen were constantly coming to him and saying that something must be done to counteract the Cuban situation." Shortly thereafter, he wrote angrily about "the expropriation of extensive American properties without acceptable provision for compensation."[31]

Nevertheless, although the expropriations were "of major concern" to U.S. policy makers, and although administration officials sympathized "deeply" with U.S. investors on the island, there is little evidence that Eisenhower launched plans for intervention primarily out of concern for U.S. private capital in Cuba. U.S. corporations denounced the agrarian reform program as "confiscatory" and appealed to the U.S. government for support, but they did not lobby for Castro's overthrow. Instead, they called on Eisenhower to impose economic sanctions on Cuba and suspend the U.S. sugar quota to pressure Castro into seeking an accommodation with U.S. investors or at least provide what they considered equitable compensation for their property losses. Indeed, throughout the June 1959–March 1960 period, many U.S. companies in Cuba were cautioning the administration "against the application of aggressive policies" and indicating their desire "to reach a modus vivendi" with Castro, while U.S. "sugar and cattle plantation owners . . . continued to operate in the hope that an acceptable arrangement could be worked out." On the rare occasions when U.S. business leaders did advocate Castro's overthrow, administration officials were unresponsive. In late June 1959, for example, Texas cattleman Robert Kleberg, whose King Ranch was about to lose holdings worth $3 million in Cuba's Camaguey province, met separately with Eisenhower, Herter, and Treasury Secretary Robert Anderson "to offer certain suggestions with regard to U.S. policy toward Cuba." Among the "immediate steps" that Kleberg recommended were a suspension of Cuba's sugar quota, seizure of all Cuban assets in the United States, deployment of a U.S. naval fleet on "Caribbean maneuvers," and a U.S. announcement that "in 1898 we fought to free Cuba from tyranny—we will not stand by now and allow Communism to permanently destroy this freedom." Herter quickly rejected Kleberg's suggestions as ill advised and informed Eisenhower that a White House reply was not necessary.[32]

Administration officials were more disturbed by the broader regional implications of Castro's property seizures. As Assistant Secretary of State Rubottom put it at the start of June, "The U.S. has investments totaling $9 billion in Latin America, and every country in the hemisphere is watching to see what U.S. reaction to Cuba's expropriation will be." U.S. embassies in the region warned that if the Latin Americans "see them getting away with taking the property in Cuba, it will happen . . . in other Latin American areas." The administration's concern was based on more than narrow considerations of U.S. economic self-interest, however. U.S. policy makers were convinced that sociopolitical stability and the prevention of anti-U.S. "extremism" in Latin America required economic growth and the improved living conditions that would presumably follow. They also believed, and relentlessly preached to Latin American government officials, that a private-enterprise/foreign-investment-based economic development model was the only viable formula for sound economic growth in the region. And in their view, nationalistic economic policies such as Cuba's agrarian reform program only discouraged the flows of private foreign investment capital that they believed were prerequisites for economic growth and regional stability. As Rubottom warned in December, "time is running out and . . . if Cuba gets by with the actions she is taking against American property owners, our whole private enterprise approach abroad would be in serious danger."[33]

Eisenhower viewed the economic dimension of the Cuban threat principally in strategic terms. He believed that Latin America was "of vital importance to the United States" as a dependable source of strategic minerals and other industrial raw materials essential to U.S. defense production. If Castro successfully seized U.S.-owned property in Cuba, nationalists elsewhere in Latin America might be emboldened to expropriate foreign-owned oil fields and mineral deposits, with potentially "disastrous and doleful consequences" for U.S. national security. On March 17, 1960, hours before he approved the CIA program of covert action against Castro, and with the "great importance" of "the Cuban situation" very much on his mind, Eisenhower warned the National Security Council (NSC) that the United States "was getting more and more to be a have-not nation as far as raw materials are concerned." Without imported iron-ore from Venezuela and Canada, the president pointed out by way of example, U.S. "steel production would be seriously curtailed." "We must have access to the South American continent," he said emphatically.[34]

In the end, however, the issues of agrarian reform and expropriation of U.S. property exerted their principal influence on Eisenhower's decision to intervene by simply reinforcing Washington's growing conviction that any accommodation with the Castro regime was impossible. The fact that Castro refused to compromise or negotiate and instead seized U.S. property without "proper" compensation—indeed, without *any* compensation, as it eventually turned out—was seen in Washington as a decisive indication that Cuba's new leaders were not going to play by the old hegemonic rules of the game and could no longer be tolerated. With the advent of agrarian reform, U.S. policy makers concluded that what Rubottom referred to as the period "of probing and testing to see what Castro would do, what he was like, and how he'd react to situations" was over. The fact that he had opted for a radical nationalist approach to land reform, one that in the State Department's view was "the recognized product of Castro's radical and extremist supporters," was sufficient evidence that, in Rubottom's words, "Castro was not going to be a man with whom the United States could work."[35]

Instead, it was Castro's "aggressively neutralist" foreign policy,[36] more than any other aspect of the revolution, that swayed Eisenhower decisively toward intervention. In 1959, as in 1953, U.S. policy makers regarded "hemispheric solidarity" and a cohesive bloc of Latin American allies as a vital cornerstone of U.S. national security in the Cold War. And in Cuba, as in Guatemala, the great U.S. concern was that the loss of a Latin American ally to neutral nonalignment would be perceived abroad as an indication of declining U.S. power, dangerously damaging the credibility of U.S. international leadership at a time when the global balance of power was growing increasingly precarious. According to a secret National Security Council policy statement approved by the president in February 1959:

> Latin America plays a key role in the security of the United States. In the face of the anticipated prolonged threat from Communist expansionism, the United States must rely heavily on the moral and political support of Latin America for U.S. policies designed to counter this threat. *A defection by any significant number*

of Latin American countries to the ranks of neutralism . . .would seriously impair the ability of the United States to exercise effective leadership of the Free World, particularly in the UN, and constitute a blow to U.S. prestige.[37]

Cuba, by its own admission, clearly represented a defection from the U.S.-led inter-American system into "the ranks of neutralism." From January 1959 through March 1960, Castro's critiques of U.S. hegemony in Latin America, his open contempt for the Organization of American States, and his expressed intention of removing Cuba from the U.S. sphere of influence in favor of a position of neutral nonalignment in the Cold War set off alarm bells in Washington. From the start, U.S. officials were appalled by "the tendency of the top revolutionary leadership to adopt an intermediate or neutral position in the East-West conflict" and by Castro's declarations "that he would not side with the United States in the cold war." In April, the U.S. ambassador in Cuba, Philip Bonsal, pointedly reminded the Cuban leader that in such a "critical time" of the Cold War, the United States was quite sensitive to Cuban expressions of "neutralism." It was uncertain, Secretary of State Herter told Eisenhower a few days later, whether Cuba "would remain in the western camp."[38]

Worse still, from Washington's perspective, were Castro's efforts to forge "a neutralistic bloc in Latin America." U.S. officials deplored the Cuban leader's early attempts to foment radical-nationalist revolutions in neighboring Caribbean states, and they blamed him for instigating revolutionary instability in Panama, the Dominican Republic, Haiti, and—by their account—Nicaragua. Rubottom later recalled that the downward trend in U.S.-Cuban relations began in April 1959, during the period when Cuba was actively preparing "filibustering expeditions against the Dominican Republic, Nicaragua, and Panama." At an April meeting of State Department officials and U.S. ambassadors from throughout the Caribbean region, "the anti-American campaign fanned by Castro" and "activities in Cuba directed at the overthrow of the Dominican, Nicaraguan and Haitian Governments" were highlighted as "problems of special concern to the U.S." Particularly disturbing to the U.S. diplomats were "Castro's indication that Cuba should be neutral in the East-West struggle" and his "backing of revolutionary activities" throughout the region. "There was agreement that United States policies and actions should be directed at containing these trends." A month later, Rubottom personally warned Castro that "we do not want to be a country isolated from our Latin American friends, nor do we want to see twenty Latin American countries united in a bloc against the United States. This would be a tragic thing." By June, Herter had concluded that "if we did not do something" to curb Cuban-sponsored nationalist revolutionary activity in the Caribbean, "the fire would spread very fast," resulting in further defections from the U.S.-led hemispheric system. It was in June that U.S. officials first decided to intervene. In drafting the State Department recommendation to Eisenhower that Castro be checked or replaced, Rubottom justified the proposed intervention by condemning the revolution's "increasingly 'neutralist'" foreign policy and its "efforts . . . to stimulate neutralism elsewhere in Latin America." By the time the recommendation reached the White House, Eisenhower was already fed up with the Cubans' "shrill anti-American diatribes" and "abortive . . . efforts to overthrow various Caribbean governments." Castro, the president complained a few weeks later, was "going wild and harming the whole American structure."[39]

During the fall of 1959, new Cuban displays of international independence exacerbated U.S. concern. In a September speech before the UN General Assembly, Cuban foreign minister Raúl Roa declared that "for the first time in its history," Cuba was "truly free, independent and sovereign" and that "its foreign policy" had "freed itself of all bondage, oppression and servitude." Roa went on to identify Cuba and Latin America with "the under-developed peoples of Africa and Asia" as an international "third group" uncommitted to either the Eastern or Western bloc. "We will never be a docile pawn on the chessboard of power politics," he said. "It is high time that the great Powers ceased arbitrarily to decide the fate of small nations." Over the next two months, Cuba successfully forged "a close working relationship with the neutralist Asian-African bloc at the United Nations," voting "with increasing frequency . . . in opposition to the United States" on important issues such as the admission of Communist China to the United Nations and "openly seeking to induce other Latin American nations. . .to follow its lead." Castro, meanwhile, was actively soliciting collaborative relations with Egypt's Nasser and Indonesia's Sukarno—two prominent neutralist leaders regarded in Washington as particularly annoying Third World troublemakers. He also attempted to organize a tricontinental "Conference of Hungry Nations" to promote unity among the world's underdeveloped countries. To U.S. officials, Cuba's promotion of a nonaligned Third World bloc was nothing less than an effort "to whittle down the free world and enlarge the number of uncommitted countries" to the detriment of the West's position in the international balance of power.[40]

Accompanying the Cuban government's neutralist initiatives were unrestrained new outbursts of anti-U.S. rhetoric. In late October, a plane flown by a Florida-based Cuban exile dropped anti-Castro leaflets on Havana, drawing Cuban anti-aircraft fire that accidentally killed three of the city's residents. Castro responded with what press observers described as his "most violently anti-American performance in some time." In a series of emotional public speeches that U.S. diplomats characterized as highly inflammatory and even hysterical, the Cuban leader charged that the "bombing" of Havana was foreign aggression carried out by counterrevolutionaries in connivance with U.S. authorities. Then, in early March 1960, when a freighter delivering Belgian munitions to the Cuban government exploded in Havana's harbor, Castro went ballistic, charging that "functionaries of the North American Government" had committed an "intentional act of sabotage." Perhaps, he speculated, the United States was planning an intervention and wanted "to show us that we can be invaded at any time." "If they think of landing troops, let them go ahead," he said. The Cuban people "would fight to the last drop of blood." The vehemence of Castro's verbal attacks infuriated U.S. officials and intensified their determination to overthrow him.[41]

Many administration analysts believed that Castro's anti-American ultranationalism and neutralism were sources of "deep satisfaction to the leaders of international communism" and provided "fertile ground for future [communist] bloc exploitation." According to a March 1960 Special National Intelligence Estimate, the Cuban leader's policies "satisfied the aims of the Latin American Communist movement by undermining the influence and prestige of the United States in the region."[42] Eisenhower, however, was not convinced that Third World nationalism and neutralism were inevitably susceptible to communist subversion.[43] And besides, the U.S. intelligence community could produce no proof that Cuba's revolution was falling under communist domination or control. Instead, the administration's apprehensions remained focused on the prospect that Castro would influence other U.S. allies in Latin America to defect from the U.S.-led hemispheric system into the ranks of nonalignment. In March 1960, one week before Eisenhower approved the CIA's covert action proposal, the State Department predicted that if Castro succeeded in consolidating his "hostile . . . neutralist" government in power, he "would undoubtedly further intensify his efforts to bring into power governments responsive to his leadership in other Caribbean and Latin American countries." It was not unlikely, the department warned, that "in view of the instability of a number of governments in the area" and the widespread "sympathy" that Castro evoked throughout the region, "he might succeed in at least a few countries. In this event, we would be in very serious difficulties in our Latin American relations. *All other dangers*—except the possibility that Cuba would be made available clandestinely or otherwise to hostile forces for operations directly against U.S. military security—*are subsidiary to this main danger.*"[44]

The message was clear: a policy of inaction would only fuel further defections from the U.S. sphere of influence. As Ambassador Bonsal warned: "The other nations of Latin America are watching the Cuban developments closely. It seems certain that they are curious to see what the response of the United States will be. A purely passive reaction might be at least partially responsible for later unfavorable developments in other nations."[45]

The "main danger," as U.S. officials perceived it, was that the erosion of "inter-American solidarity" at the hands of Cuban-sponsored neutralism would convey an image of U.S. weakness and damage U.S. prestige in the eyes of world opinion. If the United States could not enforce unity within its own hemispheric security alliance, other free world allies might conclude that the United States was a declining superpower and lose confidence in U.S. leadership. And in the world of 1959–early 1960—with the Soviet Union seemingly outpacing the United States in science and technology thanks to spectacular recent successes in the Soviet missile and space programs, and with many observers expressing concern that the United States was losing the Cold War—the Eisenhower administration could ill afford any additional appearance of national weakness.[46]

Perhaps the definitive statement of the Eisenhower administration's motives for intervening in Cuba was provided by Secretary of State Herter in his November 1959 policy memorandum to the president recommending intervention. In justifying the need for U.S. action, Herter mentioned that Castro had "tolerated and encouraged the infiltration of Communists and their sympathizers into important positions" in government and organized labor. He also criticized Castro's "drastic" economic policies for harming U.S. business interests and hindering U.S. efforts to "promote necessary private investment in Latin America." But Herter's principal justification for U.S. intervention was Castro's "deliberate fomenting of anti-American sentiment in Cuba and . . . other Latin American countries." Castro, Herter informed the president, "has veered toward a 'neutralist' anti-American foreign policy for Cuba which, *if emulated by other Latin American countries, would have serious adverse effects on Free World support of our leadership*, especially in the United Nations. . . . He has, in fact, given support to Caribbean revolutionary movements designed to bring into power governments modeled on or responsive to his government and by such interventionist activities sought to undermine the Inter-American system." The United States should move to reverse "the extremist, anti-American course of the Castro regime" by organizing an anti-Castro opposition movement in Cuba, Herter advised the president.[47] It was time to prevent the spread of anti-U.S. neutralism in Latin America by attacking the virus at its source.

Another factor, however—one seldom mentioned in policy discussions or policy memoranda—also influenced Eisenhower's decision to overthrow Castro. Again, as in Guatemala six years earlier, domestic political pressures were creating an added incentive for intervention.

State Department officials had been sensitive to the political dimension of the Cuban issue from the start. For most U.S. diplomats, the consequences of losing China in 1949—the ruined careers of State Department "China hands" during the McCarthy era, the incumbent party's defeat in the 1952 election—were still fresh memories, and the department's Latin American specialists had no desire to repeat that experience by appearing responsible for the loss of Cuba. Consequently, they argued against a renewal of the Cuban sugar quota in 1959 out of fear that such a conciliatory gesture toward Castro would lay the administration "open to charges that it was 'soft on communism.'" In September, the presidents of the leading U.S. sugar companies in Cuba delivered a thinly veiled political warning to the department that "the American people" might soon "demand" a stronger administration response to Castro's nationalistic policies, creating an impression in the minds of department officials that, as one diplomat put it, "by Cuba we will be judged." The Bureau of Inter-American Affairs subsequently concluded that a tougher U.S. approach was needed in Cuba "to avoid *domestically and internationally* any feeling that the Government is not strong-willed enough to resist Castro's attacks and depredations."[48]

State's political concerns proved to be well founded because, by the summer of 1959, Eisenhower's Cuban policy was coming under attack from several directions. In July, a bipartisan group of conservative congressmen led by Democratic Senator James Eastland of Mississippi began to publicly accuse the administration of losing Cuba. In a series of "carefully staged and televised" Senate hearings before Eastland's internal-security subcommittee, a stream of Cuban exiles and right-wing witnesses charged that administration officials knew in 1958 that Castro was a communist but permitted him to come to power nonetheless. Several State Department officials were subpoenaed, and the career of William Wieland, director of the Office of Caribbean Affairs, was destroyed by the committee's McCarthy-like innuendoes. The hearings, which continued through the second half of 1959, had an influential impact on congressional opinion, and by year's end a growing number of congressmen were calling on the administration to take more decisive action against Castro.[49] The conservative pressure from Capitol Hill was reinforced by William F. Buckley's *National Review*, which criticized Eisenhower relentlessly for allowing "patience" to "paralyze" his decision making on Cuba. By the spring of 1960, Buckley was openly calling for U.S. intervention. The criticism from conservative quarters in Congress and the press put Eisenhower on notice that, in Ambassador Bonsal's words, his "posture of moderation in the face of Castro's insulting and aggressive behavior was becoming a political liability" as the nation entered the 1960 presidential election year.[50]

Meanwhile, Senator J. William Fulbright (D-AR), the influential chairman of the Senate Foreign Relations Committee, had begun criticizing Eisenhower for mismanaging Cuba, relations with Latin America, and U.S. foreign policy in general. Fulbright believed that Eisenhower's close ties to Batista were responsible for Castro's anti-U.S. sentiments, and by September 1959, he was publicly proclaiming that "in the whole history of the presidency, with the possible exception of Herbert Hoover and James Buchanan, the performance of President Eisenhower" in foreign-policy leadership "stands on a bizarre plane of its own."[51] Then, in February 1960, a Senate Foreign Relations subcommittee chaired by liberal Senator Wayne Morse (D-OR) also issued a report expressing concern over the growth of communist influence in Cuba.[52] All in all, it did not require exceptional political foresight on Eisenhower's part to recognize that his Cuban policy was likely to be a prime target of attack in the 1960 election campaign.

In addition, however, politically induced pressure for intervention was coming from within the administration itself. By mid-1959, Vice President Richard Nixon was actively urging Eisenhower to take "a more belligerent stance" toward Castro.

Nixon hoped to succeed Eisenhower as president in the 1960 election, and Castro's overthrow would protect him from potentially damaging Democratic campaign attacks on the administration's "failed" Cuban policies. Accordingly, the vice president "assumed the leadership of a loosely knit group of hardliners" within the administration and became, in his own words, "the strongest and most persistent advocate" of forcibly overthrowing Castro by arming Cuban exiles against him.[53] During National Security Council deliberations, Nixon regularly called for a more aggressive U.S. policy toward Castro—and the political implications for his forthcoming presidential campaign seldom lay far below the surface of his arguments. In mid-December 1959, for example, he told the NSC that he "did not believe that Cuba should be handled in a routine fashion through normal diplomatic channels." "When Congress reconvened there would be a great assault on the Administration's Latin American policy," he said. "Heavy criticism of that policy was coming from the Republican as well as the Democratic members of Congress," and "a discussion of Cuba could not be avoided." The Cuban problem was already spilling out of Congress, he warned, and "would soon have far-flung" political implications. Nixon acknowledged that "radical steps with respect to Cuba would create an adverse reaction throughout Latin America," but he argued that "we needed to find a few dramatic things to do with respect to the Cuban situation in order to indicate that we would not allow ourselves to be kicked around completely."[54]

Consequently, when Eisenhower approved the CIA's covert-action proposal in March 1960, Nixon celebrated the decision as a personal victory. He would later write that "Early in 1960, the position I had been advocating for nine months finally prevailed, and the CIA was given instructions to provide arms, ammunition, and training for Cubans who had fled the Castro regime."[55] Now Nixon would only need to prod the CIA to complete its assigned project as quickly as possible and get the Cuban problem out of the way prior to the November election in order to deny the Democrats a potentially damaging weapon in their campaign arsenal against him.

The 1960 presidential campaign quickly confirmed Nixon's fears. Democratic candidate John Kennedy immediately launched an "all-out assault on the administration's foreign-policy failures," and Cuba figured prominently in his indictment. Castro's Cuba, the Massachusetts senator said, was "the most glaring failure of American foreign policy today . . . a disaster that threatens the security of the whole Western Hemisphere." "In 1952 the Republicans ran on a program of rolling back the Iron Curtain in Eastern Europe," he reminded voters. "Today the Iron Curtain is 90 miles off the coast of the United States." Thanks to the Eisenhower administration's policy of "blunder, inaction, retreat, and failure" in Cuba, he charged, U.S. international prestige had experienced a critical decline. Kennedy attacked Nixon directly by reminding campaign audiences that "I wasn't the Vice President who presided over the Communization of Cuba." "If you can't stand up to Castro," he asked, "how can you be expected to stand up to Khrushchev?" "Mr. Nixon is experienced," he remarked in an Alexandria, Virginia, speech, "experienced in policies of retreat, defeat, and weakness."[56] Kennedy was also hawkishly critical of the administration "for not doing more to remove Fidel Castro from power," and he indicated that as president he would adopt a more aggressively interventionist approach.

"For the present, Cuba is gone," he told a Cincinnati audience. "Our policies of neglect and indifference have let it slip behind the Iron Curtain." Now, he said, the United States should be giving encouragement to "those liberty-loving Cubans who are leading the resistance to Castro." Elsewhere, Kennedy lamented the fact that "these fighters for freedom have had virtually no support from our Government," and he issued a position paper recommending that "the forces fighting for freedom in exile and in the mountains of Cuba should be sustained and assisted."[57]

As a result, Nixon soon found himself trapped between his political need to match Kennedy's tough talk and his official duty to protect the secrecy of the CIA's intervention plans. In public, he tried to resolve that predicament by supporting Eisenhower's "wise policy of restraint and forbearance" while intimating vaguely that Castro "could and would be taken care of." In Detroit, the Republican candidate assured the Veterans of Foreign Wars that "the United States has the power—and Mr. Castro knows this—to throw him out of office any day that we would choose." "We could give it to Mr. Castro in 24 hours," he told reporters. On several occasions, Nixon openly invoked the possibility of a direct U.S. military invasion of Cuba but then "condemned any notion of unilateral action" as "unworthy of the United States." During his second television debate with Kennedy, the vice president assured viewers that "Cuba is not lost" and accused his opponent of defeatist talk. "The free people of Cuba, the people who want to be free, are going to be supported and . . . they will attain their freedom," he pledged.[58] Meanwhile, behind the scenes, Nixon was exerting relentless pressure on the CIA to speed up its Cuban operation. According to Peter Wyden, "The Vice President regarded the operation as a major political asset" and "was eager for the Republican administration to get credit for toppling Castro before the election." Accordingly, Nixon assigned his executive assistant for national-security affairs, Gen. Robert E. Cushman Jr., to the task of applying sustained "heat" on CIA officials. ("How are the boys doing at the Institute?" Nixon would ask Cushman. "What in the world are they doing that takes months? . . . How the hell are they coming?")[59] He also repeatedly appealed to the president to "take some action" prior to the election. Eisenhower, however, was too experienced a military commander to be rushed into an invasion before preparations had been finalized, and he consistently rejected Nixon's requests to expedite the operation.[60]

Nevertheless, the president remained sympathetic to Nixon's political plight, and as the neck-and-neck presidential race entered its critical final weeks the White House took several steps designed to strengthen the vice president's prospects.

On October 18, Nixon delivered a forceful speech before the American Legion in Miami in which he labeled Castro's government an "intolerable cancer" and announced that the administration would soon take "the strongest possible economic measures" against it. Less than twenty-four hours later, Eisenhower imposed a U.S. trade embargo on Cuba. The president had previously opposed a trade ban but reversed his position in response to Nixon's increasingly desperate entreaties for some display of strong U.S. action with which he could be personally associated. One day later, the State Department recalled Ambassador Bonsal to Washington, and as Bonsal later admitted, his recall "reflected the administration's desire to improve the Vice President's position" in the election campaign.[61] Kennedy, however, dismissed the new White House initiatives as "too little and too late" and renewed his call for efforts "to strengthen the non-Batista democratic anti-Castro forces in exile and in Cuba itself who offer eventual hope of overthrowing Castro."[62] Then, one week before the election, the White House issued a public statement pledging that the United States would fight to defend its Guantánamo naval base in Cuba. The statement, according to State Department sources, was "made for 'domestic political' reasons at the behest of Republican leaders." Shortly thereafter, "as American voters prepared to go to the polls," Eisenhower landed 1,450 U.S. marines at Guantánamo as a military show of force designed in part "to improve Nixon's chances."[63]

The president's efforts were to no avail, as Kennedy eked out a narrow electoral victory. In the end, however, the Cuban issue proved damaging to winner and loser alike. Nixon was convinced that Cuba cost him the presidency in 1960, while Kennedy's interventionist campaign rhetoric had painted him into a political corner from which, as president, he would find himself unable to cancel the CIA's disastrously ill-fated invasion project. Cuba, he was soon complaining, had now become his "albatross."[64]

Simultaneously, meanwhile, an additional factor was encouraging the U.S. government along the path toward intervention. Throughout 1960 and early 1961, anti-Castro Cubans were assuring U.S. officials that a U.S.-sponsored invasion of the island would enjoy a high probability of success. Local CIA informants in Cuba told their agency handlers that the revolutionary regime was steadily "losing popularity" and that "more and more men" were "taking to the hills to fight Castro." One Cuban source reported that "less than 30 percent of the population was still with Fidel." Another claimed that the Cuban Army had been successfully "penetrated by opposition groups and. . .will not fight in the event of a showdown." Ambassador Bonsal later acknowledged that the U.S. embassy in Havana was unduly influenced by "our anti-Castro informers."[65] At the same time, the leaders of the Miami-based Cuban exile community in Florida were informing White House officials that if an invasion were launched, "10,000 Cubans would immediately align themselves with the invading forces." Such assurances apparently contributed significantly to the U.S. government's overly optimistic expectation that a U.S.-sponsored invasion would trigger "a sizeable popular uprising" and receive "the active support of, at the very least, a quarter of the Cuban people."[66] According to Robert Hurwitch, the State Department's Special Assistant for Cuban Affairs during the Kennedy administration:

> My impression is that a great deal of influence, whether it was on the CIA or on other agencies here in the United States that dealt with these matters, came from the Cuban exiles. And I think they persuaded a number of people that things were ready to blow and all it would require was a little bit of a push to get it going. . . . I am inclined . . . to believe that Cuban exiles and refugees had a disproportionate amount of influence on the assessment the United States Government achieved in this situation.[67]

By the time of Kennedy's inauguration, U.S.-Cuban relations had deteriorated irreparably. Throughout the latter half of 1960, the two countries engaged in "a mutual economic slug match" in which Castro confiscated the remaining U.S. investments on the island and Eisenhower retaliated by suspending Cuba's sugar quota and implementing the trade embargo. Diplomatic relations were severed in early January 1961.[68] Meanwhile, Castro was moving conspicuously leftward both at home and internationally. In July 1960, Che Guevara announced for the first time that the Cuban revolution was "Marxist," and during the fall Castro began fusing the PSP and the 26th of July Movement into a single entity in preparation for the creation of the new Cuban Communist Party under his personal control. By year's end, large numbers of Cuban-owned businesses and properties were being forcibly transferred to state ownership, and free-enterprise capitalism was beginning to disappear from the island.[69] Castro also intensified his courtship of the Soviet Union. In March 1960, he asked Alekseev if Cuba could count on Soviet military and economic assistance in the event of a U.S. blockade or military attack. The Soviet reply came four months later when Premier Nikita Khrushchev announced to the world that "Soviet artillerymen" were prepared to "support the Cuban people with their rocket fire if the aggressive forces in the Pentagon dare to start intervention against Cuba." Khrushchev also offered to purchase all of the Cuban sugar that had been destined for U.S. markets prior to Eisenhower's cutoff of the sugar quota. A Soviet-Cuban defense agreement and a new trade treaty quickly formalized Khrushchev's pledges. As a result, by midsummer of 1960 Cuba's leaders felt certain that their revolution would survive in the face of U.S. hostility. The Soviets had agreed to extend the protection of their nuclear umbrella to Cuba and were quickly becoming "the guarantors of the island's economic viability." Now, Raúl Castro told Soviet military officers, "The Americans no longer dared attack us." In September, Fidel Castro and Nikita Khrushchev celebrated their new alliance with public displays of affection at the United Nations. Two months later, in Havana, Castro told a delighted audience of PSP members that he now considered himself a Marxist and regarded Moscow as "our brain and our great leader."[70]

U.S. officials watched angrily as Cuba tilted toward communism and the communist bloc. By fall, the U.S. embassy in Havana was reporting that the position of Cuba's communists had changed "from one of influence and increasing infiltration to one of effective control," and that although "Cuba is not a Soviet satellite in the traditional sense," it "must now be regarded as an extension in the Western Hemisphere of the Sino-Soviet bloc." In Assistant Secretary of State Rubottom's words, Castro had become a "commie stooge." Nevertheless, neither Eisenhower's advisers nor the incoming Kennedy team believed that the Soviet-Cuban alliance posed a direct military threat to U.S. national security. In July, Eisenhower was assured by his administration's principal Soviet specialist, Charles Bohlen, that the Soviets would not be "so foolish" as to attempt to make a military base out of Cuba, while in February 1961 Thomas Mann, Rubottom's successor as assistant secretary of state for inter-American affairs, advised new secretary of state Dean Rusk that the Department of Defense "does not currently consider Cuba to represent a threat to our national security. If later it should become a threat we are able to deal with it."[71]

Instead, U.S. officials continued to evaluate the deteriorating situation in terms of U.S. credibility and the integrity of the inter-American alliance. Now that Cuba had abandoned international neutrality for alignment with the Soviet Union, U.S. analysts considered the island "a Communist base of operations for export of similar revolutions to an already unstable and potentially explosive Latin America." If the United States did not take "immediate and forceful action," the Joint Chiefs of Staff warned Kennedy a week after he took office, the consequences for U.S. security interests could be "disastrous." The immediate threat, however, was geopolitical and psychological rather than military. If Cuban/Soviet-sponsored subversion produced additional Cuban-style defections from the U.S. hemispheric alliance, the credibility of U.S. international leadership would be seriously weakened. And that, U.S. officials believed, was the Soviets' main objective. According to the State Department, communist bloc support for the Castro regime was part of the Soviet Union's "larger efforts to isolate the United States and to weaken and eventually destroy its influence throughout the world." To that end, department analysts believed, the Soviets intended to use their new Cuban "outpost in the Americas . . . to wreck the inter-American system." With Soviet support, a December 1960 NIE predicted, "the Castro regime will continue its efforts to undermine the position of the U.S. and to spread the Castro revolution to other countries in Latin America. Given the serious social and economic pressures building up in most countries of Latin America and the weakness of many of the present governments, the chances of the establishment of one or more Castro-like regimes over the next year to 18 months are appreciable." The resulting erosion of Latin American support for U.S. leadership would have dangerous consequences for the Western position in the international balance of power. As Eisenhower told British Prime Minister Harold Macmillan, "What is involved in Cuba is a challenge to the unity and security of the Free World." The U.S. embassy in Havana succinctly summarized U.S. perceptions on the eve of the presidential transition when it reported that "the United States faces in Soviet-supported Castro's Cuba an intolerable threat to its prestige and its security which has to be eliminated."[72]

In dealing with Cuba as president, Kennedy found himself subject to the same pressures of credibility and politics as Eisenhower. Unlike Ike, however, Kennedy was a young and unproven leader with little foreign-policy experience. As a result, the new president entered office determined to demonstrate his international toughness to friends and foes at home and abroad. During the campaign, he had promised to support anti-Castro forces in Cuba, contain communist advances in southeast Asia, resist Soviet pressure on Berlin, reinvigorate the Atlantic alliance, and generally provide the United States with more vigorous Cold War leadership than his predecessor. His inaugural address put the world on notice that under his administration the United States would "pay any price, bear any burden, meet any hardship" to defend the free world; concerning Latin America, he declared: "Let all our neighbors know that we shall join with them to oppose aggression or subversion anywhere in the Americas, and let every other power know that this hemisphere intends to remain the master of its own house." Consequently, he could hardly begin his term in office with a passive or restrained policy toward Cuba. Any impression of weakness in dealing with Castro "would be a denial of Kennedy's whole approach to foreign policy, of his toughness, his courage," his bold public promises. He could not afford to "give his opponents at home or abroad reason to question his courage," Richard Welch writes. He could not "appear less resolute in his opposition to a communist Cuba" than Eisenhower.[73]

Internationally, Kennedy "excited tremendous anticipation" among U.S. allies, who were waiting expectantly for the fresh, dynamic, visionary leadership promised by the new administration. In Western Europe, a White House adviser reported, "Kennedy was considered the last best hope of the West against communism and for peace." Moscow was less impressed; the Soviet Foreign Ministry dismissed the new U.S. leader as an opportunistic politician "unlikely to possess the qualities of an outstanding person." Castro, for his part, had already expressed his open contempt for the "illiterate and ignorant millionaire" who now occupied the White House. If Kennedy failed to back up his public bravado with effective action against Cuba, government leaders in other world capitals would have cause to dismiss his policy pronouncements as little more than bluster. The ramifications could be disastrous for what Kennedy defined as the most fragile international balance of power "in the last 2,000 years." The Soviets were relentlessly "probing the West for any sign that our resolve is weakening," he believed, and Khrushchev's recent pledge of Soviet support for Third World wars of national liberation was causing major concern in the White House. If Cuban-Soviet subversion in the Western Hemisphere succeeded in creating "another Cuba," Kennedy's advisers were warning, "the game would be up through a good deal of Latin America."[74] If he could not defend the U.S. sphere of influence in Latin America, Kennedy worried, the Soviets would think him weak. How would he be able to negotiate with Khrushchev from a position of strength on Berlin, Laos, or arms control at the upcoming Vienna summit? How could he expect to build a successful foreign-policy record as president?

Domestically, political considerations virtually forced Kennedy to pursue an interventionist policy. Thanks to the inflammatory language with which he had exploited the Cuba issue in the 1960 campaign, "the political cost of scuttling the [CIA's covert] operation once he was in office" would have been steep. According to White House aide Kenneth O'Donnell, the president and his staff were well aware that if he cancelled the invasion he would look like an "appeaser of Castro" and be faced with "a major political blowup." By early 1961, "Cuba was part of American politics," deputy national-security adviser Walt W. Rostow later recalled. "Kennedy had taken an activist position during the campaign." If, as president, he had failed to carry Eisenhower's covert operation through to completion, "the Republicans could have argued that Kennedy didn't have the guts to go through with something that would have eliminated Castro once and for all. Everything unpleasant that happened subsequently in Cuba would have been directly on Kennedy." Rostow concurred fully with the observation of his friend Gunnar Myrdal: that if Kennedy had not intervened, "he would have been dead politically in the United States. The Republicans would have had an issue forever." "If we didn't do it" [i.e., intervene], Kennedy's national-security adviser McGeorge Bundy told an interviewer shortly before his death, "the Republicans would have said: 'We were all set to beat Castro, and this chicken, this antsy-pantsy bunch of liberals. . . . '" There would have been a political risk in not going through with the operation. Saying no would have brought all the hawks out of the woodwork." Robert Kennedy, the president's brother and closest adviser, also acknowledged the intervention's political motives: "If he hadn't gone ahead with it, everybody would have said it showed that he had no courage. Eisenhower trained these people, it was Eisenhower's plan; Eisenhower's people all said it would succeed—and we turned it down."[75]

Consequently, as president, Kennedy found that he had little choice but to proceed with the intervention. By the time he entered the White House, CIA preparations for a covert action were well advanced, and a paramilitary invasion force of several hundred Cuban exiles was undergoing training at secret CIA camps in Guatemala. In March, agency director Dulles warned Kennedy that cancellation of the planned invasion would create a serious "disposal problem." "If we have to take these men out of Guatemala," Dulles told the president, "we will have to transfer them to the United States, and we can't have them wandering around the country telling everyone what they have been doing." To demobilize them in Guatemala would be even worse, Dulles said, because the frustrated Cubans would disperse throughout Latin America spreading the word that the United States had "lost its nerve." Neither of Dulles' scenarios was likely to enhance the activist image that Kennedy was seeking to project for his administration. National-security adviser Bundy agreed with Dulles that "dispersal" of the Cuban strike force "would be a blow to U.S. prestige." While Kennedy himself felt that "cancellation of the operation . . . would be a show of weakness inconsistent with his worldwide stance against the Communists" and "guarantee that Castro would long be around to harass all of Latin America." In addition, the president and his senior officials were certain that if the Cuban troops in Guatemala were not unleashed against Castro and were instead brought back to the United States, they would "launch ugly political attacks on the administration" for failing to see the operation through to completion. Bundy, in a postinvasion assessment, concluded that "a quite excessive emphasis was placed, in the end, on the need to do 'something' with the Guatemala force." In Bundy's view, Kennedy and his advisers had been unduly concerned that if they called off the invasion they would be subjected to "heavy criticism from refugees and Americans for appeasing Castro." The "prospect" that anti-Castro elements would have been "noisy in complaint" played an important role in administration decision making, he implied.[76]

According to Arthur Schlesinger Jr., a White House special assistant who worked closely with the president on Cuba,

Kennedy was trapped. . . . He inherited this project from Eisenhower. When he talked to Dulles about it, Dulles kept emphasizing what he called the "disposal problem." Dulles was telling Kennedy, between the lines, that if you cancel this venture it means that the 1,200 Cubans we have been training in Guatemala will disperse around Latin America, and they'll spread the word that the U.S. government has changed its policy toward Castro. This, in turn, will be a great stimulus to the *Fidelistas* throughout Latin America. The political impact of cancellation, Dulles implied, will be very serious for the balance of force in the hemisphere.

What Dulles did not add, but what Kennedy fully understood, was that the domestic political implications of Kennedy's cancellation of this expedition would be very considerable. For a lieutenant JG [junior grade] in the Navy in the Second World War to cancel an expedition that had been advocated, sanctioned, and supported by the general who commanded the largest successful amphibious landing in history, would have been hard to explain. I think this was more important than anything else.[77]

The intervention that resulted has been variously described as a "fiasco," a "debacle," "a humiliating defeat," and "a perfect failure." Between them, Kennedy and the CIA took an operation that was at best marginal and risky and turned it into one of the worst U.S. foreign-policy disasters of the Cold War.[78] CIA planners overoptimistically assured the White House that an amphibious assault by the agency's Cuban strike force would establish a lodgment on Cuban soil, ignite a damaging civil war, and hopefully "topple the Castro regime within a period of weeks." If the invasion encountered difficulties, the CIA said, the exiles could simply melt away into the mountains and become "a powerful guerrilla force" that would "exert . . . continuing pressure on the regime."[79] Kennedy's main concern was that the intervention remain covert and "plausibly deniable" by the U.S. government. If U.S. sponsorship was too conspicuous, he feared, the provisional Cuban government that replaced Castro would be widely regarded as an illegitimate product of "Yankee imperialism," and communist accusations of U.S. "imperialist aggression" would reverberate throughout the United Nations and the Third World. Accordingly, Kennedy ordered key changes in the CIA's plan—a relocation of the landing site from a coastal population center to a more isolated area, a night deployment instead of a daytime assault, and reductions in U.S. air support—to make the operation "less noisy" and reduce the visibility of U.S. involvement. The changes doomed the invasion to defeat. The CIA accepted the president's fatal modifications in the belief that "when the chips were down" and the invasion faced impending disaster, pressures of politics and prestige would force Kennedy to send in U.S. military forces in order to prevent the operation from failing. When push came to shove, however, Kennedy refused to authorize overt U.S. military intervention, apparently out of concern that if he did so, the Soviets would move against Berlin—and in his calculus Berlin would be an even graver loss to the West than Cuba.[80] As a result, the Cuban exile brigade landed in mid-April at a hastily selected site on Cuba's southern coast, where it was immediately attacked by Castro's numerically superior forces. Lacking adequate air cover and with no viable escape route, it surrendered within seventy-two hours.[81]

The U.S. defeat at the Bay of Pigs was a traumatic experience for all concerned. At the CIA, careers were ruined and reputations sullied. At the White House, Kennedy was left feeling humiliated and "stupid."[82] His administration had embarrassed the United States, and the consequences were certain to be unpleasant. Within days, administration analysts were warning that the failed invasion would have dangerous international ramifications: the Soviets would now consider the United States to be strategically on the defensive, the underdeveloped nations would "question U.S. strength," and European allies would find the apparent "naivete and recklessness of the U.S. leadership" disturbing. Castro's military victory would also "inflame disruptive forces" throughout Latin America, the NSC's Rostow predicted. All in all, Rostow added, there was a growing perception abroad "that we are up against a game we can't handle."[83] At home, the Republicans were quick to criticize Kennedy's "disastrous handling" of the intervention. The invasion, they said, had the appearance of a Boy Scout operation. Eisenhower suggested that the Bay of Pigs story should be entitled a "Profile in Timidity and Indecision," while Nixon told reporters that Kennedy should have known that "when you commit maximum U.S. prestige you have to commit maximum U.S. power to back it up." Meanwhile, on Capitol Hill, Republican leaders eagerly prepared to make Cuba the dominant issue of the 1962 congressional election campaign. From the Bay of Pigs onward, White House aide Sorensen would later write, Cuba became "the Kennedy administration's heaviest political cross."[84]

The administration conducted internal investigations to determine what had gone wrong, and it identified numerous lessons that it claimed to have learned from the disaster.[85] The main lesson was already self-evident, however. Castro's Cuba had successfully defied U.S. power. A small Caribbean island-state had abandoned the U.S. sphere of influence for the communist bloc and inflicted a humiliating defeat on the U.S. government in the process. From a White House perspective, one conclusion outweighed all others: no U.S. president could afford to risk a repetition of the disastrous Cuban experience—the potential costs, internationally and domestically, were simply too high. For Kennedy, and for his successors in the White House over the next quarter century, a fundamental new axiom of U.S. foreign policy was etched in stone at the Bay of Pigs: there must be no "second Cuba" in the Western Hemisphere.

CHAPTER THREE
British Guiana, 1963

As the Kennedy administration struggled to contain the damage from its Bay of Pigs misadventure, a potential "second Cuba" was already appearing on Washington's radar screens. British Guiana, an obscure British colony on the northern coast of South America, was about to receive its independence with a Marxist government in power.

In 1961, after a decade and a half of anticolonial struggle, self-avowed Marxist Cheddi Jagan and his People's Progressive Party (PPP) had won control of British Guiana's colonial government and were preparing to lead the small colony's scheduled transition to nationhood. Jagan, like nearly half of the colony's 600,000 population, was the descendant of indentured East Indian "coolies" imported by the British in the nineteenth and early twentieth centuries to work on the sugar plantations that dominated the colonial economy. Ironically, it was in the United States that Jagan first became attracted to Marxism. While studying dentistry at Northwestern University in the early 1940s, he met his future wife Janet Rosenberg, a member of the Young Communist League, who introduced him to the writings of Marx, Lenin, and Stalin. Returning to British Guiana, the couple entered politics and in 1950 founded the PPP, a party dedicated to Guianese independence and "the socialist reorganization of society." The party's advocacy of a wide-ranging program of social and economic reforms—improved housing and health care for workers, redistribution of unused sugar-plantation land to peasant farmers, increased taxation of the colony's British-owned sugar industry and Canadian-owned bauxite mines—quickly attracted the political support of East Indian sugar workers and the black urban labor force, and in 1953 elections, the PPP won control of the British-supervised colonial government.[1]

With partial power in their hands, the Jagans and their supporters immediately launched a legislative attack on the established colonial order. They passed a bill empowering the colonial government to confiscate privately owned agricultural land. They introduced labor reform legislation that would have given the PPP-controlled ministry of labor indirect control of British Guiana's trade union movement. And they attempted to transfer control of the church-run educational system to secular local authorities. The colony's propertied classes counterattacked, charging that the Jagans were atheistic communists bent on the elimination of private property, and as political tensions escalated, the British government intervened militarily. In October 1953, British troops arrived, suspended British Guiana's constitution, and removed the PPP from power. The Jagans were subsequently arrested, and Cheddi received a jail sentence of six months at hard labor.

The intervention was necessary, the British announced, to "prevent Communist subversion of government and a dangerous crisis both in public order and in economic affairs." The PPP, they charged, was controlled by a clique of international communists who planned "to turn British Guiana into a totalitarian satellite of Moscow and a dangerous platform for extending Communist influence in the Western Hemisphere."[2]

Jagan steadfastly denied all allegations that he and his movement were communist, and there was nothing in the PPP's behavior during its 133 days in power to suggest that the party had any ties to the Soviet Union. There were, nonetheless, grounds for suspicion. Jagan later acknowledged that the validity of Marxist-Leninist concepts had become "pellucidly clear" to him between 1948 and 1953. A number of PPP leaders, Jagan among them, had attended communist-sponsored conferences in Eastern bloc nations, and Jagan had personally praised "the wonders" of what he had seen in East Germany and Czechoslovakia. During the mid-1950s, he also told a journalist that "he would look upon the Marxist state as his goal" but was "prepared to wait for the eventual communization of South America before implementing his Marxian theories in their extreme form." The PPP had strong international links to the British Communist Party, from which it received substantial assistance, and made no secret of its international leanings. The PPP journal *Thunder*, edited by Janet Jagan, urged the subjugated peoples of the world to wage an anti-imperialist struggle against capitalism and regularly attacked the United States and the other "imperialist" nations, which, it said, were impelled by capitalism to maintain a "war economy" in contrast to the "peace economy" of the Soviet Union. "*Thunder*," historian Jane Sillery writes, openly "affirmed the PPP's commitment to Marxist-Leninist Scientific Socialism as it was practiced in the Soviet Union" and "had nothing but praise for the USSR, for Mao's China and for the People's Democracies of Eastern Europe as peace-loving defenders of freedom." When Stalin died in 1953, the journal eulogized the Soviet leader as "the liberator of free Europe and the acknowledged pathfinder of peace."[3]

The PPP's 1953 ouster by British authorities did nothing to diminish the party's popularity among working-class voters, and in 1957 elections it again won control of the colony's government, with Jagan as "chief minister." Chastened by their 1953 experience, however, PPP leaders now adopted a more moderate pose, hoping to demonstrate to the British that they could be entrusted with the government of an independent Guiana. Jagan cast himself in the image of a democratic socialist and devoted his efforts to less confrontational social reform initiatives—village health centers, housing improvements on the sugar estates, expanded worker-compensation laws. The PPP's long-standing interest in nationalizing the sugar and bauxite industries disappeared, and Jagan began stressing the importance of attracting foreign investment capital.[4] Privately, however, in internal party deliberations, Jagan continued to employ a "Marxist-Leninist-Stalinist-Maoist" discourse. On the eve of the PPP's return to power, he lectured a party congress on the dangers of "deviationism." "Up to October 1953," he admitted, the PPP's leaders had committed adventurist "deviations to the left." "We definitely over-rated the revolutionary possibilities of our Party. We allowed our zeal to run away with us; we became swollen-headed, pompous, bombastic. . . . We were attacking everybody at the same time. We tended towards what Mao–Tse Tung called 'all struggle and no unity.'"

He reminded party members of Stalin's admonition: that "overrating the rev-olutionary possibilities of the liberation movement and . . . underrating the impor-tance of an alliance between the working class and the revolutionary bourgeoisie against imperialism" could "isolate the Communist party from the masses and turn it into a sect." To avoid that fate, Jagan indicated, the PPP needed to adopt tactics better suited to British Guiana's political realities.[5]

As an additional demonstration of his newfound moderation, Jagan assured Western leaders that his new government welcomed harmonious relations with "all friendly nations," and from 1957 onward he put his professed nonalignment into practice by soliciting economic assistance from Eastern and Western sources alike. Early attempts to acquire industrial equipment from East Germany and Hungary were vetoed by British authorities, as was a loan package that Castro's Cuba "offered on very generous terms." A 1959 Cuban agreement to purchase all of British Guiana's surplus rice at above-market prices provided Jagan with what he later de-scribed as "our biggest breakthrough" in foreign trade. At the same time, however, Jagan also sought economic aid from Western bloc nations. After his requests for a larger development budget were turned down in London, he traveled to the United States in 1959 in search of development funds. In Washington, Jagan later recalled, "I was given the 'glad-hand' treatment by officials of the various U.S. aid agencies," but "nothing tangible materialized." To force "greater aid out of the West," he then announced that he was prepared to accept a $100 million "no strings attached" loan from the Soviet Union. No Soviet loan offers were forthcoming, however, and nei-ther Washington nor London proved susceptible to attempted extortion.[6]

Jagan's strategy of moderation paid off politically if not economically. In 1961, the British government held another round of elections with the understanding that the winner would lead British Guiana to full independence by no later than the end of 1963. Given Jagan's seeming invincibility at the polls, it was assumed that he and the PPP would register another victory and lead the transition to na-tionhood. British officials recognized that Jagan was "a devoted Marxist whose whole adult thinking and study, both economic and political, have been anti-colo-nial, anti-British, and pro-Russian" and that he was "not likely to change his be-liefs." Nevertheless, they concluded that political realities had forced him "to compromise his beliefs in practice" and that the responsibilities of office would continue to channel him in a moderate, "sensible" direction.[7]

The August 1961 elections resulted in the PPP's reelection, as expected, and Jagan immediately redoubled his efforts to impress British authorities with his statesmanlike leadership. He publicly committed himself to parliamentary democracy, private ownership of the sugar and bauxite industries, and international nonalignment. He also intensified his efforts to secure the economic development funding that would make his goal of a prosperous socialist Guiana a reality. Two months after the election, he left for the United States with hopes of obtaining $40 million in development funds from the Kennedy administration's new $30 billion Alliance for Progress economic aid program. The U.S. trip would prove to be "a decisive moment" in Jagan's political career—but not in the way that he envisioned.[8]

U.S. officials had long regarded Jagan as an enemy of the United States. A 1953 State Department intelligence report labeled him "a blatant Communist propagandist," while the PPP was characterized as a communist-dominated party whose leaders were "anti-US and pro-Soviet." The PPP's 1953 electoral victory was viewed in Washington as "a serious blow to US and British interests in the region," and State Department analysts predicted that the party would now "spread Communism and anti-US ideas and . . . entrench itself politically in British Guiana." Secretary of State Dulles quickly communicated the Eisenhower administration's deep concern to British authorities, urging them to handle the incipient "Commie beachhead" with great firmness. In London, the U.S. ambassador conveyed the administration's hope that "the strongest possible action would be taken to restore the situation in British Guiana" and offered to provide U.S. assistance. When British military forces removed the PPP from power, Dulles praised the intervention and informed the British government that the United States was gratified by its action. Jagan later charged that the main cause of the 1953 British intervention "was pressure from the government of the United States."[9]

U.S. and British perceptions of Jagan began to diverge after the PPP returned to power in 1957. British officials increasingly accepted Jagan's political preeminence as an inevitability and focused their efforts on encouraging his continued moderation and willingness to work with the West. U.S. officials, on the other hand, remained skeptical of the "new" Jagan and complained that the British were being too soft on him. They strongly suspected that "rather than being tempered by political reality," he was merely temporizing and still intended to lead British Guiana "down a communist road" after it was "freed from the shackles of British sovereignty." "Even if Jagan was not a Communist," the State Department's Edwin Vallon told British authorities, "he was an obvious dupe," and it made good sense for him "to lie low until independence while he consolidated his position."[10]

Consequently, London's decision to grant the colony its independence following new elections in 1961 drew an alarmed response from Washington. Beginning in February 1961 and continuing to the eve of the election in August, Kennedy administration officials "at every level from the President down" repeatedly appealed to the British government to prevent British Guiana from gaining independence under Jagan's leadership. In early February, a State Department representative asked British officials whether something could be done to "ensure that someone other than the PPP won the August elections" and, if not, whether the colony's independence could be delayed until "alternative 'democratic' forces" had been nurtured. In April, Kennedy personally raised the matter in discussions with Prime Minister Harold Macmillan. Four months later, Secretary of State Dean Rusk, at Kennedy's request, delivered an eleventh-hour appeal to the British foreign secretary requesting urgent British action to "forestall" a Jagan victory.[11]

Each U.S. entreaty received a polite rebuff in London. British officials conceded that Jagan was "a confused thinker" whose mind was "clogged with ill-digested dogma derived from Marxist literature." Nevertheless, they argued, the Guianese leader's self-confessed Marxism did not necessarily "make him a Kremlin-controlled international communist." His moderation in office since 1957 seemed to suggest that he was now more interested in Guiana's economic development than in ideology. And besides, they reminded Washington, "there was no viable electable alternative to a Jagan government." In the British view, "the wise course" was "to give every encouragement" to PPP leaders "to feel that they are fully accepted and welcomed by the West and not regarded with suspicion." A willing acceptance of the PPP's right to govern "and the proffer of close and cordial relations" as the colony moved to independence would "create the psychological climate" most likely to persuade the party's leaders to "look . . . to the West." "If we in the West show a real willingness to try to help" Jagan develop his country, Foreign Secretary Alex Home told Rusk in August, "we think it by no means impossible that British Guiana may end up in a position not very different from that of India." Any attempt "to influence the results of the [1961] election," Home warned, would "only make matters worse." Cooperation was "the only possible policy."[12]

The British response left Washington ambivalent. On the one hand, U.S. officials doubted London's claim that Jagan was "salvageable for democracy" and instead continued to suspect that he was a "Communist-controlled 'sleeper'" who would "move to establish [a] Castro or Communist regime upon independence." On the other hand, they recognized that "the dearth of effective political leadership in British Guiana apart from Jagan" made a policy of cooperation seemingly unavoidable and that "coldness toward Jagan and withholding of aid could only result in his gravitation toward the Soviet-Castro bloc." The solution that Washington devised to resolve its dilemma was a two-track policy of overt cooperation and covert intervention. Following the PPP's August reelection, U.S. officials concluded that "we have no real choice but to feel Jagan out and see what we can do to bring . . . him into the western camp." Accordingly, they now agreed to work with the British in "a coordinated effort to get along with Jagan." In exchange, however, the Kennedy administration pressed the British to collaborate in setting up "certain auxiliary programs of a covert nature . . . designed to increase our information about the extent of communist influence in the PPP and reduce that influence." The idea, White House special assistant Arthur Schlesinger Jr. explained to Kennedy, "is to use the year or two before independence to work to tie Jagan to the political and economic framework of the hemisphere, while at the same time reinsuring against pro-Communist developments by building up anti-Communist clandestine capabilities." The clandestine track, Schlesinger indicated, would consist of "a covert program to develop information about, expose and destroy Communists in British Guiana, including, if necessary, 'the possibility of finding a substitute for Jagan himself.'" During mid-September talks with the British, U.S. officials agreed to invite Jagan to Washington for a meeting with Kennedy—"as evidence of their firm intentions to be friendly"—and to discuss with him the possibility of a $5 million U.S. aid program. As a quid pro quo, the British apparently agreed that "resources" would "be built up to enable a harder line to be put into effect if, after a reasonable time (but before British Guiana becomes independent), it is clear that British Guiana is going the way of Castro's Cuba."[13]

Jagan's October 1961 U.S. visit only strengthened the Kennedy administration's conviction that a harder-line policy was called for. During an appearance on the television program *Meet the Press* shortly after his arrival, Jagan praised communism for its ability to distribute wealth "according to needs" and offered his impression that "life in the Soviet Union" was "growing day by day better and better." In a question-and-answer session at the National Press Club, he refused to criticize Soviet nuclear testing, denied that Soviet domination of Eastern Europe constituted "imperialism," and defended the legitimacy of Fidel Castro's government.[14] His visit to the White House also went badly. Jagan first tried to reassure Kennedy and his advisers that, although he was "a socialist and a believer in state planning," he was committed to parliamentary democracy "in the British tradition." He expressed his admiration for the late Aneurin Bevan—a British Labour Party socialist critical of Soviet communism—but he inexplicably went on to confess that he also admired the writings of Paul Sweezy, Leo Huberman, and Paul Baran of the *Monthly Review*, a leftist journal that, from the Kennedy administration's perspective, was "as procommunist as *Pravda*." When Kennedy's advisers pointed out the "large difference" between Bevan and the *Monthly Review* group, Jagan equivocated, saying "Well, Bevanism, Sweezyism, Hubermanism, Baranism—I really don't get those ideological subtleties." The response "rang false" to Kennedy, who increasingly began to sense that totalitarian tendencies lurked beneath his visitor's democratic-socialist exterior. "I have a feeling," Kennedy told aides afterward, "that in a couple of years he will find ways to suspend his constitutional provisions and will cut his opposition off at the knees."[15]

From the perspective of the U.S. officials who participated in the White House meeting, Jagan "was evasive on all ideological and doctrinal issues, claiming that he was not sufficiently familiar with theory to distinguish between 'the various

forms of socialism,' within which he appeared to include communism. He spoke
. . . of the cold war as an issue in which he did not feel himself engaged or committed."[16] When Kennedy pressed him for information about "his relations with
the communist bloc," Jagan responded by asking "whether the United States
would regard a trade agreement with the Soviet Union as an unfriendly act." He
also used the occasion to complain of U.S. interference in British Guiana's internal
politics and—by his later account—accused the United States of having overthrown Brazil's Quadros government two months earlier. "It was decided after the
meeting," Schlesinger noted dryly, "that no concrete commitments could be made
to Jagan." Before leaving Washington, the Guianese leader also walked out on a
meeting with Agency for International Development Director Fowler Hamilton
after becoming "considerably upset" with Hamilton's noncommittal attitude toward Jagan's "extravagant request" for up to $250 million in U.S. economic aid.[17]

Jagan's U.S. performance sealed his fate. Less than four months later, in February 1962, Secretary of State Rusk informed British Foreign Secretary Home
that, in the Kennedy administration's view, intervention was now the only option.
"I have reached the conclusion," Rusk wrote, "that it is not possible for us to put
up with an independent British Guiana under Jagan." "*Your* policy" of promoting
cooperation with Jagan had proved unworkable, Rusk charged, and he went on to
suggest that the British government should now rig "new elections" that would remove Jagan from office prior to independence. "I hope we can agree," he concluded, "that Jagan should not accede to power again." Kennedy, meanwhile, had
already ordered "urgent action" to beef up U.S. intelligence capabilities in the
colony in preparation for a covert operation. In January, the administration agreed
to send a U.S. economic mission to British Guiana. Ostensibly designed to study
the colony's technical-assistance and planning needs, the mission's main purpose,
Hamilton later admitted, "was to get some CIA people down there."[18]

Before he could move against Jagan, however, Kennedy faced two preliminary
obstacles: the British government's reluctance to sanction intervention, and the
lack of a suitable replacement for Jagan among Guiana's politicians. The latter
problem resolved itself quickly. In May 1962, Forbes Burnham, a former PPP
leader who had split from the party in 1957 to form the rival People's National
Congress (PNC), arrived in Washington. Recognizing that Jagan's disastrous U.S.
trip created a political opportunity, Burnham shrewdly presented himself to U.S.
officials as "the very antithesis of Jagan." He spent his time in the United States
"telling the Americans what they wanted to hear"—that Jagan and other PPP leaders were "controlled communists" who were working closely with the Castro
regime to smuggle Cuban arms into British Guiana. According to Burnham,
Jagan's government was rapidly losing public confidence and could be defeated at
the polls by a PNC-led coalition of opposition parties if new elections were held.
The United States could assist the PNC in its anti-Jagan crusade, Burnham indicated, by providing an $8 million loan for the party's cooperative housing project,

scholarships for PNC-selected Guianese students to attend U.S. universities, and $100,000 in "confidential financial support" for PNC political activities.[19] U.S. officials had previously regarded Burnham as an opportunistic socialist demagogue and an Afro-Guianese racist. After his Washington visit, however, they found him to be "an intelligent, self-possessed, reasonable man, . . . stoutly anti-communist" in ideology. "He seemed a very plausible fellow," Schlesinger later recalled. "He talked a straight social democratic line. . . . He made a good impression. . . . He seemed straightforward, well spoken, articulate, and talked the right thing to please. He talked democratic socialism." According to Schlesinger, Burnham's visit left Kennedy's advisers feeling that "an independent British Guiana under Burnham . . . would cause us many fewer problems than an independent British Guiana under Jagan."[20]

Burnham was not the only Jagan opponent working to maneuver himself into Washington's favor. In the fall of 1961, conservative Guianese labor leader Richard Ishmael had come to Washington soliciting U.S. support. A bitter Jagan foe with close links to right-wing Guianese politicians and businessmen, Ishmael headed British Guiana's largest labor union—a "corrupt company union" purporting to represent workers in the sugar industry—as well as the colony's Trades Union Council, an association controlled by "right-wing and anti-PPP elements." In Washington, he briefed U.S. officials on his struggle to strengthen the "free" labor movement in British Guiana as a bulwark against the "Jaganite communist threat." Like Burnham, he also requested U.S. assistance, and in response the State Department indicated its willingness to channel U.S. aid to Ishmael through the AFL-CIO and the "international free trade union movement." Between them, Burnham's PNC and Ishmael's labor organizations offered the Kennedy administration "an admirable ready-made opposition" and a "useful tool for unseating Jagan's government."[21]

British obduracy proved a more difficult obstacle to surmount. British officials continued to express sympathy for the Kennedy administration's concerns. They even agreed to delay British Guiana's independence temporarily and to conduct another round of elections prior to granting the colony its sovereignty. But they adamantly refused to subvert democratic processes or approve any other U.S.-proposed "Machiavellianism" to remove Jagan from office. "Any attempt to dump Jagan or to manipulate the political molecules in the situation would be tricky and apt to be counter-productive," a Colonial Office spokesman told administration officials. Instead, he recommended, the United States should accept the fact that Jagan was going to run British Guiana in the future and concentrate on aligning him with the West through generous grants of development aid. As for alternative leaders, the Colonial Office said, Burnham was, "if possible, worse" than Jagan. A British embassy official in Washington summarized London's position in early 1963. The British government, he said, "remains less convinced than the U.S. that Jagan is leading BG to Communism," and it "is not inclined to make a major policy decision or take a particular action at this time, preferring to watch the situation and informally review it every three weeks or so."[22]

Unable to persuade the British to get rid of Jagan, Kennedy intervened unilaterally. In 1963, the CIA collaborated with Guiana's anti-Jagan labor unions in a campaign of economic destabilization designed to force Jagan's government from power. The specific instrument of intervention was an eleven-week general strike launched in April by Ishmael's Trades Union Council and Guiana's Civil Service Association, a pro-PNC union. The strike—the longest in the colony's history— was underwritten by the CIA, which funneled an estimated $1 million in relief benefits to striking workers through the international secretariat of the American Federation of State, County, and Municipal Employees and other AFL-CIO affiliates. Without CIA funding, Jagan estimated that "the strike would have collapsed in a couple of weeks." In addition, the AFL-CIO's government-subsidized American Institute for Free Labor Development paid the salaries of six U.S.-trained Guianese labor organizers who helped coordinate strike activities. Burnham and his PNC actively supported the strike by carrying out an antigovernment campaign of arson, bombings, and urban terrorism that left several people dead and scores injured. The colony's leading sugar companies also backed the strike by locking out nonstriking PPP sugar workers.[23]

The strike brought commercial activity to a standstill and nearly paralyzed Jagan's government. Port operations shut down, U.S. oil companies cut off supplies of petroleum products, and the major airlines suspended service to the colony. Soon, critical shortages of food and fuel developed, and when Cuban and Soviet ships arrived carrying emergency supplies, the Kennedy administration refused Jagan's request for permission to use the storage facilities of a deactivated World War II U.S. airbase outside the capital. With the economy crippled and violence spreading, Jagan was forced to ask the colonial governor to declare a state of emergency and call in British security forces.[24]

Nevertheless, Jagan managed to keep the economy limping along and eventually outlasted his adversaries. When it became clear that labor action alone would not bring down his government, the striking unions agreed to negotiate a settlement. The damage, however, had already been done. The strike and accompanying violence helped persuade British officials that Jagan could not govern the country effectively or provide the stability necessary for independence. In addition, Kennedy's demonstrated willingness to conduct a campaign of covert CIA subversion in territory that was still part of the British Empire awakened the British government to the seriousness with which its U.S. ally viewed the Guiana problem. That message was underscored at the end of June, when Kennedy and a U.S. delegation visited England for discussions with British officials. During the talks, Rusk warned Britain's colonial secretary that the ongoing disagreement over how to handle Jagan could have potentially damaging consequences for Anglo-American relations, while Kennedy informed Prime Minister Macmillan that "there would be great US resentment against the UK" if the British pulled out of Guiana leaving a communist government in control.[25]

Faced with such high-powered pressure, the British yielded to U.S. wishes. From their standpoint, there was little choice—the health of the Anglo-American "special relationship" was far more important to British interests than the future of British Guiana. Consequently, when Kennedy returned to Washington, Macmillan wrote to assure him that "we are steering things along the lines which accord with your interests." British authorities would engineer another election in Guiana prior to independence, the prime minister indicated. Unlike previous elections, however—in which the party receiving the most votes automatically formed the next government—the new election would be based on a system of proportional representation that would enable a coalition of minority parties to win control of Guiana's government. The result, Macmillan confidently predicted, would be "the defeat of Jagan and the formation of a coalition government" made up of the PPP's political opponents.[26]

The plan worked to perfection. In 1964, Burnham's PNC and Guiana's small, right-wing United Force Party forged "an effective anti-PPP coalition" and defeated Jagan in December elections, just as Macmillan had predicted. Although the PPP garnered nearly 46 percent of the vote to the PNC's 40.5 percent and the United Force's 12.4 percent, the opposition coalition's combined total gave it majority control of the colonial government under the new electoral system. Outraged at being maneuvered out of office by ostensibly democratic means, PPP leaders complained that their party had been "cheated, not defeated" and refused to step down, forcing British authorities to remove them. Burnham was then appointed premier and led the colony to independence two years later. With power in his hands, he quickly established a corrupt, quasi-socialist dictatorship that ruled the new country for the next quarter century.[27]

Why did political developments in a remote tropical backwater of the British Empire cause the Kennedy administration such acute concern? British policy makers consistently attached far less significance to British Guiana than did their U.S. counterparts. From London's perspective, the colony was a "wretched place" of little economic or strategic value—"nothing but a mud bank," in the words of a high-ranking Colonial Office official. In the British view, the affairs of the colony had been "puffed up out of all proportion to their true significance," and American policy was making "much ado about nothing." Even some U.S. officials registered occasional astonishment at "the significant extent to which British Guiana has become a major policy issue between the United States and Great Britain." As Schlesinger told Kennedy in March 1962, "British Guiana has 600,000 inhabitants. Jagan would no doubt be gratified to know that the American and British governments are spending more man-hours per capita on British Guiana than on any other current problem!" The State Department's George Ball later remarked, in a tone of understated amazement, that "a great deal of time, money, and effort—including a substantial amount of President Kennedy's own time—was expended . . . in trying to keep Mr. Cheddi Jagan from coming to power in Guyana (then British Guiana), although most Americans could not find the country on the map."[28]

Jagan later blamed the intervention on the forces of international economic imperialism, implying that he had been the victim of an "offensive" orchestrated to defend "the vested interests of. . . monopoly capitalists" and "the local and foreign capitalist class." There is no evidence, however, that economic considerations—the fear, for example, that Jagan would embark on a program of Castro-style nationalization—played any discernible role in Washington's threat perceptions. U.S. investment capital in the colony was minimal, and Kennedy had gone out of his way to personally assure Jagan during their ill-fated 1961 White House meeting that his administration was not opposed to nationalization as long as compensation was paid. And although the United States obtained some strategic minerals (bauxite and manganese) from British Guiana, it was by no means dependent on the colony as a source of supply.[29]

Instead, the British embassy in Washington had quickly identified the real basis of U.S. concern. In late January 1961, barely a week into Kennedy's presidency, the embassy reported that administration officials were anxious to discuss British Guiana with the British government and that their anxiety stemmed from fear that the colony might become "another Cuba." Thereafter, U.S. appeals to London to adopt a harder-line policy toward Jagan were consistently based on the argument that a Jagan-led Guiana was a potential second Cuba in the Americas. After discussing the issue personally with Dean Rusk in March 1962, Foreign Secretary Home reported that "the United States were really terrified of another Cuba on their continent" and hoped the British "could find ways and means of stopping Dr. Jagan from taking his country into the communist orbit." Rusk reiterated the message a month later when he warned his British counterpart that the Kennedy administration "did not believe in subsidizing Dr. Jagan, but in getting rid of him. They could not put up with another Castro in the Western Hemisphere," Home quoted Rusk as saying.[30]

U.S. intelligence analysts defined Jagan as a potential security threat. From the start, they suspected that he was bent on establishing a Cuban-style communist state in Guiana once the colony received its independence. And they worried that a communist state on the South American mainland could trigger a domino effect throughout Latin America, with potentially catastrophic consequences for U.S. security interests. Castro's Cuba was dangerous enough, but Cuba was an island isolated from its Latin American neighbors by large expanses of water. British Guiana, by contrast, shared land borders with several South American states, including Venezuela, whose oil deposits made it the richest prize in Latin America, according to administration analysts. Allied with Cuba and the Soviet Union, a communist-led British Guiana could easily become a conduit for Cuban-sponsored guerrilla infiltration into neighboring countries. And if Venezuela went "Castro or Communist," a Kennedy task force on Latin America warned, "a general explosion all the way north to Guatemala seems possible."[31]

As in the earlier Guatemalan and Cuban interventions, however, U.S. security concerns were based largely on assumptions and suspicions rather than documented evidence. Special National Intelligence Estimates (SNIEs) on British Guiana produced by the U.S. intelligence community in 1961 and 1962 openly acknowledged that their assessments of Jagan were drawn from inconclusive evidence. According to the 1961 SNIE,

> How far [to the left] a Jagan government might go after . . . independence is obscured by uncertainty about the nature and extent of his actual commitment to Communist discipline and about the tactical aims of the Bloc with respect to British Guiana. . . .
>
> It is possible that Jagan, once he had a free hand, would proceed . . . with an effort to establish an avowed Communist regime. However, we . . . would consider it more likely that an independent Jagan government would seek to portray itself as an instrument of reformist nationalism which would gradually move in the direction of Castro's Cuba. Such a regime would almost certainly be strongly encouraged and supported by Castro and the Bloc.[32]

The 1962 SNIE, which was drafted as the CIA began preparing its covert-action plan for the colony, was a masterpiece of conjectural analysis. It acknowledged that although

> the PPP leadership [had] a clear record of Communist association and of Communist-line policies, . . . the evidence does not show whether or to what extent they are under international Communist control. We believe, however, that Jagan is a Communist, though the degree of Moscow's control is not yet clear. A Jagan government in the postindependence period would probably follow a policy of nonalignment in international affairs, but would probably lean in the Soviet direction.[33]

In March 1962, the State Department also admitted that "there is no conclusive evidence that Jagan is under Communist control."[34]

In addition, the administration lacked any firm evidence of Soviet or Cuban machinations in British Guiana. The 1961 SNIE, for example, pointed out that "neither the Communist Bloc nor Castro has made any vigorous effort to exploit the British Guiana situation." And as British officials reminded Kennedy in 1962, Jagan had met "with no success" in his efforts to obtain money from the Soviet bloc.[35]

Nevertheless, in June 1962 Schlesinger authoritatively informed Kennedy that "Jagan's heart is with the Communist world. He is quite plainly a Marxist nationalist, who sees the west in terms of the old stereotypes of capitalism and imperialism and who is deeply persuaded of the superiority of Communist methods and values. There is no convincing evidence that he is a disciplined member of the Communist party, but then neither is Castro."[36]Kennedy approved the CIA's covert action plan a short time later.

Administration officials occasionally expressed concern that a second Cuba in the Western Hemisphere would be interpreted internationally as an indication of declining U.S. power. When Hugh Fraser of the British Colonial Office suggested to a group of Kennedy's advisers in March 1962 that the U.S. government was perhaps overreacting to British Guiana and that "we should all keep a sense of humor and proportion in considering the situation," U. Alexis Johnson of the State Department "interjected to say that Jagan had at least *symbolic* importance for us and we would not think it funny if another country in South America were to go communist." Nor did administration officials relish the prospect of a second Marxist state diluting the pro-Western "solidarity" of the U.S.-led hemispheric community. According to Rusk, one of the reasons why the United States could not tolerate "an independent British Guiana under Jagan" was because "the Marxist-Leninist policy he professes . . . [is] incompatible with the Inter-American system."[37]

In the Oval Office, however, British Guiana was viewed almost exclusively as a domestic political problem. From Kennedy's perspective, the emergence of a second Cuba in the hemisphere would only increase his vulnerability to Republican charges that his administration was "soft on communism" and damage his prospects for winning a second term in 1964.[38]

For Kennedy personally, the months that preceded his decision to intervene in British Guiana were the darkest of his presidency, according to White House aide Theodore Sorensen. The humiliating defeat at the Bay of Pigs was merely the first in a long series of setbacks for the administration's foreign policy during 1961. Kennedy's April decision to negotiate the neutralization of Laos was widely regarded as a U.S. retreat. In South Vietnam, advancing communist forces controlled more than 50 percent of the country by midyear. The president's "bruising encounter" with Khrushchev at the Vienna summit in June was followed by a new Berlin crisis that culminated with the construction of the Berlin Wall in August. Khrushchev's August decision to resume atmospheric nuclear testing was a major blow to the administration's arms-control initiatives. And in Cuba, a defiant Castro continued to taunt the United States—adding insult to injury when he forced Kennedy to pay ransom for the captured members of the Cuban exile brigade. As his first year in office drew to a close, Kennedy's bleak record in foreign affairs left him feeling politically vulnerable and determined to prevent any additional setbacks. "There are limits to the number of defeats I can defend in one twelve-month period," he told John Kenneth Galbraith in November. "I've had the Bay of Pigs, pulling out of Laos, and I can't accept a third."[39]

By the time Kennedy ordered preparations for covert U.S. action against Jagan in early 1962, his foreign policy record was under heavy attack from his domestic political enemies—and Cuba figured prominently in their indictments. Late in 1961, Eisenhower had publicly accused the president of "indecision and uncertainty" in his handling of Cuba and Vietnam. By 1962, the Republicans were pointing to Cuba as a symbol of the administration's "tragic irresolution." On Capitol Hill, conservative congressmen from both parties were calling for action, not "weakness," from Kennedy in his handling of Castro. Senator Barry Goldwater, who was emerging as Kennedy's likely Republican opponent in the 1964 election, had already criticized the administration for the "clumsy timidity" of its Bay of Pigs operation. In his 1962 book *Why Not Victory?* the Arizona senator blasted Kennedy and his "Fearful Foursome" of top advisers for their "disgraceful failure" to get rid of Castro. The administration's "astounding timidity and indecision" in Cuba, he charged, had given the communists "a perfect base for launching and sustaining their ideological offensive throughout the Americas." "The Communist conquest of Cuba," Goldwater wrote, was "the most important enemy victory" of the Cold War—one that had produced "a Cuban Soviet Socialist Republic" and set the stage for "a Latin American Union of Soviet Socialist Republics." He called on the administration to impose "a military blockade" on Cuba and "take whatever action is needed to dislodge communism from the front yard of the Western Hemisphere." "We must combat communist subversion throughout the Western Hemisphere . . . with every weapon in our arsenal," he concluded.[40]

For Kennedy, Goldwater's harsh criticisms and bellicose recommendations were clear harbingers of Republican campaign themes to come. As a career politician, the president knew instinctively that his Bay of Pigs defeat would complicate his plans for a second term in office in 1964. A few days after the invasion collapsed, he joked grimly to an aide that, thanks to the Cuban disaster, an appropriate title for his political biography would be "Kennedy: The Only Years."[41] To counteract the political damage, Kennedy and his brother Bobby applied unrelenting pressure on the CIA to eliminate Castro by any means necessary. "The Kennedys were on our back constantly to do more damage to Cuba, to cause an uprising, to get rid of Castro and the Castro regime," CIA official Samuel Halpern later recalled. "They were just absolutely obsessed with getting rid of Castro. . . . We felt we were doing things in Cuba because of a family vendetta and not because of the good of the United States. . . . It wasn't national security. . . . We knew we were in a political operation inside the city of Washington."[42] According to Arthur Schlesinger, "Concern for the domestic political implications of Castro and Cuba was driving both Kennedys" by 1962. "Barry Goldwater had come out . . . with a book . . . calling for the total elimination of communism from the Western Hemisphere. The supposedly enlightened Republican senator from New York, Kenneth Keating, was making a big thing of Cuba. It was a constant nag in domestic political circles for the Kennedys."[43]

As if Cuba weren't problem enough for the president, British Guiana was now threatening to go communist. From Kennedy's perspective, a second Marxist state—a second Cuba—in the hemisphere would be nothing but a political disaster, adding even more fuel to Republican charges that the incumbent administration was soft on communism and weak in its protection of U.S. security interests.

By the time Jagan visited Washington in October 1961, the White House was already under bipartisan pressure from Congress to treat the Guianese leader as a Cold War enemy. In the Senate, Thomas Dodd, a rigidly anticommunist Democrat from Connecticut, had been warning Kennedy for months that "a combination of Castro and a communist regime in British Guiana would bring us to the very brink of catastrophe in Latin America."[44] Following Jagan's reelection in August, Dodd openly criticized the administration for failing to prevent the PPP victory. "We did nothing," he charged in a speech from the Senate floor. "We sat on our hands. We sat by and allowed a government which, I predict, will be worse than the Castro regime to take over. . . . [T]his is not a situation that was inherited from a previous administration. There was ample time for this administration to take some action. But it did nothing. . . . We have lost again to communism."[45]

A month later, Dodd joined forces with his Senate colleague, Alaska Democrat Ernest Gruening, to complain in a joint letter to Kennedy that the administration was failing to take a sufficiently firm stance against Jagan and "the pro-Soviet element in British Guiana." In November, Republican Representative John H. Rousselot of California cabled the president to announce that he was "unswervingly opposed to aid of any kind to Cheddi Jagan and his Marxist-Socialist-Communist government." Representative Edna Kelly (D-NY), a key member of the House Foreign Affairs Committee, was also outspoken in her opposition to any U.S. cooperation with Jagan.[46]

In addition, by the latter part of 1961 the U.S. press was beginning to focus public attention on Jagan. In August, *U.S. News & World Report* identified British Guiana as the "Next Communist Target in Latin America." If Jagan won the 1961 elections, the news magazine warned its readers, the colony would become "a staging area for Castro-Communist operations all over South America." A month later, *U.S. News & World Report* described Jagan's successful reelection as a new "Beachhead for Reds in South America." "As long as Dr. Jagan is in power," it reported, "Fidel Castro and Nikita Khrushchev have a friend on the South American mainland." A September *Time* magazine article entitled "Old Leftist, New Game" portrayed Jagan as an erstwhile Marxist firebrand who was "now playing a much cozier game" of moderation in an opportunistic attempt to obtain U.S. economic aid. Later that month, a full-page *Saturday Evening Post* editorial warned that any steps by the Kennedy administration "to subsidize British Guiana's red regime" would only help "to entrench Communism in permanent control" of another hemispheric neighbor. Although Jagan and his communist wife had recently refrained from "roaring their redness" and "openly proclaiming the coming of Communism," the magazine reported, they were simply following Castro's example by masking their real intentions until they had Guiana under their complete totalitarian control. By October, U.S. newspapers and television commentators were also urging firmness on Kennedy's part in dealing with Jagan.[47]

Jagan's procommunist comments during his October U.S. trip did little to calm public concerns. Five months later, the State Department noted that "a vocal section of the U.S. public, several members of Congress and U.S. labor unions are strongly opposed to working with Jagan. We have received since Jagan's visit 113 Congressional letters and 2,400 public letters critical of a policy of working with him."[48]

According to the British embassy in Washington, the heavy volume of anti-Jagan mail pouring into the State Department indicated that conservative political forces were orchestrating a campaign of organized opposition to Jagan in U.S. public opinion. "Mail of these dimensions on an intrinsically minor issue must be a put up job," the embassy reported.[49]

Whether orchestrated or spontaneous, the incipient groundswell of congressional, media, and public concern had an influential impact on an administration already worried about the political consequences of its foreign-policy performance. In July 1962, when Rusk delivered the proposed covert-action plan to Kennedy for final approval, he emphasized that an independent British Guiana under Jagan would not only produce "severe adverse effects in the foreign relations field"—it would also have "obvious undesirable repercussions within this country."[50]

In their discussions with British officials, Kennedy and his top advisers candidly acknowledged that their hostility to Jagan was based on domestic political considerations. Rusk, in explaining to Foreign Secretary Home in February 1962 why it was "not possible for us to put up with an independent British Guiana under Jagan," stated frankly that "public and Congressional opinion here is incensed at the thought of our dealing with Jagan" and would not tolerate another Castro in the hemisphere. During a meeting with Colonial Office Undersecretary Hugh Fraser a month later, White House aides Schlesinger and Ralph Dungan referred to "the difficult domestic situation" that Kennedy confronted in dealing with Jagan. "The Administration," they said, "would be subject to severe criticism particularly from the right wing" if it provided Jagan with U.S. economic assistance, as the British were recommending. Kennedy, in his June 1963 discussions with Macmillan, reminded the British prime minister that 1964 was an election year in the United States and that "the great danger in 1964 was that, since Cuba would be the major American public issue, adding British Guiana to Cuba could well tip the scales, and someone would be elected who would take military action against Cuba." "The American people," the president continued, "would not stand for a situation which looked as though the Soviet Union had leapfrogged over Cuba to land on the continent in the Western Hemisphere."[51] The U.S. ambassador to Great Britain, David Bruce, reinforced Kennedy's message a few days later in a conversation with British Foreign Office Undersecretary Harold Caccia. According to Caccia, Bruce stated that of all the issues in U.S.-British relations (except for nuclear testing),

> British Guiana was the issue of far the greatest importance to the President. If British Guiana became independent under a leader commonly believed in the United States to be a Communist, the President would be vulnerable to damaging attack from all those who were far from content with the present position in Cuba. The Ambassador hoped that after what had been said we were in no doubt about the weight which the President attached to this issue. It would be of little avail to us whether the President's views coincided with our own or not on a variety of foreign issues if he was unable to be reelected next year. It was as simple as that.[52]

The administration's frank explanations merely confirmed what Macmillan had suspected all along—that Kennedy's apprehensions about Jagan "were rooted in American domestic politics." "It is clear," the prime minister had told a colleague in May 1962, "that the Americans attach great importance to achieving what they would regard as a satisfactory solution in British Guiana. They are probably moved by internal political considerations as much as by genuine fear of communism."[53]

According to Jagan, one Kennedy administration official even admitted to a member of the Guianese government that domestic politics was driving U.S. policy. In his memoirs, Jagan recounts a 1963 conversation in which "a senior member" of the U.S. delegation to the United Nations, when asked to explain the reason for U.S. antipathy to Jagan, told a member of Jagan's staff that "nothing must be done to prevent Kennedy from winning a second term with a large majority." British Guiana was "too hot to handle," the U.S. official said. The U.S. press had stirred up anticommunist feelings against Jagan in U.S. public opinion, he explained, and public opinion was a political fact of life that "Kennedy as a politician had to take into account."[54]

But the most compelling evidence that Kennedy intervened for domestic political reasons is provided by Arthur Schlesinger Jr., who served as Kennedy's chief White House point man on Guianese matters. Schlesinger represented the president in discussions with British officials about Guiana. He acted as liaison between Kennedy and Jagan during the Guianese leader's U.S. visit. He even spent three days in British Guiana in June 1962 conducting personal reconnaissance for the president.[55] Years later, Schlesinger publicly acknowledged that the U.S. intervention in Guiana was ultimately motivated by the Kennedy administration's domestic political concerns rather than by U.S. security concerns about communism in the hemisphere. In a 1990 seminar on the Guiana intervention sponsored by the editors of the *Nation*, he explained that "there was a great feeling after the Bay of Pigs, where the impression arose that Eisenhower had prepared an expedition to get rid of Castro, that Kennedy had lacked the resolution to follow through on it. It was just politically going to look very bad if the dominoes began to fall in South America."[56] When subsequently asked to assess the relative extent to which factors of economics, security, ideology, and politics influenced the U.S. decision to intervene in Guiana, Schlesinger responded that

> Kennedy wanted to avoid the domestic political consequences of a communist state on the mainland of South America. Cuba was bad enough, and another communist gain would have played into the hands of the Republicans. Barry Goldwater seems a rather sensible fellow today; but take a look at his book of 1962 *Why Not Victory?* and you will understand the national mood that JFK had to take into consideration. I do not think Kennedy otherwise gave a damn about British Guiana. There were no persuasive "economic, security or ideological" reasons for us to care.[57]

By the time Jagan was maneuvered out of office in December 1964, Lyndon Johnson had succeeded Kennedy as president and a new Labour government headed by Harold Wilson had come to power in Great Britain. Shortly before taking office, Wilson had attacked the Guianese election plan as "a fiddled constitutional arrangement," raising fears in Washington that his government might renege on Macmillan's commitment to oust Jagan. U.S. concern centered on the possibility that Wilson might postpone the Guiana election or simply grant the colony immediate independence with Jagan still in power. The latter step, a National Security Council paper warned the president, would only intensify fears in U.S. public opinion that British Guiana was about to become "a second communist beach head in the hemisphere." "This would have most unfortunate consequences in the U.S.," it noted. In response, the White House moved quickly to discourage Wilson's government from taking any steps that would "cause our BG policy to slip off the tracks at this late stage." In separate talks with Wilson and Foreign Minister Patrick Gordon Walker in late 1964, Johnson personally asked the new British leaders "not [to] change the election schedule or procedures." Wilson complied, and the arrangements for Jagan's electoral overthrow proceeded as planned.[58]

Johnson had more daunting problems to deal with, however. During his first eighteen months as president, he learned that without a large-scale U.S. military intervention South Vietnam would soon fall to the communists and that hemispheric allies Brazil and the Dominican Republic were about to become "new Cubas" in Latin America.

CHAPTER FOUR

Dominican Republic, 1965

The last thing Lyndon Johnson needed was an international crisis—in Latin America or anywhere else. Johnson's focus was on domestic affairs, and it was there that he intended to make his mark as president. Elevated to office by Kennedy's November 1963 assassination, he immediately laid out an ambitious political agenda for himself: first, to win a full four-year term of his own in 1964, and then to establish his historical reputation as a great president by carrying out the most extensive program of domestic social reforms since Franklin D. Roosevelt. Included among the Great Society reform programs that Johnson hoped to steer through Congress were civil-rights and voting-rights laws, antipoverty and jobs programs, guaranteed health care for the poor and elderly, federal aid to education, and initiatives to clean up the environment and beautify the nation. As far as foreign policy problems and international crises were concerned, Johnson regarded them essentially as unwelcome distractions from the challenges of constructing his Great Society at home. As a White House assistant observed early in his presidency, Johnson "would chop off the rest of the world if he could" in order to devote his full attention to domestic policy issues. He "wishes the rest of the world would go away and we could get ahead with the real needs of Americans," another aide noted.[1]

But the rest of the world would not go away. From the moment Johnson entered office, Vietnam intruded into virtually every aspect of his domestic political agenda. Within days of Kennedy's assassination, Johnson's national security advisers were warning him that a South Vietnamese military collapse was imminent and that the small southeast Asian ally would soon become a Communist-controlled state unless the United States intervened. "It's going to hell in a handbasket out there," Johnson told an aide after being briefed by the U.S. ambassador in Saigon, Henry Cabot Lodge, less than a week into his presidency. "If we don't do something, [Lodge] says, it'll go under—any day."[2] The principal danger, Johnson learned, was that a communist victory in Vietnam would undermine U.S. international credibility. According to the CIA, the fall of South Vietnam would be "profoundly damaging" to U.S. international prestige "and would seriously debase the credibility of U.S. will and capability to contain the spread of communism elsewhere. . . . Our enemies would be encouraged and there would be an increased tendency among other states to move toward a greater degree of accommodation with the Communists." "If we leave Vietnam with our tail between our legs," the chairman of the Joint Chiefs of Staff warned, "the consequences of this defeat in the rest of Asia, Africa, and Latin America would be disastrous."[3]

Johnson was reluctant to order a major deployment of U.S. military forces to Vietnam, fearing that to do so would divert public attention and budgetary resources from his Great Society initiatives at home.[4] Other political considerations, however, argued in favor of an expanded U.S. military commitment, and those considerations ultimately proved decisive in his calculations.

For Johnson, communist expansionism in Vietnam was not only a challenge to U.S. international credibility—it was a test of his administration's credibility and of his personal credibility as president. From the start, he worried that if he allowed Vietnam to "go under," the Soviets and Chinese would conclude that his administration was weak. "They'll think with Kennedy dead we've lost heart," he told White House assistant Bill Moyers in late November 1963; "they'll think we're yellow and don't mean what we say. . . . They'll be taking the measure of us. They'll be wondering just how far they can go." Worse still, the communists would conclude that the new president personally lacked mettle. According to Johnson, "The whole Communist world was watching to see any sign of weakness or temporizing or compromising or running on the part of the President. . . . If I'd let [communist aggression in Vietnam] go unchallenged, they'd have said, 'Well, he's a weak sister. He hasn't got any steel in his spine, and hell, we don't need to pay any attention to him. He's a pushover.'"[5]

Johnson was well aware that an image of international weakness could also have devastating domestic political repercussions. He feared that the loss of Vietnam to communism, and the conservative political firestorm that would inevitably follow, would undermine his ability to function effectively as president—just as the loss of China in 1949 and the angry right-wing backlash that it provoked had crippled an earlier Democratic president's political fortunes.[6] As Johnson later explained to historian Doris Kearns:

> I knew that if we let Communist aggression succeed in taking over South Vietnam, there would follow in this country an endless national debate—a mean and destructive debate—that would shatter my Presidency, kill my administration, and damage our democracy. I knew that Harry Truman and Dean Acheson had lost their effectiveness from the day that the Communists took over in China. I believed that the loss of China had played a large role in the rise of Joe McCarthy. And I knew that all these problems, taken together, were chickenshit compared with what might happen if we lost Vietnam.[7]

If he abandoned Vietnam to the communists, Johnson told a newspaper publisher in February 1964, the Republicans would have a field day: "God Almighty, what they said about us [Democrats] leaving China would just be warming up, compared to what they'd say now." His political concerns were more than hypothetical. By early 1964, prospective Republican presidential nominees Richard Nixon and Barry Goldwater were already attacking him for his lack of firmness in

Vietnam and for "napping" while the situation "drift[ed] toward disaster." From the start, Johnson recognized that the loss of Vietnam could undermine him politically.[8]

Above all, however, Johnson was afraid that if he failed to defend South Vietnam aggressively he would lose his effectiveness with Congress and be unable to obtain passage of the Great Society reform programs on which his dreams of presidential greatness rested. To successfully move his reform legislation through Congress, Johnson knew that he needed cooperation from conservative southern Democrats and Republicans—groups that, as historian H. W. Brands notes, "did not take kindly to weakness in Vietnam." If he let South Vietnam fall to the communists, he would only provoke the wrath of powerful conservatives who controlled the key committees that would approve or defeat his legislative proposals. To hold back from full-scale U.S. military involvement in Vietnam, Johnson concluded, would ultimately doom his Great Society to defeat.[9] "If I don't go in now," he said, "and they show later that I should have gone, then they'll be all over me in Congress. They won't be talking about my civil-rights bill or education or beautification. No sir, they'll push Vietnam up my ass every time. Vietnam. Vietnam. Vietnam. Right up my ass."[10]

If Vietnam wouldn't go away, neither would Latin America. Less than two months into Johnson's presidency, a wave of violent anti-U.S. rioting broke out in Panama. The instigators were Panamanian students protesting the hegemonic U.S. presence in their country, but LBJ interpreted the riots as another challenge by the forces of international communism, in this case "Fidel Castro, working closely with the Panamanian Communist party." Although U.S. military forces from the Canal Zone managed to restore order after three days of fighting, Johnson was only partially relieved. "We had passed our first test in Latin America," he later recalled, "but I knew it would not be the last. Castro certainly had not abandoned his plans for testing the United States and its new President."[11]

Three months later, Johnson's national-security advisers informed him that Brazil was in danger of falling under communist control. The cause of U.S. concern was a recent leftward tilt by Brazil's populist president, João Goulart. A wealthy ranch owner, Goulart had built a successful political career by cultivating the workers in Brazil's docile, state-controlled trade union movement. As president, however, he found his moderately nationalistic and mildly redistributionist programs blocked at every turn by Brazil's conservative-dominated congress. Meanwhile, his traditional power base in organized labor was growing increasingly unmanageable as communists and other radical organizers fought to free the trade union movement from its clientelistic subordination to the state. In early 1964, Goulart moved leftward in a search for political support. Working closely with radical labor leaders and left-wing nationalists, he attempted to mobilize Brazil's working-class masses as a support base for his stalemated government.[12] At a massive public rally in Rio de Janeiro in mid-March—with prominent leftist leaders seated conspicuously on the platform behind him—Goulart decreed limited land expropriations and urban rent controls, nationalized Brazil's privately owned oil refineries, and called for large-scale agrarian reform and the enfranchisement of illiterates. Other speakers demanded the legalization of Brazil's communist party and the replacement of the Brazilian Congress by "a popular Congress made up of laborers, peasants . . . and authentic men of the people." Following the rally, the Brazilian communist party announced that it had adopted "a position of firm support for President Goulart."[13] To many observers, Brazil's leader appeared to be recklessly gambling that he could harness the forces of the radical Left to his faltering populist regime without becoming their prisoner. Anticipating a disastrous outcome, nervous Brazilian conservatives cautioned Goulart to heed the ancient Chinese proverb: "He who rides the tiger dare not dismount."[14]

U.S. officials thought the odds favored the tiger. By late March, the State Department had concluded that Goulart was planning to nullify Brazil's constitution and establish "an authoritarian regime politically far to the left," after which his Marxist supporters would muscle him aside and seize complete control of the government.[15] "My considered conclusion," ambassador Lincoln Gordon reported on March 28, "is that Goulart is now definitely engaged on a campaign to seize dictatorial power, accepting the active collaboration of the Brazilian Communist Party and of other radical left revolutionaries to this end. If he were to succeed it is more than likely that Brazil would come under full Communist control, even though Goulart might hope to turn against his Communist supporters on the Peronist model which I believe he personally prefers. A desperate lunge for totalitarian power might be made at any time," Gordon warned.[16]

In the White House, Johnson and his advisers were prepared to take any action necessary to prevent a communist takeover. Brazil, after all, was no mere Guiana or Guatemala. Brazil was the fifth-largest country in the world. It was endowed with enormous resources. It held a commanding geostrategic position in the South Atlantic. It bordered on ten other Latin American states. In short, Brazil's loss to communism would have strategic consequences "far greater than the loss of South Vietnam." And the political consequences would be nothing short of catastrophic. In Johnson's view, the loss of Brazil would be the equivalent not just of "another Cuba" but of "another China" in the Western Hemisphere.[17]

Nevertheless, U.S. policy makers had reason to believe that unilateral U.S. action would not be necessary. For several weeks, right-wing Brazilian military leaders had been confidentially telling U.S. officials in Brazil that the armed forces would soon move forcefully to end Goulart's dalliance with the Left. On March 31, Brazilian army units launched a coup d'état to remove Goulart from power. Seeing the unfolding coup as "an opportunity . . . that may not recur," Johnson instructed his advisers to "take every step we can" to assure its success. Within hours, a powerful U.S. aircraft-carrier task force was headed for the Brazilian coast to demonstrate visible U.S. support for the coup and to provide air support and troops if needed. In addition, the Pentagon made preparations to deliver some 550,000 barrels of emergency fuel supplies and 110 tons of weapons and ammunition to the Brazilian armed forces to sustain them in the event of a lengthy civil war. As it turned out, however, no U.S. assistance was needed. Within days, Goulart fled the country, the military took control of the Brazilian government, and the Pentagon canceled its military support operations before U.S. forces and supplies reached their destination. Johnson had been fully prepared to carry out a large-scale U.S. military intervention—one that quite likely would have been "the largest in the history of the Western Hemisphere," according to historian Gaddis Smith. But in the end, Brazil's generals took care of the problem on their own.[18]

Thirteen months later, Johnson learned that "Castroite Communists" were about to seize control of the Dominican Republic. In April 1965, supporters of former president Juan Bosch—a democratically elected reformer who had been ousted by conservative military forces in 1963—launched a revolution aimed at restoring him to power. On April 25, pro-Bosch military officers and representatives of Bosch's Dominican Revolutionary Party (Partido Revolucionario Dominicana, or PRD) seized the presidential palace in Santo Domingo and announced plans to bring Bosch back from exile to reestablish his constitutional government. As rebel troops occupied the capital, the country's three small Marxist political parties declared their support for the pro-Bosch, or "constitutionalist," revolution. Almost immediately, however, conservative (or "loyalist") military forces counterattacked in an effort to prevent Bosch—who as president had sought to subordinate the armed forces to civilian control and curb military corruption—from regaining power. Army units from the San Isidro military base outside Santo Domingo began moving into the capital, while air force pilots strafed the presidential palace and naval commanders threatened to bombard the city. By the afternoon of April 27, the constitutionalist rebels were calling for a cease-fire and appeared ready to abandon their revolution. That night, however, a few rebel military commanders rallied their forces in a desperate, last-ditch defense of the revolutionary cause. In "the bloodiest single battle in Dominican history," rebel partisans led by Col. Francisco Caamaño Deño drove the conservative military forces out of the capital. By the twenty-eighth, rebel forces had regained their momentum, the demoralized loyalist military had retreated back to San Isidro, and Juan Bosch was preparing to return home from exile to reclaim his government.[19]

From the start, U.S. officials in Santo Domingo interpreted the constitutionalist uprising as the potential prelude to a communist takeover. Embassy reporting focused on the presence of Marxists within the rebel ranks, warning that the rebellion's PRDista leadership was in danger of being pushed aside, and the rebellion taken over, by radical elements. On the afternoon of April 25, shortly after the revolt began, the embassy cabled Washington that "all members of country team feel strongly it would be against U.S. interests for Bosch [to] return to DomRep and resume power at this time especially in view extremist participation in coup and announced Communist advocacy of Bosch's return." U.S. military attachés, the embassy added, "have already stressed . . . our strong feeling" to the country's anti-Bosch military leaders "that everything possible should be done to prevent a Communist takeover."[20] Meanwhile, the local CIA station was transmitting alarmist reports of "significant Communist participation" on the rebel side. According to CIA reports, fourteen known "Dominican Communists" were in the rebel-held presidential palace holding discussions with PRD leaders, at least two of whom were themselves possible "Communist sympathizers," while in the streets, "trained communist guerrilla fighters" were organizing popular resistance, distributing weapons, and forming paramilitary commando units. As the fighting intensified, both the embassy and the CIA station filed frightening reports of radical "Castroite" behavior on the constitutionalist side: bearded men with machine guns had appeared on rebel television "spouting pure Castroism" and providing instructions in the making of Molotov cocktails; captured policemen were being placed, Cuban-style, against a *paredón* (wall) and shot; the severed heads of murdered loyalists were being paraded through the streets.[21]

On April 28, after rebel forces turned back the loyalist military advance and the tide of battle suddenly turned in their favor, U.S. ambassador William Tapley Bennett informed Washington that the situation was deteriorating rapidly. Loyalist forces were "tired . . . discouraged . . . [and] disorganized," he reported, while at San Isidro the general atmosphere was "dejected and emotional, with [a] number of officers weeping." On the rebel side, many moderate PRD leaders had abandoned the struggle on the twenty-seventh, when defeat seemed certain, and, according to Bennett, Marxist activists had filled the leadership vacuum. "Leadership of rebellious forces," he cabled Washington, was "now clearly extreme left, Castro-type with some befuddled military officers." "The issue here now," he stated categorically, "is a fight between Castro-type elements and those who oppose." Bennett recommended that "serious thought be given in Washington to armed intervention which would go beyond the mere protection of Americans." If loyalist forces failed to defeat the constitutionalists, he warned, "power will be assumed by groups clearly identified with the Communist party." "My own recommmendation and that of [the] country team," he concluded, "is that we should intervene to prevent another Cuba from arising out of the ashes of this uncontrollable situation." Within hours, Johnson landed a 1,500-man Marine Corps expeditionary unit in Santo Domingo.[22]

The Marines were deployed primarily for psychological effect rather than for combat purposes. U.S. officials hoped that the arrival of U.S. troops would boost the loyalists' sagging morale and encourage them to resume offensive military operations against the constitutionalists. Such hopes quickly faded. Instead of launching an offensive, loyalist forces remained inactive, apparently concluding that they could now "safely withdraw from the frontline" and let U.S. forces restore order. By April 29, U.S. officials in Santo Domingo were painting an increasingly bleak picture of the situation. Communist-led mob violence was spreading, and rebel atrocities were increasing, embassy and CIA cables reported. According to the embassy, the rebels were gaining rapidly in confidence and firepower; they were reportedly capturing police strongholds throughout the capital and distributing weapons to street followers in preparation for a decisive assault on San Isidro. Ambassador Bennett estimated that rebel forces numbered approximately 1,500 paramilitaries "under the direct leadership of experienced Communist-trained fighters," along with nearly 1,000 pro-Bosch army troops, and between 1,000 and 4,000 young "hangers-on." Arrayed against that communist-led insurrectionary force, he reported, were a mere 1,700 loyalist troops scattered at locations in and around the city, troops that in Bennett's view probably lacked the will "to see this thing through." Against the backdrop of Bennett's increasingly pessimistic cables, the CIA now confirmed that as many as eight of the rebels' top leadership posts were held by communists.[23]

Based on these reports, the White House quickly ordered a massive deployment of U.S. military forces to Santo Domingo. In the early hours of April 30, units of the U.S. Army's 82nd Airborne Division began landing at San Isidro. Within days, nearly 23,000 U.S. troops were in the country carrying out a full-scale military intervention. First, U.S. forces set up a defense perimeter around San Isidro to secure the base from rebel attack. They then advanced into Santo Domingo, cutting a military corridor through the heart of the city that split the constitutionalists' forces in two. Confronted by insurmountable U.S. firepower, rebel leaders agreed to a truce in early May. Four months later—weary, demoralized, and besieged by U.S. and loyalist forces—they accepted a U.S.-brokered peace agreement that left power largely in the hands of Dominican conservatives.[24]

What Johnson did not know was that his decision to intervene had been made on the basis of inaccurate information. From the start, the embassy and CIA station grossly exaggerated the extent of communist influence in the rebellion. The three small Marxist-Leninist organizations that supported the constitutionalist side—the Popular Socialist Party (Partido Socialista Popular), the 14th of June Revolutionary Movement (Movimiento Revolucionario 14 de Junio), and the Dominican People's Movement (Movimiento Popular Dominicana)—had few members, fewer weapons, no charismatic leaders, and little popular support; they were also wracked by bitter internal divisions within their ranks. They participated in the fighting. They helped mobilize the residents of Santo Domingo's lower-class *barrios*. They may have been partially responsible for some of the isolated atrocities and occasional excesses of "popular justice" that occurred during the fighting.

And their spokesmen occasionally appeared on rebel television. But Dominican Marxists exercised little influence within the constitutionalist leadership and certainly never dominated the rebel movement. From the uprising's inception down to the final peace settlement, civilian moderates and anticommunist military officers remained in control of the movement. Weak and divided, with only "a handful of leaders and a few hundred followers," the Dominican Republic's "communists" had little prospect of emerging as the revolution's vanguard. As Juan Bosch later remarked, "There were not enough communists in my country to run a good hotel, let alone the country."[25]

Why then did U.S. officials overstate the communists' influence so fervidly in their field reports? In part, to protect their careers. By 1965, U.S. diplomats in the Dominican Republic and throughout Latin America suffered from a nervous condition that journalist Philip Geyelin dubbed the "Cuban syndrome." After the Cuban revolution, Geyelin suggests, U.S. Foreign Service officers "were quite aware that fortune had not smiled upon the hapless colleague who happened to be holding down the Cuban desk when Fidel Castro delivered himself up to communism." In subsequent outbreaks of revolutionary violence in the region, therefore, U.S. diplomats tended instinctively to err on the safe side by highlighting any and all evidence of Marxist influence in order to safeguard themselves against accusations that they had failed to identify a potential "second Cuba" in formation.[26] In the Dominican case, Ambassador Bennett later admitted to political scientist Howard Wiarda that the embassy staff had overreacted to the threat of a communist takeover because they knew that failure to predict events earlier in China and Cuba, and the loss of those countries to communism, had destroyed the careers of many of their Foreign Service colleagues. Based on Bennett's candid admission and interviews with other U.S. officials, Wiarda concludes that "the Embassy knew, given the weakness of the Dominican leftist groups," that a second Cuba in the Dominican Republic "was an unlikely possibility; but it was unwilling to take a chance." Faced with a violent power struggle between the moderate but communist-supported Bosch and "an authoritarian but 'anti-communist' military," it unhesitatingly reduced the conflict to a Cold War confrontation between communism and anticommunism. "The main reason the Embassy took this stand," Wiarda believes,

> was not because it reflected accurately the real situation in the DR but because of career considerations on the part of the foreign service officers. Knowing what had happened to those State Department officials who had failed to see the Marxism-Leninism of the earlier Chinese and Cuban revolutionaries and who had been professionally disgraced or drummed out of the foreign service for their oversight, the [foreign service officers] in Santo Domingo were determined not to make the same mistake. So even if the chances of a Marxist triumph in the Dominican Republic were only 1 or 2 percent, the Embassy could

not take that chance. Better to err on the safe "anti-communist" side than to risk a definite career-ender by saying the revolution was non-communist.[27]

Similar considerations apparently influenced the CIA station's reporting. Bennett's predecessor, John Bartlow Martin, noticed on several occasions during his ambassadorship that "routine CIA reports on the Castro/Communists . . . gave rumors a credibility far higher than I would have. . . . In reporting a Castro/Communist plot, however wildly implausible," Martin noted, "it is obviously safer to evaluate it as 'could be true' than as nonsense."[28]

Another reason why U.S. diplomats and intelligence officers overstated the communist role was because they had been badly misled by their loyalist allies. At the time of the 1965 revolution, the embassy maintained an extremely close relationship with the country's conservative elites. State Department undersecretary George Ball later described Ambassador Bennett as "a conservative Georgian who instinctively tended to favor the established hierarchy" and whose "basic sympathies were clearly with Colonel Wessin," the loyalists' chief military commander. Conversely, neither Bennett nor his second in command, Deputy Chief of Mission William Connett, had any significant ties to the PRD or the country's leftist parties. "Tap [Bennett] didn't seem to know anyone to the left of the Rotary Club," an embassy colleague noted, while Connett "seemed to be ill at ease with people who were not correctly dressed."[29] As a result, when the fighting broke out, the embassy relied heavily on its conservative contacts as sources of intelligence information about the rebels. Those conservative contacts, in turn, quickly took advantage of the opportunity to manipulate U.S. perceptions. In an apparently coordinated campaign to enlist U.S. support on their behalf, loyalist leaders and their supporters immediately inundated local U.S. officials with warnings that the constitutionalist uprising was a Marxist-led revolution and that "the return of Bosch would mean surrendering the country to communists." They informed their U.S. contacts that Bosch's movement had fallen under the control of "Fidelista communist elements" and "Moscow." They fed them false stories of rebel atrocities and exaggerated reports of rebel extremism. They claimed to have communications intercepts linking the rebel leadership to Cuba. Under stress and fearful of underestimating the danger, the embassy and CIA station forwarded the loyalist reports to Washington as information obtained from reliable sources.[30]

The loyalists not only influenced U.S. perceptions—they openly invited the United States to intervene on their behalf. Before the first day of fighting had ended, the embassy reported that San Isidro's military commanders were already inquiring about "what U.S. support they could expect." Their first request for U.S. troops came the following day. By April 28, as military momentum swung toward the rebel side, they were openly begging for U.S. intervention. That afternoon, loyalist leader Col. Pedro Bartolomé Benoit delivered a formal written request to U.S. officials in Santo Domingo asking the U.S. government to "lend us its unlimited and immediate military assistance" to help put down the rebellion. In justifying the request, Benoit claimed that the "revolutionary movement . . . is directed by Communists and is of authentic Communist stamp, as shown by the excesses committed against the population, mass assassinations, sacking of private property, and constant incitations to fight broadcast by Radio Havana." If the rebels were victorious, he warned, they would "convert this country into another Cuba." Benoit continued his entreaties on the twenty-ninth, when, according to the embassy, he "appealed repeatedly for U.S. military assistance."[31]

Consequently, U.S. officials in Washington could hardly be blamed for concluding that a communist takeover of the Dominican Republic was imminent and that only U.S. intervention could prevent it. A steady influx of distorted information and exaggerated reports from Santo Domingo had led them to believe that the country's anticommunist military forces were collapsing in the face of uncontrollable revolutionary violence and that Castro-type communists were about to seize power. The U.S. ambassador and Dominican military leaders were urgently calling for immediate U.S. intervention. From the information available in Washington, the situation seemed "ominously reminiscent of the last days of Batista" in Cuba. There seemed little choice but to intervene.[32]

It was evident by April 30 that the White House was operating on the basis of erroneous impressions. That morning, as Johnson ordered the 82nd Airborne to Santo Domingo, he informed his top national-security advisers that he could not permit the Dominican Republic to become a second Cuba and that he was "not going to sit here and let Castro take that island." That evening, in a brief public announcement of the troop deployment, he told the nation that "there are signs that people trained outside the Dominican Republic are seeking to gain control." In a national television address two days later, he justified the intervention by explaining that "Communist leaders, many of them trained in Cuba, seeing a chance to increase disorder, to gain a foothold, joined the revolution. They took increasing control. And what began as a popular democratic revolution, committed to democracy and social justice, very shortly moved and was taken over and really seized and placed in the hands of Communist conspirators."[33] Judged by such statements, presidential perceptions bore little resemblance to Dominican realities.

A standard interpretation of the Dominican intervention is that Johnson overreacted to the exaggerated threat of a communist takeover because he was misled by faulty intelligence.[34] To conclude, however, that the president and his advisers were merely unwitting and gullible victims of bad intelligence information would not be entirely accurate. Although their knowledge of the situation in Santo Domingo came from embassy and CIA reports, White House officials were by no means uncritical consumers of that information. They discounted some of the more exaggerated CIA allegations. They also acknowledged privately that U.S. intelligence sources had failed to produce any conclusive proof that the rebellion was communist-dominated. In an off-the-record interview with journalist Arthur Krock on April 29, for example, Johnson dismissed CIA claims that as many as eight of the top rebel leaders were communists by remarking that "for all we know there are 800 leaders." In reality, Johnson told Krock, "no one on earth knew if this was a pro-Castro or Communist affair." The following day, as Johnson was preparing to explain the intervention in a national television address, Defense Secretary Robert McNamara warned him that he would have "a pretty tough job proving" that people trained outside the Dominican Republic were "seeking to gain control." When the president "asked if the CIA could document Castro's involvement . . . McNamara replied that he didn't think so." National Security Adviser McGeorge Bundy also expressed doubt that the "Communists were that much in control" of the rebel movement and advised Johnson not to "point the finger that hard at the Communists" in his speech. On the thirtieth, as U.S. troops poured into Santo Domingo, George Ball of the State Department cautioned *New York Times* columnist James Reston to avoid giving too much emphasis to communist participation in the rebellion because, according to Ball, the situation was "highly confused." There were "some Communist elements . . . fighting on the rebel side," Ball said, but "there is no evidence that this thing has been captured" by communists. Lt. Gen. Bruce Palmer Jr., the military officer who commanded U.S. forces during the intervention, states that Johnson's principal advisers all "recommended against immediate intervention" on April 30 because they believed the administration needed more "time to . . . gather credible, hard evidence of the imminent danger of a Communist coup." According to Palmer, "The truth was that no one had a handle on what was going on in Santo Domingo" when Johnson made the decision to intervene.[35]

In the end, however, no matter how confused the picture or how thin the evidence, Johnson proved to be as susceptible to the "Cuban syndrome" as his subordinates in Santo Domingo. As the reports of escalating violence and growing communist influence poured in, he too concluded that it was better to err on the safe side and not risk the possibility, however remote, that the handful of Marxists participating on the constitutionalist side might somehow seize control of the rebellion. After all, as administration officials high and low were fond of noting, Fidel Castro had launched *his* successful revolution with only twelve men. The Castro analogy was clearly in Johnson's mind as he unleashed U.S. military forces on the constitutionalists. When Secretary of State Rusk pointed out in an April 29 White House meeting that not all of the Dominican rebels were communists, the president immediately reminded him that not all of the Cubans who had helped Castro come to power had been communists, either.[36] According to Philip Geyelin, who covered the intervention for the *Wall Street Journal* and subsequently published an insightful book about Johnson's foreign policy, the prevailing view in Washington during the Dominican crisis "was that a dozen trained Communists, in the right place at the right time, might have captured control, or at least gained a solid foothold, in any rebel movement coming to power under such chaotic conditions. This was the crux of Johnson's thinking, according to those closest to him. For him, it was never necessary to satisfy himself that the revolution was Communist-controlled, or that it *would* produce another Cuba. The point was that it *might*. That risk he found unacceptable."[37]

It was unacceptable to Johnson because a second Cuba in the Western Hemisphere could undermine his entire domestic political agenda. Johnson knew that a communist takeover of the Dominican Republic would inevitably provoke an angry domestic backlash against his administration. He was acutely aware, in Piero Gleijeses' words, "that he would incur the wrath of the American people if he allowed a 'second Cuba'" and that "American public opinion and the U.S. Congress would be pitiless to a president" who permitted the loss of another Caribbean ally to communism. Throughout the crisis, Johnson repeatedly expressed his fear that a failure on his part to prevent a leftist victory in the Dominican civil war would cost him the political support of the American people. "If I send in Marines, I can't live in the Hemisphere," he confided to congressional leaders early in the crisis, but "if I don't, I can't live at home." "I realize I am running the risk of being called a gunboat diplomat," he told his aides, "but that is nothing compared to what I'd be called if the Dominican Republic went down the drain." "I know what the editorials will say," he added, "but it would be a hell of a lot worse if we sit here and don't do anything and the Communists take that country."[38]

Domestic political considerations were clearly in the minds of the president and his top advisers when they made the decision to intervene on April 30. During the morning meeting at which the decision was finalized, McGeorge Bundy remarked that "one thing is clear: a Castro victory in the D.R. would be the worst domestic political disaster we could possibly suffer." After the meeting, the president used nearly identical language when he told his long-time friend and adviser Abe Fortas: "I think that the worst domestic political disaster we could suffer would be for Castro to take over." The Republican hawks will "eat us up if I let Cuba come in there," he told Senator Mike Mansfield that same morning. "They'll say, 'Why did you sit on your big fat tail?'"[39] Meanwhile, Jack Valenti, the president's aide and media adviser, was reinforcing Johnson's concern that a second Cuba in the Caribbean would be a domestic political nightmare. Valenti, however, saw an opportunity for the administration to turn a dangerous situation to its political advantage. If the president could successfully persuade U.S. public opinion that the threat of a communist takeover was serious, Valenti suggested, Johnson could turn a potential disaster into a resounding political victory.[40]

Several U.S. officials who were intimately involved in the intervention subsequently confirmed that political considerations played a central role in Johnson's decision to intervene. According to General Palmer, the commander of U.S. military forces in Santo Domingo during the intervention, the president "faced a large domestic political problem. Having seen Eisenhower criticized for 'losing' Cuba and Kennedy humiliated by the Bay of Pigs failure, Johnson was determined that no similar disaster would befall him: there would be no 'second Cuba' while he was president."[41] John Bartlow Martin, who served as Johnson's special envoy to Santo Domingo during the intervention, concurred. "It was politically impossible in the United States to accept a revolutionary Communist regime in the Dominican Republic," he wrote. "We could not permit it on the simple ground that public opinion in the United States would not have tolerated a second Cuba in the Caribbean."[42] Undersecretary of State George Ball, who was present at most of the key White House meetings leading up to the intervention, later referred to the public clamor that would have arisen if the Dominican Republic had been taken over by Marxists. "I think this very deeply concerned the President," Ball wrote.[43]

Johnson's principal political concern was that a foreign-policy disaster in the Dominican Republic might derail his Great Society legislative initiatives at home. Arthur Schlesinger Jr. had already warned the White House that failure "to avert a Communist takeover" would "probably" mean "losing the House of Representatives next year." Few scenarios could have been more disturbing to a president determined to achieve greatness by enacting a far-reaching program of domestic reforms. More immediately, the White House was busy steering some of its most ambitious proposals—including a landmark voting-rights bill, increased funding for a "war on poverty," and Medicare—through Congress as the Dominican crisis unfolded. Any failure on Johnson's part to hold the line against further communist expansionism in the Caribbean would be certain to antagonize the powerful congressional conservatives who held the fate of the president's legislative proposals in their hands, damaging the fragile coalition he was cobbling together in support of his domestic reform programs. On the other hand, an aggressive U.S. military response to the ostensible Marxist threat in Santo Domingo would emphatically strengthen the president's stature in the eyes of the hardcore anticommunists on Capitol Hill. By opting for military intervention in the Dominican Republic, historian Peter Felten suggests, Johnson was attempting "to appease conservatives on foreign policy in order to win their tolerance of reform at home."[44]

From the initial Marine landing of April 28 onward, Johnson and his foreign-policy team orchestrated a series of White House briefings and "targeted leaks" to persuade key congressional leaders that Castro-trained agents were active within the rebel leadership and that the administration was taking effective measures to prevent a "Moscow-financed, Havana-directed plot" from taking over the Dominican Republic. Soon, influential conservative Democrats—Carl Albert of Oklahoma, L. Mendel Rivers of South Carolina, and Armistead Selden Jr. of Alabama, among others—were publicly praising the president's decision to land the Marines as "absolutely necessary." According to Felten, Johnson used the crisis in part to rally conservative southern Democrats behind him, "distracting them from intra-party disputes over reform" and helping them "swallow the bitter pill of voting rights legislation which was making its way through Congress."[45] At the same time, intervention effectively precluded the administration's Republican opponents from impeding Johnson's legislative efforts on Capitol Hill with charges that he was "soft on communism." On the evening of April 28, shortly after ordering the first contingents of U.S. Marines into Santo Domingo, Johnson summoned Everett Dirksen and Gerald Ford, the Republican minority leaders of the Senate and House respectively, to the White House. "I want you to know," he reportedly told the two GOP leaders, "that I have just taken an action that will prove that Democratic presidents can deal with Communists as strongly as Republicans."[46] From the start, Felten concludes, it was clear that "domestic political calculations played the largest role in determining [Johnson's] actions."[47]

And then, of course, there was always Vietnam to worry about. Johnson's decision to intervene in the Dominican Republic coincided directly with his fateful and wrenching decision to defend South Vietnam with U.S. military forces. In February 1965, the president had accepted his advisers' recommendation to carry out a sustained campaign of U.S. bombing attacks against North Vietnam in an effort to relieve communist military pressure on Saigon and force the North Vietnamese government to the negotiating table. Within weeks, however, he was advised that the bombing campaign—Operation Rolling Thunder—would not, by itself, stave off the imminent fall of South Vietnam. Accordingly, in early April, Johnson ordered an initial deployment of 20,000 U.S. ground troops to South Vietnam to combat communist insurgents. Then, three days before the constitutionalist uprising broke out in Santo Domingo, he agreed to commit an additional 50,000 U.S. troops by midyear.[48]

The deepening U.S. involvement in Vietnam directly influenced Johnson's response to the Dominican situation in several ways. He was concerned, among other things, that the emergence of a potential second Cuba in the Caribbean would complicate his ability to build public support for a major U.S. military intervention in southeast Asia. How could he persuade the American people that U.S. soldiers should risk their lives fighting communists in an obscure country half way around the world if, at the same time, he allowed a seemingly Marxist-hued revolution to proceed unchallenged on the very doorstep of the United States? According to George Ball, "Johnson's use of excessive power and effort in the Dominican Republic reflected a wider preoccupation. We were just on the verge of committing large numbers of American combat forces to Vietnam and the President feared that a disaster close to home might lead more Americans to challenge our adventure ten thousand miles away."[49]

Strategic military considerations also played a role in Johnson's decision to intervene. General Palmer recalls that "on the eve of the 1965 Dominican crisis . . . hostilities in southeast Asia had taken center stage. The Caribbean, however, was no less strategically important to the United States than before, and the Dominican question confronted President Johnson with the need to take swift, decisive action in this area if U.S. forces were to undertake a major commitment in Vietnam halfway around the world." According to Palmer, Johnson was "determined to bring an end to the fighting in Santo Domingo and avoid a festering sore" in the Caribbean so that the United States could "commit its power in southeast Asia without having to worry about the security of the Western Hemisphere."[50]

Concern for U.S. international credibility also intruded heavily into the decision-making process. Johnson and his advisers saw a direct connection between the Dominican crisis and the credibility of U.S. policy in Vietnam. In their view, the upheaval in Santo Domingo was in some respects "a litmus test of U.S. resolve" in the fight against communism in Asia. With a major U.S. military intervention just getting under way to deter communist aggression in South Vietnam, administration officials worried that a weak or passive response on their part to a potential communist challenge in the Caribbean would send entirely the wrong signal to the North Vietnamese government at a critical juncture in the war. Any appearance of U.S. weakness or vacillation in the Dominican Republic, they feared, might cause Hanoi's communist leaders to doubt the seriousness of the U.S. military commitment in Vietnam. If the North Vietnamese didn't take the administration's threats seriously, they would continue their military operations in the south, refuse to participate in peace talks, and generally remain undeterred in their drive to bring all of Vietnam under communist control. Dean Rusk, among others, argued that the administration would weaken its hand in Vietnam if it failed to demonstrate its strength in Santo Domingo. Johnson "reportedly wondered aloud how anyone could believe his determination in Indochina if he appeared weak in the Caribbean." "What can we do in Vietnam if we can't clean up the Dominican Republic?" he asked his advisers on April 30.[51]

If the administration regarded the Dominican crisis as a test of U.S. resolve in Vietnam, it looked upon Vietnam as a test of U.S. credibility worldwide. Like Kennedy before him, Johnson believed that if the United States did not come to South Vietnam's defense, the damage to U.S. prestige around the world would be irreparable. "Our allies not just in Asia but throughout the world would conclude that our word was worth little or nothing," he later wrote. "Those who had counted so long for their security on American commitments would be deeply shaken and vulnerable." Worse still, he feared, a U.S. failure to stand firm in Vietnam would only encourage new communist aggressions elsewhere. "I was as sure as a man could be," Johnson recalled, "that if we did not live up to our commitment in Southeast Asia," the Soviets and Chinese Communists

> would move to exploit the disarray in the United States and in the alliances of the Free World. They might move independently or they might move together. But move they would—whether through nuclear blackmail, through subversion, with regular armed forces, or in some other manner. As nearly as one can be certain of anything, I knew they could not resist the opportunity to expand their control into the vacuum of power we would leave behind us.[52]

Above all, however, Johnson feared that the fall of South Vietnam would cripple him politically at home just as the loss of China had crippled Truman. Throughout the spring of 1965, he remained "terrified" by the prospect that the loss of Vietnam to communism would trigger a devastating backlash of right-wing political recrimination in the United States—one that, in his words, would "shatter" his presidency and "kill" his administration. And, as always, his deepest fear was that "those damn conservatives in Congress" would punish him for losing Vietnam by rejecting his domestic reform proposals and in the process destroy the Great Society on which his hopes of presidential greatness were founded.[53] Unknowingly, and to their grave misfortune, the Dominican Republic's constitutionalist rebels had launched their revolution at precisely the moment in U.S. political history when, in LBJ's words, "two great streams in our national life"—"the dream of a Great Society at home and the inescapable demands" of U.S. "obligations" in Vietnam—were converging to decide the fate of Johnson's presidency.[54]

For Johnson, then, the Dominican crisis was essentially an unwelcome distraction from what he regarded as far larger and more pressing issues. Yet the possibility, however remote, that a constitutionalist victory might usher in a second Cuba in the Caribbean made it a crisis that he could ill afford to treat lightly. And so Johnson intervened in Santo Domingo with massive military force, unleashing 23,000 U.S. troops on the constitutionalists in what George Ball describes as a deliberate display of "Texan overkill."[55] He did so precisely in order to send an unmistakable message to multiple audiences, foreign and domestic: that under the Johnson administration, and under Lyndon Johnson's personal presidential leadership, the United States was fully prepared to project its power internationally in defense of its interests.

The intervention was in part a demonstration to communist leaders in Hanoi, Moscow, Beijing, and Havana that America's new president was tough enough to stand up to them—that he would respond forcefully to their international challenges. From the earliest days of his presidency, Johnson believed that the communist world was testing him to see whether he was "a weak sister" or "yellow." In the Caribbean, he later recalled, he had no doubt that Fidel Castro "had decided, perhaps with Soviet encouragement, to take the measure of the new President of the United States, to push me a little and see what my response would be."[56] A strong response, Johnson hoped, would deter the communists from testing him further; a show of strength—a large-scale U.S. military response in the Dominican Republic, in Vietnam, or in both if necessary—might persuade them to leave him alone. And Johnson desperately wanted the communists to leave him alone internationally because—as he said in reference to Vietnam—he had "bigger things to do right here at home."[57]

The intervention was also a demonstration to domestic U.S. audiences that Lyndon Johnson was a strong president—a president who would take swift and decisive action to prevent a potential new security threat from arising in the hemisphere, a president to whom the political epithet "soft on communism" could not be applied. Among the intended recipients of that message were conservative forces in Congress and the American electorate generally, an electorate that in Johnson's view would "forgive you for anything except being weak."[58] Both of those domestic audiences LBJ regarded as critical components of the political support base that he needed to complete his Great Society reform agenda and secure a prominent place in history.

In the end, however, Johnson's efforts at message-sending produced only mixed results at best. The intervention blocked a constitutionalist victory and prevented the restoration of a Juan Bosch government under which the Dominican Republic's minuscule Marxist Left might have enjoyed increased freedom and perhaps even a small degree of influence. On the other hand, communist leaders elsewhere in the world remained unintimidated by the display of U.S. power. If anything, the Cubans accelerated their promotion of Marxist revolutionary movements in Latin America in the latter half of the 1960s, while Vietnam's communists persevered doggedly in their campaign to conquer the south, eventually forcing the United States to accept a humiliating military withdrawal and consolidating their control over the entire country in 1975.

At home, meanwhile, Johnson's assertive interventionism produced short-term gains, but at a heavy long-term cost. The intervention proved to be popular with the U.S. public; according to a mid-May Gallup poll, 76 percent of those surveyed approved the sending of U.S. troops to Santo Domingo, while only 17 percent objected. Republicans and conservatives heaped accolades on the White House for its handling of the crisis. Former president Eisenhower praised Johnson's decision to send in U.S. military forces as "exactly right," while Richard Nixon publicly supported the intervention as a necessary step to thwart what he called "the taking over of another independent country by Communists." Even Barry Goldwater, the Republican candidate trounced by Johnson in the 1964 election, called the president's action "just as right as the day is long." On Capitol Hill, the intervention helped lessen the rancor of southern conservatives as they grudgingly accepted defeat in their efforts to block the administration's voting-rights legislation.[59] Johnson also used the intervention to secure congressional ratification of his controversial decision to expand U.S. military operations in Vietnam. On May 4, two days after informing the nation that U.S. troops were fighting in Santo Domingo to prevent "Communist conspirators" from taking over the Dominican Republic, the president presented Congress with an urgent request for $700 million in emergency military appropriations. The funds were needed, he told congressional leaders, to meet the "unusual and unanticipated" challenges that the administration faced "in both the Viet-Nam theater and the Dominican Republic." To reject the request, Johnson implied, would mean denying support to "those brave men" who at that moment were "risking their lives" fighting communism in the field. Congress quickly passed the appropriation with only 10 dissenting votes, thereby giving its tacit consent, almost without debate, to the escalating U.S. military involvement in southeast Asia. By tying his Vietnam funding request to the fight against communist aggression in the Caribbean, Johnson had managed to obtain what historian Lloyd Gardner describes as "a new 'small-scale Tonkin Gulf Resolution'" that "substituted . . . Dominican rebels for . . . North Vietnamese PT boats."[60]

What Johnson had not foreseen, however, was the havoc that the intervention would wreak on his own liberal political base. Many U.S. liberals regarded Juan Bosch as the Dominican Republic's best hope for democratic reform, and for them the intervention was nothing less than a tragically misguided U.S. attack on the forces of progressive change in Latin America. The administration's grossly exaggerated allegations of communist influence in the rebellion struck many liberals as evidence that U.S. foreign policy was suffering from delusions of anticommunist paranoia, while the White House's heavy-handed military response to the crisis seemed disturbingly reminiscent of an earlier era of benighted U.S. imperialism in the Caribbean that Franklin Roosevelt's enlightened Good Neighbor policy had brought to an end. "In short," Brian VanDeMark writes, the Dominican intervention "outraged American liberals"—and the "angry liberal reaction" that it provoked quickly "sheared away the left wing of Lyndon Johnson's Great Society consensus."[61] Within days, *New York Times* and *Washington Post* editorials were questioning the president's decision to return to the policy of the "Big Stick." By early May, Democratic senators Mike Mansfield of Montana and Joseph Clark of Pennsylvania were expressing concern that the intervention would reignite Latin American fears of U.S. gunboat diplomacy and thereby strengthen Fidel Castro's hand throughout the hemisphere. Soon other prominent Democrats, including liberal senators Robert Kennedy and Frank Church, together with J. William Fulbright, the influential chairman of the Senate Foreign Relations Committee, were openly criticizing Johnson's handling of the crisis. By the summer of 1965, the intervention had opened a serious breach between the president and his liberal supporters in Congress, the press, and the academic community.[62] Over the next three years, the administration's escalating military commitments in Vietnam then widened that breach beyond repair, ultimately destroying Johnson's presidency.

CHAPTER FIVE

Chile, 1970

President Nixon was enraged. When Ambassador Edward Korry entered the Oval Office on October 13, 1970, to discuss U.S.-Chilean relations with the president, Nixon was slamming his fist into the palm of his hand and fuming, "That sonofabitch, that sonofabitch!" The "sonofabitch" in question, Nixon quickly explained, was "that bastard Allende"—a profane reference to the newly elected president of Chile, Salvador Allende.[1]

Nixon had ample reason to dislike Allende. The new Chilean president was, after Fidel Castro, one of Latin America's most prominent Marxist political leaders. Allende and Castro were close friends and fellow revolutionaries. Allende, however, rejected the Cuban model of insurrectionary violence and armed struggle as a strategy for socialist revolution in Chile. Instead, he was committed to pursuing a peaceful, democratic "road to socialism" in his country—a *vía parlamentaria*, or "parliamentary path," in which Chile's Marxist forces would first mobilize mass-based electoral support to win power democratically and then, once in control of the government, use constitutional processes and legislative enactments in the congress to construct a socialist society. The end result, Allende promised, would be a uniquely Chilean experience—a socialist revolution carried out in a framework of "democracy, pluralism, and liberty." If his revolutionary strategy succeeded, he believed, Chile would become a "second model of the transition to a socialist society," a peaceful, democratic alternative to the Soviet, Chinese, and Cuban models.[2]

Allende's commitment to the *vía parlamentaria* spanned some four decades. A founding member of Chile's Socialist Party in 1932, minister of health in a Popular Front government during World War II, and a senator in the Chilean congress from 1945 to 1970, he had spent his entire political career as "a normal, democratic politician" working for socialist change from within Chile's traditional institutional structures.[3] Now, with his electoral victory in the 1970 presidential election, he had an historic opportunity to make his vision of a nonviolent, democratic Marxist revolution in Chile a reality.

Not all of Allende's supporters shared their leader's commitment to parliamentary democracy, however. Allende had campaigned for the presidency as the candidate of Unidad Popular (Popular Unity, or UP), a heterogeneous and fractious electoral coalition of leftist parties consisting of Chile's Socialists and Communists along with four smaller organizations. The Chilean Communist Party—generally regarded as "the largest, best-organized, and most disciplined of its kind in Latin America"—was pursuing the *vía parlamentaria* largely for reasons of tactical opportunism. Following orthodox Leninist strategy, the Communists had for years been embarked on a "long march through the institutions," participating in Chile's democratic political system in the hope of gaining power and introducing revolutionary changes without resorting to armed insurrection or civil war. The Communists viewed their participation in the 1970 Unidad Popular electoral coalition as an appropriate strategy for the party during a preliminary "national-democratic stage" of the revolution—when the Communists, in alliance with other "popular forces" and "progressive" sectors of "the bourgeoisie," would win power electorally and implement broad reforms, attacking, weakening, and isolating Chile's capitalist elites in preparation for a full transition to socialism and the eventual establishment of a Soviet-style "dictatorship of the masses."[4]

Ironically, a majority of Allende's own Socialist Party was skeptical of the peaceful, parliamentary road to socialism and believed instead that a true socialist revolution could ultimately be achieved only through a process of revolutionary violence that would destroy socialism's capitalist enemies. During the mid-1960s, the party's leadership had fallen under the control of radicals, "mainly Trotskyites," who looked to the Cuban revolution as their source of political inspiration. A 1967 party congress declared that "revolutionary violence is inevitable and legitimate" and that "peaceful and legal forms of struggle are limited instruments of action" in a political process that inevitably would end in armed struggle. Party radicals accepted the Socialists' participation in the 1970 Unidad Popular electoral coalition for tactical reasons, but they made no secret of their belief that, if elected, Allende would at some point have to abandon "bourgeois legalism and constitutionality" and mobilize the working classes and popular masses for a decisive revolutionary assault on Chile's entrenched elites.[5] Indeed, at the time of Allende's election, many Socialist radicals openly supported the guerrilla-warfare tactics of the Movimiento de Izquierda Revolucionaria (Movement of the Revolutionary Left, or MIR), an organization of ultraleft Marxist militants that was carrying out a campaign of bombing attacks, hijackings, bank robberies, and illegal land seizures throughout the country.[6] Whether Allende would be able to control the radical elements in his own coalition when the peaceful road to socialism turned bumpy remained problematical as he prepared for his November 1970 inauguration.

Some of Allende's political opponents even questioned the depth of *his* commitment to democratic processes. Both outgoing president Eduardo Frei of the center-left Christian Democratic Party and Jorge Alessandri, the defeated 1970 candidate of the conservative National Party, expressed fears that if Allende found the *vía parlamentaria* blocked by centrist and right-wing forces in the Chilean congress, he might, under pressure from his radical-left supporters, suspend constitutional procedures and resort to authoritarian governance. To allay such concerns, Allende agreed prior to his inauguration to abide by a new constitutional "statute of democratic guarantees" that reaffirmed his commitment to preserve "the norms

of pluralistic constitutional democracy."[7] Less reassuring, however, was the president-elect's proposed plan to replace Chile's traditional two-house legislature
with a unicameral "assembly of the people" that would be empowered to select
Chile's supreme-court judges and supervise the nation's judicial system. Given
the pivotal role that Chile's courts would play in sanctioning any socialist reform
initiatives passed by the congress, Allende's proposal only increased the fears of his
political opponents that under his presidency Chilean democracy might mutate
into an increasingly totalitarian system.[8]

Salvador Allende was no friend of the United States. Like the Guatemalan and
Cuban revolutionaries before him, he ascribed his country's underdevelopment
and poverty to an exploitative "symbiotic alliance" that Chile's upper-class oligarchy had forged with U.S. private investors. Unidad Popular's basic "Program"
(which in effect served as Allende's 1970 campaign platform) explicitly blamed
Chile's problems on "the imperialists and the ruling class," "reactionary interests,
both national and foreign," and the "large-scale capitalists, both native and foreign" who "totally controlled" the country. Together, the UP Program claimed,
"Imperialist capital and a privileged group of less than 10 per cent of the population monopolize half the national income," condemning the majority of Chile's citizens to deprivation and poverty. Chile was poor, the Program charged, because it
was "a capitalist country, dependent upon imperialism, and dominated by sectors
[of society] allied to foreign capital." The solution, according to the Program, was
"to end the rule of the imperialists, of the monopolies, of the landed oligarchy,
and to begin the construction of socialism."[9] As Allende's first minister of economy, Pedro Vuskovic, put it shortly after taking office, the whole purpose of state
control was "to destroy the economic bases of imperialism and the ruling class by
putting an end to the private ownership of the means of production."[10]

"Imperialism," of course, was a UP synonym for "U.S. economic domination."
In 1970, U.S. corporations had more than $1 billion of capital invested in Chile,
the bulk of it in the mining and communications industries. Allende and his followers were convinced that this "imperialist" capital had milked unconscionably
large profits from the country—profits that by their calculations were "equivalent
to twice the amount of capital invested" in Chile in its entire history.[11] Allende's
socialist remedy was state ownership of Chile's economic infrastructure and resources, and his highest and most immediate priority was the nationalization of
Chile's U.S.-owned copper industry. Copper was "the single dominant element in
Chilean economic life"—"Chile's bread," in local parlance. Copper exports generated approximately three fourths of the country's foreign-exchange earnings and
a substantial percentage of the Chilean government's revenues. The industry, however, was dominated by three U.S.-based copper companies—Anaconda, Ken-
necott, and Cerro—which together accounted for nearly 80 percent of the
country's annual production. Allende charged that the U.S. companies were reap-
ing excess profits from their Chilean operations; by his calculations, they had repa-

triated more than $4 billion in profits on initial investments of "no more than $30 million," leaving far too little money behind to finance economic development or social progress. As one of his supporters put it, the U.S. companies "pulled the treasure from the earth, took it home, and left us the hole." From Allende's perspective, nationalization of the copper industry was the key to "controlling our economic destiny" and "winning our second independence." It would restore Chilean control over Chile's own resources and in the process provide his government with the financial resources to build "a strong internal market" and "raise the standard of living of the masses." Unidad Popular's Program promised financial compensation to the owners of all expropriated properties, but if—as seemed likely—Allende factored his estimates of the copper companies' "excess" profits into his compensation figures, the copper companies could easily end up *owing* Allende's government hundreds of millions of dollars after their expropriation.[12]

In his foreign-policy pronouncements, Allende frequently drew a distinction between his hostility to "imperialistic" foreign capital and his desire for harmonious relations with the U.S. government. During the 1970 election campaign, he promised to adopt an independent, nonaligned foreign policy that would maintain relations "with all . . . countries regardless of their ideological or political position, based upon respect for self-determination and the interests of the people of Chile." After his election, he went out of his way to assure Washington that his government, although Marxist, posed no threat to the United States. Immediately following his swearing-in ceremony, he informed the head of the visiting U.S. inaugural delegation that although his government intended to nationalize the copper industry and other U.S.-owned enterprises, he nevertheless hoped to have "the best possible relations with the United States" and that U.S. security would "never be endangered by Chile or by anything that happens there." Even though "the interests of the United States and the interests of Latin America" had "nothing in common," he stated a few weeks later, Chile wanted "to maintain cordial and cooperative relations with all nations in the world and most particularly with the United States." Shortly thereafter, he publicly reaffirmed that "we will never do anything against the United States or contribute to injuring its sovereignty."[13]

The public record was nonetheless replete with less comforting statements. Allende had long advocated Chile's withdrawal from the Rio Pact—the U.S.-led hemispheric security system that he contemptuously characterized as "one cat and twenty mice"—and he regularly disparaged the Organization of American States and other manifestations of inter-American collaboration. During a July 1970 campaign speech, he allegedly referred to the United States as "public enemy number one" in the Western Hemisphere. His Unidad Popular campaign platform conveyed strong tones of anti-Americanism. Among other things, the UP Program promised that Allende's government would resist "any form of Pan-Americanism," reject the OAS as "the tool and agency of North American imperialism," and "revise, denounce and cancel" all "treaties of reciprocal assistance and mutual aid" between Chile and the United States; it also expressed Unidad Popular's "solidarity with the Cuban Revolution" and condemned "North American aggression in Vietnam."[14] Allende himself was an outspoken supporter of Castro's Cuba. Although he rejected insurrectionary violence as a revolutionary strategy in Chile, he nevertheless praised the Cuban revolution as "a revolution for all of Latin America" that had "shown the way for the liberation of all our peoples." In the aftermath of the Bay of Pigs debacle, he publicly condemned U.S. "aggression against Cuba" as "an aggression against the small nations of the world, against Latin America, and against Chile." He played a prominent role in helping Castro establish the Organización Latino América de Solidaridad, a Havana-based "mini-Comintern" created in 1966 to promote the spread of Marxist insurrections in the hemisphere, and served as the organization's first president.[15] Secretly, meanwhile, Allende was functioning as a longtime "confidential contact" of the Soviet KGB, providing information on political conditions in Chile and neighboring countries as a self-avowed "friend of the Soviet Union" and receiving "personal subsidies" of up to $50,000 from the Politburo for his services.[16]

All in all, Allende's Marxist revolutionary agenda, nationalistic designs on U.S. investment capital, anti-imperialist rhetoric, close association with Castro's Cuba, and secret collaboration with Soviet intelligence made it highly unlikely that the immediate future of U.S.-Chilean relations would be either "cordial" or "cooperative" as he prepared to begin his presidency.

Richard Nixon was not the first U.S. president to regard Salvador Allende as an enemy. In 1962, four years after Allende had lost the 1958 presidential election by less than three percentage points, the Kennedy administration mounted a covert campaign to prevent him from winning Chile's next presidential election, in 1964. According to U.S. ambassador Korry, "The Kennedys utilized every means—illegal and unconstitutional as well as legitimate—to defeat . . . Allende." Between 1962 and 1964, the CIA spent nearly $4 million on some fifteen covert action projects in Chile. Some of the money helped to finance the campaign of the center-left Christian Democrats and their candidate Eduardo Frei, whose opposition to communism was, by his own definition, unalterable and whose international orientation was, in his words, irrevocably with the West. Much of the rest was used to fund "a massive anti-communist propaganda campaign" designed, in Thomas Powers' words, "to scare the living daylights out of Chileans at the prospect of a victory by Allende." CIA-generated campaign materials depicted Chile's Socialists as "nakedly Stalinist," while Agency-produced "posters of Russian tanks in the streets of Budapest and of Cubans in front of Castro's firing squads proliferated on Chilean walls." In the end, Frei's landslide victory in the 1964 election owed at least a partial debt to the CIA-induced atmosphere of fear that helped to polarize Chile's voters during the campaign.[17]

The Nixon administration, by contrast, was notably lax in its response to Allende's 1970 presidential bid. During 1969, embassy and CIA proposals for new covert operations to block Allende elicited no action by Nixon's National Security Council. Instead, preoccupied with serious international crises elsewhere and lulled into complacency by Chilean polls that showed conservative candidate Alessandri well in the lead, the White House failed to focus on the Chilean political situation until well into 1970. In late March, a small "spoiling" operation, modeled on the 1964 CIA propaganda campaign, was approved, with funding that eventually totaled some $435,000. But, according to Henry Kissinger, Nixon's national security adviser, this U.S. "token effort" was "much too little . . . far too late" and was carried out "in only the most minimal and ineffectual fashion." By August, as the Chilean election campaign entered its final phase and Kissinger finally began to "focus on the dangers" inherent in the situation, he was appalled to discover "that nothing further could now be done before the election."[18]

Allende's dramatic election victory on September 4, 1970, left Washington in a state of stunned surprise, Kissinger recalls; "Nixon was beside himself" and desperate to do "something, *anything*, that would reverse the previous neglect." Over the course of the next eleven days, in an atmosphere that Kissinger describes as frantic and frenzied, the White House hastily improvised a two-track strategy of covert initiatives designed to prevent Allende from taking office. In Track I, U.S. officials in Chile were ordered to secretly promote a constitutional coup d'état. Because Allende had won only a 36 percent plurality in the three-candidate presidential contest, he faced a congressional runoff election on October 24 in which the Chilean congress would choose between Allende and the runner-up candidate Alessandri. The Nixon administration's Track I strategy consisted of various plans to prevent Allende's election in the congress. One option (the "Frei reelection gambit") involved the bribing of Chilean congressmen to vote for Alessandri, who would immediately resign the presidency, forcing a new election in which the popular Frei—constitutionally barred from succeeding himself in office—would be free to run for a second term. Another Track I option consisted of applying pressure on Frei to "voluntarily yield power to an interim military regime" prior to Allende's confirmation, again opening the way to fresh elections, which Frei would presumably win.[19]

Track II took form on September 15 when Nixon ordered CIA director Richard Helms to instigate a military coup in Chile that would "prevent Allende from taking power or . . . unseat him" if he took office. According to Helms' oft-quoted notes from the meeting, the president recognized that there was probably only a one-in-ten chance of success, but he was determined to "save Chile" and was "not concerned [with the] risks involved." Nixon indicated that he was prepared to make "$10,000,000 available, more if necessary." Helms was instructed to assign the "best men we have" to the project, and to "make the [Chilean] economy scream," presumably as a pressure tactic to prod Chile's armed forces into moving against Allende. As Helms later testified, "The President came down very hard that he wanted something done, and he didn't much care how." Within days of the September 15 meeting, the CIA found itself under "constant . . . continual pressure . . . from the White House" to accomplish its assigned mission.[20]

In the end, however, Nixon's two-track strategy turned out to be "a real-life 'Mission Impossible'"—primarily because neither Frei nor any of Chile's key military officers would go along. As a result, Allende was confirmed as president-elect by the Chilean congress on October 24 and duly inaugurated on November 3.[21] Having failed to block the Chilean Marxist's accession to power, the Nixon administration then settled into a public policy of "cool but correct" behavior toward Allende's government combined with a covert program of economic destabilization designed to wreak havoc on Allende's socialist experiment and force the Chilean military to oust him. That Janus-like policy remained in effect until September 1973, when Chile's armed forces overthrew Allende's government in a bloody military coup that left Allende dead in the presidential palace.[22]

Any number of authors have attributed Nixon's Chilean intervention to economic motives. According to Seymour Hersh, "There is compelling evidence that Nixon's tough stance against Allende in 1970 was principally shaped by his concern for the future of the American corporations whose assets, he believed, would be seized by an Allende government." In his efforts to deny Allende the presidency, Hersh concludes, "Nixon was primarily protecting the interests of his corporate benefactors."[23] James Petras and Morris Morley characterize Nixon's interventionism as the effort of an imperial state to defend the interests of U.S.-based multinational corporations in Chile.[24] Allende and his advisers had said as much while they were still in office. In a 1972 speech to the UN General Assembly, Allende charged that his country was the victim of serious U.S. "aggression . . . designed to take revenge on the Chilean people for its decision to nationalize its copper." A 1973 internal report prepared by Allende's government also attributed Nixon's hostility to his anger at Allende's nationalization of the copper industry. "What the United States cannot accept," the report concluded, "is the existence of a government like Popular Unity that can decide to nationalize without indemnification, using legal methods that paralyze the U.S. capacity to respond."[25]

The available evidence, however, is less "compelling" than economic interpretations would suggest. That U.S. companies lobbied the administration to intervene in Chile in 1970 is beyond dispute. In April, the board chairman of Anaconda Copper and a group of worried U.S. business leaders offered the State Department $500,000 to assist in financing anti-Allende campaign efforts. In July and September, senior officials of the International Telephone & Telegraph Company, a corporation with Chilean investments totaling $150 million, offered the CIA up to $1 million to help block Allende's accession to power. (International Telephone & Telegraph officials warned the White House that their company would be "in deep financial trouble" if it lost its Chilean holdings.)[26] Meanwhile, the administration's own intelligence assessments were predicting that Allende's election would lead to "harsh measures against U.S. business interests in Chile," resulting in "tangible economic losses" for the United States.[27] Nixon later acknowledged that he was aware of Allende's plans to expropriate U.S.-owned property at the time that he ordered the CIA to instigate a military coup.[28]

Nevertheless, no conclusive evidence has yet emerged that the intervention was based on Nixon's concern for the welfare of U.S. investors in Chile. Kissinger has categorically denied that economic factors played a role in the White House's policy formulations. "Nationalization of American-owned property was not the issue," he wrote in his memoirs; "the Nixon Administration did not view our foreign policy interests through the prism of the financial concerns of American companies." Colleagues have described Kissinger's own attitude toward U.S. businesses overseas as "contemptuous"—"He never gave a shit about the business community," one recalled.[29] Nor did administration officials accept any corporate financial support for the intervention effort; every private offer to contribute funds was quickly rejected as inappropriate.[30]

Nixon and Kissinger themselves, in their few public references to Chile, consistently defined their concerns in terms of U.S. national security. In his memoirs, Kissinger states categorically that "Our concern with Allende was based on national security, not on economics."[31] Nixon, in a 1977 television interview with journalist David Frost, recalled that in 1970 he considered "a leftwing dictatorship" in Chile to be a threat to "our security interests."[32] More specifically, both Nixon and Kissinger defined their security fears in terms of geopolitical "falling dominos." "I don't mean that [an Allende government] was an immediate threat," Nixon told Frost, "but I mean that if you let one go, you're going to have some problems with others. . . . Now we had one country in the Western Hemisphere, Cuba, that is, exporting revolution, and we didn't want another one, Chile, doing it." "Months before Allende came to power," Nixon recalled, "an Italian businessman came to call on me in the Oval Office and he said 'If Allende should win the election in Chile, and then you have Castro in Cuba, what you will in effect have in Latin America is a red sandwich, and eventually it will all be red.' And that's what we confronted."[33] Kissinger, in his memoirs, describes Allende as

not merely an economic nuisance or a political critic but a geopolitical challenge. Chile bordered Peru, Argentina, and Bolivia, all plagued by radical movements. As a continental country, a militant Chile had a capacity to undermine other nations and support radical insurgency that was far greater than Cuba's, and Cuba has managed to do damage enough. If Chile had followed the Cuban pattern,

Communist ideology would in time have been supported by Soviet forces and Soviet arms in the southern cone of the South American continent.[34]

Nixon's and Kissinger's retrospective public explanations conflict sharply, however, with the views of their own security analysts at the time. In August, Ambassador Korry had informed Washington that the U.S. embassy in Santiago was "unable to identify any vital U.S. security interests in Chile. The fall of Chile to Marxist totalitarianism," he wrote, "cannot. . .be considered a threat to the nation in military terms." Three days after Allende's election, the administration's interdepartmental Group for Inter-American Affairs—made up of representatives from the CIA, the State Department, the Department of Defense, and the White House—reported that the United States had "no vital national interests within Chile," that "the world military balance of power would not be significantly altered by an Allende government," and that an Allende-led Chile would not pose "any likely threat to the peace of the region." It would be "hard to argue" that Allende constituted "a mortal threat to the U.S.," the National Security Council's chief Latin American specialist advised Kissinger a week later.[35] A National Intelligence Estimate prepared in July concluded that although Allende would attempt to take Chile "a long way down the Marxist-Socialist road" during a six-year term in office, he would first have to surmount a long list of powerful domestic obstacles, "such as Chile's security forces, the Christian Democratic Party, some elements of organized labor, the Congress, and the Catholic Church."[36]

The intelligence community specifically discounted any likelihood that Allende's government would attempt to subvert its Andean neighbors and trigger a domino effect in South America. A CIA intelligence memorandum produced shortly after Allende's electoral victory predicted that the new Chilean president would be "cautious in providing assistance to extremists" in neighboring countries because of his "fear of provoking a military reaction in his own country." The memorandum also concluded that "the degree to which [foreign] revolutionary groups would be allowed to use Chile as a base of operations would be limited" because the Chilean Communist Party—Allende's partner in the Unidad Popular coalition—was opposed to "violence-prone groups."[37] Meanwhile, the U.S. embassy was continuing to assure Washington that an Allende government would pose no direct security threat to the region or to the United States. "Chile is really an island" isolated from its neighbors by geography, Ambassador Korry reported on September 5, the day after the election. Furthermore, Korry pointed out, "There is no country on earth that is so far from the two super-powers and Red China." Chile "is not Poland nor is it Mexico," he wrote, and "it will not require any massive commitment from anyone." Nor would the Soviet Union take advantage of Allende's victory to "expand its base" of influence in Chile, the ambassador informed Washington; instead, the Soviets would "move with caution" and not let Chile become "another Cuban drain of Moscow's resources."[38] Kissinger's off-the-cuff quip to reporters that Chile was "a dagger pointed at the heart of Antarctica" suggests that, despite his "official" explanations for the public record, the national security adviser may have privately shared his security bureaucracy's skepticism that an Allende-led Chile was a threat to U.S. security.[39]

In actuality, Nixon's hatred of Allende—and the U.S. intervention that resulted—can best be understood in the context of the goals that Nixon had set for his presidency. In direct contrast to his immediate predecessor in the White House, Nixon intended to achieve presidential greatness in the realm of foreign policy. He personally regarded himself as an expert in international affairs and confided to friends that he considered his life "dedicated to great foreign policy purposes." According to historian Melvin Small, Nixon also understood that politically "a president enjoyed considerable freedom of action in international relations and that the chances of achieving successes there were far greater than in trying to resolve intractable domestic problems." "I've always thought this country could run itself domestically without a President," he told an interviewer a year before his election; "All you need is a competent Cabinet to run the country at home. You need a President for foreign policy." He also thought the stakes were higher in international politics. "The American economy is so strong it would take a genius to ruin it," he later observed, "whereas one small mistake in foreign policy could blow up the world."[40]

Nixon entered office with an ambitious—even visionary—objective for his presidency: to lead the United States out of the draining environment of Cold War confrontation and into "a new era of peaceful coexistence with the communist world." Negotiations with the Soviet Union would produce a détente based on the concept of "linkage," in which Soviet political and military restraint in such international trouble spots as Vietnam, Berlin, and the Middle East would be rewarded with U.S. cooperation on issues of vital interest to the Soviet Union, such as strategic arms limitation, increased access to Western food and technology, and recognition of existing boundaries in Eastern Europe. Normalization of relations with Communist China would place the United States in "a balancing position" vis-à-vis the two leading communist bloc powers, providing the Nixon administration with "a great strategic opportunity" to construct a more stable and peaceful world. The "subtle triangle of relations between Washington, Peking, and Moscow" that would result would first enable Nixon to end the Vietnam War, by giving his administration the increased bargaining leverage that would induce the Soviets and Chinese to apply pressure on Hanoi to "moderate its requirements for a cease-fire." The broader long-term result would be a more stable international balance of power—a new multipolar "global equilibrium" based, in Kissinger's words, on mutual restraint and "even eventual cooperation" among the major world powers.[41] If his grand design worked, Nixon—the quintessential U.S. cold warrior—would establish an historical legacy for himself as one of the twentieth-century's great peacemakers.

The vision proved easier to conceptualize than to implement. In the twenty months between Nixon's inauguration and Salvador Allende's election, the administration's efforts to give birth to a new international "structure for peace" ended mainly in what Nixon characterized as miscarriages. The communist world greeted the new administration with intransigence and acts of military aggression. In February 1969, a month after Nixon's inauguration, the North Vietnamese launched what he described as "a small-scale but savage offensive into South Vietnam." In April, North Korea shot down an unarmed U.S. EC–121 reconnaissance aircraft over the Sea of Japan, killing all thirty-one crew members. That summer, Hanoi bluntly rejected Nixon's offer to negotiate a speedy end to the Vietnam War; in rebuffing Nixon's conciliatory proposals, Ho Chi Minh "blamed the United States for the war, reiterated his determination to settle for nothing less than full independence of his country, and called for a complete U.S. withdrawal from Vietnam." For their part, the Soviets displayed little interest in "linkage"-induced behavior modification; in his memoirs, Kissinger criticizes them for refusing to reduce tensions in the Middle East or Berlin and for failing to assist the United States in its efforts to disengage from Vietnam. By October 1969, Nixon was complaining that Moscow had done "nothing to help" settle the war in Vietnam except to arrange for an oblong negotiating table at the Paris peace talks.[42]

The year 1970 brought more international crises. In March, the Soviets began a dramatic expansion of their military presence in the Middle East, pouring combat forces and advanced armaments into Egypt in support of the Nasser regime's military buildup along the Egyptian-Israeli frontier. In early September, fighting broke out in Jordan when radical Palestinian refugees, backed by pro-Soviet Syria, attempted to overthrow the moderate, pro-Western government of King Hussein. Nixon captured the tension of the moment in his memoir *RN*:

> One thing was clear. We could not allow Hussein to be overthrown by a Soviet-inspired insurrection. If it succeeded, the entire Middle East might erupt in war; the Israelis would almost certainly take pre-emptive measures against a Syrian-dominated radical government in Jordan; the Egyptians were tied to Syria by military alliances; and Soviet prestige was on the line with both the Syrians and the Egyptians. Since the United States could not stand idly by and watch Israel being driven into the sea, the possibility of a direct U.S.-Soviet confrontation was uncomfortably high. It was like a ghastly game of dominoes, with a nuclear war waiting at the end."[43]

Simultaneously, halfway across the world, U.S. U-2 spy planes were producing evidence that a Soviet nuclear submarine base was under construction in Cienfuegos, Cuba; when completed, Kissinger informed Nixon, the base would mark "a quantum leap in the strategic capability of the Soviet Union against the United States."[44] Then, on September 4, the election returns from Chile presented the administration with yet another crisis situation.

For Nixon and Kissinger, the international crises of 1969–1970 represented "different facets of a global Communist challenge." Both men believed that communists respected only "power and strength" and that Soviet foreign policy was predicated on a relentless probing for points of international weakness. Now, the White House concluded, Moscow was probing "in several directions at once" in order to test the credibility of U.S. power under Nixon's stewardship. North Korea's shoot-down of the EC-121 was, in Kissinger's words, "a test of the new administration's decisiveness." The Jordanian crisis was "yet another test of U.S. resolve." And the construction of the Soviet submarine base in Cuba was also "part of a process of testing under way in different parts of the world."[45]

Above all, the administration looked upon the Vietnam War as a *decisive* test of U.S. global credibility—and the one that would determine the success or failure of Nixon's international grand design. According to Melvin Small, "Nixon and Kissinger were . . . certain that how the United States ended the war in Vietnam would influence upcoming negotiations with the Russians and Chinese. Relations with the communists could not be stabilized unless the United States left Vietnam with dignity." Kissinger had been warning since 1966 that a U.S. defeat at the hands of a "third-class Communist peasant state" like North Vietnam would "strengthen" America's enemies, "demoralize" her allies, "lessen the credibility" of the United States throughout the world, and tempt other countries to shift their alignments to the communist bloc.[46] In his memoirs, Kissinger writes that it was crucial for the United States to avoid the perception of having been "routed" in Vietnam:

> As the leader of democratic alliances we had to remember that scores of countries and millions of people relied for their security on our willingness to stand by allies. . . . No serious policymaker could allow himself to succumb to the fashionable debunking of "prestige" or "honor" or "credibility." For a great power to abandon a small country to tyranny simply to obtain a respite from our own travail seemed to me . . . profoundly immoral and destructive of our efforts to build a new and ultimately more peaceful pattern of international relations. We could not revitalize the Atlantic Alliance if its governments were assailed by doubt about American staying power. We would not be able to move the Soviet Union toward the imperative of mutual restraint against the backdrop of capitulation in a major war. We might not achieve our opening to China if our value as a counterweight seemed nullified by a collapse that showed us irrelevant to Asian security. Our success in Middle East diplomacy would depend on convincing our ally of our reliability and its adversaries that we were impervious to threats of military pressure or blackmail.[47]

Kissinger's views mirrored those of the president. "I am utterly convinced that how we end this war will determine the future of the U.S. in the world," Nixon told several top advisers in July 1970. "We can maintain the American position in Europe and Asia if we come out well."[48]

Nixon interpreted the North Vietnamese military offensive of February 1969 as "a deliberate test, clearly designed to take the measure of me and my administration at the outset." He immediately responded by ordering the secret bombing of Vietnamese communist sanctuaries in Cambodia as a demonstration to Hanoi that his administration was "different and tougher" than its predecessors.[49] A year later, in April 1970, he told a national television audience that his controversial decision to widen the war by deploying U.S. ground forces into Cambodia was designed to put

> the leaders of North Vietnam on notice that . . . we will not be humiliated. We will not be defeated. . . .
>
> If, when the chips are down, the world's most powerful nation, the United States of America, acts like a pitiful, helpless giant, the forces of totalitarianism and anarchy will threaten free nations and free institutions throughout the world. . . .
>
> If we fail to meet this challenge, all other nations will be on notice that despite its overwhelming power the United States, when a real crisis comes, will be found wanting.[50]

Allende's election victory was seen in the White House as yet another communist challenge to U.S. interests—the latest in an accelerating series of communist "tests" of U.S. power under Nixon's leadership. Nixon recalled in his memoirs that "America was being tested in the fall of 1970—by war in Vietnam; by the threat of war in the Middle East; by the introduction of threatening nuclear capabilities in Cuba. In Chile the test was just as real, although much subtler." According to Kissinger, "We were faced simultaneously with a civil war in Jordan, a Soviet attempt to build a submarine base in Cuba, and the coming to power of Allende in Chile. It was at once *the most dangerous and decisive period of the new administration.*"[51] "The Chilean election results," Kissinger continued,

> came in just as Moscow and Cairo were rejecting our protests of Middle East cease-fire violations; Jordan feared an imminent move by Iraqi troops against the King; a Soviet naval force was steaming toward Cuba. By September 8, the day the Chilean developments were first discussed by an interagency committee, several airplanes had just been hijacked in the Middle East and the Soviet flotilla was nearing the port of Cienfuegos. Six days later, on September 14, when Chile was next considered, the Jordan situation had deteriorated, and Cuban MiGs intercepted a U-2 flight seeking to photograph Cienfuegos and

the mission had to be aborted. In the weeks that followed, our government pondered Chilean events not in isolation but against the backdrop of the Syrian invasion of Jordan and our effort to force the Soviet Union to dismantle its installation for servicing nuclear submarines in the Caribbean. The reaction must be seen in that context.[52]

From Nixon's and Kissinger's perspective, the Soviets were now probing for new weak points in the Western Hemisphere. If they encountered "mush," they would proceed; if they encountered "steel," they would withdraw. The administration felt that it had to demonstrate its steel in Chile. The United States could not be "found wanting." The stakes were too high.[53]

Most immediately, a Marxist-led Chile would further erode the unity of the United States' hemispheric alliance system. According to Kissinger, Allende's government would represent "a permanent challenge to our position in the Western Hemisphere," while Nixon worried that the Chilean election would have "profound implications . . . for the inter-American system."[54]

But the implications extended far beyond Latin America. At the time of Allende's election, the administration was preparing for a new round of peace talks with North Vietnamese representatives in Paris, and Nixon was finalizing secret plans to withdraw 150,000 U.S. troops from Vietnam over the next several months. He feared that if the United States passively accepted the establishment of a new Marxist state in its own hemisphere, Hanoi would have even less reason to believe that the new president was "tougher" than his predecessors or that the United States had the strength of will to remain in Vietnam "for the duration." Why, then, would the North Vietnamese agree to a negotiated settlement of the war? More broadly still, why would Soviet and Chinese leaders agree to "mutual restraint," détente, or rapprochement with a "pitiful, helpless giant" that could no longer maintain hegemony in its Latin American sphere of influence? Ambassador Korry later acknowledged that the Nixon administration's "number one" concern in Chile was its fear, "at a time that we were about to . . . begin the scale down and withdrawal from Vietnam, and . . . launch new initiatives with Moscow and Peking, that for the United States to act indifferent to the disappearing of a democracy, of a unique democracy in what was viewed throughout the world as its back yard, could have a significant effect on those who made policy in the Soviet Union and the People's Republic of China."[55] The principal concern in Washington, Korry told Senator Frank Church, was

the probability that the governments in Moscow and Peking would misread US indifference in Chile. . . . At the time of the Chilean election campaign, the US [was] engaged in the reordering of its relations with the USSR and the PRC. I speculated to and in Washington that if the US did nothing to sustain a democracy of the caliber of Chile . . . then either or both of the two major Communist powers might conclude that the US disasters in Indochina, the subsequent demoralization within the US and abandonment in Chile—in our own hemisphere—taken together with the evident crises in Western Europe at that time, signified a general Western collapse in the offing. They might, I said, adopt the analysis of the leadership of Allende's own Socialist Party—that the US was incapable of defending its interests and, as the leader of the Socialist Party, Sr. Altamirano, kept emphasizing in Chile, the collapse of the US would be hastened by kicking it hard and often.[56]

The administration's "number two" concern, according to Korry, was the "certain effect" that Allende's Chilean model would have on political trends in Western Europe. Kissinger in particular was worried about the growing strength of communist parties in Italy and France. He feared that the successful example of a freely elected Marxist coalition government in Chile would encourage the "Eurocommunists" to seek political alliances with Socialists and Christian Democrats in upcoming elections and gain control of the Italian or French government as members of leftist popular-front coalitions. If communists came to power in Italy or France, Kissinger believed, the consequences would be devastating for the West's position in the Cold War and for the Nixon administration's goal of achieving peaceful coexistence. "The world balance of power," he wrote in 1969, "depends on our ability to deny the resources and manpower of Western Europe to an aggressor," while any "true relaxation in [East-West] tensions presupposes Western unity." In his view, there was "no doubt that a Communist breakthrough to power or a share of power in one country will have a major psychological effect on the others, by making Communist parties seem respectable, or suggesting that the tide of history in Europe is moving in their direction. . . . [T]he accession to power of Communists in an allied country would represent a massive change in European politics . . . [and] would have fundamental consequences for the structure of the postwar world as we have known it and for America's relationship to its most important alliances." According to political scientist Robert H. Johnson, "Kissinger argued that the military strength of NATO would be 'gravely weakened' because governments containing Communists would have to be excluded from discussions of classified subjects, [and] because they would seek to weaken NATO defense efforts. . . . With NATO weakened, member countries would be forced to accommodate to Soviet power and 'massive shifts against us would occur.'" In short, from Kissinger's perspective, "Allende's success would have had implications . . . for the future of Communist parties in Western Europe, whose policies would inevitably undermine the Western Alliance." "The political evolution of Chile," he remarked soon after Allende's victory, "is a very serious matter for the national security interests of the United States because of its effects in France and Italy."[57]

Ambassador Korry shared "the conviction that were the U.S. to act indifferently to [Chile's] fate . . . , the effects would be devastating in other countries where a communist party had meaningful political influence or where ultra-Marxist-Leninists might play a significant role. I had in mind not only, or even primarily, Latin America," the ambassador recalled; "Chile seemed to share Western European political structure and outlook, so I spoke then to Washington of France, Italy, Spain—even Japan."[58]

Kissinger worried that the Chilean model of a democratic road to Marxist revolution could also have a harmful effect on Latin American politics. One of his staff assistants later recalled that "Henry saw Allende as being a far more dangerous threat than Castro. If Latin America ever became unraveled, it would never happen with a Castro. Allende was a living example of democratic social reform in Latin America. All kinds of cataclysmic events rolled around, but Chile scared him. He talked about Eurocommunism the same way he talked about Chile early on. Chile scared him."[59]

According to another aide, "Henry thought that Allende might lead an anti-U.S. move in Latin America more effectively than Castro, just because it *was* the democratic route to power."[60] It was this aspect of the Chilean situation that the U.S. intelligence community found to be the most worrisome. An interagency intelligence assessment produced three days after the Chilean election warned that although the United States had "no vital national interests within Chile," an Allende government "would . . . create considerable political and psychological costs. . . . Hemispheric cohesion would be threatened by the challenge that an Allende government would pose to the [Organization of American States], and by the reactions that it would create in other countries." "An Allende victory," the assessment concluded, "would represent a definite psychological set-back to the U.S. and a definite psychological advance for the Marxist idea."[61] Nixon personally underscored the dangerous effect that the Chilean model could have on international politics when, three days after Allende's inauguration, he told the National Security Council: "Our main concern in Chile is the prospect that [Allende] can consolidate himself and the picture projected to the world will be his success.[62]

The available evidence suggests, then, that the United States intervened in Chile in 1970 not for reasons of economic self-interest or military defense but because the Nixon administration viewed Salvador Allende as a dangerous challenge to its international credibility and strategic goals. The White House believed that it had to respond aggressively to what it regarded as a new communist "test" in Chile if it hoped to end the Vietnam War "with honor" and persuade the Soviets and Chinese to participate in a new global "structure for peace." The administration feared that a perception of U.S. weakness in Chile would damage its credibility in the eyes of communist bloc governments and hinder its "efforts to build a new and ultimately more peaceful pattern of international relations." "If . . . we are accommodating" to Allende, Kissinger told his Senior Review Group shortly after Unidad Popular's election victory, "we risk giving the appearance of weakness or of indifference to the establishment of a Marxist government in the Hemisphere." "If [Allende] is inaugurated," Korry advised from Santiago, "the United States has admitted its impotence." The communist world respected "power and strength," not impotence, and as Kissinger put it, "displays of American impotence in one part of the world . . . would inevitably erode our credibility in other parts of the world." In the national security adviser's evocative metaphor, the administration simply could not afford to look like "a sort of mother hen clucking nervous irrelevancies from the sidelines"—especially not in the middle of its "most dangerous and decisive period" in office.[63]

Administration officials likewise believed that the mere example of an Allende government could disrupt the East-West balance of power and endanger their plans to forge a more stable relationship with the communist bloc. In their view, the Chilean model had the capability of undermining the Western Alliance—first by fueling the political momentum of communist parties in Western Europe, with potentially disastrous consequences for NATO, and second by damaging the inter-American system, eroding "hemispheric cohesion," and possibly leading to Latin America's eventual "unraveling." Nixon and Kissinger believed that a "true relaxation in [Cold War] tensions" required "Western unity"—because communists compromised only when confronted by strength. There consequently could be little hope for successful negotiations with Moscow, Beijing, or Hanoi if the U.S. alliance system appeared to be falling apart in Western Europe and Latin America. To an administration that already considered itself under assault from communist "tests" and "challenges," Allende's government was an unacceptable threat to the stable new international system that Nixon was seeking to construct as his great historical legacy.

There was also a domestic political dimension to the intervention. More primal even than Nixon's hope for great achievements in international affairs was his desire to be a two-term president. As one of his presidential biographers writes, "Nixon began to think about his second term almost as soon as he took office" in 1969. Kissinger recalls that "Nixon had three goals" as he entered the White House: "to win [reelection in 1972] by the biggest electoral landslide in history; to be remembered as a peacemaker; and to be accepted by the 'Establishment' as an equal."[64]

From the start, Nixon understood that his reelection prospects hinged on his ability to extricate the United States from Vietnam. Domestic opposition to the war had forced Lyndon Johnson to abandon plans to seek a second full term in 1968, and Nixon was already being warned as he entered office that he too would be a one-term president unless he found a way to end the war quickly. His early reliance, however, on military escalation to push Hanoi toward a negotiated settlement not only failed to achieve the desired result—it triggered massive and increasingly violent antiwar protests at home. By mid-1970, the White House was literally besieged by antiwar demonstrators, and the president and his advisers found themselves embroiled in what they regarded as a virtual civil war in the United States. In September, when Chile added itself to the list of the administration's worries, Nixon's public-approval rating dropped below 50 percent for the first time in his twenty months as president. It was clear, he told Kissinger, that the war in Vietnam was "sapping his domestic support and therefore had to be ended before 1972."[65]

In the days leading up to his decision to intervene in Chile, Nixon was focusing heavily on his 1972 reelection strategy. On September 12, 1970, according to White House Chief of Staff H. R. Haldeman, the president ordered his aides to "gear everything to '72, reelection and winning Congress." According to Haldeman, Nixon spent the morning of September 15—the day he ordered the intervention— working on his "basic political approach" to reelection in 1972.[66]

Chile complicated his plans. A Marxist takeover of a second Latin American country would increase the already embattled president's political vulnerability. Nixon had built his political career on what Kissinger characterizes as "a tough, occasionally strident anti-Communism"; from his 1946 campaign for the House of Representatives onward, he had routinely accused his campaign opponents of weakness in combating communism. He believed that the reason he had lost the 1960 presidential election was because, as he wrote in his memoirs, "Kennedy conveyed the image . . . that he was tougher on Castro and communism than I was"; according to Kissinger, "Nixon was determined that no one would ever be able to make this charge again." During the early 1960s, he had heaped criticism on the Kennedy administration for its handling of Cuba—for having "goofed an invasion [and] given the Soviets squatters' rights in our backyard." Thanks to Kennedy's policies, he charged in 1963, "Cuba is western Russia, and the rest of Latin America is in deadly peril."[67] Now, in 1970, Nixon feared that it was payback time—the Democrats would blame him for having "lost Chile," for having been "asleep at the wheel" "on his watch."[68] To make matters worse, he knew that he was exceedingly vulnerable to such charges. Throughout 1969 and early 1970, his administration had taken no action to prevent Allende's election, despite recommendations from Korry and the CIA that covert anti-Allende blocking efforts should be initiated. According to Kissinger, the reason Nixon was "beside himself" when he received the news of Allende's election victory was because "for over a decade he had lambasted Democratic administrations for permitting the establishment of Communist power in Cuba. And now what he perceived—not wrongly—as another Cuba had come into being during his own Administration. . . . This explains the virulence of his reaction and his insistence on doing something, *anything*, that would reverse the previous neglect."[69]

The National Security Council reinforced Nixon's political concerns. On November 3, 1970—the day Allende was inaugurated—it warned that "the U.S. Congress and knowledgeable sectors of the public will follow with interest the political course which Chile takes internally and its attitudes and actions with regard to the United States. . . . As the actions of the Allende government become more overtly hostile to U.S. interests . . . we may expect adverse reaction by some sectors of the U.S. public, press, and Congress to the 'establishment of another communist government in the hemisphere.'" Failure on the administration's part "to take any steps" against Allende, the NSC concluded, "would leave the initiative in his hands, discourage opposition to Allende in Chile, weaken our hemisphere leadership, and create serious problems with public and Congressional opinion in the United States."[70] The following morning, Kissinger defined the danger in terms that went to the heart of Nixon's fears. "Chile," the national security adviser told White House aide Dwight Chapin, "could end up being the worst failure in our administration—'our Cuba' by 1972."[71]

And so Richard Nixon intervened in Chile because he viewed Allende's Unidad Popular government as a threat not only to his foreign-policy goals but to his domestic political ambitions as well. It was this dual nature of the threat that Ambassador Korry highlighted in his September 5 cable to Washington informing the administration of Allende's election victory. "Chile," he wrote, "voted calmly to have a Marxist-Leninist state, the first nation in the world to make this choice freely and knowingly. . . . *It will have the most profound effect on Latin America and beyond; we have suffered a grievous defeat; the consequences will be domestic and international.* . . ." According to Kissinger, Nixon underlined the italicized sentence on his copy of Korry's cable.[72]

Finally, Nixon's decision to intervene was also influenced by the lobbying efforts of Allende's Chilean political enemies. A few days after Allende's election, Agustín Edwards, Chile's "most powerful businessman," called on Ambassador Korry in Santiago and asked whether the United States intended to "do anything militarily—directly or indirectly" to block Allende's accession to power. Korry's answer was no. Edwards then traveled to Washington, D.C., on what a Nixon administration official later described as "a last-minute effort" to recruit U.S. support for a plan to prevent Allende from taking office. In the United States, the wealthy Chilean capitalist—whose business empire included the conservative *El Mercurio* publishing chain, Chile's largest granary, a major poultry business, and a Pepsi Cola bottling plant—was the houseguest of PepsiCo chairman Donald Kendall, one of Nixon's "closest friends and largest campaign contributors." On September 14, Kendall visited the White House and personally conveyed Edwards' thoughts on the Chilean political situation to Nixon. The following morning, September 15, Edwards was granted a one-hour breakfast meeting with Kissinger and Attorney General John Mitchell and a separate meeting with CIA director Richard Helms. Although the details of his conversations with Nixon's senior advisers remain classified, he likely warned them that Allende was "a Soviet dupe" who would transform Chile into "another Cuba." The suggested courses of action that he urged the U.S. government to consider bore a striking resemblance to the Track I and Track II covert operations that the administration subsequently implemented. A few hours after the meetings, Nixon ordered the intervention—and Edwards' input clearly had a significant impact on his decision to do so. Helms later testified that he had the "impression" that the president took action on the fifteenth "because of Edwards' presence in Washington and what he heard from Kendall about what Edwards was saying about conditions in Chile and what was happening there." Kissinger goes further, stating frankly that Nixon was "triggered into action . . . by Augustin [sic] Edwards . . . who had come to Washington to warn of the consequences of an Allende takeover."[73]

Edwards' lobbying activities were by no means an isolated phenomenon. Korry recalls being "propositioned by key Chileans anxious to involve the United States in hair-brained plots" against Allende. He later told a Senate subcommittee that "there were a great many Chileans who wanted the United States to do their bidding, a great many, and who were very active in Washington, who tried to manipulate the pressures on me in Chile. And in certain instances . . . they were very successful, indeed." "There were Chileans very anxious to involve us," he reiterated later in his testimony—"so many Chileans that were trying to entrap us, one way or another in this thing."[74]

Korry also mentions a "provocative" and "highly inflammatory" anti-Allende letter that outgoing president Frei sent to Nixon "the week before" September 15.[75] The impact of the letter is unclear, but Frei subsequently played a significant role in shaping Nixon's policy toward Chile after Allende was sworn in as president. On November 3, the day of Allende's inauguration, the National Security Council produced an "Options Paper on Chile" that outlined several alternative courses of action available to the United States in dealing with Allende's government. Option D called for the Nixon administration to "maintain an outwardly correct but adversary posture, [and] adopt without delay economic, political and diplomatic measures designed to prevent Allende from consolidating his position." "This option," the NSC paper noted, "reflects the reported evaluation of the situation by ex-President Frei . . . that Chile is dead, without any future except as a fully Marxist state, and that the only miracle that might save it would be the incapacity of the government to handle the economic situation."[76] Option D became the basis of U.S. policy toward Chile from 1971 to the military coup of September 1973 that destroyed Allende and his Unidad Popular government.

Quietly, behind the scenes, Chile's political and economic elites worked to instigate a U.S. intervention and helped conceive the program of U.S. economic destabilization that contributed to Allende's eventual demise. Richard Nixon ordered the U.S. intervention in Chile because he believed that core elements of his presidential agenda—a reduction in Cold War tensions, an honorable withdrawal from Vietnam, reelection in 1972—were at stake, but Allende's Chilean opponents played an influential background role in the affair.

CHAPTER SIX

Nicaragua, 1981

In November 1981, ten months into his presidency, Ronald Reagan ordered the Central Intelligence Agency to begin covert paramilitary operations against Nicaragua's Sandinista government. The following March, CIA-sponsored Nicaraguan counterrevolutionaries carried out bombing attacks on transportation facilities in northern Nicaragua. The attacks marked the start of Reagan's "Contra war" against the Sandinistas, a war that would drag on for the remainder of his two terms in office, resulting in some 43,000 Nicaraguan casualties and more than $1 billion in damage to the Nicaraguan economy. The desired outcome eventually came in 1990 when Nicaragua's electorate, exhausted by the years of crisis and conflict, voted the Sandinistas out of power.[1]

Reagan and his Republican supporters had made little secret of their hostile intentions prior to winning the White House. The 1980 Republican Party platform "deplore[d] the Marxist Sandinista takeover of Nicaragua" and committed the Republicans to "support the efforts of the Nicaraguan people to establish a free and independent government." During the election campaign, candidate Reagan attacked the Sandinistas as Marxist-Leninists and accused them of promoting the spread of communism among their neighbors. Under their control, he charged, the Nicaraguan government bore a distinctly "Cuban label" and had become nothing less than a Russian "bear's paw" in Central America.[2]

The Reaganites' charges were not entirely without foundation. That the top Sandinista leaders were Marxist-Leninists is beyond dispute. Their organization, the Frente Sandinista de Liberación Nacional (Sandinista National Liberation Front, or FSLN), had been founded in 1961 by young members of Nicaragua's "Moscow-line" communist party (the Partido Socialista Nicaraguense) frustrated by their party's "Soviet-dictated orthodoxy" and its reluctance to engage in revolutionary armed struggle against the country's long-entrenched Somoza family dictatorship. Carlos Fonseca, the FSLN's principal founder and chief theorist, conceived the Sandinistas as a Leninist-style vanguard organization whose objective was to ignite a people's revolution that would destroy the Somoza dictatorship and replace it with "a revolutionary government based on [a] worker-peasant alliance." "Marxism," Fonseca wrote in 1968, "is now the ideology of the most ardent defenders of Latin American humanity. It is high time for all Nicaraguan revolutionaries to embrace the goal of proletarian liberation." Humberto Ortega, who emerged as the Sandinistas' leading theorist after Fonseca was killed in battle in 1976, stated explicitly that the FSLN was "guided by the scientific doctrine of revolution, by Marxism-Leninism."[3]

After a decade of sporadic guerrilla operations against the Somoza dictatorship's security forces, however, the Sandinistas had little to show for their efforts. By the early 1970s, the movement had fewer than 100 members and controlled no Nicaraguan territory. Small, weak, isolated, and battered, the FSLN—in the words of founding member Tomás Borge—"totally lacked an internal base of support, or even the minimum infrastructure" necessary to play the role of revolutionary vanguard.[4]

By 1972, internal disputes over military strategy had led to the emergence of three separate FSLN factions. A "Prolonged Popular War" faction advocated a Cuban- or Chinese-style guerrilla war of attrition utilizing "peasant support in remote mountain areas." A "Proletarian" faction favored a more orthodox Marxist-Leninist strategy of organizing urban workers and *barrio* dwellers as the essential revolutionary power base. A "Tercerista" ("third," or "insurrectional") faction argued that the FSLN must first broaden the revolutionary movement's support base by forming alliances with non–Marxist anti-Somoza elements, including middle-class professionals, disaffected businessmen, and progressive priests from the liberation-theology wing of the Catholic Church. Once a broad-based revolutionary front had been created, the Terceristas believed that a series of high-profile Sandinista-led armed strikes could trigger a successful popular insurrection against the dictatorship. In 1977, the Terceristas gained control of the FSLN's national directorate, and it was their strategy that propelled the Sandinistas to their dramatic seizure of power at the head of a popular multiclass insurrection in July 1979.[5]

Their emphasis on collaboration with non–Marxist elements suggested to many outside observers that the Terceristas were political moderates. In reality, they were as committed to a Marxist-Leninist agenda as the Sandinistas' other two factions. A 1977 FSLN General Political-Military Platform prepared shortly after the Terceristas emerged as the dominant force on the national directorate defined the proposed alliance with the anti-Somoza "bourgeoisie" as "temporary and tactical." Once a broad-based FSLN-led revolution had succeeded in toppling Somoza, the platform stated, an initial phase of democratic government would provide the opportunity for

> the conquest of real political power by the Sandinista forces. . . . With the development of the Popular Sandinista Revolution, with the triumph over the dictatorship and the development of a revolutionary popular-democratic government, our present Marxist-Leninist vanguard organization will be able to develop to the maximum its organic structure until it becomes an iron-hard Leninist party, created and strengthened by the process itself and with the capacity for developing to the maximum the organization and mobilization of the masses.[6]

A few months prior to Somoza's overthrow, Humberto Ortega reaffirmed the Tercerista strategy and lauded its effectiveness. "Without slogans of 'Marxist orthodoxy,' without ultra-leftist phrases such as 'power only for the workers,' 'toward the dictatorship of the Proletariat,' etc., we have been able—without losing at any time our revolutionary Marxist-Leninist Sandinista identity—to rally all our people around the FSLN." "The fact that we [cannot] establish socialism immediately after overthrowing Somoza," Ortega added, "does not mean that we are planning a capitalist type social-democratic or similar development policy; what we propose is a broad, democratic and popular government which, although the bourgeoisie has participation, is a means and not an end, so that in its time it can make the advance towards a more genuinely popular form of government, which guarantees the movement towards socialism."[7]

Once in power, the Sandinistas moved quickly to implement what they regarded as the "intermediate" or "democratic transition stage" of their revolution. A new Government of National Reconstruction was installed that included Catholic clergy, Nicaraguan business leaders, and representatives of the country's democratic political parties alongside Sandinista *comandantes*. In public, FSLN leaders spoke of their commitment to political pluralism and a "mixed economy." Simultaneously, however, Sandinista hard-liners were consolidating their control over the principal organs of armed power: the police, the state security agencies, and a new "Sandinista People's Army." In September 1979, two months after the victory over Somoza, a secret congress of FSLN leaders proclaimed triumphantly that the "Sandinista Front" had now "emerged as the hegemonic force of the Nicaraguan revolution" and that "internally there is no force other than that represented by *Sandinismo*." "However," the congress report noted, "despite its sweeping victory, *Sandinismo* has not made radical moves to transform all this power once and for all into the power of the workers and peasants, because political expediency dictates that more favorable conditions be developed for the revolution and requires that first the more urgent task of its political, economic, and military consolidation be obtained in order to move on to greater revolutionary transformations." Nicaragua's "centrist and bourgeois" political parties, Sandinista leaders secretly informed a sympathetic foreign visitor a month later, would be permitted to exist "only because they presented no danger and served as a convenient façade for the outside world."[8] Sandinista public pronouncements notwithstanding, Nicaragua's revolution was not heading in a pluralistic direction.

Reagan's claims that the Sandinistas were Soviet allies also had at least some basis in fact. Sandinista leaders had long looked upon the Soviet Union as an attractive model of national development. After visiting Moscow and Kiev in 1957 as a Partido Socialista Nicaraguense delegate to a socialist youth festival, Carlos Fonseca wrote what even a sympathetic biographer describes as an uncritical and one-sided travel account that glorified the Soviet Union. According to Fonseca, the Soviets had eliminated economic crises, unemployment, and discrimination; Soviet leaders lived humble lifestyles, and Soviet newspapers were one of the country's "main means of criticism." He even put a positive spin on the Soviets' brutal suppression of the 1956 Hungarian uprising. After founding the FSLN in 1961, Fonseca accepted Soviet financial backing and became a "trusted agent" of the KGB.[9]

Throughout the 1970s, FSLN writings continued to praise the Soviet experiment. The 1977 General Political-Military Platform celebrated "the glorious October Revolution in Russia" as the decisive moment when "world capitalism was profoundly shaken and . . . its historical agony and death commenced."[10] After seizing power in 1979, Sandinista leaders operated on the assumption that the Soviet Union was the ascendant superpower in world affairs, "equal in strength to the United States, economically as well as militarily." "We thought the Soviet Union was as rich as the United States," Humberto Ortega later recalled. "We truly believed that the utopia existed."[11]

The Soviet Union's chief allure to the Sandinistas, however, was as a protector and patron. In 1979, the FSLN national directorate came to the same conclusion that Cuba's revolutionary leaders had reached twenty years earlier: that to consolidate their revolution and survive in power in the face of predictable U.S. hostility, they would need to forge a strategic alliance with the Soviet bloc. The Sandinistas' cultivation of the Soviets commenced in October 1979 when the head of the new revolutionary government, former Tercerista *comandante* Daniel Ortega, told a visiting Soviet KBG official, Nicolai Leonov, that the FSLN "regarded the USSR . . . as a class and strategic ally, and saw the Soviet experience . . . as a model to be studied and used" in Nicaragua. "Our strategy," Ortega confided to Leonov, "is to tear Nicaragua from the capitalist orbit and, in time, become a member of . . . Comecon" (the Soviet bloc international economic organization). Six months later, in March 1980, a high-level Sandinista delegation arrived in Moscow seeking—in *comandante* Jaime Wheelock's words—"support and solidarity." The visit yielded bilateral commercial, scientific, and cultural-exchange agreements, along with secret military protocols that committed the Soviets to supply the Sandinista army with weaponry. In addition, formal party-to-party relations were established between the FSLN and the Communist Party of the Soviet Union.[12] Thereafter, however, although the Sandinistas remained "eager suitors of Soviet patronage," the Soviets proved less than eager to serve as patrons. Military deliveries in 1980 and 1981 were modest, and the unreliable East German trucks and World War II–era tanks that the Soviets supplied did little to strengthen the Sandinistas' military power. Moreover, the military aid was accompanied by Soviet warnings that if attacked the Sandinistas would have to defend themselves—in other words, that the Soviets were not prepared to add Nicaragua to their list of protectorates. Sandinista requests for hard-currency economic assistance were ignored in Moscow, and no major commitments of Soviet development aid were forthcoming. By late 1981, when the CIA received its orders to intervene, the Sandinistas were hardly the "puppets of Moscow" that Reagan administration officials claimed them to be, but their foreign policy was considerably less "nonaligned" than their public statements suggested.[13]

Reagan's allegations that the FSLN bore a "Cuban label" were also fairly close to the mark. In many respects, the Sandinistas were Cuban clones. It was Fidel Castro's 1959 revolution that inspired the FSLN's founders to leave the Nicaraguan communist party and form their own guerrilla revolutionary movement in 1961, and from the beginning they looked upon Castro and Che Guevara as heroic role models. Castro's government reciprocated by taking the fledgling organization under its wing, harboring Sandinista leaders in exile and providing them with military training, weapons, and tactical advice.[14] In 1978, Fidel's personal influence was instrumental in unifying the three FSLN factions in preparation for the Sandinistas' final offensive the following year.[15] Some sources claim that special troops from the Cuban Interior Ministry accompanied Sandinista military columns on their victorious march into Managua.[16]

Once in power, the Sandinistas relied heavily on Cuban advisers and Cuban models in constructing their revolutionary state structures. Lacking sufficient cadre from within their own small guerrilla organization, they immediately turned to Cuban-supplied specialists to assist them in running the armed forces and police, the intelligence services and security agencies, the government ministries, the nationalized industrial and agricultural enterprises, and a new Cuban-style literacy crusade and public-health program. Soon, according to the U.S. ambassador in Managua, "the Cubans had an in that nobody was going to compete with." The generous support provided by the Cuban government further increased Castro's influence over the FSLN's leaders. To reach the top of the Sandinista power hierarchy after 1979, Humberto Ortega later told an interviewer, an ambitious power contender "had to get closer to Fidel."[17]

But above all, the "deep fraternal ties" that linked the Nicaraguan and Cuban revolutionaries rested on a commonly shared worldview. Like Guatemala's revolutionaries before them, both groups were, at their ideological core, anti-American nationalists who interpreted their national realities in terms of international systems of domination and symbiotic alliances between "Yankee imperialists" and reactionary local collaborators. Just as Castro and his *compañeros* in the 26th of July Movement attributed their country's underdevelopment and poverty to the Cuban elites' self-serving subordination to U.S. interests, so the Sandinistas blamed the wretched living conditions of the Nicaraguan masses on a "three-sided reactionary force represented by armed Yankee intervention, the oligarchy, and the bourgeoisie." And just as Cuba's revolutionaries regarded Fulgencio Batista's dictatorship as the immediate instrument of U.S. domination in Cuba, so the Sandinistas viewed the Somoza dictatorship as "the Yankee empire['s] . . . present instrument for ruling" Nicaragua. Carlos Fonseca was merely echoing Fidel Castro when he remarked that "American imperialism and the local oligarchy" were "two sides of the same coin."[18]

Like the Cubans twenty years earlier, the Sandinistas believed that genuine revolutionary change required the destruction of the transnational symbiotic alliance that held their country in bondage—the alliance formed by "the *Somocista* clique and its protector, Yankee imperialism." As Fonseca put it in a 1970 interview, "Inspired by the victorious Cuban revolution, inspired by sublime Vietnam, inspired by the heroic *comandante* Ernesto Che Guevara . . . the Frente Sandinista has the profoundly revolutionary goals of wiping out *not only* imperialist domination in Nicaragua but also the domination of all the exploiting classes."[19] According to the FSLN's General Political-Military Platform:

> More than 40 years of Somocista dictatorial rule have allowed, on the one hand, the subjugation of our nation by North American imperialism and, on the other, the exploitation and oppression of our masses by the backward, dependent-capitalist, agro-exporting system of Nicaragua.
>
> To break the chains that bind our country to the yoke of foreign imperialism is the determining factor in our struggle for *national liberation*. Breaking the yoke of exploitation and oppression imposed by the dominant reactionary forces over our masses determines our process of *social liberation*. Both historical enterprises will advance together, indissolubly, if there exists a Marxist-Leninist cause and a solid vanguard to direct the process.[20]

After Somoza's 1979 overthrow, the Sandinistas knew that—like the Cuban and Guatemalan revolutionaries before them—they would have to defend their revolution "against the inevitable attack by the reactionary forces of the country and Yankee imperialism." Nevertheless, they were confident that—as new President Daniel Ortega told the nation—the FSLN's "popular revolution" had brought Nicaragua's long history of "submissions and sell outs" to an end.[21]

The Sandinistas had an abundance of historical evidence to draw upon in support of their views. It was true, as Fonseca charged, that Nicaragua had been "a victim of Yankee aggression for more than a century," dating back to William Walker's infamous 1855–1857 filibuster. It was also true that in the early decades of the twentieth century the country had endured a succession of U.S. military interventions and occupations facilitated by Nicaragua's "Liberal-Conservative oligarchy." It was equally true that, in Fonseca's words, "The people of Nicaragua ha[d] been suffering under the yoke of a reactionary clique imposed by Yankee imperialism virtually since 1932, the year in which Anastasio Somoza [Sr.] was named commander-in-chief of the [U.S.-created] National Guard." And it was at least partially true, as Daniel Ortega charged, that for forty years the Somoza dynasty had "based and justified its power in the support which the United States always offered it."[22] More debatable, perhaps, were Sandinista claims that Nicaragua had been impoverished by the "indiscriminate looting" of "Yankee monopolies" and "foreign companies."[23]

Given the similarities in historical experience and ideological perspective, it was not surprising that the Sandinistas' anti-U.S. rhetoric rivaled that of the

Cubans in sheer vitriol. Carlos Fonseca referred to Americans as "blond beasts," while FSLN statements of principle identified "Yankee imperialism" as the common enemy of "the peoples of Asia, Africa, and Latin America" and "the rabid enemy of all peoples who are struggling to achieve their definitive liberation." Ronald Reagan and his supporters denounced the Sandinistas as Cuban surrogates in Central America, but from the Sandinistas' point of view, Americans were nothing less than the "enemy of humanity."[24]

The Nicaraguan revolution occurred at a time when President Jimmy Carter was attempting to carry out a revolution of his own—one designed to move U.S. foreign policy away from its emphasis on Cold War containment and East-West confrontation to a new focus on human rights issues and "North-South dialogue." Improved U.S. relations with Latin America were central to Carter's plans. He openly criticized U.S. interventionism in the Dominican Republic and Chile and pledged that no Latin American government would be overthrown by his administration. To distance the United States from the region's dictatorships and align it instead with the forces of "progressive change," he announced that U.S. economic and military assistance would be tied to the recipient's human rights performance. And to demonstrate that U.S. hegemonic behavior in the hemisphere was a thing of the past, he promised to transfer the Panama Canal—the ultimate symbol of U.S. imperialism in Latin America—back to Panama. So central to Carter's international agenda were improved relations with Latin America that the negotiation and ratification of a new set of Panama Canal treaties became "his highest foreign policy priority" during the first year and a half of his presidency.[25]

Carter's emphasis on human rights immediately produced tensions in U.S. relations with the notoriously repressive Somoza dictatorship. Shortly after entering office, the new administration withheld more than $13 million in U.S. economic and military assistance to Nicaragua in an effort to pressure Somoza to reform.[26] Counterpressure from Somoza's friends in the U.S. Congress quickly constrained Carter from taking further action, however. Representative Jack Murphy, a conservative Democrat from New York and leader of a core group of Somoza supporters on Capitol Hill (the self-proclaimed Dirty Thirty), threatened to sabotage the Panama Canal treaties—the symbolic centerpiece of Carter's foreign policy— if the administration did not "lay off Somoza." Murphy had the power to make good on his threat; he chaired the House Merchant Marine and Fisheries Committee, through which the Canal treaties' enabling legislation had to pass before reaching the House floor for final approval.[27]

Carter backed off. Facing "a bruising political battle" over the treaties—with Congress almost evenly split between supporters and opponents—and, in the words of Assistant Secretary of State for Inter-American Affairs Viron Vaky, "a little intimidated" by the tactics of the "Somoza lobby" on the Hill, the president chose not to provoke the dictator's congressional allies. He reportedly told Panamanian leaders that he "could not do anything about Nicaragua until the Canal treaties cleared the House." In coming to that decision, Carter adhered to the advice of his White House chief of staff, Hamilton Jordan, who repeatedly warned the president that "you can endanger the greatest achievement of your administration, the Panama Canal legislation. And for what? Nicaragua!"[28]

In mid-June 1979, as the dictatorship suddenly and unexpectedly began to unravel in the face of a massive, FSLN-led insurrection, some of Carter's aides urged the president to take aggressive action to prevent a Sandinista victory. White House National Security Adviser Zbigniew Brzezinski warned that the loss of Nicaragua would badly damage the administration both at home and abroad. "A Castroite take-over in Nicaragua," he predicted, would have "major domestic and international implications"—it "would impact on U.S.-Soviet relations and on the President's domestic political standing, particularly in the South and the West." Internationally, Brzezinski warned, the United States "would be considered as being incapable of dealing with problems in our own backyard and impotent in the face of Cuban intervention." "This" would in turn "have devastating domestic implications," he added ominously.[29]

To block the Sandinistas from coming to power, Brzezinski initially suggested sending a multinational Organization of American States "peace-keeping" force to Nicaragua to impose a cease-fire and arrange a transfer of power from Somoza to a moderate, pro-U.S. "third force." The administration's ensuing efforts to promote what one U.S. diplomat called "an intervention without it being our intervention" failed to enlist the support of a single Latin American nation, however—at which point Brzezinski recommended direct U.S. military intervention.[30] His arguments fell on deaf ears. Carter refused to abandon his commitment to noninterventionism as a basic component of his administration's foreign policy—first, because, as a matter of principle, he believed that U.S. intervention in Latin America was morally wrong; second, because a central tenet of his foreign policy (improved relations with the Third World) would lose its credibility among the underdeveloped nations if he resorted to old-fashioned U.S. intervention in Latin America; and third, because Carter was well aware of the heavy political penalties that his two immediate Democratic predecessors in the White House, John Kennedy and Lyndon Johnson, had paid for their failed interventions in Cuba and Vietnam, respectively, and he was reluctant to risk the political consequences of a U.S. failure in Nicaragua.[31] But above all, the Panama Canal treaties still needed to be finessed through Congress. By late June 1979, the Senate and House had yet to approve the treaties' enabling legislation, and with difficult political battles still looming on Capitol Hill, Carter was that much more reluctant to undertake what would inevitably be a controversial intervention in Nicaragua.[32]

The White House was subsequently "dismayed" by the Sandinista victory but quickly shifted into "damage limitation" mode. Convinced that U.S. hostility would only accelerate the revolution's radicalization, Carter opted instead for a policy of "conditional accommodation" and restraint. During the Sandinistas' first two and a half months in power, his administration shipped $26.3 million in food, medicine, and other relief supplies to Nicaragua. It also promised the new FSLN government a long-term $75 million U.S. economic aid package, on the condition that the Sandinistas respected human rights, practiced political plural-ism, and refrained from aiding Marxist insurrections in neighboring Central American countries. In September, Carter hosted President Daniel Ortega and other high-ranking Nicaraguan officials at a White House breakfast, telling his guests that "if you don't hold me responsible for everything that happened under my predecessors, I will not hold you responsible for everything that occurred under your predecessors."[33]

"Few" administration officials "had illusions about the Sandinista Directorate's preferences for Cuba and Marxism, and its visceral hatred of the United States," recalls the NSC's director of Latin American affairs, Robert Pastor:[34]

> But we didn't believe that the game was over by a long shot! We didn't believe that the entire leadership was Marxist-Leninist or even that those [who] con-sidered themselves Marxist-Leninist were incapable of evolving within a more conducive climate. Thus, we thought that the policy that made the most sense for the United States was one which creates a climate that encourages those whose minds were not yet frozen to realize that to succeed in meeting the needs of their people . . . they needed to reach an accommodation with the U.S. To have this relationship with the U.S. they would have to dispense with their re-flexive anti-Americanism and moderate their behavior.[35]

Besides, Pastor adds, "no one saw any other viable option other than to seek a good relationship with the new government."[36]

Carter's strategy was doomed to disappointment. The Sandinistas' vituperative anti-U.S. rhetoric, ongoing closeness to Cuba, and disinclination to hold elections produced growing doubts within the administration that a policy of accommoda-tion would induce moderation in Managua. Then, in mid-1980, U.S. intelligence began to produce mounting evidence that the Sandinistas were actively facilitating the flow of weapons from Cuba to Marxist guerrillas in neighboring El Salvador—in direct defiance of Carter's conditions for the receipt of U.S. aid.[37] By the time the 1980 U.S. presidential election campaign got under way, Nicaragua was in-creasingly looking like a Carter foreign-policy failure.

Carter was overwhelmed with international problems as he launched his bid for reelection. Early in 1979, the United States lost a key ally in the Persian Gulf when Islamic revolutionaries overthrew the government of the Shah of Iran. Months later, the Iranian revolutionaries seized the personnel of the U.S. embassy in Tehran and proceeded to taunt and humiliate Carter in a hostage crisis that dragged on for the remainder of his presidency. Then in December 1979, after expanding its presence in South Yemen and Ethiopia, the Soviet Union invaded Afghanistan to prop up that country's pro-Soviet government. Soon U.S. officials were referring to an "arc of crisis" extending from the Persian Gulf through the Horn of Africa. Meanwhile, the second Organization of Petroleum Exporting Countries (OPEC) oil shock of the decade had doubled the price of oil, triggering a domestic energy crisis in the United States in which "angry motorists," forced to endure four-hour lines at gas stations, "punched each other, pulled guns on line jumpers, and cursed President Carter." As the 1980 election campaign approached, opinion polls showed that a majority of the U.S. public viewed Carter as "weak" in foreign policy, and "editorialists and cartoonists were portraying the president in cruel, diminutive terms."[38]

By 1980, many of Carter's closest advisers were urging him to adopt a tougher policy against Marxist revolutions in Central America—precisely in order to protect himself from Republican campaign charges that his foreign policy was "soft" on communism. National Security Adviser Brzezinski, Defense Secretary Harold Brown, White House political advisers Hamilton Jordan and Jody Powell, even First Lady Rosalynn Carter, all warned the president that after "losing" Nicaragua and Iran "he could not afford to 'lose' El Salvador . . . and still win reelection."[39]

Carter heeded their warnings. He approved a "covert political-action program" to strengthen anti-Sandinista opposition forces in Nicaragua, authorizing the CIA to pass $19.5 million in funds to "private business groups, organized labor, political parties, and the press" in a clandestine operation that, according to the National Security Archive's Peter Kornbluh, "resembl[ed] the agency's destabilization campaign against the socialist government of Salvador Allende a decade earlier."[40] He renewed U.S. military aid (suspended "since 1977 on human-rights grounds") to the government of El Salvador to strengthen it against attacks by Salvadoran Marxist insurgents. And near the end of his presidency he terminated his $75 million U.S. aid program to Nicaragua in response to "conclusive proof" that the Sandinistas were continuing to transship arms from Cuba to the Salvadoran guerrillas. By the time Carter left office, his policy approach toward Nicaragua was shifting rapidly from accommodation to confrontation.[41] Confrontation was a policy that his successor in the White House would pursue with a vengeance.

Ronald Reagan also entered office with what he and his advisers regarded as a revolutionary agenda: to rebuild U.S. national power and restore self-confidence in the American public after more than a decade of domestic traumas and foreign-policy disasters. The cumulative effect of Vietnam, Watergate, OPEC-induced energy crises, the Iranian hostage crisis, a major recession, and ever-worsening economic "stagflation" was what outgoing President Carter had described as a deepening "malaise" in American society. The "Reagan revolution" was dedicated, first and foremost, to reviving the nation's vitality and morale—and the new administration's highest priority as it took up the reins of power was to improve the U.S. economy. At the time of Reagan's inauguration, the United States was suffering from double-digit inflation, 20 percent interest rates, and 7 percent unemployment. During the previous five years, workers' real wages had declined by 5 percent while federal taxes for the average family had increased by 67 percent. To reverse these trends and stimulate economic growth, Reagan and his advisers were determined to implement a comprehensive economic program of large-scale tax cuts, reductions in government spending, deregulation of business and industry, and a balanced budget. So preoccupied was the new administration with economic revival during its first several months in office that all other policy initiatives, both domestic and foreign, were deliberately subordinated to its economic policy goals.[42]

Not that foreign policy was insignificant in Reagan's agenda. Convinced that the United States was "losing ground to Communism in much of the globe" and that its "strategic forces were growing obsolete," the new administration planned to undertake the largest defense build-up in U.S. history—$1.6 trillion over five years—and then launch a "strategic offensive" designed to "checkmate" the Soviets and "roll them back" from vulnerable points along Cold War frontiers. For far too long, the Reaganites believed, the United States had been reluctant to project its power as an assertive international superpower. Paralyzed by defeat in Vietnam, distracted by Watergate, and further weakened by what they characterized as "the Carter experiment in obsequiousness" and "vacillation," the nation had allowed the Soviets to gain the strategic advantage in the Cold War. "Seduced by the weakness of the American will," Reagan's secretary of state Alexander Haig would later write, the Soviet Union had "extended itself far beyond the natural limits of its interests and influence." The end result was the incorporation of a long list of new Marxist client states into the Soviet sphere of influence between 1974 and 1980: Vietnam, Cambodia, Laos, Afghanistan, Ethiopia, Zimbabwe, Angola, Mozambique, Guinea-Bissau, São Tomé, Cape Verde, Grenada, Suriname, Nicaragua—clients positioned (by "grand design," according to the Reaganites) to give the Soviets control over key "strategic chokepoints" and the maritime "lifelines of Western commerce" in the Persian Gulf, the Red Sea, the Indian Ocean, the Straits of Malacca, and the Caribbean.[43]

To counter Soviet expansionism, the Reagan administration believed that it must first reestablish the credibility of U.S. power. In his memoirs Reagan recalls:

> During the late seventies, I felt our country had begun to abdicate [its] historical role as the spiritual leader of the Free World. . . . Some of our resolve was gone. . . . the previous administration for some reason had accepted the notion that America was no longer the world power it had once been, that it had become powerless to shape world events. Consciously or unconsciously, we had sent out

a message to the world that Washington was no longer sure of itself, its ideals, or its commitments to our allies, and that it seemed to accept as inevitable the advance of Soviet expansionism, especially in the poor and underdeveloped countries of the world. . . .

Predictably, the Soviets had interpreted our hesitation and reluctance to act and our reduced sense of national self-confidence as a weakness, and had tried to exploit it to the fullest, moving ahead with their agenda to achieve a Communist-dominated world. . . .

As the foundation of my foreign policy, I decided we had to send as powerful a message as we could to the Russians that we weren't going to stand by anymore while they armed and financed terrorists and subverted democratic governments. . . .

I deliberately set out . . . to let them know that there were some new fellows in Washington who had a realistic view of what they were up to and weren't going to let them keep it up.[44]

Elsewhere, Reagan writes that he "wanted to send a message to others in the world that there was a new management in the White House."[45] "American strength and American integrity must . . . be taken seriously—by friends and potential foes alike," he told a New York City audience early in his presidency. "Restoring both our strength and our credibility is a major objective of this administration."[46]

According to Secretary of State Haig, "Soviet diplomacy" was

based on tests of will. Since Vietnam, the United States had largely failed these tests. Like the assiduous students of tactics and Western vulnerabilities that they are, the Russians would send out a probe—now in Angola, again in Ethiopia, finally in El Salvador—to test the strength of Western determination. Finding the line unmanned, or only thinly held, they would exploit the gap.

The Soviets [needed to be made to] believe that it was better to accommodate to the United States and the West than to go on marauding against their interests and security. Rhetoric would not lead them to this conclusion. Only a credible show of will and strength could do so.[47]

Other nations had also lost confidence in U.S. power, Haig contended. "Especially in the Third World, deep doubts existed about the United States and its capacity to project its power in defense of its own interests. . . . Vietnam and its aftermath had made a deep impression."[48]

We had coldly abandoned our faithful ally, the Shah of Iran, an act that sent a tremor of apprehension through every moderate Arab leader in the Middle

East. . . . In Europe . . . our allies urged us to take up our fallen leadership. In Southeast Asia, we had abandoned our influence almost totally, and if it had not been for the Chinese, who were doing America's work for it in that region, the rest of the dominoes might have fallen after South Vietnam and Cambodia and Laos. . . . The Chinese leaders were wondering exactly what point or advantage there could be in a relationship with a United States too enfeebled by its malaise to resist the spread of Soviet hegemony throughout the Far East. . . .

There was, in short, a worldwide climate of uncertainty. . . . Our friends felt fearful and alone; they did not know whether we would ever face up to the Soviets again.[49]

It was precisely that "climate of uncertainty" that the new administration intended to change. "In the morning of an Administration," Haig writes,

the air is fresh and still relatively quiet, and friends and adversaries are alert and watchful. It is the best time to send signals. Our signal to the Soviets had to be a plain warning that their time of unresisted adventuring in the Third World was over. . . . Our signal to other nations must be equally simple and believable: once again, a relationship with the United States brings dividends, not just risks.[50]

And where better to send a watchful world the requisite "signals" of renewed U.S. power and resolve than in Central America—where, in Haig's melodramatic phrasing, "the fires of insurrection, fed by the Soviets and fanned by their surrogates, the Cubans, spread unchecked." Close to home and far from the Soviet Union, Central America seemed to offer the incoming administration an ideal opportunity to achieve—"at minimal risk and cost," in Raymond Garthoff's words— "a victory that would demonstrate to all—to the Soviet leaders, to U.S. allies and others in the world, and to the American people—that American will and strength, reasserted, were effective in countering continuing Soviet efforts around the world to expand at American expense."[51]

In justifying anticommunist interventionism in Central America to the American public, administration officials often resorted to apocalyptic imagery. Reagan predicted that successful Marxist revolutions in Nicaragua and El Salvador could easily set off a chain reaction of communist victories south into Panama and South America and north through Guatemala to Mexico. "We are the last domino," he warned.[52] Haig told Congress that "what we are watching is a four-phase operation. Phase one has been completed, the seizure of Nicaragua. Next is El Salvador, to be followed by Honduras and Guatemala. It is clear and explicit. . . . I wouldn't call it necessarily a domino theory. I would call it a priority target list, a hit list if you will, for the ultimate takeover of Central America."[53]

The president also warned that "if Communism prevailed in Central America," there would be dire consequences for the U.S. economy. "Two-thirds of all our foreign trade and petroleum pass through the Panama Canal and the Caribbean," he claimed. There was also "the security of our borders to think about, and the question of our economy's ability to absorb an endless flow of refugees." Marxist victories in Central America, Reagan said, "would accelerate the flow of illegal immigrants who, propelled by poverty, were already overwhelming welfare agencies and schools in some parts of our nation."[54] Other administration officials suggested that "the major Soviet objective in Central America" was "to disrupt the American 'strategic rear'" and force the United States to divert its forces from other Cold War frontiers. CIA director William Casey, for instance, told *Washington Post* reporter Bob Woodward that the Soviets' overall goal in Central America was to "divert our attention from the real battleground, the Middle East" and its "oil fields."[55]

From the start, however, Reagan and his top advisers looked upon Central America primarily as a credibility issue. As Dario Moreno writes:

> The unrest in Central America presented [Reagan] with both an opportunity to demonstrate U.S. power and a dangerous crisis that could cost his administration its credibility. He and his advisers felt that it was important that the Soviet Union realize that the United States was once again determined to contain its expansion. The knowledge that the United States would respond forcefully to prevent further Soviet gains in Central America would constrain the Kremlin leadership from undertaking even more dangerous adventures, such as testing the U.S. commitment to defend the Persian Gulf or Western Europe. Resolving the crisis in Central America was vital to the efforts of the administration to reaffirm U.S. worldwide credibility.[56]

State Department official Elliott Abrams later acknowledged that the United States had "no significant tangible interests in Central America." The real issue, Abrams said, was one of international perceptions. "If people see that the Americans are not going to move against the Sandinistas in their own backyard," he asked rhetorically, "what will they do ten thousand miles away?"[57] According to Haig, "Reagan . . . knew that a failure to carry through on this challenge at the heart of our sphere of interest would result in a loss of credibility in all our dealings with the Soviets."[58] The president himself placed Central America squarely in the context of U.S. international credibility when he asked a joint session of Congress:

> If Central America were to fall, what would the consequences be for our position in Asia, Europe, and for alliances such as NATO? If the United States cannot respond to a threat near our own borders, why should Europeans or Asians believe that we're seriously concerned about threats to them? If the Soviets can

assume that nothing short of an actual attack on the United States will provoke an American response, which ally, which friend will trust us then? . . .

The national security of all the Americas is at stake in Central America. If we cannot defend ourselves there, we cannot expect to prevail elsewhere. Our credibility would collapse, our alliances would crumble, and the safety of our homeland would be put in jeopardy. [59]

But where in Central America should the United States take up the communist challenge? Initially, the new administration decided that El Salvador, not Nicaragua, was where the "determined show of American will and power" needed to be made. The decision was at least partly political. According to Robert Kagan, a member of the State Department's Policy Planning staff,

Reagan officials believed the Carter administration had bungled badly in Nicaragua, but Nicaragua had been Carter's "loss." If the Salvadoran government fell, on the other hand, it would be Reagan's loss. American intelligence officials predicted that the government of El Salvador might fall by the end of the year and that the government of Guatemala could fall soon thereafter. Senior officials in the new administration feared that their first year in office could be plagued by communist triumphs in Central America. From the very first days, they were preoccupied with putting out the fire in El Salvador.[60]

Accordingly, El Salvador was chosen as the symbolic test case of the administration's "determination to resist Soviet and Cuban imperialism."[61] In the minds of many administration officials, Dario Moreno writes, "that country . . . would be 'the first step' in a conscious effort to repair the U.S. image. . . . By drawing the line in El Salvador, Reagan thought he could win a quick victory and in so doing could forever wipe out the stigma of Vietnam and erase the so-called Vietnam syndrome. Reagan was privately assured of an easy victory when Haig confidently reported, 'Mr. President, this is one you can win.'"[62]

As for Nicaragua, Kagan writes that "Reagan officials worried almost exclusively about the Sandinistas' continuing support for the Salvadoran guerrillas. El Salvador remained the main problem in Central America, and . . . held a much higher priority than Nicaragua." A few days after the inauguration, U.S. intelligence provided the White House with what Reagan describes as "firm and incontrovertible evidence that the Marxist government of Nicaragua was transferring hundreds of tons of Soviet arms from Cuba to rebel groups in El Salvador." In February, Haig told reporters: "Our most important objective is to stop the large flow of arms through Nicaragua into El Salvador. We consider what is happening as part of the global communist campaign coordinated by Havana and Moscow to support the Marxist guerrillas in El Salvador." For the next several months, the administration's Nicaragua policy was geared almost entirely toward preventing the Sandinistas from acting as "the bridgehead and arsenal for insurgency" in El Salvador.[63] Discussions about how to achieve that objective, however, quickly produced factional divisions within the upper ranks of the administration.

Some of Reagan's advisers favored a policy of direct U.S. military intervention to sever the arms pipeline. Among them, Haig quickly emerged as the most vocal advocate of a hard-line approach. Shortly after his swearing-in as secretary of state, he ordered his aides to "put together a strategy for toppling Castro" and indicated his intention to "eliminate this lodgement in Nicaragua from the mainland" as well. A subsequent Haig-generated options paper entitled "Taking the War to Nicaragua" proposed as one contingency "the open use of military force against Cuban ships and planes as well as a naval blockade of Nicaragua." Convinced that Cuba was the main instigator of Marxist insurgency in Central America, he told Reagan: "Give me the word and I'll make that island a fucking parking lot."[64]

Haig also worked aggressively to generate public support for U.S. intervention. In a series of strident speeches and bellicose public statements, he stressed the imminent danger of a Soviet- and Cuban-sponsored communist takeover of Central America and called for a forceful U.S. response. In February, he issued a State Department White Paper purporting to document the involvement of the Soviets, Cubans, and Nicaraguans in arming and directing the Salvadoran insurgents. At a Washington, D.C., cocktail party, he told Nicaragua's ambassador to the United States that the Reagan administration was "prepared not only to cut off all aid" to Nicaragua "but to do other things as well." Soon, Haig's strong statements and dire warnings were attracting front-page headlines and primetime television coverage. By March, he had succeeded almost single-handedly in transforming Central America into the new administration's highest-profile policy issue.[65]

Haig's interventionist activism garnered little support elsewhere in the administration. The Pentagon argued that a U.S. military intervention in Central America so soon after Vietnam would be so unpopular in Congress that it would jeopardize the administration's budgetary proposals for massive increases in defense spending.[66] Reagan's White House advisers—Chief of Staff James Baker, Baker's deputy Michael Deaver, and Presidential Counselor Edwin Meese—also opposed Haig's proposals. For them, the secretary of state's Central American crusade was "a surefire political loser" certain to be unpopular among a U.S. public still traumatized by the recent disaster in Vietnam. During the first half of 1981, the White House remained fixated on enacting the president's economic program, and Reagan's White House aides feared that Haig's headline-grabbing pronouncements on Central America were upstaging the president's efforts to focus public attention on economic issues. Baker was particularly concerned that a politically draining foreign-policy controversy over Central America would undermine the bipartisan congressional support that he was trying to cultivate for the administration's economic initiatives. "The crazies want to get us into war," he told his staff; "we cannot get this economic recovery program going if we get involved in a land war in

Central America." Baker and Deaver also worried that Haig's "menacing talk" might appear to confirm the Democrats' portrayal of Reagan as a trigger-happy warmonger bent on embroiling the country in another Vietnam, and in the process endanger Republican prospects in the 1982 midterm elections.[67]

There was evidence to support their concerns. By early March, public communications to the White House were running ten-to-one against Haig's militant approach, and White House polls were confirming Baker's fears.[68] According to Reagan's White House communications director David Gergen:

> At the time, we were taking surveys week to week and we saw some slippage in Reagan's popularity. Our domestic stuff had dominated the news play in the first few weeks, and Reagan's polls went up. Then we got the Salvadoran news, and Reagan's polls fell because it brought up the trigger-happy stuff. People got afraid of what Reagan would do. We were losing control of the agenda. We had a different game we wanted to play. Important as Central America was, it diverted attention from our top priority, which was economic recovery, which we wanted to be the only priority. Haig didn't understand that. We decided we had to cut off his story.[69]

Hedrick Smith reports that when subsequent White House polls continued to "show . . . the public reacting negatively to Haig's bellicose talk and opposed to embargos and military action against Cuba," Baker "took the poll results to the president to persuade him that Haig's tactics were hurting Reagan politically; the president got the message. According to one White House account, Baker telephoned Haig in late March and told him the president wanted him 'to knock it off.' Haig complied."[70]

The rejection of Haig's hard-line approach left the administration with no Central American policy at all. Matters continued to drift for several months while Reagan recovered from a March 30 assassination attempt. Then, in late summer, as U.S. intelligence continued to report heavy Sandinista involvement in arms shipments to El Salvador, Assistant Secretary of State for Inter-American Affairs Thomas Enders obtained permission to try a new strategy: he would begin a "secret dialogue" with the Sandinistas, and—through a combination of persuasion and intimidation—attempt to reach a "negotiated settlement" in which the Nicaraguans would agree to terminate their support for the Salvadoran insurgents.[71]

The result was a diplomatic train wreck. In August, Enders visited Managua for two days of secret talks with Daniel Ortega and other top Sandinista officials. Participants in the meetings described the U.S. envoy's tone as threatening, confrontational, accusatory, and arrogant. He began by offering the Sandinistas a deal: the Reagan administration was prepared to enter into a bilateral nonaggression pact and consider resumption of U.S. aid in exchange for a Sandinista pledge to end support for guerrillas in neighboring countries. "We don't like your regime," Enders reportedly told the Nicaraguans, "but there is not much we can do about it. But you have to get out of El Salvador." He went on to tell the Sandinistas that relations between the Reagan administration and their government were "now at a crossroads." Relations in the future, he said, could be based on accommodation or confrontation, and to avoid confrontation the Sandinistas must "take the necessary steps to ensure that the flow of arms to El Salvador is . . . halted."[72]

Ortega would later tell Fidel Castro that Enders came to Nicaragua

> as President Reagan's representative to say that Nicaragua had been given up as lost—that it was the problem of the Democratic Party in the U.S., and that the Republicans' problem was not Nicaragua, but El Salvador, which they had no intention of losing. [Enders said] that the Nicaraguans could do whatever they wished—that they could impose communism, they could take over *La Prensa* [Nicaragua's leading newspaper], they could expropriate private property, they could suit themselves—but they must not continue meddling in El Salvador, dragging Nicaragua into an East-West confrontation, and if they continued along those lines . . . , they would be smashed.[73]

Ortega responded by informing Enders that the Sandinistas had already "seen the crossroads" and "considered the two alternatives." They had "decided to defend our revolution by force of arms, even if we are crushed, and to take the war to the whole of Central America if that is the consequence." The Nicaraguan leader stated frankly that the Sandinistas were "interested in seeing the guerrillas in El Salvador and Guatemala triumph." "The Salvadoran revolution is our shield," he said—"it makes our revolution safer."[74]

Enders ridiculed the notion that the Sandinistas could defend themselves against a U.S. military invasion. According to one account, he warned Ortega: "You can forget defending yourselves because we are one hundred times bigger than you are."[75] During a particularly heated exchange, Enders told *comandante* Bayardo Arce: "You can do your thing, but do it within your own borders, or else we're going to hurt you." To which Arce replied: "All right, come on in! We'll meet you man to man. You will kill us, but you will pay for it. You will have to kill us all to do it."[76] Summarizing the meetings, one U.S. official "said he had never seen anything so dramatic, so direct, and so lacking in subtlety in three decades of negotiations in Latin America."[77]

Rebuffed in Managua, the administration nonetheless continued to pursue Enders' persuasion-and-intimidation strategy for another two and a half months. Between late August and mid-September, the State Department sent the Nicaraguan government three diplomatic notes proposing terms for a joint agreement. The Pentagon followed up in early October by conducting military maneuvers off the Caribbean coast of Honduras in a threat-posturing exercise "designed to signal that the United States was in a position to intervene militarily if the FSLN did not acquiesce" to Enders' proposals.[78] The Sandinistas remained defiant and unyielding. Daniel Ortega responded to the U.S. military maneuvers by denouncing U.S. imperialism before the United Nations. In mid-October, anticipating a U.S. invasion, his brother Humberto publicly called on the Sandinista militias to draw up lists of the revolution's internal enemies and warned that any Nicaraguans who supported "the plans of North American imperialism" would "be the first to appear hanging by the lamp posts along the roads and highways of the country." At the end of the month, the Sandinistas formally rejected Enders' proposals as "sterile."[79]

The collapse of Enders' diplomatic initiative proved to be the decisive turning point in Reagan's relations with the Sandinistas. With a negotiated settlement seemingly unattainable and direct U.S. military intervention ruled out, administration hard-liners now proposed a new alternative: a covert paramilitary intervention utilizing a proxy army of anti-Sandinista Nicaraguans.[80] On November 16, two weeks after the final breakdown in negotiations, the NSC endorsed a plan to create a secret U.S.-funded, CIA-directed paramilitary force of "non-Americans" to attack the "Cuban-Sandinista support infrastructure in Nicaragua and elsewhere in Central America." The plan had been drawn up by a Restricted Interagency Group composed predominantly of zealous ultraconservative hawks: Duane Clarridge, the chief of the CIA's Latin America division; Nestor Sanchez, a former CIA chief of operations for Latin America now serving as Deputy Assistant Secretary of Defense; Alfonso Sapia-Bosch, a conservative Cuban-American CIA analyst representing the NSC staff; General Paul Gorman from the Joint Chiefs of Staff; and Enders.[81] The plan's principal advocate in the NSC deliberations was CIA director William Casey. Throughout 1981, Casey had been urging Reagan to turn the tables on the Soviets—to "bleed them"—by providing covert U.S. assistance to anticommunist "national liberation movements" fighting against Soviet-backed regimes in the Third World. High on Casey's list of promising covert allies were Afghanistan's mujahedin and anticommunist insurgents in Angola, Cambodia, and Laos. In the November 16 NSC meeting, the CIA director argued that a U.S.-backed anti-Sandinista resistance movement in Nicaragua would provide the United States with another effective weapon in the struggle to regain the strategic initiative against international communism.[82]

Although the NSC endorsed the covert-intervention plan, most of its members did so for essentially negative reasons, seeing it as merely the least unattractive of available options. Secretary of Defense Casper Weinberger supported the proposal primarily because it left the Pentagon out and was "infinitely preferable to any plan involving the use of U.S. combat forces." Haig had a low opinion of covert operations, which he regarded as the worst sort of Vietnam-style "incrementalism," but he went along with the plan "largely because everything else had been rejected, and he believed that doing something was better than doing nothing." James Baker and Reagan's other White House advisers considered covert action less dangerous politically than direct U.S. military intervention, and with the administration's tax and budget bills now having been enacted, they were prepared for political reasons to "throw a foreign-policy bone" to the Republican right wing. Enders supported the plan because he viewed an anti-Sandinista military force as a weapon that the administration could use to pressure the Sandinistas into ending their support of the Salvadoran guerrillas.[83]

The president did not make a final decision on the proposed plan at the November 16 NSC meeting. On November 23, however—after a week of lobbying by Casey, UN ambassador Jeane Kirkpatrick, and other members of what Reagan official Otto Reich characterized as "a hard-line group working together behind the scenes"—he signed National Security Decision Directive 17 authorizing the covert-action program.[84]

From the president's perspective, a policy of covert intervention had much to recommend it. It offered first of all an attractive compromise between a politically controversial deployment of U.S. military forces in Central America, on the one hand, and Reagan's strategic and political concerns about losing El Salvador on the other. "Reagan intended to stop the advance of communism in Central America," Robert Kagan writes, "but he wanted to do so in the least violent and least controversial manner possible." In that sense, a particular virtue of covert action was that "it required no public explanation, no public defense, and no public vote in Congress." By secretly backing a proxy army of anti-Sandinista Nicaraguans, the administration could presumably achieve its strategic goals in Central America without incurring heavy political costs at home.[85] Finally, and perhaps best of all, launching a covert intervention would not require a massive effort on the administration's part—because by November 1981, military units of Nicaraguan counterrevolutionaries had already formed and were eagerly soliciting U.S. sponsorship.

Although most accounts of Reagan's intervention in Nicaragua portray the Contras as a U.S. creation, the Reagan administration did not create the Contras—Latin Americans did. More specifically, anti-Sandinista Nicaraguans, Argentine military officers, and elements of Honduras' governing elite collaborated in putting together the initial nucleus for a counterrevolutionary army and then sold the enterprise to the Reagan administration as an instrument of U.S. intervention.

Following the Somoza regime's collapse in 1979, small bands of Nicaraguan National Guardsmen had taken refuge in neighboring Honduras and Guatemala. By 1980, several anti-Sandinista leaders, including former Guard colonel Enrique Bermúdez, were struggling to organize the scattered and ill-equipped groups into a unified fighting force. In Honduras, their efforts were assisted by members of the Policarpo Paz García government, notably the head of the national police, Army Colonel Gustavo Alvarez, who feared a potential spillover of Nicaragua's radical revolution into Honduras.[86]

Bermúdez and the other Nicaraguans working to organize an armed resistance movement spent much of 1980 traveling around the hemisphere in search of outside backing. By the time of Reagan's election in November, they had begun working with conservative contacts in the United States and were lobbying the Republican Party for support. In April 1981, Bermúdez visited Buenos Aires and won the backing of Argentina's rabidly anticommunist military dictatorship. Having recently completed a brutally successful "dirty war" against Marxist insurgents in their own country, the Argentines looked upon Sandinista Nicaragua as the Cold War's new "ideological frontier" in the Western Hemisphere and a dangerous sanctuary where the surviving remnants of Argentina's decimated Montonero and Ejército Revolucionario del Pueblo guerrillas had fled to regroup. Soon the Argentines were providing Bermúdez and his men with money, advisers, and military training.[87]

Simultaneously with Bermúdez's visit to Argentina, Gustavo Álvarez, the Honduran police chief, traveled to Washington, D.C., and presented CIA director Casey with a solution to Reagan's Nicaraguan problem. With covert U.S. support, Alvarez said, the rag-tag bands of former Nicaraguan Guardsmen in Honduras could be built up into a powerful military force; they could then be sent into Nicaragua to ignite civil war and hopefully provoke the Sandinistas into launching a retaliatory strike against Honduras. If the Sandinistas fell into the trap and attacked Honduras, the United States could then come to the defense of its Honduran ally and invade Nicaragua, getting rid of the Sandinistas once and for all.[88]

Casey, already a strong proponent of covert action and proxy armies as the United States' best weapons against Third World Marxist states, promised to give Alvarez's proposal careful study. By August, with Enders heading for Managua on his ill-fated diplomatic mission and an Argentine-trained Nicaraguan resistance force beginning to emerge in Honduras, the CIA director concluded that a U.S.-backed Contra army was the administration's most promising policy option. In early August, apparently without White House authorization, Casey dispatched Duane Clarridge, the CIA's Latin American division chief, to Honduras to inform Alvarez that the United States was prepared to support anti-Sandinista military actions by the resistance forces. Later that month, Clarridge returned to Tegucigalpa, where he met with Honduran officials, Argentine officers, and representatives of Bermúdez's movement and drafted a program of tripartite support for Contra military operations in Nicaragua; under the plan, the United States would supply the money and weapons, the Argentines would supervise the military operations, and the Hondurans would allow their country to be used as a territorial base and sanctuary for Contra forces.[89]

In November, once Enders' efforts to achieve a negotiated settlement had crashed and burned, Casey presented the tripartite plan to the NSC and Reagan for approval. In selling the project to the president, the CIA director emphasized that the Argentines were already training 1,000 Nicaraguan exiles in Honduras and that consequently the United States would merely be "buying in" to an existing operation.[90]

But what precisely was the goal of the operation that the United States was buying into? The secret presidential document authorizing the intervention—National Security Decision Directive 17, signed by Reagan on November 23, 1981—instructed the CIA to employ paramilitary "action teams" of Nicaraguan exiles to attack the "Cuban presence and Cuban-Sandinista support infrastructure in Nicaragua and elsewhere in Central America."[91] From the start, however, views within the administration differed as to the covert operation's ultimate objective. Some officials regarded it as a pressure campaign to force the Sandinistas to moderate their behavior. Thomas Enders, for example, viewed the Contras primarily as a "bargaining chip," a military lever to "up . . . the heat on Nicaragua"—to "harass the government, waste it," in Enders' words—"until we could get a negotiated settlement" and an agreement from the Sandinistas to stop supplying arms to the Salvadoran guerrillas. Casey, in his initial briefings before congressional intelligence committees, implied that the Contras' principal function would be to interdict weapons flows from Nicaragua to El Salvador and "make the Sandinistas amenable to negotiations."[92]

Privately, however, Casey and his CIA colleagues—together with Jeane Kirkpatrick, Casper Weinberger, and other administration hard-liners—apparently regarded the Contras as a weapon to overthrow the Sandinista regime and "roll back" communism in Central America. "In truth," the CIA's Clarridge recalls, "no one in the Agency was going to shed any tears if Daniel Ortega, Tomás Borge, and the rest of the Sandinista ruling directorate found unemployment as a result of our efforts." Recognizing that the Nicaraguan exiles were unlikely to develop into a fighting force "capable of marching into Managua," the hard-liners instead anticipated that Contra sabotage activities would destabilize the Nicaraguan economy and force the Sandinistas to make mistakes—such as eliminating civil liberties and intensifying their internal crackdown on opponents—that would eventually erode their domestic and international support.[93] Reagan's initial expectations for the Contras remain unclear, although as a combination of "hidebound ideologue" and "pragmatic politician" he may well have regarded either outcome—overthrow or a forced settlement—as acceptable.[94]

Almost immediately, confusion over the covert operation's ultimate aims brought the administration into conflict with Congress. During 1982, amid mounting evidence that—contrary to Casey's briefings to the House and Senate intelligence committees—the Contras were bent on overthrow, not interdiction, Democratic congressmen wrote into the fiscal 1983 intelligence authorization and defense appropriations bills language prohibiting the use of government funds "for the purpose of overthrowing the government of Nicaragua." By 1983, anti-interventionist Democrats in both houses were actively seeking to cut off all U.S. funding of Contra operations. As partisan battle lines hardened and a Contra funding cutoff loomed, however, the administration was suddenly presented with an auspicious new opportunity to rally public support for a renewed policy of aggressive anticommunism—and in the process send a new signal of revitalized U.S. strength and assertiveness to Marxist adversaries, Western allies, and the American people alike—when, in October 1983, factional warfare within the Marxist government of Grenada gave Reagan the pretext he needed to invade that Caribbean microstate.[95]

CHAPTER SEVEN

Grenada, 1983

Midway through his first term, Ronald Reagan's presidency was in trouble. As 1983 began, he and his administration were rapidly losing popular support. The principal cause of public discontent was Reagan's handling of the economy. Since late 1981, the U.S. economy had been mired in a severe recession—one that proved to be the country's worst economic downturn since the Great Depression. During 1982, U.S. business failures and home foreclosures set new post-Depression records, domestic unemployment skyrocketed to levels not seen since the pre–World War II period, and the poverty rate reached its highest level in 15 years—dubious achievements for a president who, as a candidate in the 1980 election, had promised to revitalize the U.S. economy.[1] To make matters worse, Reagan's large-scale tax cuts, combined with his massive military spending, had produced staggering new budget deficits—another ironic accomplishment for a president who had campaigned on a pledge to balance the federal budget. By 1982, Reagan's own budget director had already warned of a "budget hemorrhage" that could "wreck the president's entire economic program," and White House pollster Richard Wirthlin was acknowledging privately that Reagan had "failed miserably" in his promise to bring the budget into balance. "We really are in trouble," Reagan recorded in his diary in late 1982. "Our one-time projections, pre-recession, are all out the window and we look at $200 million deficits if we can't pull some miracles."[2]

Nor was Reagan's foreign-policy performance winning many accolades as he began his third year in office. During the 1980 campaign, candidate Reagan had trumpeted his determination to restore U.S. power and prestige in world affairs and to return the country to the position of international primacy that it had enjoyed prior to its recent humiliations at the hands of North Vietnam and Iran.[3] As president, however, Reagan initially seemed more given to tough talk than to assertive action. Despite some eyebrow-raising public references to the Soviet Union as an "evil empire" and "the focus of evil in the modern world," he treated the Soviets with consummate caution—doggedly pursuing arms-control negotiations with them even as Soviet troops intensified their heavy-handed military occupation of Afghanistan and after martial law was imposed in Poland. When the Soviets shot down a Korean civilian airliner that they mistook for a U.S. spy plane, killing 269 passengers (including 61 Americans, one of them a U.S. congressman), Reagan's rhetoric was "tough as nails" but his follow-up actions were so restrained that they "went almost unnoticed." When he tried to persuade the United States' European allies not to assist the Soviets in constructing a natural-gas pipeline from

Siberia to western Europe, he was rebuffed; and "when he then imposed economic sanctions against the Europeans after their refusal to heed him on the issue, he was forced first to weaken his punitive measures, and later to abandon the whole effort behind a thin smoke screen of diplomatic word play." And although candidate Reagan had pledged his unwavering support for Taiwan, President Reagan was forced by the Chinese Communists to limit (and eventually terminate) U.S. arms sales to the Taiwanese.[4] By mid-1983, there was "little discernible enthusiasm" for Reagan's foreign policy, even among traditional right-wing Republicans and Reagan's die-hard neoconservative supporters.[5]

Public dissatisfaction with Reagan's performance in office was quick to express itself. In the midterm elections of November 1982, the Democrats gained twenty-six seats in the House of Representatives, effectively destroying the working majority of Republicans and conservative Democrats that had delivered Reagan's legislative victories a year earlier. The following month, White House pollster Wirthlin warned Reagan that he was losing his aura of strong leadership and that the resulting "perceptual changes" could endanger his presidency. Opinion polls steadily reinforced Wirthlin's warning. A January 1983 Gallup poll placed Reagan's presidential approval rating at 35 percent, lower than that of any of his four elected predecessors, including the much maligned Jimmy Carter, after two years in office. That same month, the *New York Times* editorialized that "the stench of failure hangs over Ronald Reagan's White House." By May, early polls forecasting the 1984 presidential election race showed Reagan trailing both of the leading Democratic contenders, John Glenn and Walter Mondale, with Glenn holding a seventeen-point lead over the president. To many observers, including some of his own White House advisers, Reagan was increasingly beginning to look like "another failed one-term president."[6]

During the summer of 1983, the domestic economy finally began to show signs of recovery, but Reagan's foreign-policy difficulties continued unabated. In particular, the deepening U.S. military involvement in Central America—one of the few areas where Reagan appeared to be backing up his tough anticommunist rhetoric with action—was becoming ever more controversial. As the number of U.S. military advisers in El Salvador increased and details of the CIA's covert operation in Nicaragua became known, the specter of "another Vietnam" proved frightening to many Americans. Opinion polls throughout 1983 consistently showed 60–80 percent of the U.S. public opposed to Reagan's Central American policies.[7] The numbers paralleled Americans' attitudes toward Reagan's management of U.S. foreign relations more generally: an August Gallup poll found that only 31 percent of respondents approved of the way the president was handling the nation's foreign affairs. By autumn, with the economy beginning to recede as a political issue, Reagan's Democratic rivals were increasingly focusing their campaigns on what they perceived to be Reagan's Achilles' heel: his conduct of foreign policy.[8]

Then, in October, disaster struck. On Sunday the twenty-third, a suicide truck bomber blew up a U.S. military barracks in Beirut, Lebanon, killing 241 Marines and wounding scores of others. The casualty figures were as high as any suffered on a single day of fighting in Vietnam. The bombing stunned Reagan. He had deployed the Marines in Lebanon in a controversial effort to impose pro-U.S. stability in that war-wracked Middle Eastern nation and had "repeatedly ignored the warnings of his military advisers" that the U.S. troops were vulnerable to terrorist attacks. The following day—as Democratic critics in Congress lambasted him for the stupidity of his decision to put the Marines in Lebanon and with overnight polls showing another precipitous decline in his approval rating—Reagan took a decisive step that reversed his political fortunes and restored forward momentum to his presidency: he ordered U.S. military forces to invade Grenada.[9]

If Reagan was looking for an easy Cold War victory over communism, it would have been difficult to pick a weaker, lower-risk adversary than Grenada. The tiny island nation, a former British colony in the eastern Caribbean, was barely the size of Martha's Vineyard, with a total population of 110,000. Its defense forces consisted of a 2,000-man army, and it had no navy or air force. In short, a prospective U.S.-Grenada military conflict had all the trappings of a *Mouse That Roared*–level mismatch.

In 1979, a seventy-member Marxist political organization calling itself the New Jewel Movement (NJM) seized control of Grenada's government and attempted to carry out a socialist revolution on the island. Inspired by the Cuban revolution and the militant "black power" philosophies in vogue at the time among Caribbean intellectuals, the New Jewel Movement established a new People's Revolutionary Government (PRG) and launched an ambitious program of structural transformation. In doing so, it neglected to reveal that its leaders had secretly defined their organization as a Marxist-Leninist vanguard party.[10]

What followed was in some respects reminiscent of the early days of the Cuban and Nicaraguan revolutions.[11] Notable improvements in education, health care, and basic infrastructure were accompanied by the inevitable darker features of Marxist revolutions: suspension of the constitution; an absence of free elections; imprisonment without trial for prominent members of the "bourgeoisie" and "those who stood in the way of progress"; forced closure of opposition newspapers; drastic declines in investment activity by the private business community; inefficient, poorly run state enterprises; "political cronyism, as the New Jewel Movement repeatedly placed supporters in influential positions for which they were not qualified"; and incessant efforts at "popular mobilization." It soon became apparent, however, that the Grenadian people were a less-fertile mass base for a Marxist revolution than their Cuban or Nicaraguan counterparts. A majority of the island's population consisted of socially conservative, Catholic or Anglican peasant smallholders—inauspicious clay from which to mold a Marxist society. They were also the products of a British colonial heritage in which respect for parliamentary democracy and civil liberties had been deeply ingrained. By 1983, most of Grenada's population was "either hostile to the revolution or disillusioned with it,"[12] and the New Jewel Movement's Central Committee was acknowledging that the party had lost much of its popular support. "At present," it concluded in August, "the Revolution is facing its worst crisis ever and the most serious danger in 4 ½ years. The mood of the masses is characterized at worst by open dissatisfaction and cynicism, and at best by serious demoralization. Overall the mood is 1–2 on a scale of 5."[13]

The revolution's deterioration and eventual disintegration owed much to the New Jewel Movement's international policies. Desperate for foreign aid from virtually any source, the PRG publicly committed itself to international nonalignment and good relations with all nations, including the United States. Privately, however, the revolution's leaders were working tirelessly to establish the radical credentials necessary for Grenada to gain membership in the Soviet bloc.[14]

From the start, the New Jewel Movement's closest ties were with Cuba. Like the Sandinistas and other Latin American guerrilla movements of the period, the organization had received "significant financial support and military training" from Fidel Castro's government during its formative years. NJM founder Maurice Bishop personally revered Castro, and the two men developed a close friendship that Bishop's mother would later describe as almost a father-son relationship. Accordingly, when the New Jewel Movement seized power in 1979, Castro provided immediate and extensive support: weapons and military trainers; civilian advisers for a wide range of new revolutionary programs, including health care, education, and propaganda; and pledges of generous financial assistance for airport construction, fisheries, and other infrastructure development projects.[15]

In return, Grenada's revolutionaries made no secret of their gratitude or their determination to function as Cuba's ally. "We look to the people of Cuba," Bishop (now Grenada's prime minister) told a Havana audience during a May 1980 state visit; "we look to your revolution and your leadership to ensure that the revolutionary process in the Caribbean and Central American region continues to go forward with strength."[16] That same year, Bishop openly acknowledged that the PRG was using the Cuban revolution as its model. Cuba was "the best example in the world of what a small country under socialism can achieve," he declared; "if there had been no Cuban revolution in 1959 there could have been no Grenadian revolution in 1979."[17] Privately, meanwhile, Bishop was assuring Castro that "in whatever ways and at whatever price[,] the heroic internationalist people of Cuba can always count on [the] total solidarity, support and cooperation of the Grenada revolution." So "profound" was Castro's influence on Bishop and his colleagues that the Cuban ambassador to Grenada reportedly participated in PRG cabinet meetings.[18]

Working through Cuban contacts, the Grenadians also pursued an "intensive courtship" of the Soviet Union and other members of the Eastern bloc. The PRG established diplomatic relations with the Soviet Union in December 1979. Six months later, the NJM's chief theoretician, Bernard Coard, traveled to Moscow and signed a party-to-party accord with the Soviet Communist Party. Simultaneously, the PRG cultivated the Soviets' friendship by voting "unfailingly" in support of their positions in the United Nations—most conspicuously in January 1980 when Grenada joined Cuba as the only Western Hemisphere nations to oppose a UN resolution condemning the 1979 Soviet intervention in Afghanistan.[19] Grenada also played host to various international "solidarity meetings" at which Marxist and other leftist groups from the eastern Caribbean joined with counterparts from Cuba and Central America and "fraternal" delegations from the Soviet bloc to discuss issues of ideology and organization.[20]

Rewards came primarily in the form of military assistance. Secret Soviet-Grenadian military agreements were completed in Havana in October 1980 and February 1981 providing Grenada with Soviet weaponry and training valued at some 9.4 million rubles. A third and even larger military agreement was signed in Moscow in July 1982. Other agreements followed, including one with North Korea that promised Grenada another $12 million in military aid. In addition, trade agreements were negotiated with East Germany, Bulgaria, and Czechoslovakia.[21]

Like the Sandinistas, however, Grenada's revolutionaries soon learned that the Soviets were hard-headed pragmatists when it came to economic assistance and commercial agreements. People's Revolutionary Government requests for multimillion-dollar loans and grants were turned down by Moscow, and the Soviets refused a Grenadian request to purchase 1,000 tons of nutmeg at a time when the Soviet Union consumed only 200–300 tons per year.[22]

By 1983, Grenada's ambassador in Moscow was complaining that the Soviets had been exceedingly cautious and "sometimes maddingly [sic] slow" in providing support. "Considering the risks that we have taken," he said, referring specifically to Grenada's 1980 UN vote condoning Soviet intervention in Afghanistan, "it might be fair to say that their support for us is actually below our support for them." The problem, the ambassador continued, was that "they regard Grenada as a small distant country. . . . Grenada's distance from the USSR, and its small size, . . . mean that we . . . figure in a very minute way in the USSR's global relationships." To develop closer relations with the Soviets, he advised, the PRG needed to "lift our profile and highten [sic] our priority." "Our legitimate begging operations have to be cast in the larger world context," he said.

> Our revolution has to be viewed as a world-wide process with its original roots in the Great October Revolution. For Grenada to assume a position of increasingly greater importance, we have to be seen as influencing at least regional events. We have to establish ourselves as the authority on events in at least the English-speaking Caribbean, and be the sponsor of revolutionary activity and progressive developments in this region at least. . . .

To the extent that we can take credit for bringing any other country into the progressive fold, our prestige and influence would be greatly enhanced.[23]

Specifically, the ambassador identified Suriname and Belize as promising targets of opportunity. Before his superiors back in Grenada could move to implement his recommendations, however, factional warfare within the New Jewel Movement gave Reagan his opportunity to invade the island and destroy the Grenadian revolution.

That the PRG's relations with the United States quickly deteriorated should have surprised no one. From its inception, the New Jewel Movement had defined the United States as "the main imperialist power on earth" and the NJM's "No. 1 enemy." A 1973 NJM manifesto openly "condemn[ed] in the strongest possible terms the intervention of the U.S.A. in the internal affairs of the South East Asian countries and the genocidal practices being committed on their peoples." The manifesto went on to announce the New Jewel Movement's support for "the heroic struggle of the people of Vietnam and Cambodia" and "reject[ed] the right of the U.S.A. or any other big power to control the economies and the lives of any people anywhere."[24]

When Bishop and his colleagues seized power in March 1979, the Carter administration was aware of their radical nature but believed that they might still be "co-optable."[25] Accordingly, U.S. emissaries soon arrived on the island offering the revolutionaries U.S. economic assistance in exchange for "cooperative relations" and "prompt elections." The U.S. aid offer included more than $1.3 million in U.S. Agency for International Development loans plus a number of $5,000 rapid-disbursement grants for community-development projects. Bishop expressed interest but never followed up with a formal request for aid. On April 10, as Cuban arms and advisers poured into Grenada, U.S. ambassador Frank Ortiz reiterated the U.S. offers of economic assistance but "pressed Bishop again on elections" and warned him that the United States "would view with displeasure any tendency on the part of Grenada to develop closer ties with Cuba."[26]

Three days later, Bishop responded with a public speech blasting the United States. He ridiculed the offers of U.S. assistance as paltry. Were a few $5,000 grants "all that the wealthiest country in the world can offer to a poor but proud people?" he asked. Bishop also attacked Ambassador Ortiz as a hegemonic bully who had rudely attempted to "meddl[e] in our affairs." "We reject entirely the argument of the American Ambassador," he said. "If the government of Cuba is willing to offer us assistance, we would be more than happy to receive it." Bishop concluded with a stirring proclamation of defiant nationalism: "No country has the right to tell us what to do or how to run our country, or who to be friendly with. . . .We are not in anybody's backyard, and we are definitely not for sale. . . . We would sooner give up our lives before we compromise, sell out, or betray our sovereignty, our independence, our integrity, our manhood, and the right of our people to national self-determination and social progress."[27] Co-optation did not appear to be working.

The Carter administration next considered covert intervention. On May 8, National Security Adviser Zbigniew Brzezinski informed the CIA of "the President's concern about the growing Cuban presence on Grenada" and suggested "a covert effort to focus international press attention on it." The agency responded a week later with "a political action program going beyond Brzezinski's suggestion and intended to counter the Cubans on the island." On July 3, Carter signed a presidential "finding" authorizing covert action "to promote the democratic process on Grenada and. . . support resistance to the Marxist government there." When the finding reached the Senate Intelligence Committee on July 19, however, "all hell broke loose," the CIA's Robert Gates recalls. The committee expressed its strong displeasure with the proposed covert operation, pointing to "the divergence between the . . . proposal and the administration's position on human rights and noninterference." The White House backed off, and on July 23 the CIA "ceased all covert activity relating to Grenada."[28] From that point until the end of its term in office, the Carter administration adopted a policy of distancing itself from the PRG and worked to isolate Grenada by extending development aid to its regional neighbors in the eastern Caribbean.[29]

The Reagan administration opted for a tougher approach. Its central thrust, initially, was a program of economic destabilization aimed at undermining the PRG's political support base. Shortly after entering office, Secretary of State Alexander Haig ordered officials in the Bureau of Inter-American Affairs to see to it that Grenada did not receive "one penny" from any international financial institution. Over the course of 1981, administration officials blocked a $3 million World Bank grant to the PRG, lobbied the International Monetary Fund to significantly reduce its loan commitments to Grenada, applied pressure on the Caribbean Development Bank to exclude Grenada from its lending programs, and tried, with only partial success, to dissuade the United States' European allies from providing the PRG with any economic assistance. In February 1982, Reagan specifically excluded Grenada from participation in his new Caribbean Basin Initiative, a "mini-Marshall Plan" for the region.[30] Meanwhile, the CIA drew up new plans for a covert operation designed "to cause economic difficulty for Grenada" and provide "aid" to opposition groups. In July 1981, however, that plan also encountered unanimous opposition in the Senate Intelligence Committee, and Reagan—like his predecessor—dropped the proposal.[31]

Reagan also subjected the PRG to a heavy dose of military intimidation. From August to mid-October 1981, the United States and its NATO allies conducted the largest joint naval maneuvers ever held in the Caribbean—maneuvers that included some 250 warships, 1,000 aircraft, and more than 120,000 troops. One component of the maneuvers—dubbed "Amber and the Amberdines" in a thinly veiled allusion to Grenada and the Grenadines—featured a mock amphibious invasion to "liberate" an island described in the operation's scenario as "our enemy in the eastern Caribbean where U.S. hostages were in need of rescue." The real purpose of the exercise, a participating U.S. admiral explained, was to send a message to unfriendly countries in the region.[32] Another round of U.S. naval maneuvers followed in 1982, and in 1983 a "training exercise" named "Readex 83" featured the deployment of another large fleet of U.S. and allied warships six miles off the Grenadian coast.[33]

Reagan and his advisers accompanied their threat posturing with public statements portraying Grenada as a threat to U.S. national security. From the start, their charges centered on a new international airport that the PRG was constructing, with Cuban assistance, at Point Salines on the island's southwestern tip. According to the Grenadians, the $71 million airport project was the centerpiece of their economic-development program. Grenada's existing airport was an antiquated and isolated facility equipped with a short (5,300-foot), unlighted, grass runway that could accommodate only small, propeller-driven aircraft. By replacing it with a modern airport featuring a 9,800-foot runway capable of handling large, wide-body commercial jets, Grenada would be able to develop a competitive tourism industry, which in turn would provide the foreign exchange needed to finance the revolution's social and economic programs. In a gesture of "fraternal" support, the Cuban government had generously agreed to contribute some $60 million in material and labor to the project. Construction began in March 1980.[34]

The Reagan administration claimed that the Point Salines airport was a Trojan horse of communist military expansionism. In December 1981, State Department officials warned the Senate Foreign Relations Committee that the airport would be a Cuban-Soviet base that could threaten the oil fields of Venezuela, interdict maritime shipping routes throughout the Caribbean, and give Cuban military aircraft "a guaranteed refueling stop" as they transported Cuban troops and equipment to Marxist wars of national liberation in Africa. In March 1982, Undersecretary of Defense Fred Iklé, citing unverified sources, told a Senate subcommittee that Grenada's minister of national mobilization, Selwyn Strachan, had "publicly boasted that Cuba will eventually use the new airport . . . to supply troops in Angola" and that "the airport may also be used by the Soviet Union." Three months later, in testimony before the House Subcommittee on Inter-American Affairs, Deputy Assistant Secretary of State for Inter-American Affairs Stephen D. Bosworth stated that the construction of the airport added "a new and serious dimension to our security concerns" and predicted that Grenada would "no doubt repay its debt to Cuba" by giving Cuban military aircraft access to the airport for transit flights to Africa and other military bases.[35]

The administration's rhetoric ratcheted up noticeably in early 1983. In an effort to mobilize congressional and public support for their anticommunist operations in Central America, Reagan and his advisers now seized upon Grenada's airport project as proof that Marxist forces were gaining a dangerous military advantage in the Caribbean basin. In February, Deputy Assistant Secretary of State Nestor Sanchez suggested that nothing less than another Cuban missile crisis was looming in Grenada; the island's new military facilities, Sanchez predicted, "would provide air and naval bases . . . for the recovery of Soviet aircraft after strategic missions" and "might also furnish missile sites for launching attacks against the United States with short and intermediate range missiles."[36] In a March 10 speech to the National Association of Manufacturers, Reagan himself chided those who claimed that Grenada was too small and weak to pose a security threat to the United States:

> Grenada, that tiny little island—with Cuba at the western end of the Caribbean, Grenada at the eastern end—that tiny little island is building now, or having built for it, on its shores, a naval base, a superior air base, storage bases and facilities for the storage of munitions, barracks, and training grounds for the military. I'm sure all of that is simply to encourage the export of nutmeg.
>
> People who make these arguments haven't taken a good look at a map lately or followed the extraordinary buildup of Soviet and Cuban military power in the region or read the Soviets' discussions about why the region is important to them and how they intend to use it.
>
> It isn't nutmeg that's at stake in the Caribbean and Central America. It is the United States national security.[37]

Thirteen days later, during a nationally televised speech announcing the administration's Strategic Defense Initiative, the president held up a U.S. satellite-reconnaissance photograph of the airport and exclaimed dramatically: "On the small island of Grenada, at the southern end of the Caribbean chain, the Cubans, with Soviet financing and backing, are in the process of building an airport with a 10,000 foot runway. Grenada does not even have an air force. Who is it intended for? . . . The Soviet-Cuban militarization of Grenada . . . can only be seen as power projection into the region." The following month, Reagan informed a joint session of Congress that in the event of a global conflict, the Soviet Union would use Grenada's new airfield to intercept U.S. reinforcements to Europe and the Middle East.[38] By the spring of 1983, if the Reagan administration was to be believed, Grenada's airport construction project had become a major threat to Western security in the Cold War.

The increasingly ominous-sounding U.S. charges alarmed Maurice Bishop. The Grenadian leader had never been known for restraint in his characterizations of Reagan and his advisers, labeling them "reactionaries," "imperialists," "neutron warmongers," and the "fascist clique in Washington," among other epithets. U.S. claims that the Point Salines airport was destined for Soviet-Cuban military use were, Bishop said, nothing but "a pack of lies."[39] Nevertheless, the increasingly apocalyptic tone of Reagan's March–April 1983 rhetoric, and the realization that the president of the most powerful nation on earth was now identifying minuscule Grenada as a serious threat to its national security, apparently persuaded Bishop that survival required a new policy of prudence and conciliation. On May 31, he arrived in Washington, D.C., on a public-relations trip designed to improve the revolution's image in the eyes of the American people and Congress "in order to restrain the U.S. government from attacking Grenada militarily." During the visit, Bishop repeatedly indicated that he would welcome the opportunity for a "dialogue" with Reagan administration officials to "personally clear up the misconceptions that exist." After several days of administration stonewalling, National Security Adviser William Clark and Deputy Secretary of State Kenneth Dam agreed to meet with the Grenadian leader for thirty minutes on June 7. The meeting produced nothing of substance. Bishop tried to assure the U.S. officials that Grenada posed no threat to the United States, and he went on to propose that the two countries should "move toward better relations." Clark responded that the United States was primarily interested in a change in Grenada's behavior and warned Bishop that Soviet influence in the eastern Caribbean was "not acceptable."[40]

Bishop's unrequited attempt at rapprochement with the United States complicated his political situation back in Grenada. By mid-1983, hard-core Leninists within the New Jewel Movement were growing increasingly disenchanted with Bishop's leadership. Led by Deputy Prime Minister Bernard Coard and counting high-ranking officers of the People's Revolutionary Army (PRA) among their members, the dissidents criticized Bishop for his conduct in Washington, complaining that he had exceeded his authority in meeting with Clark and Dam and that his conciliatory gestures came dangerously close to "right opportunism" and the compromising of revolutionary principles. Rumors circulated within the party hierarchy that Bishop had inadvertently "sold out" the revolution during his U.S. trip.[41]

The dispute reflected a deeper power struggle that was developing within the revolutionary leadership. At a series of NJM Central Committee meetings between July and September 1983, Coard and his followers charged that the revolution was unraveling. The general populace, they pointed out, was increasingly dissatisfied and hostile; party members were demoralized; efforts at mass mobilization were weak and ineffective, and the PRG was "dangerously close . . . to losing its links with the masses." Unless the regime immediately applied "firm Leninist leadership" and instilled "a Leninist level of organization and discipline" within the party, they warned, Grenada's revolution would "disintegrate within 3–6 months."[42] Blame for the sorry state of affairs was placed squarely on Bishop's shoulders. "The most fundamental problem" and "number one weakness," Coard's followers charged, was "the quality of leadership of the Central Committee and party provided by Comrade Maurice Bishop." Bishop, they said, was disorganized, undisciplined, vacillating, ideologically weak, soft, and too much inclined toward humanitarianism. Some of Bishop's critics urged him to adopt a "Marxist-Leninist-Stalinist" approach, while others expressed doubt that he was capable of providing the firm leadership required by the crisis situation.[43]

In mid-September, the dissidents proposed a joint-leadership arrangement in which Bishop and Coard would share power—with Bishop's responsibilities limited to international relations and the development of mass organizations and "organs of popular democracy," while Coard would be in charge of "party organization, the ideological development of party members, and party strategy and tactics." Bishop temporized, hoping to find an alternative political formula that would prevent him from becoming a mere figurehead. By early October, the political atmosphere had degenerated into "emotional vilification, hatred, and militarism," with rumors spreading that each side was planning to physically eliminate the other. On October 13, Coard and the Central Committee placed Bishop under house arrest and stripped him of his governmental authority. It was time for "Bolshevik staunchness," one of Coard's followers remarked; "Communists without belly better hop the next plane."[44]

Six days later, on October 19, as Bishop rallied his followers in a desperate attempt to regain control of the situation, PRA troops opened fire on a mass demonstration, killing "over 100." Bishop and seven of his aides were then placed before a firing squad and executed, at the direct order of Coard and the Central Committee. As the PRA soldiers prepared to open fire, Jacqueline Creft, the PRG's minister of education and Bishop's mistress, screamed "Comrades, you mean you're going to shoot us? To kill us?" To which a PRA officer replied: "You fucking bitch, who are you calling comrades? You're one of those who was going to let the imperialists in."[45]

Coard's forces quickly established a new provisional government—a Revolutionary Military Council (RMC) headed by PRA commander in chief Gen. Hudson Austin—and announced that they intended to "govern with absolute strictness." As confirmation, a twenty-four-hour shoot-on-sight curfew was declared in effect.[46] Within a matter of days, however, a U.S. military invasion brought the Coard faction's Leninist project to an abrupt end. In the early hours of October 25, six days after Bishop's murder, the first of some 6,000 U.S. troops began their assault on the island. After four days of fighting, and some seventy-six American, Grenadian, and Cuban casualties, they seized control of the island, arrested Coard, Austin, and their colleagues, and removed the NJM revolutionaries from power. The following year, representatives of Grenada's traditional, pre-1979 political system were installed as the island's new leaders.[47]

Reagan explained his motives for ordering U.S. forces into Grenada in a nationally televised press conference on the morning of October 25. With Eugenia Charles, the prime minister of Dominica and head of the Organization of Eastern

Caribbean States (OECS), at his side, the president listed three reasons why the invasion was deemed necessary: first, to protect the "personal safety" of U.S. citizens in Grenada; second, "to forestall further chaos"; and third, "to assist in the restoration of conditions of law and order and of governmental institutions" on the island.[48]

There was more to it than that. As Eugenia Charles' presence at Reagan's press conference suggested, Grenada's island neighbors in the eastern Caribbean played a prominent role in the U.S. decision to intervene. The 1979 NJM coup—an unprecedented act of political violence in the English-speaking Caribbean—had deeply alarmed the region's conservative elites, who were "terrified" that the Marxist revolutionary "virus" in Grenada would spread, infect their own islands, and "bring about their downfall." Accordingly, although the governments of neighboring islands maintained diplomatic relations with Bishop's regime, nervous leaders in Barbados, Jamaica, Dominica, St. Lucia, St. Vincent, Trinidad, and elsewhere privately longed for the Grenadian revolutionaries' removal from power.[49] The outbreak of factional warfare within the ranks of the NJM leadership in October 1983 provided them with an unparalleled opportunity to achieve that goal by enlisting U.S. military might on their behalf.

On October 17, four days after the Coard faction placed Bishop under house arrest, Prime Minister Tom Adams of Barbados suggested to U.S. Ambassador Milan Bish that the United States should launch a military operation against Grenada. Adams—whose conservative ideology had earned him the nickname "Uncle Tom" from Bishop—told Bish that the PRG's internal instability now provided the United States with a golden opportunity to oust Grenada's unpopular Marxist-Leninist regime and reduce Soviet-Cuban influence in the Caribbean. That same day, Dominica's Charles—admired by the Reaganites as "a Caribbean Jeane Kirkpatrick"—informed the State Department that U.S. military assistance was needed "to address the Grenada situation"; Reagan should "deal severely" with the PRG's Leninist hard-liners, she advised. On the nineteenth, the day Bishop was murdered, Adams again called on the United States to invade Grenada and offered Barbados as a staging base. The following day, Adams and Prime Minister John Compton of St. Lucia concluded that the situation in Grenada had become too dangerous and that, if something were not done, Coard's newly installed Revolutionary Military Council "would attempt to push the entire Caribbean community into the communist camp." That night, Adams took his case directly to the American people. Appearing on the ABC News *Nightline* program, he told host Ted Koppel that most West Indians hoped the United States would intervene militarily in Grenada.[50]

On October 20, the State Department informed the White House that "Caribbean leaders were deeply frightened by the bloodshed on Grenada and wanted action taken." The Reagan administration had not yet decided to intervene, however. Some of the president's advisers were concerned that the United States lacked any plausible legal grounds for a full-scale military invasion. As Assistant Secretary of State for Inter-American Affairs Langhorne Motley later recalled, "I didn't want 9,000 years of [postinvasion] Security Council debate" in the United Nations. What might be useful, Secretary of State George Shultz thought, was a formal request for U.S. assistance from the Organization of Eastern Caribbean States, which would provide a legal basis for U.S. intervention.[51]

The OECS was already moving in that direction. At a summit meeting in Barbados on the twenty-first, the organization's members "voted to invite the United States to participate in an invasion of Grenada." Motley quickly informed Shultz that Grenada's neighbors "are now out in front, and we want to keep it that way." Two days later, as the OECS leaders drafted their formal written invitation, special U.S. emissary Frank McNeil cautioned them that the Reagan administration "had not yet decided how the United States would respond to the OECS invitation" and listed several "essential points" that would need to be included in any formal invitation before the United States could accept.[52] Adams, Compton, Charles, and Jamaica's Edward Seaga responded by giving McNeil the "hard sell." American citizens in Grenada "appeared vulnerable," they warned, and "a bloody civil war seemed likely," in which case "the Cubans and Soviets would probably become involved." Eventually, the Caribbean leaders feared, "democracy would be at risk throughout the region." Charles stressed that none of the OECS member states had military forces capable of withstanding "air attacks and the army of Cuban advisers amassing in Grenada." The People's Revolutionary Army, she reminded McNeil, now had access to the nearly 10,000-foot airstrip that the Cubans were building, "clearly for military use," and "a thousand armed Cuban advisers" were there to assist them. "That's what it's all about," she warned: "to point a dagger at the eastern Caribbean states."[53]

McNeil considered the Caribbean leaders' arguments compelling. "I . . . found the reasoning of the OECS leaders entirely persuasive as to the dangers to the neighboring small islands if the thugs who massacred Bishop and his followers kept power," he later wrote. Charles and her colleagues "had a good sense of what was happening on Grenada," he recalled—"better than U.S. intelligence had." Accordingly, McNeil quickly telephoned Washington recommending prompt U.S. military action. Before he left Barbados, the OECS leaders provided him with a formal written request that covered all of the administration's "essential points."[54] Reagan now had the legal fig leaf that he needed to launch a military invasion.

But it was not the welfare of the eastern Caribbean's governing elites that motivated the Reagan administration to intervene. From the start, the president and his top advisers were primarily concerned that the instability in Grenada might give rise to a politically damaging hostage crisis like the one in Iran that had undermined Jimmy Carter's presidency three years earlier. In October 1983, memories of the

1979–1980 Iranian hostage crisis and its political consequences remained vivid in the minds of Washington policy makers. That crisis had begun in November 1979, when militant followers of Iran's Islamic fundamentalist leader Ayatollah Khomeini stormed the U.S. embassy in Tehran and seized sixty-six American diplomats and staff as hostages. For the next fifteen months, the American captives were paraded before news cameras, threatened with execution, and generally exploited as symbols of American powerlessness in the face of Iran's Islamic revolution. The humiliating experience, amplified nightly on U.S. television news programs, eventually crippled Carter politically as his inability to secure the hostages' release made him appear increasingly ineffectual—particularly after a poorly conceived military rescue mission in April 1980 went horribly awry, resulting in the deaths of eight U.S. servicemen.[55]

The Iranian hostage crisis doomed Carter to defeat in the 1980 presidential election. During the campaign, Reagan and the Republicans pounded him relentlessly for his alleged mishandling of the situation. The whole humiliating episode, Reagan suggested, was symbolic both of Carter's incompetence and the depths of international weakness to which the United States had sunk in the aftermath of Vietnam. If he had been president in 1979, Reagan implied, the U.S. hostages would never have been seized in the first place.[56]

Consequently, once they were installed in the White House, Reagan and his advisers were understandably hypersensitive to any possibility of another politically debilitating U.S. hostage crisis anywhere in the world. By October 1983, with Reagan's public approval ratings at dangerously low levels and the 1984 presidential election barely a year away, that hypersensitivity was acute. Politically, Reagan simply could "not afford to look and sound like Carter, wringing his hands helplessly about the sad fate of Americans in some foreign country." As he frequently reminded his advisers, there must not be "another Teheran" on his watch.[57]

As a result, administration officials were quick to take notice when early intelligence reports about the outbreak of political violence in Grenada mentioned the possibility that "Americans on the island might now be in danger." At meetings of the administration's Restricted Interagency Group in Washington on October 14 and 17, State Department representatives argued that an emergency evacuation of U.S. citizens—a "noncombatant evacuation operation" (or NEO, in D.C. bureaucratese)—might soon be necessary and that planning should commence immediately. In advocating preparations for an evacuation, the group's chair, Assistant Secretary of State for Inter-American Affairs Motley, and his State Department colleagues were "driven by the Iran analogy" and the certainty "that Reagan would not tolerate a hostage situation." Following the October 17 meeting, Reagan was briefed by his newly appointed national security adviser Robert McFarlane and ordered that planning for an evacuation should proceed.[58]

On the nineteenth, U.S. diplomats in Barbados cabled a "red-coded" message to Washington reporting Bishop's murder and indicating that U.S. citizens in

Grenada appeared to be in imminent danger. That evening, Motley discussed the situation with Secretary of State George Shultz, and the two men concluded that conditions were ripe for hostage taking. Describing the conversation in his memoirs, Shultz recalled that "we both had the searing memory of Tehran and the sixty-six Americans seized from our embassy on November 4, 1979, and held hostage for well over a year. We both knew what Ronald Reagan's reaction would be to such a development in Grenada. He would not stand still while American hostages were held for 444 days. In fact, he probably wouldn't stand still for a week."[59]

The following afternoon, the administration's highest-level crisis management unit, the Special Situations Group, convened in the White House to discuss the instability in Grenada. Participants included Vice President George Bush, Shultz, McFarlane, Secretary of Defense Caspar Weinberger, Chairman of the Joint Chiefs of Staff General John Vessey, Acting CIA Director John McMahon, White House Counselor Ed Meese, and several aides. Fear of hostage taking pervaded the discussion. The meeting opened with a "pessimistic intelligence appraisal of General Austin and his RMC colleagues," and included information suggesting "that those now in charge on Grenada were ruthless and might possibly try to hold American hostages." Undersecretary of State for Political Affairs Lawrence Eagleburger "specifically raised the specter of the Teheran hostages." When the discussion turned to contingency plans for a mission to "rescue" U.S. citizens on the island, JCS Chairman Vessey "observed . . . that a surgical strike simply to remove the Americans would be extremely difficult without securing the entire island." Accordingly, following the meeting, a naval amphibious task force en route to Lebanon was redeployed to the eastern Caribbean—"within easy sailing distance of Grenada"—in order to put sufficient U.S. military power in place if Reagan opted for a full-scale invasion.[60]

No one in the administration, of course, had more to lose from a Grenadian hostage crisis than the president himself. And as Robert Beck notes, Reagan had concluded early on that U.S. intervention was "politically desirable." "He couldn't wait," national security adviser McFarlane recalled. Nevertheless, as the Pentagon raced to complete its military planning and the White House awaited receipt of a formal OECS invitation, the devastating Beirut terrorist bombing on October 23 suddenly forced Reagan to reconsider the wisdom of going ahead with the intervention. Throughout the day, he and his advisers vigorously debated the political risks of a military invasion. If, fresh on the heels of the disaster in Lebanon, the operation went badly, with a significant loss of American lives, the negative consequences for Reagan's presidency would be severe. According to Weinberger and Meese, "Reagan was informed in no uncertain terms that he could hardly afford another foreign policy debacle." On the other hand, one administration official recalled, "The President and those around him thought it was risky to abort the operation. There was concern that news of it might leak out and that Americans would be seized before the Marines could land." "I'm no better off than Jimmy Carter," Reagan reportedly lamented.[61]

Late that night, from Barbados, U.S. special emissary Frank McNeil informed Washington that the OECS had officially invited the United States to invade Grenada. "I recommended sending in the troops," he later recalled, "so long as it was done quickly before surprise was lost. In doing so, I was mindful of Teheran, where colleagues had languished as hostages for so long." "The make-or-break factor for me," McNeil remembered, was the "growing danger" to Americans on the island. The following day, after receiving assurances from the Pentagon that the operation would succeed and that "casualties would be light," Reagan gave the "final order" to launch the invasion. In the president's mind, the political risk of a potential hostage crisis apparently outweighed the risk of incurring new U.S. military casualties so soon after Beirut.[62]

The main problem with the administration's fear of a Grenadian hostage crisis, however, was that from the start it was based entirely on conjecture. None of the U.S. citizens living in Grenada—approximately 1,000 in all, including some 600 medical students studying at the St. George's University School of Medicine—had been harmed or even threatened by Grenada's Leninist revolutionaries. To the contrary, throughout the period leading up to the U.S. invasion, the RMC's leaders repeatedly assured the Reagan administration that they were committed to ensuring the safety of all U.S. nationals on the island. After imposing their draconian shoot-on-sight curfew on the nineteenth, Hudson Austin and his military colleagues went out of their way to look after the welfare of the medical students—providing them with emergency supplies of food and water and offering transportation to the airport for any who wished to leave. By October 23, only about 10 percent of the students had expressed any interest in being evacuated; and that evening the parents of some 500 of the students sent Reagan a cable informing him of their children's safety and asking him "not to . . . take any precipitous action at this time."[63] The CIA's Duane Clarridge later admitted that as late as the twenty-third "there was still some question in Washington as to whether the medical students on Grenada were frightened and really wanted to leave." The State Department's Kenneth Dam later testified before Congress that he had no information that any Americans were threatened or harmed during the entire period.[64]

Practical considerations alone made it highly unlikely that the RMC would have even contemplated seizing Americans as hostages. The St. George's medical school was a major source of revenue for the Grenadian government, and the island was heavily dependent on North American tourist dollars. Consequently, a hostage crisis would almost certainly have wrecked Grenada's economy and the revolution's development plans. Above all, the taking of U.S. hostages would have provided the Reagan administration with a perfect pretext for military intervention. Indeed, the RMC's only rational motive for hostage taking would have been to bargain for its survival in the face of a U.S. invasion, making the Reagan administration's decision to intervene a potentially self-fulfilling prophecy if there ever was one. "The assertion that the students were in danger is the lie of the twentieth century," Hudson Austin later charged. "It was really Ronald Reagan and the White House, trying to justify the invasion. . . . We had no plans to take the students hostage. Where would we put them if we took them hostage? What would we do with them?"[65]

How, then, does one account for the warnings that top administration officials received about an imminent and growing danger to U.S. citizens in Grenada? Certainly, the conservative leaders of Grenada's eastern Caribbean neighbors played on that theme in their conversations with Milan Bish, Frank McNeil, and other U.S. diplomats who were instrumental in influencing Washington's understanding of conditions on the island. In addition, U.S. security analysts at the lower and intermediate levels of the information pipeline may have been subject to career pressures similar to those that colored the field reporting of their counterparts in the Dominican Republic two decades earlier (see chap. 4). Just as U.S. diplomats and intelligence agents in the Dominican Republic grossly exaggerated the implausible threat of a "Castroite Communist takeover" of that Caribbean nation in 1965 in order to protect themselves against subsequent accusations that they had failed to identify a "second Cuba" in formation, intermediate-level Reagan administration officials—acutely aware of the White House's paranoid fear of hostage crises—may have overemphasized the highly unlikely possibility of a hostage situation in Grenada in order to safeguard themselves from later recrimination in the event that the unlikely occurred. Whatever the explanation, however, it seems clear that Reagan intervened in Grenada at least in part to protect himself from the threat—no matter how remote—of a politically scarring hostage situation. As Defense Secretary Weinberger later admitted, "The costs of not doing Grenada were obviously greater than the cost of doing it. We didn't want students held 440 days as hostages."[66]

But the intervention had more proactive motives as well. Reagan and his advisers saw the invasion of Grenada as the perfect opportunity to achieve a Cold War victory over communism. As CIA director William Casey proudly informed journalist Bob Woodward three days into the operation, Grenada was "an 'opportunity' to finally turn things our way" and reverse Soviet/Cuban expansionism in the Caribbean. The removal of Grenada's Leninist revolutionaries, Casey said, would be the first Soviet setback, the first "rollback" of communism, since World War II.[67] In fact, Grenada seemed almost made-to-order for an easy U.S. victory: a tiny, virtually defenseless island close to the United States, weakened by internal turmoil, and ruled by "a bloodstained left-wing regime with Cuban and Soviet connections." U.S. intervention would almost certainly be quick, inexpensive, and popular, with few American casualties. In that sense, Russell Burgos notes, the Grenada invasion was even better than rollback; it was "Rollback-Lite—Looks Great, Costs Less."[68]

As initial reports of Bishop's October 13 house arrest reached Washington, members of the National Security Council staff began lobbying informally for a military operation that would not only evacuate U.S. citizens but force regime change as well. When the idea was formally presented at an NSC meeting on the eighteenth, national security adviser McFarlane gave it his personal okay. By the twenty-second, Reagan and his top advisers were all "gung-ho" for a full-scale invasion that would remove the revolutionaries from power.[69]

Their enthusiasm was heightened by another prospective benefit of intervention, one that struck a particularly powerful chord in Reagan's administration. A U.S. military victory in Grenada would send a powerful message to the world: that after a long interlude of "enfeeblement" and malaise in the aftermath of Vietnam, the United States once again had the capability, and the will, to project its military power in defense of its interests. With the administration's "signal-sending" efforts in Central America constrained by congressional and public opposition, Grenada offered an extremely attractive alternative venue in which to demonstrate that U.S. power must again be taken seriously. According to Secretary of State Shultz, Grenada was "a shot heard round the world. . . . The report was sharp and clear: some Western democracies were again ready to use the military strength they had harbored and built up over the years in defense of their principles and interests. It raised the credibility of the U.S." As a member of the National Security Council staff put it: "The Grenada incursion reflected a sense of the Reagan administration from the very beginning that it was time to show, in the administration's words, that America was back, that we were cured of the post-Vietnam syndrome." In the words of another administration insider, the Grenada intervention "was not something terribly important in its own right but a symbol that 'America was back.'"[70]

The Beirut disaster reinforced the administration's determination to go ahead with the invasion as an urgently needed "symbolic" display of U.S. strength. Reagan viewed the crises in Lebanon and Grenada as closely related challenges to U.S. global influence by "sinister forces"—terrorists linked to Soviet proxy Syria in the case of Lebanon, communists supported by Soviet proxy Cuba in Grenada. In White House meetings on the twenty-third, the president and his top advisers debated whether the carnage in Beirut made the potential loss of U.S. lives in a Grenada invasion too risky or whether, conversely, Beirut made the planned invasion "all the more imperative as a sign of U.S. determination to stand up in defense of its perceived national interests." Some of Reagan's advisers argued the first view, but as one participant told a British journalist, "the President felt . . . that America was being kicked around as it had been when Carter was in charge. And . . . as he struggled mainly to cope with Beirut where he could *not* react, it crystallised in his mind that here [in Grenada] he bloody well could react—and would." In the end, Assistant Secretary of State Eagleburger told an interviewer, the events in Beirut increased the need to "demonstrate American resolve."[71]

The demonstration was intended for multiple audiences. Reagan and his advisers considered the invasion "a big message" to the Soviet Union that their administration was ready and willing to confront communism with military force—a "signal," in Secretary of State Shultz's words, that "Ronald Reagan [was] capable of action beyond rhetoric."[72] That warning, they believed, would have a particularly beneficial impact in Latin America. CIA director Casey told Bob Woodward that the Grenada invasion was important because it was sending the Soviets and Cubans a message: "That we might strike in Nicaragua." "Reagan was very conscious" of the invasion's potential effect on the Sandinistas, McFarlane recalls. "Also, he thought it would probably send some shivers up Castro's spine about whether or not they might be next." Staffers at the NSC repeatedly advised that the intervention would "have a positive political effect in Central America and throughout the Caribbean, encouraging our friends and demoralizing the violent communist groups." On the other hand, they warned, "our failure to act would be perceived in the region as weakness." Reagan, too, believed that U.S. credibility was at stake. In his view, the Beirut bombings made it imperative that the United States accept the OECS invitation and take decisive action against Grenada. "We cannot let an act of terrorism determine whether we aid or assist our allies in the region," he said. "If we do that, who will ever trust us again?" "The real issue here," Reagan told his staff, "is that we have four countries—the East Caribbean states—asking us to help. And if we get that request and say no, what signal does that send to NATO, to London, Bonn, Tokyo, and the industrial countries who are relying on us?"[73]

The intervention also sent a morale-boosting—and for Reagan, a politically beneficial—message to the American people. Reagan had entered office promising "to restore the morale and power of America." By October 1983, however, he had little to show for his efforts. A decisive military victory over Communist "thugs" in Grenada would help to restore Americans' self-confidence, rekindle the national spirit, and assuage the recent humiliations in Vietnam and Iran. It would show the American people that, thanks to his administration's leadership, the United States was, in his words, "back on its feet and standing tall."[74]

Beirut again reinforced the urgency of Reagan's need to convey that message. From a military standpoint, Steven Emerson writes, the Beirut bombings appeared to be

> the latest installment of an apparent curse of [U.S.] incompetence. The disaster threatened to become the Reagan Administration's equivalent of the Iranian hostage debacle. Once more the United States seemed helpless, either to protect its own people or to strike back. Again, American military men seemed unable to provide security or to gather intelligence about their country's enemies. All the technology, all the money, all the expertise that the United States possessed appeared worthless. Something was very deeply wrong. . . .

Moreover, this was the Reagan Presidency, whose leader had spoken of "standing tall" and making America first again. He had condemned his predecessor for failing to retaliate for terrorism and kidnapping. How would Reagan himself respond to the challenge?[75]

According to Reynold Burrowes, Reagan "had been elected on the basis that he would be tough with challenges to U.S. power in the Third World." Consequently, his "tragic" and "embarrassing" foreign-policy failure in Lebanon required "a bold move, one that would restore the president's credibility, especially as new elections approached."[76]

The "bold move" that resulted was Reagan's decision to proceed with the Grenada operation. In its political dimension, his response exemplified the "Teflon" nature of his presidency. As presidential biographer Lou Cannon notes, Reagan managed to avoid political damage from the bloodshed in Lebanon—"the greatest disaster" of his presidency, as measured by the loss of U.S. lives—"largely because the invasion of Grenada two days after the bombing in Beirut provided Americans with a victory to celebrate." When later asked how Reagan had been able to remain politically unscathed by the Beirut disaster, his White House communications director David Gergen replied: "Because two days later we were in Grenada, and everyone knew that Ronald Reagan would bomb the hell out of somewhere."[77]

The intervention in Grenada was the first major foreign-policy victory of Reagan's presidency, and he milked the accomplishment for all it was worth. Over the course of the next year—in public speeches and press conferences, in White House photo-ops with returned U.S. medical students, and elsewhere—the president and his advisers skillfully exploited the military triumph to bolster Reagan's domestic image in the run-up to the 1984 election.

Three days into the operation, Reagan was already claiming that his assertive response to the situation had protected the United States from an imminent and dangerous communist threat. In a national television address on the twenty-seventh, he stated that U.S. forces in Grenada had "discovered a complete [Cuban military] base with weapons and communications equipment, which makes it clear that a Cuban occupation of the island had been planned." One warehouse, Reagan continued, "contained weapons and ammunition stacked almost to the ceiling, enough to supply thousands of terrorists. Grenada, we were told, was a friendly island paradise for tourism. Well, it wasn't. It was a Soviet-Cuban colony, being readied as a major military bastion to export terror and undermine democracy. We got there just in time."[78] The president also took the occasion to remind the American people that his swift action had prevented the 1,000 U.S. citizens on the island from being "harmed or held as hostages."[79]

The administration also claimed that the U.S. military victory in Grenada had gone a long way toward restoring the United States' international credibility. "Four years ago," Reagan told a Houston audience, "our adversaries and even our friends were counting us out. Defeatism was the order of the day." But "We took action" in Grenada, he said, and in the process "we have again assumed our role as the leading force for freedom in the world." "We have put America back on the map," he declared three weeks later.[80]

Secretary of State Shultz was more specific. "There were many signals sent by the Grenada operation," he wrote:

In many different parts of the world, people began to get the message: Ronald Reagan is capable of action beyond rhetoric. Latin Americans in particular saw that if a country went nose to nose with Uncle Sam, Fidel Castro could not, or would not, come to its rescue.

A few days after the Grenada operation, [leftist leader] Desi Bouterse in Suriname abruptly changed course. He threw out the large Cuban contingent and all but broke diplomatic relations with Cuba. Within a week of the Grenada operation, Tomas Borge, a Nicaraguan *comandante*, called on our ambassador, Anthony Quainton, to inform him that if the United States ever wanted to evacuate Americans from Nicaragua, please call Borge and he would facilitate their departure. I saw some of the same reactions . . . in Paris when I heard reports of Syrian concerns that they might be next. Grenada had a strong rippling effect in faraway places.[81]

In Reagan's spin, the U.S. victory in Grenada not only garnered renewed international respect for the United States, it was an important first step in restoring the nation's self-confidence as well. "During the latter part of the 1970s," he recalled in a 1984 White House address,

America passed through a period of self-doubt and national confusion. We talked and acted like a nation in decline, and the world believed us. Many questioned our will to continue as a leader of the Western alliance and to remain a force for good in the world. But I believe this period of self-doubt is over. History will record that one of the turning points came on a small island in the Caribbean where America went to take care of her own and to rescue a neighboring nation from a growing tyranny.[82]

In his public speeches during the 1984 election campaign, Reagan routinely and—according to Lou Cannon, "shamelessly"—invoked Grenada as a symbol of his strong leadership. "Because we were willing to take decisive action," he told the Veterans of Foreign Wars in August, "our students today are safe, Grenada is free, and that region of the Caribbean is more peaceful and secure than before."[83]

"When we got to Washington," he declared at a Corpus Christi rally, "the enemies of freedom were on the move. They were encouraged by what they saw as a lack of will in the previous administration. . . . Well, I'm proud to say that . . . [i]n the last four years, not one square inch of territory has been lost to Communist aggression. And, in one case, with quick and decisive action, we protected hundreds of American medical students from a potential hostile situation and restored freedom to the people of Grenada."[84] Three weeks later, in a flag-draped White House ceremony marking the intervention's first anniversary, Reagan told a carefully selected group of "rescued" medical students that

> using military force is . . . the most serious decision any President must make. It's an awesome responsibility. But the evidence to me was clear. At stake was the freedom of 110,000 Grenadians, the security of the democracies of the Eastern Caribbean and, most important, the safety and well-being of you American medical students. . . . So, we approved a military operation to rescue you, to help the people of Grenada, and to prevent the spread of chaos and totalitarianism throughout the Caribbean.[85]

References to Grenada in the president's campaign speeches were usually accompanied by stirring, and implicitly self-congratulatory, proclamations that the United States' post-Vietnam era of "paralyzing self-doubt" had ended, that "our days of weakness" were over, and that America was "back."[86]

The results were all that the president could have hoped for. Within two weeks of the invasion, public opinion polls showed that 71 percent of the American people approved of the intervention, and Reagan suddenly found himself leading his two principal Democratic presidential challengers for the first time in months. By January 1984, when he announced his intention to run for a second term, his presidential approval rating had skyrocketed from the thirties into the sixties. Ahead lay "a free ride" to his uncontested renomination—"the first for any incumbent president since Dwight Eisenhower in 1956"—and "a strong running start" toward his eventual landslide victory in November.[87] A quick and easy military victory in Grenada—a "nine-day pushover," as one account describes it—had proven to be a healthy tonic for a faltering presidency. Skillfully exploited by a media-savvy White House, the intervention had diverted the nation's attention away from economic recession, high unemployment, budget deficits, and a foreign-policy catastrophe in the Middle East, and allowed Reagan to refurbish his image as a strong, effective, and popular president.[88]

CHAPTER EIGHT

Panama, 1989

In an early morning television address from the Oval Office on December 20, 1989, President George H. W. Bush informed the American people that he had just ordered U.S. military forces to invade Panama. Bush offered four reasons for the invasion: (1) "to safeguard the lives of . . . the 35,000 American citizens in Panama"; (2) "to combat drug trafficking" and "bring [Panamanian dictator Manuel] Noriega, . . . an indicted drug trafficker, . . . to justice"; (3) "to defend democracy in Panama"; and (4) "to protect the integrity of the [1977] Panama Canal treaty."[1] For anyone familiar with U.S.-Panamanian relations in the period leading up to the intervention, there was ample reason to question the validity of each of the president's stated motives.

First, although members of Noriega's Panamanian Defense Forces (PDF) had killed a U.S. Marine and roughed up a U.S. naval lieutenant and his wife on December 16, the acts of violence were precipitated by a war of nerves that the Bush administration had initiated two months earlier in an apparent effort to provoke Noriega into providing a justification for intervention. If Bush's primary concern was the safety of U.S. citizens in Panama, he might first have terminated the U.S. campaign of provocation and stopped trying to bait Noriega into committing violent acts against Americans. A large-scale U.S. military invasion that resulted in the deaths of twenty-four Americans (along with hundreds, if not thousands, of Panamanians) seemed a rather incongruous strategy if the goal was to save lives.[2]

Second, if Bush was seeking to stanch the massive flow of narcotics entering the United States from Latin America at the end of the 1980s, there were many more significant targets for U.S. military action than Manuel Noriega. It was true that Noriega had profited handsomely from business dealings with Colombia's Medellín drug cartel, but his involvement consisted primarily of allowing the cartel to transship drugs and launder money in Panama in exchange for millions of dollars in kickbacks. He was never more than a minor player in the world of international narcotics trafficking, and—as U.S. officials were well aware at the time of the intervention—he had retired from active participation in the drug trade in March 1986. Paradoxically, Noriega had also worked closely with the U.S. Drug Enforcement Agency, providing so much valuable assistance to its drug-interdiction operations in Panama that agency officials considered him a key ally and trusted collaborator in the U.S. war on drugs. (In fact, several agency officials were prepared to testify in Noriega's defense when he was eventually brought to trial on drug-trafficking charges in the United States.) Consequently, Bush's antinarcotics rationale for the 1989 intervention seemed, as Thomas Carothers puts it, "hollow" at best.[3]

Third, the track record of U.S. policy toward Panama during Noriega's years in power made it difficult to believe that a desire to defend democracy was a decisive determinant of Bush's decision to intervene. If a democratizing impulse impelled Bush to order the December 1989 invasion, no such dedication to ideological activism had been evident five months earlier when Noriega's bloody quashing of a Panamanian presidential election elicited little more than verbal protests from the United States. A few years earlier, President Reagan and Vice President George Bush had responded to Noriega's blatant theft of a 1984 election and subsequent ouster of incumbent president Nicolás Ardito Barletta in 1985 with a policy of passive acquiescence bordering on approval. Moreover, as critics of the 1989 intervention pointed out at the time, Bush's concern with democracy in Panama seemed curiously selective; why—if democracy was the issue—did he not unleash U.S. military power on Libya's Muammar Khaddafi, Syria's Hafez Assad, Indonesia's Suharto, or the many other Third World dictators who were at least as unsavory as Manuel Noriega?[4]

Fourth, Noriega had done nothing to threaten either the Panama Canal treaties or the canal itself. No Panamanian leader of any political persuasion was likely to place in jeopardy treaties that mandated the transfer of the canal to Panamanian sovereignty by the year 2000. And as Pentagon officials privately acknowledged at the time of the intervention, the waterway itself was in no danger whatsoever. Nor had Noriega threatened U.S. access to the canal.[5]

Why, then, *did* Bush invade Panama? A more accurate and candid explanation would have required the president to discuss factors unmentioned in his December 20 television address: namely, the successful manipulation of U.S. public opinion by Noriega's Panamanian political enemies and the resulting U.S. domestic political pressures that eventually led Bush to carry out a military intervention.

The Panama invasion was a major departure from preceding U.S. interventions in the region in the sense that the target of U.S. hostility was not a Marxist leader or movement but a right-wing military officer who had worked closely with the United States for three decades. Manuel Noriega was, in fact, precisely the kind of Latin American leader the United States had so often accepted as an ally in the struggle against international communism. By virtually all accounts, he was ruthless, sadistic, utterly amoral, thoroughly corrupt, and authoritarian to his core.[6]

A career in the military had enabled Noriega to overcome unpromising origins in the slums of Panama City. As a young junior officer, he attached himself to the coattails of his politically ambitious garrison commander, Col. Omar Torrijos, and advanced rapidly—earning a notorious reputation for raping prostitutes, torturing prisoners, and killing leftists along the way. After Torrijos seized power in a 1968 coup, Noriega was promoted to high-level positions, first as a military zone commander, then in 1970 as chief of national intelligence—a position that made him the second most powerful man in Torrijos' dictatorship, with powers equivalent to those of the directors of the CIA and FBI combined. Noriega exploited his new power to amass personal wealth from a variety of illicit activities, including arms smuggling and money laundering. After Torrijos died mysteriously in a 1981 plane crash, Noriega quickly muscled rival officers aside and became Panama's military commander in chief, giving him de facto control of the country. Elevated power offered him new sources of outside income, particularly in the emerging growth industry of international narcotics trafficking. A 1989 report by the Senate Foreign Relations Committee's Narcotics Subcommittee described the basic dynamics of Noriega's dictatorship: by 1983,

> Noriega [had] gained control of the Customs, Immigration, and Passport Services, Civil Aeronautics, the National Bank of Panama, and the Attorney General's Office, which together represented the major Panamanian institutions with jurisdiction over the narcotics trade. Noriega pushed legislation through the National Assembly consolidating the National Guard, Air Force, Navy, police and Customs under a single command called the Panamanian Defense Forces (PDF). As head of the PDF, Noriega now controlled all elements of the Panamanian government essential to the protection of drug trafficking and money laundering, thus accomplishing two goals simultaneously: increasing his control over Panama and enriching himself. Noriega turned Panama's political system into what one [committee] witness called a "narcokleptocracy," a system in which Panamanian government became controlled by personal loyalties to Noriega, cemented by graft and corruption, and substantially funded with narcotics money.[7]

The financial rewards were impressive. Working in partnership with Colombia's newly formed Medellín drug cartel, Noriega pocketed $100,000 to $200,000 for each planeload of cocaine and marijuana that the cartel transshipped through Panama to the United States. For helping his Medellín partners launder their drug profits in Panamanian banks, he received monthly commissions of up to $4 million. By the time of his ouster in 1989, his net worth was estimated at between $200 million and $800 million.[8]

Noriega's ties to the United States dated back to his military-cadet days in the late 1950s, when the CIA recruited him as a paid informant. During the 1960s, U.S. training at the School of the Americas , Fort Bragg, and other installations helped him develop his intelligence-gathering and counterintelligence capabilities. His value to the United States increased significantly during the 1970s, when, as Panama's chief of intelligence, he regularly supplied U.S. intelligence agencies with what they regarded as some of their best information about Cuba, Latin American guerrilla movements, and—beginning in 1979—Nicaragua's Sandinista government. As his services to the United States increased in importance, so did his compensation: by the mid-1970s, the CIA was secretly paying him $110,000 per year—by the early 1980s, $200,000.[9]

The high point in Noriega's collaboration with the United States came between 1981 and 1985, when—as Panama's new military strongman—he helped the Reagan administration conduct its anticommunist crusade in the Caribbean basin. During this period, the intelligence information he provided about Castro's Cuba was considered so valuable that Reagan's CIA director, William Casey, traveled to Panama for personal briefings by the Panamanian dictator. Noriega's active support for Reagan's Contra war in Nicaragua won him even greater esteem in Washington. From the start, he worked hand in hand with Casey, Oliver North, and Reagan's other key Central American operatives—facilitating arms shipments to Contra units; providing them with money, training facilities, and safe transit through Panama; conducting espionage operations in Nicaragua on behalf of the United States; helping to blow up a major Sandinista military arsenal in 1985; and even offering at one point to assassinate the entire Sandinista leadership. So important was his support of U.S. policy in Central America and the Caribbean that by the mid-1980s CIA and Pentagon officials regarded him as an indispensable and crucial ally.[10]

An indispensable ally Noriega may have been, but a trustworthy friend he was not. Always the consummate opportunist, he habitually worked both sides of every street, selling his services to anyone who would pay for them. During the 1970s, while earning hefty paychecks on the CIA's payroll, he simultaneously worked for the Cuban intelligence service—supplying Fidel Castro's government with sensitive information about U.S. operations; facilitating shipments of Cuban weapons to Marxist insurgents in El Salvador, Guatemala, and Colombia and helping arm the Sandinistas in their insurrection against Somoza; helping Castro circumvent the U.S. trade embargo against Cuba by permitting Cuban companies to secretly purchase U.S. computers and other advanced technology in Panama's Colón Free Zone; and granting base rights at the Panamanian port of Vacamonte to Cuba's Pacific fishing fleet as it conducted intelligence missions and smuggled weapons to leftist forces up and down the Pacific coast of Latin America.[11] In 1976, in what journalist Kevin Buckley described as "one of the largest intelligence thefts against the United States in recent history," Noriega bribed several employees of a U.S. National Security Agency electronic-eavesdropping facility in the Canal Zone to supply him with copies of the agency's communications intercepts and other top-secret documents about U.S. electronic-surveillance operations in the hemisphere—a gold mine of classified information that U.S. officials suspected ended up in Castro's hands.[12] He also worked both sides of the drug war—assisting the U.S. Drug Enforcement Agency in drug busts against small-time Panamanian drug dealers he disliked while simultaneously raking in massive profits as a business partner of Colombia's drug lords.[13]

U.S. officials were well aware of their Panamanian ally's duplicity and criminality, but they valued his services too greatly to sever ties with him. After all, as Reagan's national security adviser Colin Powell explained matter-of-factly, "Cold War politics sometimes made for creepy bedfellows." Or as one CIA official put it: "Not all our sources are people you'd take home to meet mother. You have to use them anyway." Noriega was always regarded as useful despite his proclivity for double-dealing. His links to Cuba, for example, were known and accepted by U.S. intelligence agencies because they believed that the information he supplied them about Cuba far outweighed the information he was providing Castro about the United States. ("Sure, Noriega worked for the Cubans," a U.S. agent later recalled, "but we calculated he belonged twenty percent to them and eighty percent to us.") The Reagan administration continued to "coddle" Panama's dictator through the mid-1980s because it believed that his criminality and authoritarianism were far less important than his support of U.S. policy in Nicaragua. It was Reagan's CIA director Casey who perhaps best summed up the prevailing U.S. view of Noriega when he said of the Panamanian leader: "He's a bastard, but he's our bastard."[14]

By the mid-1980s, Noriega's Panamanian political opponents were waging war on him—not in the streets of Panama City but in the U.S. news media and on Capitol Hill. Based mainly in the urban middle class, their ranks included civilian politicians seeking free elections, businessmen and professionals demanding commercial freedom and respect for civil liberties, and defectors from the dictatorship maneuvering to take over Noriega's authoritarian system and maintain "business as usual" without Noriega. Weak and disunited, lacking a mass base of popular support, and reluctant to physically confront the dictator's PDF troops and riot police, they turned instead to the United States for help. According to scholar Richard Millett, most members of the opposition "blamed their plight on U.S. policies. In their view, Noriega and the PDF were U.S. creations," armed and trained by the United States, and sustained in power by U.S. economic and military assistance. Some opposition leaders were convinced that if they could change U.S. policy and persuade Washington to withdraw its support of Noriega, they would be able to overthrow the dictatorship relatively easily. Others believed that a U.S. military intervention would be needed to oust Noriega. (As one opposition leader informed a U.S. newspaper reporter: "You created the monster, so you kick him out.")[15] But they all shared one strategic goal in common: to bring Noriega down by turning the United States against him.

In June 1985, Panamanian newspaper publisher Roberto Eisenmann arrived in the United States to begin a yearlong fellowship at Harvard University's Nieman Foundation for Journalism. Eisenmann had long been a vocal critic of military rule in Panama, and his feisty opposition daily *La Prensa* had at various times been shut down and "viciously vandalized" by Noriega's troops for printing exposés of government corruption and PDF involvement in the drug trade. In 1978, he gained valuable insight into the process of influencing U.S. policy when he testified before a U.S. congressional subcommittee that was investigating the Torrijos dictatorship's human-rights abuses. After describing Torrijos' frequent practice of forcing his political enemies into exile, Eisenmann became frustrated with the subcommittee members for failing to express sufficient concern over his revelations. When he asked the congressmen, in exasperation, if 40,000 Panamanian political refugees living in the United States would upset Congress, Representative Clarence D. Long (D-MD) replied: "If they voted in our district it would." For Eisenmann, the message was clear and the lesson obvious: the U.S. Congress was more concerned with the U.S. electorate than with human-rights violations in Panama. Political pressure from the U.S. voting public must therefore be the key to influencing U.S. policy makers.[16]

It was that tactical premise that guided Eisenmann's efforts when he returned to the United States in 1985. Convinced that the Reagan administration would not abandon Noriega "unless domestic politics made it unavoidable," he immediately launched a campaign to discredit the Panamanian dictator in the eyes of the U.S. public by generating negative coverage of him in the U.S. news media. From his Harvard base, he utilized the Nieman Foundation's influence networks to cultivate important U.S. media contacts. Playing on the issue of press censorship in Panama and his experience as the publisher of a victimized newspaper, he quickly gained the attention of influential East Coast journalists; with his insider's knowledge of the media, he was able to give them the "hard leads and verifiable facts" they required. His fluency in English also helped. Soon he was showing up on the *MacNeil-Lehrer NewsHour*, ABC's *Nightline*, and other television news programs, detailing Noriega's crimes before national U.S. viewing audiences, charging that the PDF had a "Made in the U.S.A." label on it, and publicly chastising U.S. policy makers for their moral bankruptcy in giving aid to a "Mafia gang" like the Noriega regime.[17]

In December 1985, another of Noriega's Panamanian political enemies, attorney Winston Spadafora, arrived in the United States to lobby against the dictator. Three months earlier, Spadafora's brother Hugo—a charismatic political activist and one of Noriega's harshest critics—had been savagely murdered by the dictator's PDF henchmen. When Panama's compromised Justice Ministry failed to file charges in the case, Spadafora traveled to Washington, D.C., to enlist support from the United States and the Organization of American States in a crusade to see Noriega prosecuted for murder. In January 1986, he called on Senator Jesse Helms (R-NC), the chairman of the Senate Foreign Relations Committee's Western Hemisphere subcommittee. Helms, who had fiercely opposed the 1978 Panama Canal treaties, was always looking for new evidence to back his contention that "Panama's leaders were simply too corrupt to be entrusted with the Canal." Spadafora described for the senator the gruesome details of Hugo's murder—which included lengthy torture, homosexual rape, and decapitation—and showed him grisly photographs from the autopsy. Sickened, Helms told Spadafora: "I'm going to promise to work my hardest to get justice for your brother and to raise the issue to the level of President Reagan's agenda." True to his word, Helms quickly convened Senate subcommittee hearings in March and April to provide the Panamanian opposition with a forum. Among the witnesses was Norman Bailey, a former U.S. National Security Council staff member, who testified that drug trafficking was endemic in Panama's government and that Noriega was widely suspected of ordering Hugo Spadafora's murder. Helms' hearings produced no spectacular headlines in the United States, but they caught the attention of other influential congressmen and a few D.C.-based journalists.[18]

Meanwhile, Eisenmann's media campaign was about to pull off a major coup. At the Nieman Foundation, Eisenmann persuaded director Howard Simon, a former *Washington Post* managing editor, that Noriega's relationship with the United States was "a great story waiting to be told." Simon put the Panamanian publisher in contact with Seymour Hersh, the prominent investigative reporter who had won a Pulitzer Prize for uncovering the My Lai massacre in Vietnam. Hersh's interest in Noriega had already been piqued by the Helms hearings, and he was eager to talk with Eisenmann. The two men met on May 22, 1986, and afterward Eisenmann sent the reporter a note that read: "I don't want to sound dramatic, but two million freedom-loving Panamanians could be depending on your success in breaking this [Reagan administration] cover-up and support of a terrible man. . . . I'll be in touch."[19] Three weeks later, an explosive Hersh article examining the U.S.-Noriega connection appeared on the front page of the *New York Times*. According to the article, U.S. officials were well aware that their longtime Panamanian ally was a drug-dealing murderer and a Cuban double agent. Citing "senior State Department, White House, Pentagon and intelligence officials" as his sources, Hersh described Noriega's deep involvement in "illicit money laundering and drug activities," his role in helping Cuba acquire "restricted American technology" and highly sensitive National Security Agency intelligence materials, and his smuggling of arms to Cuban-trained Marxist guerrillas in Colombia. The article claimed that the U.S. Defense Intelligence Agency had communications intercepts "demonstrating that General Noriega ordered the killing" of Hugo Spadafora. And it reported that "officials of the Reagan administration and past administrations" admitted "in interviews" that they had deliberately "overlooked General Noriega's illegal activities" because they considered him to be "a valuable asset."[20]

Hersh's exposé was the big break Eisenmann had been hoping for in his effort to make Noriega a public issue in the United States. The embarrassing reality of the U.S. government's long and "immoral" alliance with a corrupt, sadistic dictator had suddenly been thrust before the U.S. public eye by the nation's preeminent newspaper, as reported by a highly respected U.S. journalist and backed up, not by politically self-interested members of the Panamanian opposition, but by authoritative-sounding "senior" U.S. government sources. Better still, the article had an immediate multiplier effect in the U.S. media. Within days, three other major U.S.

news outlets—the *Washington Post*, NBC News, and the *Miami Herald*—ran independently reported stories on Noriega, and the *MacNeil-Lehrer NewsHour* aired a feature segment examining Hersh's charges in detail.[21]

Eisenmann quickly followed up with a new round of media appearances to inform the American people of the plight that Panamanians were suffering under their U.S.-supported military regime. Meanwhile, Helms' efforts were beginning to attract bipartisan interest on Capitol Hill. After sitting in on a few of Helms' subcommittee hearings in the spring, Senator John Kerry, a liberal Democrat from Massachusetts, sensed that his North Carolina colleague was "onto something." In September, the two senators co-sponsored an amendment to the Intelligence Appropriations bill requiring the CIA to report to the House and Senate intelligence committees on the PDF's involvement in criminal activities, including the Spadafora killing. The amendment passed. Four months later, Kerry's Senate Subcommittee on Terrorism, Narcotics, and International Communications launched "an exhaustive investigation" into Noriega's links to the drug world. The subcommittee hearings, which featured colorful testimony from imprisoned drug pilots and money launderers, generated substantial press coverage. By early 1987, Noriega's photograph was appearing daily in the U.S. news media, and increasing numbers of congressmen were asking why the Reagan administration was continuing to do business with such a repugnant dictator.[22]

June 1987 was a particularly busy month for Panama's opposition. In a series of sensational press interviews in Panama City on the sixth and seventh, Col. Roberto Díaz Herrera—whom Noriega had forcibly retired as his second in command a week earlier—revealed inside details about PDF corruption and directly implicated Noriega in the deaths of both Spadafora and Torrijos. Díaz Herrera's revelations sparked a wave of public protests in the Panamanian capital and prompted the opposition's newly created umbrella organization, the National Civic Crusade, to organize demonstrations demanding an end to military rule. Noriega responded with a vicious crackdown, deploying his riot police—aptly named the "Dobermans"—to beat and arrest the demonstrators. The violent repression immediately became a nightly feature of U.S. television news and provided Eisenmann with new opportunities to influence U.S. public opinion. In a June 18 appearance on the *MacNeil-Lehrer NewsHour*, he charged that the Reagan administration found it easier and more efficient to achieve its policy goals in Panama by dealing with a dictator than by working with an elected government. U.S. support of Noriega, he implied, was trampling democracy in Panama. "For God's sake," he implored his American viewing audience, "get on the right side, get on the democratic side before it's too late."[23]

A few days earlier, another of Noriega's Panamanian political enemies, Gabriel Lewis, arrived in Washington. A multimillionaire businessman, Lewis had served as Panama's ambassador to the United States during the Panama Canal treaty negotiations, and in the process he had acquired influential friends in the U.S. Congress, including Senator Edward Kennedy (D-MA) and other Democrats who supported the treaties' ratification. After clashing repeatedly with Noriega over business matters, Lewis was forced to flee Panama in June 1987 when he suggested that the dictator should consider stepping down for the good of the country. In D.C., he immediately set up a branch office of the National Civic Crusade and launched "a vigorous lobbying campaign" aimed at pressuring the Reagan administration to reverse policy and force Noriega from power. Through his tireless efforts on Capitol Hill, he soon succeeded in welding together a strong bipartisan coalition of anti-Noriega senators led by Democrats Kennedy and Kerry and Republicans Helms and Alphonse D'Amato of New York, another of Lewis' friends. Eisenmann would later call Lewis' bipartisan base of Senate support "a vital ingredient" in the opposition's drive "to disconnect the U.S. government from Noriega. . . . We [now] had both sides of the aisle, right and left, committed to our Cause," thereby "avoiding an ideological seal on our efforts." Tangible results came quickly. Working closely with Kennedy's staff, Lewis helped draft a Senate resolution that called for a public accounting of Díaz Herrera's allegations and urged the Reagan administration to "direct the current commander of the Panama Defense Forces and any other implicated officials to relinquish their duties pending the outcome of the independent investigation." The resolution passed on June 26, by a nearly unanimous vote. [24]

Then, in December 1987, José Blandón, one of Noriega's closest confidantes and most trusted political advisers, defected to the opposition from his post as Panama's consul in New York City. Blandón had been intimately involved in many of Noriega's secret diplomatic and business dealings, and the sordid details that he was soon divulging in congressional testimony and media interviews made Hersh's *New York Times* exposé seem bland by comparison. In one anecdote, Blandón recounted a 1984 episode in which the Medellín drug lords put out a contract to kill Noriega in the belief that he had stolen $5 million from them, and Fidel Castro mediated the dispute, saving the dictator's life. Such fascinating new revelations provided another "bonanza for American newspapers, radio stations, and TV networks" and helped keep Noriega in the forefront of U.S. public attention. [25]

As 1988 began, Eisenmann and his colleagues had reason to be proud of their accomplishments. Thanks to the media coverage they had generated and the bipartisan support they had mobilized in Congress, the Reagan administration was under growing pressure to "do something" about Noriega. And with a U.S. presidential election campaign about to get under way, the administration's relationship with the dictator was certain to be one of the "hot-button" issues in American politics in the months ahead. The opposition's strategy was working to perfection.

The initial spate of anti-Noriega publicity in the United States had what former U.S. ambassador to Panama Ambler Moss describes as "considerable . . . repercussions" on the Reagan administration, and it quickly forced the administration to take a "new look" at its Panama policy. In June 1986, shortly after the publication of Hersh's *New York Times* exposé, the *Washington Post* reported that U.S. officials were split between "those who favored 'overlooking' the problem and those who argued that Noriega's vices could no longer be 'ignored.'" According to the *Post* story, a senior administration official admitted that "'in the past we've needed' Noriega but that Hersh's charges might force a reevaluation of the relationship."[26] Nevertheless, Noriega's supporters in the CIA, Defense Department, and National Security Council successfully argued that the Panamanian leader's assistance, particularly to the Nicaraguan Contras, made him too valuable an asset to lose. As a result, the administration's existing policy was reaffirmed, and as the State Department's Frank McNeil recalls: "A decision was made to put Noriega on the shelf until Nicaragua was settled." [27]

Events soon "settled" Nicaragua, although not in the way that Reagan would have chosen. During the autumn of 1986 it was revealed that the administration had violated U.S. law by secretly supplying the Contras with funds diverted from covert arms sales to the government of Iran. The Iran-Contra scandal and the political firestorm that it ignited brought an ignominious end to the administration's counterrevolutionary operations in Nicaragua—and in the process significantly reduced Noriega's value as a U.S. ally. Concurrently, Noriega was losing two of his strongest administration supporters. In late 1986, Oliver North was forced to resign from the National Security Council because of his involvement in Iran-Contra, and CIA director Casey was hospitalized with brain cancer. Casey died five months later. [28]

June 1987 generated new pressures on the administration to reconsider its relationship with Noriega. The dictator's violent suppression of the mass protests that followed Col. Díaz Herrera's revelations graphically heightened U.S. public awareness of Noriega's brutality. When the U.S. Senate, spurred on by Gabriel Lewis' lobbying activities, passed its resolution calling on Noriega to step down, the infuriated dictator again responded with violence. Four days after the Senate action, a pro-Noriega mob attacked the U.S. embassy in Panama City, causing extensive damage. The fact that Panamanian police assigned to guard the embassy were withdrawn shortly before the mob arrived suggested strongly that the Panamanian government had orchestrated the attack—presumably as a warning to the Senate that Noriega would not be intimidated by U.S. criticism. [29]

The embassy attack forced the Reagan administration to conclude that a working relationship with Noriega was no longer politically sustainable. In July, the administration suspended U.S. economic and military assistance to Panama and removed Noriega from the CIA payroll. Five months later, Assistant Secretary of Defense Richard Armitage visited Panama and informed Noriega that the Reagan administration now viewed him as a problem and wanted him to resign. By the end of 1987, Washington's indispensable intelligence asset in Panama had become an embarrassing political liability.[30]

He became even more of a liability in February 1988, when two U.S. federal grand juries, operating independently of the Reagan administration, indicted Noriega on multiple counts of narcotics trafficking. The indictments left the administration with no choice but to adopt a more aggressive anti-Noriega policy. Politically, Thomas Carothers writes, Reagan simply "could not afford to be seen tolerating" an indicted drug dealer—not at a time when the toxic political fallout from Iran-Contra was threatening to undermine his presidency, and certainly not in an election year in which his own vice president was campaigning to succeed him in the White House. A "get tough" policy toward Noriega now became "an unquestionable political necessity."[31]

Less than three weeks after the indictments were announced, Reagan told a White House press conference that he wanted to see "a return to democracy and a civilian government in Panama." Secretary of State George Shultz reinforced that message in early March when he told reporters: "We are anxious to see General Noriega get out of there." At the same time, however, the administration openly disavowed military intervention as a policy option. In March, Reagan stated publicly that the United States would not use military force to push Noriega out of power. A month later, Treasury Secretary James Baker reiterated that the administration had ruled out "putting our military assets into play" in Panama.[32]

Instead, the administration opted for a combination of economic pressure and diplomatic negotiations to secure Noriega's removal. In March, Reagan imposed economic sanctions, freezing Panamanian assets in the United States and suspending U.S. payments to Noriega's government. Delays and exemptions, however, prevented the sanctions from achieving the desired result.[33] Then in May, U.S. diplomats offered the dictator a deal: the United States would drop the indictments and end its economic sanctions in exchange for Noriega's voluntary retirement and the restoration of civilian government in Panama. Noriega mulled the offer over for a while but eventually declined, telling a reporter that he enjoyed being "a pain in the rear" of the United States.[34]

By mid-1988, Reagan's efforts to rid himself of his erstwhile Panamanian ally had gone nowhere. Worse still, his offer to lift Noriega's U.S. drug indictments had inadvertently damaged Vice President Bush's presidential election campaign. Behind the scenes of White House policy making, Panama's dictator had become a divisive issue in Republican Party campaign politics.

For the Bush campaign, Manuel Noriega was a potential Achilles' heel from the very beginning. "Noriega was one of those things that fell into the category of the less you had to say about it, the better," Craig Fuller, the vice president's chief of staff, later recalled. "We felt at all times that George Bush was vulnerable on the issue, in the sense that we thought the other side would raise it." Fuller was correct. During the Republican primaries, Senator Robert Dole of Kansas—Bush's principal rival for the party's nomination—charged that Bush had known about, and condoned, Noriega's criminal activities both as the Ford administration's CIA director in 1976–1977 and as Reagan's vice president after 1980. According to Dole, Bush and other U.S. officials had been "playing footsie with this guy" for years even though they "knew, or . . . ought to have known" that Noriega "was up to his eyeballs in dirty drugs and anti-American politics."[35]

The Democrats were also quick to play the Noriega card. By April, Massachusetts governor Michael Dukakis, the Democratic front-runner, was raising questions about Bush's past ties to the Panamanian strongman. "How about telling us who in this administration was dealing with Noriega," he asked during a party debate. "Who was paying Noriega? Who was ignoring the fact that we knew he was dealing in drugs and making millions and we're still doing business with him?" Soon, Democratic bumper stickers reading "Bush-Noriega '88—You Know They Can Work Together" were rolling off the party's printing presses.[36]

The Bush camp responded to the attacks with what journalist Frederick Kempe describes as "a maze of . . . confusing and contradictory statements." Initially, Bush tried to claim that he had never met Noriega. When a photograph appeared showing the two men together, his aides were forced to admit that at least two personal meetings had taken place—one in 1976 and another in 1983. Bush also maintained that he had known nothing about Noriega's involvement in the drug trade until the February 1988 indictments. Going further, he tried to take partial credit for the indictments, telling a group of Ohio high-school students in early May that "when it became demonstrably clear that Noriega was involved in drugs we moved against him, with an indictment." "It is our administration," Bush said, "that is trying to bring this man to justice, once we found out he had gone bad." A few days later, however, a *New York Times* story, citing White House and State Department sources, reported that the U.S. ambassador to Panama had briefed the vice president in 1985 about Noriega's drug trafficking. Bush categorically denied the story's charges. But when his foreign-policy adviser, Donald Gregg, testified under oath that the 1985 briefing had in fact covered drugs, at least "in a general way," Bush's staff was forced into damage-control mode. The vice president wasn't "trying to suggest that he didn't know Panama had a narcotics problem and that Noriega . . . might have some involvement," Fuller explained. "What he was really saying is that" he had no "*certain* knowledge" or hard evidence linking Noriega to drugs "until after the indictments."[37]

By mid-May, the drug issue was threatening to derail Bush's campaign. A majority of Americans believed that narcotics were now the most dangerous security threat facing the nation—more dangerous even than communism. And, as journalist Kevin Buckley writes, "Noriega had become the ugly symbol of the reigning evil." According to *New York Times* and *Washington Post*/ABC News polls, 58 percent of voters disapproved of the Reagan administration's Panama policies, while only 36 percent believed the administration was dealing successfully with international narcotics trafficking; a mere 24 percent thought that Bush would conduct the U.S. war on drugs as effectively as Dukakis. Overall, the vice president trailed his Democratic rival by ten points in the race for the presidency.[38]

Consequently, Reagan's decision on May 11 to offer to throw out Noriega's U.S. drug indictments in exchange for the dictator's retirement produced near-panic in the Bush camp. In a series of White House meetings that Secretary of State George Shultz described as "wild" and "wilder," the vice president and his campaign advisers vehemently opposed the president's decision, arguing that it would be "political suicide in an election year" for Bush to appear to be "going soft" on Panama's "drug dictator" by letting him "go free of the drug charges." "The Democrats will eat us up on this," Bush's campaign manager James Baker warned. "How can we make the argument we're getting tough on drug dealers if we let this guy off?" Bush asked the president. For the next 12 days, a policy dispute that one administration official characterized as "monumental" raged inside the White House, with Reagan and Bush going "toe-to-toe" over the issue.[39]

Reagan remained adamant, arguing that the indictments forced him to take some form of action to remove Noriega, and that the only available options were to persuade the dictator to leave power voluntarily or to intervene militarily and force him out. "There is no alternative to this deal except troops," Reagan told Bush. "What you guys are settling for," the president complained, "is that we have to go in there with considerable loss of life, and how does that look to the rest of Latin America?" Secretary of State Shultz energetically backed Reagan's position, warning that if "fearful" members of the administration "kill this deal [with Noriega], then we have to support tougher measures—like go in and get him."[40]

Meanwhile, press leaks about an impending deal with the dictator had set off a storm of "scathing and bipartisan" public criticism in the United States. Reporters began hounding Bush with difficult questions at every campaign stop. Smelling blood, Dukakis also criticized the reported deal, asking campaign audiences "how I and people like me can go to . . . children and their parents today and tell them to say 'no' to drugs when we've got an Administration in Washington that can't say 'no' to Noriega." "There will be no more dealing with drug-running Panamanian dictators" in a Dukakis administration, the Democratic candidate promised.[41]

Soon the vice president's aides were complaining that "Bush can't make a speech these days with any credibility about drugs if we're dealing with the drug kingpin of the world." Bush's campaign handlers now frantically urged him to break publicly with the president over the Noriega issue and to do so as quickly as possible. "We have really got to pull the plug on this one," aide Sam Watson advised, or else "George Bush is going to be trapped by Panama." Accordingly, in a May 19 campaign speech in Los Angeles, the vice president pointedly distanced himself from Reagan by declaring: "I won't bargain with drug dealers . . . whether they're on U.S. or foreign soil." The following day, the Bush staff announced that the vice president was opposed to negotiations with Noriega.[42]

The dictator's reluctance to accept the U.S. deal soon made the issue moot. But Bush had begun to paint himself into a corner. To save his political campaign, he had unequivocally rejected diplomatic negotiations as a strategy for securing Noriega's removal. If Reagan and Shultz were correct that the only alternative option was U.S. military intervention, Bush, as president, would have only two choices available: intervene militarily, or accept Noriega's continuance in power and look weak and irresolute in the process. In November, that eventuality became reality when the vice president won a massive electoral victory with a 53 percent majority and 426 electoral-college votes. "If we had known we would win the election by so much," campaign manager James Baker commented "only half-jokingly," "we would not have dug such a deep hole for ourselves."[43]

Following the collapse of negotiations with Noriega in late May, Reagan had assisted Bush's campaign by endeavoring to keep Panama out of the headlines until the election was over. U.S. diplomats and military officers in the country were instructed to tone down their public statements and activities in order to avoid roiling the waters. The commander of U.S. military forces in the Canal Zone, General Frederick Woerner, later recalled that "before the elections, as we started to get into active campaigning, the word was out: 'Put Panama on the back burner'" and "keep it out of the news" for the remainder of the campaign. Throughout the summer and fall, according to Woerner, U.S. policy in Panama was "based blatantly on partisan politics and no other . . . consideration."[44] The strategy worked. Although Dukakis continued to raise questions about Bush's past involvement with Noriega, and although Bush was frequently confronted with chants of "What about Noriega?" at campaign appearances, the vice president successfully deflected the issue and swept to victory in November.[45]

Nevertheless, as they prepared to take office, Bush and his advisers still regarded Noriega as one of their most pressing problems. Bush continued to talk tough, declaring publicly that "there must be no misunderstanding about our policy. Our policy will be that Noriega must go."[46] To that end, the new administration focused its initial efforts on Panama's upcoming May 1989 presidential election, in which an opposition coalition headed by attorney Guillermo Endara was running against one of Noriega's handpicked puppets. Bush secretly funneled $10 million in campaign funds to the opposition and authorized the CIA to conduct clandestine anti-regime radio broadcasts inside Panama in a campaign designed to defeat the dictator at the polls. The new president also invested some of his own personal prestige in the outcome by publicly challenging Noriega to conduct an honest election and warning that his administration would not accept the "results of a fraudulent election engineered simply to keep Noriega in power." In addition, the White House dispatched a U.S. delegation headed by former presidents Carter and Ford to monitor the voting. Consequently, as the *Washington Post* noted, the

Panamanian election quickly came "to be regarded by Panamanians and the outside world as a test of whether the United States [could] end [Noriega's] defiance."[47]

The result was an unmitigated disaster. When early returns on election day showed the opposition leading by a three-to-one margin, Noriega ordered Panama's Electoral Tribunal to suspend vote counting and sent his supporters out to destroy the ballots. Three days later, during an opposition-led protest march through the streets of Panama City, the dictator unleashed his newly organized paramilitary goon squads, the "Dignity Battalions," on the marchers. With the international media on hand to record the event, the Dignity Battalions beat the opposition's leaders with metal pipes, rubber hoses, and two-by-fours studded with rusty nails. Within hours, photographs of the savagery, including jarring images of Endara's vice-presidential running mate Guillermo ("Billy") Ford drenched in blood, were appearing on U.S. television screens, newspapers, and the covers of news magazines—chilling new symbols of Noriega's contempt for democracy and graphic evidence that George Bush's first attempt to oust the Panamanian strongman had ended in humiliating failure. As if to underscore the latter point, Noriega now went out of his way to taunt the new U.S. administration. "No one is going to tell me when I have to go," he declared defiantly, "much less the United States."[48]

Bush responded with more tough talk but little action. He issued outraged public statements demanding that Noriega "honor the will of the people." He said that the United States would "not be intimidated by [the dictator's] bullying tactics." He called on the Organization of American States to seek a constitutional solution to Panama's political difficulties. And in a rhetorical outburst that would soon come back to haunt him, he called on the Panamanian Defense Forces to rebel against their leader and remove him from power. "They ought to do everything they can to get Mr. Noriega out of there," he told reporters on May 13. "He's one man, and they have a well-trained force." "I would love to see them get him out." But other than recalling the U.S. ambassador and reinforcing the U.S. military presence in the Canal Zone, Bush did nothing. Nor did he even seem to be considering more muscular action at this point. When asked if U.S. military forces in Panama would be prepared to assist the PDF in overthrowing Noriega, Bush's Defense Secretary, Richard Cheney, responded that the administration did not see "any role for U.S. troops" in "deciding who governs Panama."[49]

Bush's less-than-forceful response to the election debacle was undoubtedly a reflection of his instinctive political caution. As he told his staff shortly after his inauguration: "I don't want to make any early term mistakes like Kennedy and the Bay of Pigs." "I don't want to do anything dumb."[50] Nevertheless, his restraint left him looking weak in the eyes of many observers. Almost immediately, reporters began bombarding him with pointed questions about the effectiveness of his foreign-policy leadership, and Bush's replies did little to inspire confidence that he had any plan in place to resolve the Noriega problem. During an interview with the White House press corps on May 9, two days after the aborted election, a reporter asked him: "Did you put yourself in a box here by making such a public point of being upset about these elections, and if Noriega decides to stay anyhow, that it looks like the U.S. has been ineffective?" Bush rejected the suggestion that he had been boxed in but offered no indication that he had a strategy for ousting the dictator. Four days later, another journalist pressed the president on his Panama policy: "So far, you have struck out—and so did President Reagan—in trying to get [Noriega] out of power. Do you have any other options?" "No," Bush replied. At a White House news conference in early June, he again faced harsh questioning: "Mr. President, some of your critics say that, despite your rhetoric, General Noriega can sit in Panama for as long as he wishes, in effect laughing at you, sir, laughing at the United States. Can you do anything about it?" Bush's response was that he was "not going to give up on this." The following month, a reporter again pushed him for his plan to remove the dictator: "Mr. President, Noriega is still in charge in Panama. The GAO [Government Accounting Office] says the sanctions haven't worked. Where are you going on Panama? What are you going to do? Are you going to accept the situation the way it is?" To which Bush replied: "I wish I could give you a much clearer answer, that there is some plan that is going to solve this problem."[51] By midsummer of 1989, an unflattering perception of the new U.S. president was beginning to spread. During his two terms as vice president, Bush had been derided in various circles as an unassertive "yes man," Reagan's "lap dog," and a "wimp." Now, six months into his first term as president, Manuel Noriega was making him look like an ineffectual leader.[52]

But Bush's image problem extended far beyond Panama. Throughout 1989, he often seemed almost detached and disengaged as a series of cataclysmic internal transformations destabilized the communist bloc. In the Soviet Union, Mikhail Gorbachev was implementing a far-reaching program of political and economic liberalization, calling for an end to the East-West conflict, and proposing international initiatives in Europe that would render the principal Cold War security alliances, NATO and the Warsaw Pact, obsolescent. Meanwhile, in Poland, Hungary, and Czechoslovakia, communist regimes were unraveling in the face of popular democratic revolutions. In June, Gorbachev began a unilateral withdrawal of Soviet military forces from Eastern Europe, in effect dismantling the Warsaw Pact. That same month, government forces in the People's Republic of China crushed a prodemocracy movement in Beijing's Tiananmen Square, killing hundreds. As democratic ferment swept through the communist world and the Iron Curtain crumbled, Bush remained a silent and passive spectator. From his perspective, it was only prudent to avoid any potentially inflammatory U.S. statements or actions that communist governments might interpret as internal meddling or gloating. To many observers, however, his cautious response to the remarkable changes taking place in the Eastern bloc was a further indication of weak, indecisive leadership: the West's Cold War arch-adversary—the communist bloc—was falling apart, and the president of the United States was doing nothing to encourage the process.

Soon Bush was being "vilified for his inaction." In the U.S. Senate, Democratic majority leader George Mitchell charged that the president appeared "frightened" by the uncertainties and opportunities that the unfolding world events were producing. The press was equally critical. According to *Time* magazine, Bush seemed "almost recklessly timid, unwilling to respond with the imagination and articulation that the situation requires." The *New York Times* reported that the new administration was "widely viewed as having failed so far" and indicted Bush for being "hyper-cautious by nature, a reactor rather than an initiator." Bush's national security adviser Brent Scowcroft recalls that by midsummer the White House was already worrying about how to "turn around the sharply negative image the press had drawn of the performance and even the capability of the President and the Administration in foreign policy."[53]

Consequently, Bush's difficulties in Panama were increasingly perceived as symptomatic of a larger problem: the new president's weak leadership in foreign affairs generally. As Noriega clung stubbornly to power in the face of U.S. opposition, he became in many eyes a symbol of Bush's inadequacies in the international arena. Given the historical moment—with the communist bloc collapsing and the Cold War seemingly coming to an end—the implications were enormous; if George Bush—"the leader of the Free World"—could be "pushed around by a small-time thug" in a small country like Panama, his prospects for maintaining U.S. global leadership in the emerging post–Cold War world seemed unpromising at best.[54]

Then suddenly, in early October, Bush got what he had wished for in Panama. On the third, dissident elements of the Panamanian Defense Forces led by Major Moisés Giroldi launched a coup d'état, seizing Noriega at the PDF's Comandancia headquarters in Panama City and announcing publicly that the dictator and his top commanders were being forcibly retired. Giroldi had informed the United States of his coup plans two days earlier and had asked U.S. military forces in the Canal Zone to support the operation by setting up roadblocks and disrupting air traffic in order to prevent pro-Noriega troops from coming to the dictator's defense. Bush initially agreed to the request but grew cautious when U.S. authorities in Panama warned that Giroldi might be a Noriega plant trying to lure the United States into an embarrassing display of imperialist behavior. Then, on the day of the coup, a hectic White House schedule—featuring visits by the Soviet defense minister and the president of Mexico—partially distracted the administration from events in Panama, to the extent that no National Security Council meetings were convened to monitor the situation. Consequently, when the coup got under way, U.S. military forces failed to carry out the full range of "blocking" activities that Giroldi had initially been led to expect. Within hours of Noriega's capture, loyalist PDF units from outside the capital had moved into the city and surrounded the Comandancia. In desperation, Giroldi offered to turn Noriega over to U.S. forces in the Canal Zone, but it took two hours to elicit a response from Washington, and by the time Bush authorized U.S. officials in Panama to take custody of the dictator, it was too late—Noriega loyalists had freed their leader and forced Giroldi to surrender. Giroldi and at least ten of his co-conspirators were quickly executed.[55]

Noriega immediately denounced U.S. involvement in the uprising and taunted Bush again. "The gringo piranhas want to do away with me" and "install a government of sellouts," he told a crowd of cheering supporters two days after his rescue, but the Bush administration "left its agents in the lurch." Laughing at how badly Bush had "screwed up," he compared the episode to the Bay of Pigs debacle and dared the president to try again.[56]

The administration's performance in the failed coup generated a new torrent of public criticism in the United States. In Congress, Democrats excoriated the president for his handling of the affair. David Boren, chairman of the Senate Intelligence Committee, accused Bush of "talking tough but acting less than courageously." "We had an insurrection of some very courageous people . . . and the United States did nothing," Boren charged. Chairman Sam Nunn of the Senate Armed Services Committee complained that despite its "longstanding policy . . . of encouraging a coup" in Panama, the administration had "no real plans for our people on the ground on how to proceed if [such an event] occurred." "We should anticipate that our policy might succeed," he remarked acidly. In the House, Chairman of the Select Committee on Intelligence Dave McCurdy (D-OK) suggested that Bush's handling of the coup made "Jimmy Carter look like a man of resolve." The result, according to McCurdy, was "a resurgence of the wimp factor" that had long plagued Bush's public image. "It's hard to imagine Lyndon Johnson or Ronald Reagan hesitating," another House Democrat with extensive foreign-policy experience noted.[57] Republicans were equally vociferous in their criticism. In the Senate, Jesse Helms labeled the administration "a bunch of Keystone Kops, bumping into each other." "After this," he declared, "no member of the PDF can be expected to act against Noriega." In the House, Henry Hyde, the ranking Republican on the Intelligence Committee, also blasted the administration, complaining that "we look indecisive, vacillating, and weak."[58]

The U.S. press heaped ridicule on the administration. The *New York Times* characterized Bush's handling of the coup as "a model of incompetence," while the *Washington Post* described the president as "absolutely paralyzed" during the coup—"All he could do was 'dither.'" *Newsweek* magazine, in a cover article entitled "Amateur Hour," charged that the administration's "management of [the] crisis smacked of inexperience and unpreparedness." The coup had been the new president's first "test by fire," the article asserted, and the results were "not comforting"; the White House had managed to reap "the worst of both sides: a loss of face in a world where that matters, and Noriega still in power." All in all, the magazine concluded, Bush's performance "made for a poor contrast with his predecessor." The conservative weekly *Human Events* was even more vitriolic, charging that Bush's failure to support Giroldi revealed an "incompetence and timidity bordering on appeasement."[59] Syndicated columnists had a field day. Charles Krauthammer wrote that the failed coup reflected the administration's "halfway-ness—halfway policy backed by halfway measures." A George Will column enti-tled "An Unserious Presidency" suggested that the symbol of Bush's presidency "should be a wetted finger held up to the breezes," while William Safire, in a piece entitled "A Man With No Plan," concluded that Bush's "fiasco quota has now been filled." Retired colonel Harry G. Summers Jr., a former holder of the Doug-las MacArthur Chair at the U.S. Army War College, detected graver issues at stake. In a syndicated column titled "Panama Coup Bumbling Is the Least of Our Wor-ries," he wrote that the coup had given the American people "a glimpse into the abyss. Our national security decision-making process, the very heart and soul of our national defenses, was revealed to be in chaos. It was a frightening revelation. . . . If our national leaders bungled so badly on a minor crisis like Panama, what would they do in the face of a major threat? Would they still be shuffling papers . . . while enemy missiles were inbound?"[60]

The Panamanian opposition also took the president sharply to task. In a *Wash-ington Post* op-ed headlined "You Yanquis Can't Handle a Coup," Roberto Eisen-mann expressed his "great disillusionment" with the administration. Bush's "bungling" response to the crisis made it "clear," Eisenmann wrote, "that there is no coherent policy behind the presidential rhetoric, that . . . contingencies had not been contemplated, much less planned for, [and] that in the campaign to dis-lodge Noriega, U.S. rhetoric can safely be ignored." "A dog that barks [had] better have a bite behind its bark," another opposition leader warned angrily, "or other-wise it better shut up."[61]

But the most damaging criticism came from administration officials themselves. For several days following the attempted coup, stories in leading U.S. newspapers quoted administration insiders "expressing criticisms or doubts regarding the White House's handling of the affair." In a *Washington Post* article headlined "U.S. Was Caught Off Guard by Coup Attempt," "top Bush aides" described the "cloud of uncertainty" that hampered the president's decision making about whether to support Giroldi. A *New York Times* story quoted "White House officials" as ad-mitting that "the Bush Administration's team performed badly in a major test." Another *Times* story, citing unnamed "administration officials" as its sources, de-scribed "tension between the [White House] chief of staff and Brent Scowcroft, the national security adviser, over the fact that contingency planning . . . did not take into account the kind of fast-moving . . . events that led to the collapse of the rebellion."[62] By October 6, Bush had had enough. Early that morning, according to *Washington Post* reporter Ann Devroy,

an "enraged" President Bush ordered his top advisers to put a stop to internal criticism of the administration's handling of the coup attempt. . . . [For three days] officials in many departments told reporters that the administration had been ill-prepared for its first unexpected international crisis, had no contingency plans for dealing with it, and reacted clumsily to unfolding events. . . . Bush's anger . . . , aides to senior officials said, was based on reading the morning newspapers, many of which quoted senior officials lamenting how the crisis had been mishandled, and suggesting an efficient crisis management operation was lacking and that the president was either too cautious or too hampered in information he was receiving to make informed decisions.[63]

The October coup debacle was, in Secretary of State James Baker's words, a watershed in Bush's policy toward Panama. The administration's stumbling response to the rebellion produced a crisis of credibility for the White House, fueling public perceptions of Bush as an overcautious, vacillating "incompetent." Underlying the "frenzy" of public criticism that followed the coup, Joint Chiefs of Staff chairman Colin Powell observed, "was the question of presidential image—lingering doubts about Bush as wimp. Nine months into his presidency, Bush still had not defined himself" as an effective commander in chief, "and this failure left open a basic question" in the public mind: "Was the essential Bush indecisive and hesitant?"[64] Did he really "have the *stuff* to be President of the United States? Was he equal to the job?"[65]

"Rattled by the criticism" (according to Vice President Dan Quayle) and desperate to improve his public image, Bush immediately began preparations for a show of strength that would demonstrate his capacity for bold, decisive leadership. A week after the coup, he ordered the Pentagon to initiate planning for a full-scale U.S. military invasion of Panama. "Amateur hour," he told his advisers, "is over."[66]

An awkward problem immediately became apparent, however: the White House needed a legitimate reason to invade Panama. As Vice President Quayle put it, "before we could [act], we needed a pretext for moving against the dictator." "We knew that in order to implement the full [invasion] plan," chief Pentagon planner Lt. Gen. Carl Stiner later recalled, "it would take some kind of a trigger that would be acceptable as morally justifiable—like protecting lives—in the minds of the American people and the world." What the administration specifically needed, Secretary of State Baker writes, was "a blatant provocation against American citizens that would arouse public sentiment and make intervention more palatable."[67]

Accordingly, to provide the requisite "pretext" for intervention, U.S. military forces in Panama proceeded to conduct a series of aggressive combat-training maneuvers deliberately designed "to raise the level of tension" and "draw Noriega into a confrontation." According to one postinvasion investigating commission, the exercises included "searching Panamanian citizens, confronting PDF forces, occupying small towns for a number of hours, buzzing Panamanian air space with military aircraft, and surrounding public buildings with troops." Two months after the Giroldi coup, the Council on Hemispheric Affairs reported that "Canal Zone-based U.S. forces in recent weeks have been regularly trespassing on Panamanian soil, almost inviting an incident with the Panamanian Defense Force." Soon U.S. forces were carrying out "intimidation games" and "intense, high-adventure night exercises" "three or four times a week," producing an environment of "heightened open friction" and an escalating "war of nerves" between U.S. and Panamanian troops. "We had young soldiers, locked and loaded, facing PDF, also locked and loaded, where any one person on either side could easily get scared or do something wrong, and start a fight," a U.S. infantry officer later recalled. In late November, as invasion planning neared completion and dangerous confrontations with PDF forces increased in number, the commander of U.S. military forces in Panama assured the Pentagon's General Stiner that if "there's a single American killed, we're going to blow [Noriega] away."[68]

Meanwhile, events on the broader world stage were exerting additional pressure on Bush to move aggressively in Panama. In early November, East German authorities responded to escalating popular unrest by opening the Berlin Wall and standing aside as tens of thousands of their countrymen fled to freedom in the West. Within days, the wall itself—"for three decades the symbol of communist enslavement of half of Europe"—was being sledge-hammered into rubble by crowds of jubilant Berliners. As the Western world celebrated the dramatic events, Bush again remained cautious and restrained. His public response—a terse, emotionless, unenthusiastic-sounding statement praising the East German communists' decision making—subjected him to more criticism for failing to provide any inspirational or visionary leadership during a period of momentous historical change. In the press, syndicated columnist William Pfaff warned that the United States appeared to be "court[ing] irrelevance," while on Capitol Hill, the House majority leader, Richard Gephardt (D-MO), complained that "even as the walls of the modern Jericho come tumbling down, we have a president who is inadequate to the moment."[69]

By December, the Cold War was clearly ending and administration strategists were excitedly drafting blueprints for the U.S.-dominated "new world order" that they hoped would follow. The post–Cold War international system that they envisioned was a stable world of capitalist democracies, in which the United States, as the only remaining superpower, would utilize its overwhelming military superiority to guarantee global stability, working with cooperative allies and the United Nations to reduce international conflict, prevent aggression, and promote liberal models of national development—a world in which, as Bush would put it a year later in the run-up to the Persian Gulf War, "what we say goes." Not all Americans necessarily shared the administration's vision of a hegemonic U.S. role in the post–Cold War world, however. By late 1989, speculation was rife in U.S. intellectual circles that the nation—having exhausted itself in the victorious struggle against communism—would now share the fate of previous great powers by entering a period of inevitable decline, in which its international power would diminish and it would lose its preeminent position in the world. From the administration's perspective, alarming early indicators of a potential "declinist" scenario were already appearing on Capitol Hill, where some members of Congress had begun to call for drastic reductions in U.S. defense spending and the allocation of the resulting "peace dividend" to domestic social programs.[70]

It was no coincidence that the U.S. invasion of Panama occurred at a time when the White House was preoccupied with these broader strategic challenges. For Bush and his advisers, Manuel Noriega's successful defiance of the United States raised inconvenient questions about U.S. power at a critical moment when the nation was preparing to assume new responsibilities of global leadership. The U.S. inability to oust Noriega could easily be read as a sign of growing impotence— "the sort of foreign policy weakness exhibited by [great] powers in decline, not by vigorous world leaders." As a prominent international-relations specialist noted at the time, "The contrast between America's position in the world today and its position only a few decades ago is sobering. U.S. influence in the Western Hemisphere—so enormous in the 1950s that Washington could overthrow a left-leaning Guatemalan government with a minimal covert effort—had so diminished by the late 1980s that the Reagan administration was unable to force out of office a minor-league dictator in Panama, a country actually created by Washington and controlled by American officials for decades." If the United States was incapable of ousting a petty tyrant in its own Caribbean backyard, would it still command the deferential respect in other world capitals that effective global leadership required? Would other nations unhesitatingly follow the United States' lead as it set out to construct a new world order in its own image? Would future "rogue states" be emboldened to pursue their own aims in defiance of America's will? From the Bush administration's perspective, a demonstration of U.S. power in Panama would reassure the world that the United States was still the superpower it claimed to be. In his memoirs, Colin Powell describes a pervasive sense of outrage in the White House in late 1989 that "a third-rate [Panamanian] dictator" was "thumbing his nose at the United States." In Powell's view, "this sort of challenge" to U.S. international credibility, coming at a watershed point in global affairs, "was intolerable"—an "affront to the country" that demanded a powerful U.S. response. It was time, he advised the president, for the United States "to put a shingle outside our door saying, 'Superpower Lives Here.'" The "shingle" was Panama.[71]

By December, the administration's two-month campaign of military provocations in Panama had raised tensions to an explosive level. Early in the month, Noriega's courts issued arrest warrants for the two highest-ranking U.S. military commanders in the Canal Zone on charges of "constant harassment" of Panamanian citizens. Adding to the tension was the administration's announcement, also in early December, that no vessels flying the Panamanian flag would be allowed to enter U.S. ports, effective February 1990. For Panama, which registered a significant proportion of the world's merchant ships and depended heavily on maritime commerce for its income, the port ban was a major economic blow—and Noriega's government reacted angrily. On December 15, the Panamanian national assembly passed a resolution calling the U.S. action tantamount to a declaration of war against Panama. In a public speech the same day, Noriega declared that "the North American scheme" of constant harassment had "created a state of war in Panama." Brandishing a machete over his head for effect, he told a crowd of cheering supporters: "We will sit by the canal and watch the bodies of our enemies float by."[72]

A day later, the now-all-but-inevitable incident of violence occurred. On the evening of the sixteenth, an automobile carrying four U.S. Marines ran through a PDF checkpoint outside Noriega's Comandancia headquarters in a section of Panama City officially designated off-limits to U.S. military personnel. When the car approached the checkpoint, Panamanian soldiers armed with AK-47s tried to inspect the Marines' identification documents and "words were exchanged," at which point the car's driver panicked and floored the accelerator. As the car sped off, one of its occupants, Lt. Robert Paz, reportedly "gave the finger" to the PDF soldiers, who opened fire, killing Paz. The incident was witnessed by a U.S. naval officer and his wife, who were detained by the PDF and subjected to four hours of physical and psychological abuse before being released. What four U.S. Marines were doing in a sensitive off-limits area of the capital at a time of acute tension between the two countries remains a matter of controversy. The Marines claimed that they "got lost" while driving back to their base from a Panama City restaurant; investigative reports by the *Armed Forces Journal International* and *Los Angeles Times*, however, identified them as intelligence officers affiliated with a secret group of "gung-ho" Marine provocateurs called the "Hard Chargers," who may have been probing Noriega's defenses on the evening of the sixteenth. Whatever the reality, the incident sealed Noriega's fate. Although the PDF quickly sent word to U.S. officials that Paz's killing had been an unintended accident and an isolated incident, it was too late. The White House now had the "trigger event" that it had been waiting for. "They had a plan" to invade Panama, a Pentagon official told *Newsweek* magazine, "and they were just waiting for an excuse to use it."[73]

The following day, a few hours after learning of Paz's death, Bush and his top advisers reviewed the invasion plan, code-named Operation Just Cause. After receiving assurances from Colin Powell that there would be "no repeat of the failure at Desert One," Jimmy Carter's disastrous military mission to rescue U.S. hostages in Iran nine years earlier, the president ordered the Pentagon to proceed with the operation. U.S. combat forces began parachuting into Panama in the early hours of December 20 and quickly overwhelmed the PDF. Two weeks later, Noriega surrendered to U.S. authorities. The dictator was then transported to Miami, where in 1992, after a seven-month trial, he was convicted of cocaine trafficking, racketeering, and money laundering and sentenced to forty years in a U.S. prison.[74]

Among the beneficiaries of the U.S. invasion, none had greater cause for celebration than Panama's political opposition. In a fundamental respect, the intervention was the culmination of their efforts. Four years earlier, Roberto Eisenmann and his colleagues had set out to turn the United States against Manuel Noriega. The strategy they adopted was based on an astute premise: that by galvanizing U.S. public opinion against the dictator, they could generate political pressure on the U.S. government to terminate its alliance with him. Over the course of the next two years, their skillful media campaign and energetic lobbying activities achieved precisely that result. By 1987, thanks largely to the opposition's efforts, Noriega's public image in the United States was so bad that the Reagan administration had little choice but to distance itself from him. From that point on, the downward spiral in U.S.-Panamanian relations developed a momentum of its own. But the subsequent key events—Reagan's decision to sever ties with Noriega, candidate Bush's move to rescue his presidential campaign by renouncing negotiations with the dictator, President Bush's image-driven decision to intervene—all unfolded in the context of anti-Noriega sentiment that the Panamanian opposition had fostered in U.S. domestic politics. The payoff came on December 20, 1989, when, shortly before the invasion began, U.S. forces transported Guillermo Endara and his colleagues to a U.S. base in the Canal Zone and arranged for them to be sworn in as the new leaders of the Panamanian government. Endara knew that he was assuming Panama's presidency "under occupation" by an American invasion force and that, as he later recalled, history would condemn him as a U.S. puppet. Nevertheless, the opportunity to take power and end military rule in Panama was too irresistible to turn down.[75]

The invasion also enhanced the credibility of U.S. claims to the role of dominant superpower in the emerging post–Cold War international system. In its operational aspects, Kevin Buckley writes, it was designed to provide "a showcase spectacle" of U.S. military power and "a demonstration of Pentagon prowess." To assure an overwhelming victory, Bush and his advisers opted for a massive air and ground assault, deploying some 26,000 troops in the largest U.S. military combat operation since Vietnam (and the largest American paratroop drop since World War II). Reflecting Colin Powell's belief in the "disproportionate use of force," U.S. forces outnumbered PDF combatants by a ratio of six to one. The operation also provided the Pentagon with an opportunity to display (and test) many of the newest and most sophisticated items in its formidable arsenal of high-tech weaponry, including Abrams tanks, Apache attack helicopters, AC-130 "Spectre" gunships equipped with 105-mm howitzers, and the new supersonic Stealth fighter-bomber. Some of the weapons were utilized, in Powell's words, "just for show." For example, the Stealth fighter-bomber—an aircraft uniquely engineered to evade enemy air defenses—was deployed against a PDF adversary that "lacked military radar, anti-aircraft batteries, or a true air force."[76] The end result was a military cakewalk in which the PDF was quickly routed and replaced in power by the civilian politicians who had been denied victory in Panama's May 1989 elections. The UN General Assembly condemned the invasion as a "flagrant violation" of international law, and Panama's new democratic leaders quickly proved disappointing (drug trafficking in Panama actually *increased* under Endara, while the new government soon became so unpopular that in December 1990 the Bush administration was forced to intervene militarily again to protect it from overthrow).[77] Nevertheless, the Panama invasion sent a powerful signal to the rest of the world: that after a potentially exhausting forty-year struggle against communism, U.S. power was alive and well—and that in the new world order that lay ahead the United States was fully prepared to use its overwhelming might to crush "rogue" dictators and promote democracy.[78]

Finally, Operation Just Cause established George Bush's credentials as a strong, decisive president. Throughout his first year in office, Manuel Noriega had made him look ineffectual, "wimpish," and weak, damaging his domestic political credibility and raising questions about his ability to project U.S. leadership internationally at a pivotal moment in world history. By overthrowing Noriega militarily, he not only rid himself of a major foreign-policy embarrassment. He demonstrated in the process that he could be a forceful leader and an effective commander in chief—one who "had the guts to send kids into battle," in Herbert Parmet's words. Bush's supporters were elated—and relieved. According to the *Wall Street Journal,* the invasion provided Bush "with new political momentum, displaying him as decisive and tough and blunting criticism that his sense of prudence precludes bold action." In Colin Powell's view, the president's "bold political decision" to invade Panama had "vindicated" him as a leader. Even Bush's critics acknowledged that the invasion had "solidified [his] political identity at last." The *New York Times* observed that "for President Bush—a man widely criticized as recently as a month ago for his purported timidity, a man assailed on Capitol Hill and elsewhere for failing to fully support an attempted coup against General Noriega . . . in October, a man still portrayed in the Doonesbury comic strip as the invisible President— showing his steel [in Panama] had a particular significance. . . . It has shown him [to be] a man capable of bold action." As journalists Jack Germond and Jules Witcover put it: "No one will make the mistake of taking President Bush lightly again."[79] That, for Bush, was probably the crux of the matter all along. Prior to the intervention, he had confided to close friends that he would never "feel fully settled into the job" of president until he had passed his "first test as commander-in-chief of the armed forces."[80] Now, in Panama, he had a military victory under his belt.

He had passed the test. He had shown that he did in fact have "the stuff" to be a successful president—that he was not to be taken lightly. Thirteen months later, he would draw on the heightened stature that he had gained from Operation Just Cause to galvanize domestic and international support for a considerably greater challenge: a U.S.-led war in the Middle East against the "rogue" dictator of Iraq.

Conclusion

"In its relations with Latin America," historian Fredrick Pike noted in an influential 1974 essay, "the United States has been motivated primarily by security and economic considerations." "Such a trite observation could scarcely provoke challenge," Pike added, "although authorities have disagreed heatedly through the years over whether it is security or economic interests that have been paramount."[1] Pike's formulation undoubtedly reflected the conventional wisdom of academic scholarship at the time, but as the preceding chapters make clear, it provides an inadequate framework for explaining recent U.S. interventionism in the region.

No conclusive evidence has yet come to light to support the claim that economic self-interest played a decisive role in any of the U.S. decisions to intervene. In some cases (British Guiana, the Dominican Republic, Nicaragua, Grenada), U.S. trade and investments were simply too insignificant to have exerted a decisive influence on U.S. policy. There seems little reason to doubt Ronald Reagan's statement that it wasn't nutmeg that was at stake in Grenada, for example, while Reagan's alarmist warnings about the damaging impact that hoards of Central American political refugees and the loss of Caribbean sea lanes would have on the U.S. economy sound, in retrospect, more like justifications for aggressive U.S. action than articulations of policy motivation. In those cases where evidence of U.S. presidents' economic concerns seems most substantive (Cuba and, to a much lesser extent, Panama), other factors clearly predominated in White House decision making. Eisenhower and his advisers reacted angrily to Castro's expropriations of U.S.-owned property and worried that the Cuban revolution's nationalist economic model would inspire a wave of attacks on U.S. investment capital throughout Latin America, but in the end they viewed Cuban economic nationalism as merely one manifestation of the broader strategic threat that the revolution posed to U.S. hegemony in the region. In Panama, Bush occasionally expressed concern for the safety of the Panama Canal as relations with Noriega deteriorated, but his concern centered primarily on the Canal's strategic significance to the United States rather than on its commercial value. Even in the two cases where influential U.S. corporations actively lobbied for U.S. intervention (Guatemala and Chile), no hard evidence exists that the subsequent policy decisions of White House officials were made on the basis of the corporations' interests. In Guatemala, the United Fruit Company's appeals for U.S. intervention emphasized the security dimension rather than the company's economic interests, and its anti-Arbenz publicity campaign was designed to generate domestic political pressure on Eisenhower to protect the United States from a Central American security threat. The CIA's Richard Bissell, one of Operation PBSUCCESS's planners, later recalled that United Fruit "had quite a lot to do with causing the State Department and others in Washington to focus on Guatemala as the locus of a major communist threat" but that "when it came to decisions to plan an operation and . . . launch it," there is "absolutely no reason to believe that the desire to pull the fruit company's chestnuts out of the fire played any significant role"[2]—a conclusion reinforced by Guatemalan communist leader José Manuel Fortuny's statement that "they would have overthrown us even if we had grown no bananas." In Chile, the Nixon administration had extensive interactions with International Telephone &Telegraph, Anaconda Copper, and other threatened U.S. corporations, but "smoking gun" evidence that Nixon intervened to defend U.S. investment capital has yet to be discovered, while Henry Kissinger, in the inelegant words of a colleague, "never gave a shit about the business community."

Nor were any of the interventions driven by fundamental national-security concerns—that is, by fear of a foreign military attack on the United States. U.S. officials consistently regarded the radical elements that became the targets of U.S. intervention as allies or potential allies of the Soviet Union and "international communism," and in the vast majority of cases their perceptions were accurate. By their own admission, Jacobo Arbenz, Raúl Castro, Che Guevara, Bernard Coard, and the highest-ranking Sandinista *comandantes* were all attracted to Soviet development models, while—for reasons of ideological affinity, geopolitical opportunism, or both—revolutionary leaders in Guatemala, Cuba, Chile,[3] Nicaragua, and Grenada actively solicited close relations with Moscow. Salvador Allende, Daniel Ortega,[4] and Sandinista founder Carlos Fonseca served as secret intelligence assets of the Soviet KGB, while both Cheddi Jagan and Maurice Bishop were committed Marxists with deep ties to Castro's Cuba. Only in the Dominican Republic (where Lyndon Johnson later admitted to having been "misled" about the extent of radical influence in the 1965 civil war)[5] and Panama (essentially an early post–Cold War intervention against a former Cold War ally) were the targets of U.S. intervention *not* Marxists with strong pro-Soviet leanings.[6]

And yet in none of these interventions was fear of Soviet military aggression the principal White House concern. The Eisenhower administration's defense analysts had concluded that Arbenz's Guatemala posed no military threat to the United States and that if, in the future, the Soviet Union were to develop a military presence there, "a battalion or two" of U.S. troops could easily eliminate it. In March 1960, when planning for the Bay of Pigs invasion commenced, the Eisenhower administration did not consider Fidel Castro's government communist dominated or susceptible to foreign control. Four months later, the administration's leading Soviet specialist informed the president that a Soviet military presence in Cuba was highly unlikely, while as late as February 1961—two months before the U.S. invasion—the Defense Department was advising the Kennedy administration that Castro's Cuba did not constitute a threat to U.S. security and could be "dealt with" if it ever became one. U.S. diplomats and senior intelligence analysts repeatedly counseled President Nixon that the United States had no vital security interests in Chile and that an Allende government would not pose a military threat to the United States; while Kissinger's description of Chile as "a dagger pointed at the heart of Antarctica" would seem to suggest that the principal architect of the U.S. intervention held similar views. No Soviet military bases, missiles, aircraft, or troops were to be found in British Guiana, the Dominican Republic, Nicaragua, or Grenada at the time of the U.S. interventions in those countries, and they could undoubtedly have been neutralized by U.S. military strikes in the unlikely event that they materialized. In several cases (Guatemala, Cuba, Chile, Nicaragua), White House officials expressed concern that the Marxist governments in power would export their revolutions to neighboring countries, stimulating a domino effect that might eventually confront the United States with a hostile region to the south, but here, too, White House threat perceptions focused primarily on issues other than military defense.

A less conventional—and much vaguer—security concern *did*, on the other hand, factor significantly into every decision to intervene. Cold War presidents and their senior advisers consistently believed that a passive U.S. response to Marxist or otherwise unfriendly regimes in the Western Hemisphere would create a perception of U.S. weakness in the eyes of the international community, with potentially serious long-range consequences for the nation's security. Cold War U.S. foreign policy was predicated on the belief that U.S. power must be credible—that, in Stephen Van Evers' words, "America's worldwide alliance system and its ability to deter Soviet aggression depend[ed] on the credibility of America's threats and promises" and that "leftist challenges" in Latin America and elsewhere had to be defeated "in order to maintain [that] credibility." Throughout the Cold War, U.S. leaders worried that failure on their part to maintain firm hegemonic control over the United States' traditional sphere of influence in the Western Hemisphere—a passive response, for example, to the takeover of a neighboring republic by Marxist or other anti-American forces, or failure to prevent the defection of a Latin American or Caribbean ally from the United States' inter-American alliance system—would be interpreted by other governments as an indication of U.S. weakness, a sign, perhaps, that the United States no longer had the capability, or the will, to project its power in defense of its interests. The principal danger to U.S. interests in Latin America, the 1984 Kissinger Commission report concluded, was that "the triumph of hostile forces in what the Soviets call the 'strategic rear' of the United States would be read as a sign of U.S. impotence." If the United States appeared impotent in its own "backyard," if it appeared incapable of controlling events in its own regional sphere of influence, the forces of international communism might be emboldened to accelerate their "reckless" expansionism and "adventurism"; U.S. allies in Latin America, Western Europe, Asia, and the Persian Gulf might lose confidence in the United States' ability to defend them and begin to reconsider their international alignments; while neutral governments would presumably draw similarly negative inferences. From the U.S. perspective, in short, perceptions of U.S. weakness—perceptions that U.S. power and resolve might no longer be credible—could lead to dangerous shifts in the fragile Cold War balance of power, leaving the United States in an increasingly perilous position. The quintessential expression of that concern was Ronald Reagan's 1983 warning to Congress that if the United States failed to respond aggressively to Marxist revolutionary threats in Central America, "Our credibility would collapse, our alliances would crumble, and the safety of our homeland would be put in jeopardy."[7]

This U.S. "fixation with credibility"—what historian Robert McMahon calls "a preoccupation with images, appearances, and perceptions"—was in fact a key determinant of U.S. interventionism. Every nation that became the target of a U.S. intervention was being viewed by White House officials at the time not as a place where tangible U.S. interests were at stake but as a "symbolic battlefield" in a global geopolitical power struggle, a battlefield where hostile forces had chosen to test U.S. power and resoluteness, "a battlefield where—above all—the international credibility and prestige of the United States [were] being tested and challenged."[8] To the Eisenhower administration, Arbenz's Guatemala represented "a frontal test" of U.S. "strength" by the forces of international communism. The administration's top advisers believed that the successful establishment of an ostensibly "neutralist" Soviet satellite in the heart of the United States' Central American sphere of influence would constitute "a tremendous propaganda victory" for the international communist movement—one that would "strengthen the power of Communist forces in every free nation of the world" and cause U.S. allies in Latin America and Western Europe to question "whether the U.S. could be counted on to defend them." The "main danger" in Cuba, the Eisenhower administration concluded, was that Fidel Castro's campaign to "undermine the inter-American system" by forging an anti-American "neutralist bloc" of Latin American states would, if it succeeded, "constitute a blow to U.S. prestige" and have "serious adverse effects on Free World support of our leadership." In British Guiana, the Kennedy administration believed that the threat posed by Cheddi Jagan's Marxist government had "at least symbolic importance" for the United States. Lyndon Johnson viewed the alleged threat of a "Castroite Communist" victory in the 1965 civil war in the Dominican Republic as "a litmus test of U.S. resolve" in the global fight against communist expansionism, and Johnson's immediate concern was that a weak or passive U.S. response to a Marxist challenge in the Caribbean—a U.S. failure to "clean up the Dominican Republic"—would cause communist leaders in Hanoi and elsewhere to doubt the seriousness of the U.S. military commitment in Vietnam. The U.S. intervention in Chile stemmed from the Nixon administration's belief that the Soviet Union was aggressively "testing" the United States in Latin America and elsewhere and that, in Henry Kissinger's words, any "appearance of [U.S.] weakness or indifference to the establishment of a Marxist government in the Hemisphere" would weaken the credibility of U.S. power in the eyes of communist leaders in Moscow, Beijing, and Hanoi. The administration's "main concern" in Chile was that Salvador Allende's model of Marxist electoral success would have a pernicious "psychological effect" on the international balance of power and, in particular, that his Chilean model would fuel the political momentum of communist parties in Western Europe. The Contra war in Nicaragua was essentially an expression of the Reagan administration's determination to overcome the United States' post-Vietnam "reputation for strategic passivity" and reluctance to combat communist "adventurism," and the administration's overarching concern was that a U.S. failure to confront the Marxist "challenge at the heart of our sphere of influence would result in a loss of credibility in all our dealings with the Soviets." The "real issue" in Grenada, Reagan and his national security adviser Robert McFarlane believed, was that a U.S. failure to respond positively to the Organization of Eastern Caribbean States' request for U.S. intervention "would have a very damaging effect on the credibility of the United States"[9] and send an unhealthy signal to NATO and the Western industrial democracies who were "relying on us" for defense. The Bush administration's invasion of Panama occurred during a period of growing debate about the United States' ability, after an exhausting four-decade struggle against communism, to function as the principal guarantor of global stability in the post–Cold War international system.

At the same time, U.S. leaders consistently regarded successful interventions as important U.S. victories in these "symbolic battlefields"—victories that sent unambiguous and beneficial "signals of [U.S.] strength and resolution" to the rest of the world.[10] The Eisenhower administration overthrew Arbenz in an effort to demonstrate that the United States was capable of defeating communist expansionism and in the belief that a U.S. tactical victory in Guatemala could help to "restore the prestige of the West" and "create a climate of victory" in the Western alliance after years of uninterrupted communist advances. The Reagan administration's Central American and Caribbean interventions were deliberately intended "to send as powerful a message" as possible to "friends and potential foes alike" that after years of "hesitation and reluctance to act" the United States once again had the strength and determination to forcefully resist Soviet/Cuban expansionism in the Western Hemisphere. The Grenada invasion, in the administration's view, was "not something terribly important in its own right but a symbol that 'America was back.'" The massive (some would say excessive) use of U.S. military force in the Dominican Republic and Panama was, in each case, deliberately designed to assure an overwhelming victory and impress international observers with the military might of the United States—a deliberate demonstration to the world that U.S. power was not only credible but invincible.

U.S. credibility concerns, in turn, had powerful domestic political connotations. A fundamental axiom of U.S. politics from the early 1950s onward was that incumbent presidents and their parties could expect to pay a heavy political price for "losing one on their watch"—that is, for failing to prevent the loss of a former ally to communism or the defection of an ally from the U.S. alliance system. Political scientist Robert H. Johnson suggests that "the traumatic effects on U.S. politics of the 'loss' of China to the Communists in 1949" and the successful "exploitation of that 'loss'" by the Republicans in the 1952 presidential election "predisposed" subsequent Cold War presidents to interventionism for political reasons: to protect themselves from partisan charges that they had mismanaged U.S. security interests.[11] That concern was clearly central in several Latin American and Caribbean interventions. President Kennedy went ahead with Eisenhower's planned invasion of Cuba because he wanted to avoid politically damaging Republican charges that he "didn't have the guts" to go through with it. According to Kennedy's White House special assistant Arthur Schlesinger Jr., "the domestic political implications" of the Bay of Pigs project were "more important than anything else" in the president's ill-fated decision to proceed. Schlesinger also stated that Kennedy's intervention in British Guiana was motivated exclusively by his desire "to avoid the domestic political consequences of a communist state on the mainland of South America." "Cuba was bad enough," Schlesinger later recalled, "and another communist gain would have played into the hands of the Republicans," jeopardizing Kennedy's prospects for reelection in 1964. President Johnson feared that failure on his part to prevent a leftist takeover of the Dominican Republic would be "the worst domestic political disaster [he] could suffer" and that the Republican "hawks" would "eat [him] up" on the issue, potentially costing the Democrats control of the House of Representatives in 1966 and endangering his 1968 election prospects. The Nixon White House feared that failure to block a Marxist takeover of Chile "could end up being the worst failure in our administration—'our Cuba' by 1972," fueling Democratic charges that Nixon had "lost Chile" through neglect and jeopardizing his plans for reelection to a second term in office. The intervention in Grenada was driven to a significant extent by the Reagan administration's fear of a politically debilitating hostage crisis similar to the one that had crippled Jimmy Carter's presidency three years earlier.[12]

In several cases, interventions occurred when presidents found themselves under political pressure to live up to their own militant campaign promises. The Guatemalan intervention took place at a time when President Eisenhower was under sharp attack from the Republican Right for failing to deliver on the party's 1952 campaign promise to reverse the tide of communist expansionism. As presidential candidates, John F. Kennedy and George H. W. Bush both painted themselves into political corners with campaign rhetoric that, once elected, left them little choice but to conduct interventions or risk damaging their political credibility. Kennedy, operating on the premise that "what China was to the GOP in 1952, Cuba [could] be to the Democrats" in 1960,[13] harshly criticized the Eisenhower administration during the 1960 campaign for "not doing more to remove Fidel Castro from power" and strongly implied that he would adopt a more aggressively interventionist approach as president—thereby limiting his future options "by raising the political cost of scuttling [Eisenhower's] operation once he was in office."[14] During the 1988 campaign, Bush publicly committed himself to removing Manuel Noriega from power, and as a result his subsequent "failure to do anything about" the Panamanian dictator during his first eleven months in the White House looked, in Vice President Dan Quayle's words, "like a broken campaign promise."[15] During the campaign, Bush had also rejected diplomatic negotiations to secure Noriega's ouster, leaving military intervention as his only realistic option.

Interventions also transmitted powerful, image-laden messages of strong presidential leadership to domestic political audiences, enhancing the president's political standing, strengthening public perceptions of him as an assertive commander in chief, and boosting his public-opinion approval ratings. Prior to the Guatemalan intervention, Eisenhower leaked hints of the impending operation to influential Republican congressmen in an effort to shore up his eroding base of support among party conservatives, while afterward he and his senior advisers exploited Arbenz's overthrow in the media by citing it as evidence of their administration's effectiveness in combating communism. Two days after a horrendous foreign-policy disaster in the Middle East, and with his presidency languishing in the political doldrums, Ronald Reagan used the invasion of Grenada to refurbish his public image as a strong leader and achieve a much-needed foreign-policy victory a year before the 1984 presidential election. Following a series of embarrassing failures to remove Noriega, George Bush ordered a military invasion that proved his presidential mettle and demonstrated to the American people that he was a "tough," decisive leader "capable of bold action." The political gains were immediate: the interventions in Grenada and Panama produced spikes of 4 and 9 percent, respectively, in Reagan's and Bush's presidential approval ratings, according to Gallup polls (while the Dominican Republic intervention immediately elevated Lyndon Johnson's poll numbers by 6 percent).[16]

To describe the political motives of interventionism exclusively in terms of partisan self-interest and public-opinion polls, however, oversimplifies the context in which presidents formulate foreign policy. Virtually every Cold War president came to office with an ambitious legislative and programmatic agenda designed to advance the public interest and secure his reputation in history as a successful— ideally, a "great"—president. In a number of cases, the emergence or threatened emergence of a Marxist regime to the south interfered with those broader presidential goals and ambitions to the extent that intervention was deemed necessary. According to CIA sources, Eisenhower ultimately looked upon Arbenz's Guatemala as a "critical test. . .of his ability as a leader"; if he could not find "creative" and cost-effective "responses to Communist penetration of peripheral areas like Guatemala," Eisenhower believed, one of the central goals of his presidency— strengthening the U.S. position in the Cold War—was doomed to failure. Kennedy similarly concluded that a restrained policy on his part toward Castro's Cuba would be "a denial of [his] whole approach to foreign policy." The Dominican intervention can be fully understood only when placed in the context of Lyndon Johnson's aspirations for presidential greatness. To secure passage of the Great Society programs that he hoped would win him a prominent place in history, Johnson knew that he would have to "hang tough" in Vietnam or provoke an angry conservative backlash in Congress that would doom his legislative initiatives to defeat; and he feared that if he allowed the Dominican Republic to become a "second Cuba," he would be unlikely to prevail either in Vietnam or on Capitol Hill. The Chilean intervention must similarly be seen in the context of the broader goals that Richard Nixon had set for his presidency. Nixon, who according to White House aides was "preoccupied . . . with his place in history,"[17] hoped to establish his legacy of greatness as an international peacemaker—first by ending the war in Vietnam and then by constructing a stable new international system based on "global equilibrium." If Nixon permitted the consolidation of a Marxist government in Chile, he believed that the resulting image of weakness, combined with the corrosive effect of an Allende regime on U.S. allies in Western Europe and Latin America, would leave little hope for successful negotiations with Moscow, Beijing, or Hanoi—wrecking prospects for the international "structure for peace" that was to be his great historical achievement.

In some cases, in fact, it is difficult to determine the extent to which the decision to intervene was driven primarily by concern for the national interest or for the incumbent administration's self-interest. Presidents frequently conflated the two concepts, believing that U.S. international credibility, their administrations' credibility, and their personal credibility as presidents were fundamentally indistinguishable from one another, and that the prestige of the United States and the prestige of the president were inseparably interconnected. In his memoirs, Lyndon Johnson recalled that when he took office in 1963, "The most important foreign policy problem I faced was signaling to the world what kind of man I was and what sorts of policies I intended to carry out."[18] The communists had decided "to take the measure of the new President of the United States," Johnson believed, and they were testing him, in Vietnam, in the Caribbean, and elsewhere, watching for "any sign of weakness or temporizing or compromising or running on [his] part." If he failed to respond aggressively to communist expansionism, LBJ concluded, communist leaders would think he was "a weak sister" and wonder "just how far they [could] go." A strong—that is, interventionist—response on his part, on the other hand, would show that he was tough enough to stand up to them, and U.S. security would accordingly be safeguarded. Like Johnson, Richard Nixon believed that the communists were deliberately "taking [his] measure" at the onset of his presidency and that they would curtail their international aggressions only after he had demonstrated that his administration was "different and tougher" than its Democratic predecessors. Perhaps no Cold War president personalized his foreign-policy challenges more habitually than George H. W. Bush. By late 1989,

Bush was treating the confrontation between the United States and Manuel Noriega as "a personal test of wills" between himself and the Panamanian dictator,[19] while the ensuing U.S. military intervention appears to have been motivated in large part by Bush's determination to establish his credentials as a successful commander in chief and thereby silence his many critics who were questioning his capacity to lead the nation, and the world, into a new post–Cold War era.

Ultimately, then, the Cold War hemispheric interventions of the United States can best be understood as exercises in imagery—efforts by U.S. leaders to project images of strength to multiple audiences, foreign and domestic. Each intervention was meant to impress other governments with U.S. power *and* with the willingness of the incumbent president to deploy that power in defense of U.S. interests. Each intervention was also a demonstration to that president's domestic political constituents that he was managing U.S. security interests vigilantly and effectively. Given White House officials' dual concern for U.S. international credibility and their administration's domestic political interests, once a challenge to U.S. hemispheric hegemony gained sufficient visibility, intervention was perhaps all but inevitable.

But finally, none of the interventions was entirely unilateral in nature. In every case, local political actors influenced the U.S. decision to intervene. Guatemalan conservatives and the governing elites of neighboring Central American states played what Zachary Karabell describes as a "pivotal" role "in convincing the Eisenhower administration that Arbenz . . . had to be removed,"[20] while dissident army officer Carlos Castillo Armas and his Nicaraguan patron Anastasio Somoza Sr. repeatedly volunteered their services as instruments of U.S. intervention. Misleading reports from anti-Castro Cubans about rising levels of political discontent on the island exerted what the Kennedy administration's Cuba desk officer characterized as "a disproportionate amount of influence" on the administration's overly optimistic assessment of the Bay of Pigs invasion's prospects. In British Guiana, opposition political and labor leaders opportunistically reinforced the Kennedy administration's suspicions by characterizing Cheddi Jagan as a "controlled communist" and offered themselves as "a useful tool for unseating" him. The distorted intelligence information that Dominican conservatives fed to U.S. officials helped foster Lyndon Johnson's political paranoia about Marxist influence in the 1965 civil war, while "loyalist" military officers repeatedly invited the United States to intervene militarily on their behalf. The White House–level lobbying activities of a prominent Chilean businessman helped spur Richard Nixon into action against Salvador Allende. Anti-Sandinista Nicaraguans, Argentine military officers, and members of the Honduran governing elite offered the Reagan administration their Contra army as an instrument of U.S. intervention in Nicaragua. The conservative leaders of Grenada's island neighbors in the eastern Caribbean had been urging the Reagan administration to "deal severely" with the New Jewel Movement's hard-line leadership even before Maurice Bishop was murdered, and their regional organization's subsequent formal request for U.S. military intervention played a key role in Reagan's decision to act. The Panamanian opposition's anti-Noriega media campaign and lobbying efforts in the United States were instrumental in creating the climate of opinion in U.S. domestic politics that led the Reagan and Bush administrations down a path toward eventual intervention.

In two of the interventions, in fact, the roles played by local elites appear to have been not only influential but decisive. According to Henry Kissinger and former CIA director Richard Helms, Nixon's decision to intervene in Chile was directly triggered by the alarming reports that he had received hours earlier from Chilean millionaire Agustín Edwards. And in the Panamanian case, George Bush eventually found himself compelled to intervene because of political pressures emanating from the anti-Noriega environment in the United States that the dictator's Panamanian opponents had played a central role in fostering.

Throughout the Cold War, Latin American radicals routinely blamed their nations' plights on a "symbiotic alliance" composed of foreign "imperialism" and domestic "reaction." That hypothesis could perhaps be stretched to fit some cases of U.S. interventionism—Guatemala, Chile, Nicaragua, possibly the Dominican Republic—but not others. In the Bay of Pigs invasion, the United States' Cuban collaborators were not reactionary oligarchs but anti-Batista middle-class elements and disillusioned former members of Castro's 26th of July Movement. In British Guiana, Washington's favored alternative to Cheddi Jagan was Forbes Burnham, a socialist and former member of Jagan's People's Progressive Party. The Panamanian opposition essentially represented the interests of their nation's urban middle classes. Even in Guatemala, Castillo Armas, the instrument of U.S. intervention, was the protégé of a military hero of the 1944 revolution (Francisco Arana) and had served as an officer in Juan Jose Arévalo's army.[21] But nevertheless, whatever the political or class background of the specific local partner, the record clearly indicates that Latin American or Caribbean actors were, in every case, important "architects" of U.S. intervention.[22]

In 1954, David Atlee Phillips overcame his personal moral qualms and participated in the Eisenhower administration's Guatemalan intervention in the belief that he was helping to protect the national security of the United States. What he did not know—and what the thousands of other U.S. intelligence operatives and military personnel who carried out their presidents' Cold War hemispheric interventions did not know—was that the policy decisions that committed them to action had been shaped predominantly by factors of image, prestige, political self-interest, and foreign manipulation.

Notes

Preface

1. David Atlee Phillips, *The Night Watch* (New York: Ballantine, 1982), 37, 42–43, 45.
2. Ibid., 66–67.
3. The reference is to Geir Lundestad's article "Empire by Invitation? The United States and Western Europe, 1945–1952," *Journal of Peace Research* 23, no. 3 (1986), 263–277 in which he argues that the growth of the U.S. economic and military presence in Western Europe following World War II was in substantial part at the invitation of Western European governments.

Chapter One. Guatemala, 1954

1. Stephen G. Rabe, *Eisenhower and Latin America: The Foreign Policy of Anticommunism* (Chapel Hill: University of North Carolina Press, 1988), 60; Stephen Schlesinger and Stephen Kinzer, *Bitter Fruit: The Untold Story of the American Coup in Guatemala* (New York: Doubleday, 1984), 216; Evan Thomas, *The Very Best Men—Four Who Dared: The Early Years of the CIA* (New York: Simon & Schuster, 1995), 122–124.

2. The following brief overview of the intervention's operational aspects is drawn from four basic sources: Schlesinger and Kinzer, *Bitter Fruit;* Richard H. Immerman, *The CIA in Guatemala: The Foreign Policy of Intervention* (Austin: University of Texas Press, 1982); Piero Gleijeses, *Shattered Hope: The Guatemalan Revolution and the United States, 1944–1954* (Princeton, NJ: Princeton University Press, 1991); and Nick Cullather, *Secret History: The CIA's Classified Account of Its Operations in Guatemala, 1952–1954* (Stanford, CA: Stanford University Press, 1999).

3. CIA memorandum to Eisenhower, quoted in Immerman, *CIA in Guatemala*, 161 (emphasis in original).

4. Gleijeses, *Shattered Hope*, 246–247, 304–305, 307, 335; Cullather, *Secret History*, 68, 96–97. On 15 June 1954, the CIA station chief in Guatemala informed a high-ranking Guatemalan army officer that the time had come to "get moving and take over the Army," warning that this was "the last opportunity for the Army to salvage its honor and even its existence" (ibid., 84).

5. Several authors have argued that U.S. economic self-interest was the primary motivation for the 1954 intervention. In *Bitter Fruit*, Schlesinger and Kinzer write that Arbenz's "takeover of United Fruit land was probably the decisive factor pushing the Americans into action" (106). According to Jonas, "The U.S. could not tolerate the Guatemalan Revolution essentially because a nationalistic independent capitalism directly threatened existing U.S. interests there and called into question the feasibility of maintaining the area as a 'safe' preserve for future investments" (Suzanne Jonas, "Guatemala: Land of Eternal Struggle," in *Latin America: The Struggle with Dependency and Beyond*, ed. Ronald H. Chilcote and Joel C. Edelstein [New York: Wiley, 1974], 165). Also see José M. Aybar de Soto, *Dependency and Intervention: The Case of Guatemala in 1954* (Boulder, CO: Westview, 1978). Immerman, on the other hand, concludes that "the Eisenhower admin-

istration approved the CIA operation because all concerned officials believed that Communists dominated Guatemala's government and leading institutions. . . . The United States did not ultimately intervene in Guatemala to protect United Fruit. It intervened to halt what it believed to be the spread of the international Communist conspiracy" (*CIA in Guatemala*, 68, 82). Gleijeses offers a more holistic explanation: that "a complex interplay of imperial hubris, security concerns, and economic interests" produced the U.S. intervention (*Shattered Hope*, 7).

6. Dwight D. Eisenhower, *Mandate for Change, 1953–1956* (Garden City, NY: Doubleday, 1963), 3.

7. Mario Rosenthal, *Guatemala: The Story of an Emerging Latin American Democracy* (New York: Twayne, 1962), 235–237; Gleijeses, *Shattered Hope*, chaps. 1–2; Immerman, *CIA in Guatemala*, chaps. 2–3; Schlesinger and Kinzer, *Bitter Fruit*, chap. 3; Jonas, "Guatemala: Land of Eternal Struggle," 150–153.

8. For valuable interpretive overviews of Latin American political trends in the 1940s, see Fredrick Pike, *Spanish America, 1900–1970: Tradition and Social Innovation* (New York: Norton, 1973); and James Malloy, "Authoritarianism and Corporatism in Latin America: The Modal Pattern," in *Authoritarianism and Corporatism in Latin America,* ed. James Malloy (Pittsburgh: University of Pittsburgh Press, 1977).

9. Thomas Melville and Marjorie Melville, *Guatemala—Another Vietnam?* (Middlesex, UK: Penguin, 1971), 70–71; Gleijeses, *Shattered Hope*, 19–22, 86–93; Immerman, *CIA in Guatemala*, 68–75, 79, 82–83; Schlesinger and Kinzer, *Bitter Fruit*, 65–71, 75; U.S. Department of State, *Foreign Relations of the United States* (hereafter cited as *FRUS*), *1952–1954*, vol. 4: *The American Republics* (Washington, DC: Government Printing Office, 1983), 1060. On UFCO's pre-1944 role in Guatemala, see Paul Dosal, *Doing Business with the Dictators: A Political History of United Fruit in Guatemala, 1899–1944* (Wilmington, DE: SR Books, 1993).

10. Juan José Arévalo, *Escritos políticos y discursos* (Havana: Cultural, 1953), 115, 165–166, 310, 395 (my translations).

11. Jonas, "Guatemala: Land of Eternal Struggle," 153. According to Jonas, "The Arévalo government made no attempt to facilitate rural unionization, and on some occasions obstructed it" (ibid.).

12. Ibid., 154; Immerman, *CIA in Guatemala*, 75–79; Gleijeses, *Shattered Hope*, 93, 103.

13. Jonas, "Guatemala: Land of Eternal Struggle," 154, 160; Gleijeses, *Shattered Hope*, 107–115, 118–119; Immerman, *CIA in Guatemala*, 97.

14. Immerman, *CIA in Guatemala*, 37; Gleijeses, *Shattered Hope*, 23–24, 86, 117, 121–122; Schlesinger and Kinzer, *Bitter Fruit*, 26, 30, 34. In July 1950, Arévalo told U.S. Assistant Secretary of State for Inter-American Affairs Edward G. Miller that Guatemala's "destiny" was "of geographic necessity economically and politically tied to the United States and the Western Hemisphere" (*FRUS, 1950*, vol. 2: *United Nations; Western Hemisphere* [Washington, DC: Government Printing Office, 1976], 907).

15. U.S. Department of State, Office of Intelligence Research, "Guatemala: Communist Influence," Intelligence Report no. 5123, 23 October 1950, 48–49, in *OSS/State Department Intelligence and Research Reports: Latin America, 1941–1961,* ed. Paul Kesaris (Washington, DC: University Publications of America, 1979), microfilm, reel 9, frame 0082; Gleijeses, *Shattered Hope*, 39, 175.

16. Gleijeses, *Shattered Hope*, 40, 42, 175; Ronald M. Schneider, *Communism in Guatemala, 1944–1954* (New York: Praeger, 1959), 42.

17. Gleijeses, *Shattered Hope*, 76–81, 134–143, 147–148.

18. Schneider, *Communism in Guatemala*, 193; Gleijeses, *Shattered Hope*, 147, 182, 189.

19. *FRUS, 1952–1954*, 4: 1093.

20. Gleijeses, *Shattered Hope*, 147–148; Schneider, *Communism in Guatemala*, 80. According to José Manuel Fortuny, "The Guatemalan Labor Party does not propose to fight immediately for a socialist society in Guatemala. It fights now against the backward feudalism and imperialist oppression from which our country suffers, especially the oppression of North American imperialism which plunders our wealth, monopolizes our foreign trade and tries to impose upon us its political dictates and drag us into its warlike adventures. We fight for the economic development of Guatemala along capitalist lines, not because capitalism is 'good,' but because existing national and international conditions suggest that Guatemala take the path of liquidating feudalism and the backward forms of production which obtain today in our country" (quoted in Daniel James, *Red Design for the Americas: Guatemalan Prelude* [New York: Day, 1954], 95).

21. Gleijeses, *Shattered Hope*, 149–156; Immerman, *CIA in Guatemala*, 63–65; Jonas, "Guatemala: Land of Eternal Struggle," 156–159.

22. Gleijeses, *Shattered Hope*, 144–147, 152; Schneider, *Communism in Guatemala*, 80.

23. Gleijeses, *Shattered Hope*, 155–156, 164, 194–196; Immerman, *CIA in Guatemala*, 65–67, 81. Also see U.S. Department of State, Office of Intelligence Research, "Agrarian Reform in Guatemala," Intelligence Report no. 6001, 5 March 1953, 5–6, in Kesaris, ed., *OSS/State Department Intelligence*, microfilm, reel 9, frame 0208. Among the landholdings expropriated under the agrarian reform program were 1,700 acres owned by Arbenz and 1,200 belonging to his friend and future foreign minister Guillermo Toriello. See Schlesinger and Kinzer, *Bitter Fruit*, 55.

24. Gleijeses, *Shattered Hope*, 178–182; U.S. Department of State, Office of Intelligence Research, "Guatemalan Support of Subversion and Communist Objectives (1950–1953)," Intelligence Report no. 6185, 30 April 1953, 18–19, in Kesaris, ed., *OSS/State Department Intelligence*, microfilm, reel 9, frame 0220.

25. Gleijeses, *Shattered Hope*, 141, 178, 180, 184–189.

26. Ibid., 148, 177.

27. Ibid., 94, 99; Immerman, *CIA in Guatemala*, 75–78.

28. *FRUS, 1947*, vol. 8: *American Republics* (Washington, DC: Government Printing Office, 1972), 713.

29. Gleijeses, *Shattered Hope*, 93–94, 96, 103; Alex Roberto Hybel, *How Leaders Reason: US Intervention in the Caribbean Basin and Latin America* (Oxford, UK, and Cambridge, MA: Basil Blackwell, 1990), 55; Harold A. Scott, "Dismantling the Good Neighbor: Domestic Politics and the Overthrow of the Guatemalan Revolution" (unpublished paper, University of Pittsburgh, Graduate School of Public and International Affairs), 20–21; Bryce Wood, *The Dismantling of the Good Neighbor Policy* (Austin: University of Texas Press, 1985), 154.

30. Gleijeses, *Shattered Hope*, 9, 12, 48–49, 99, 217–219, 337; Schlesinger and Kinzer, *Bitter Fruit*, 40, 74; Arévalo radio address, reprinted in Arévalo, *Escritos políticos y discursos*, 406–407. Also see Zachary Karabell, *Architects of Intervention: The United States, the Third World, and the Cold War, 1946–1962* (Baton Rouge: Louisiana State University Press, 1999), 114. During Arévalo's six-year term as president, "Some 25 to 35 uprisings either occurred or were uncovered in the planning stage." Max Gordon, "A Case History of U.S. Subversion: Guatemala, 1954," in *Guatemala in Rebellion: Unfinished History*, ed. Jonathan Fried, Marvin Gettleman, Deborah Levenson, and Nancy Peckenham (New York: Grove, 1983), 53.

31. Immerman, *CIA in Guatemala*, 89, 120, 129; Gleijeses, *Shattered Hope*, 365; Karabell, *Architects of Intervention*, 122–123. Also see Cullather, *Secret History*, 34. In March 1953, Guatemala's ambassador to the United States told State Department officials that "Guatemala's neighbors were professing alarm over Guatemalan Communism, but in reality their alarm was only that of the wealthy landowners over agrarian reform" (*FRUS, 1952–1954*, 4: 1060). In 1954, Castillo Armas received "generous amounts of cash and arms" from the dictatorships of Somoza in Nicaragua, Rafael Trujillo in the Dominican Republic, and Marcos Pérez Jiménez in Venezuela. See Frederick W. Marks III, "The CIA and Castillo Armas in Guatemala, 1954: New Clues to an Old Puzzle," *Diplomatic History* 14, no. 1 (Winter 1990): 76. In preparation for the 1954 invasion, Somoza allowed Castillo Armas and the CIA to set up training bases in Nicaragua, including one on a Somoza-owned plantation. The invasion was launched from staging areas in Honduras, and the governments of Nicaragua and Honduras permitted the CIA to use their territory for radio warfare and aircraft sorties against the Arbenz government. See Schlesinger and Kinzer, *Bitter Fruit*, 114–116, 169–170. According to the CIA's internal history of the intervention, "Somoza's support became essential to PBSUCCESS" (Cullather, *Secret History*, 48).

32. Gleijeses, *Shattered Hope*, 95–104, 362–363.

33. Ibid., 101–102; Immerman, *CIA in Guatemala*, 89; *FRUS, 1950*, 2: 912; "Guatemala," CIA research report, 27 July 1950, 1, in *CIA Research Reports: Latin America, 1946–1976*, ed. Paul Kesaris (Frederick, MD: University Publications of America, 1982), microfilm, reel 5, frame 0073.

34. Gleijeses, *Shattered Hope*, 76, 80, 102, 142–143, 183, 195; Gutiérrez quoted in U.S. Department of State, Office of Intelligence Research, "Guatemala: Communist Influence," Intelligence Report no. 5123, 23 October 1950, 102, in Kesaris, ed., *OSS/State Department Intelligence*, Appendix C, microfilm, reel 9, frame 0082. A predecessor to the PGT had been crushed by Ubico in 1932. See Gleijeses, *Shattered Hope*, 8–10.

35. Immerman, *CIA in Guatemala*, 99; *FRUS, 1950*, 2: 866. Jonas charges that Patterson "carried his involvement with the opposition beyond cocktail parties to the point of attending clandestine meetings plotting Arévalo's overthrow" ("Guatemala: Land of Eternal Struggle," 160–161). Also see Schlesinger and Kinzer, *Bitter Fruit*, 86.

36. Immerman, *CIA in Guatemala*, 109–110; Gleijeses, *Shattered Hope*, 128–129; *FRUS, 1952–1954*, 4: 1144.

37. Scott, "Dismantling the Good Neighbor," 15–17; Gleijeses, *Shattered Hope*, 129. As Robert F. Woodward, deputy assistant secretary of state for inter-American affairs in 1953–1954, later recalled: "So far as 'indoctrination' is concerned, there was no deliberate, planned or systematic training in policy for the Foreign Service Officers (FSOs) who were working on Latin American relations. But 'non-intervention' was so much the centerpiece of all relations with Latin America that it loomed like Mount Hood or Mount Rainier on the landscape. It was just there. You took it for granted as being something big and immovable" (quoted in Wood, *The Dismantling of the Good Neighbor Policy*, 160).

38. Gleijeses, *Shattered Hope*, 125–127.

39. *FRUS, 1951*, vol. 2: *United Nations; Western Hemisphere* (Washington, DC: Government Printing Office, 1979), 1437; Cullather, *Secret History*, 17, 24, 27. In August 1950, the CIA began recruiting "suitable indigenous Guatemalan personnel" as assets, but as late as December 1953 the agency's Guatemalan station had "no penetrations of the PGT, government agencies, armed forces, or labor unions"—raising questions about the agency's sources of field information (Cullather, *Secret History*, 18, 46).

40. Cullather, *Secret History*, 28–32; Gleijeses, *Shattered Hope*, 228–230; Immerman,

CIA in Guatemala, 120–121; *FRUS, 1952–1954: Guatemala Supplement* (Washington, DC: Government Printing Office, 2003), 1, 28–29, 31–32, 34–35. Former CIA director Richard Helms told interviewer Piero Gleijeses in 1989 that "Truman okayed a good many decisions for covert operations that in later years he said he knew nothing about. It's all presidential deniability" (Gleijeses, *Shattered Hope*, 366–367n17).

41. Among the Eisenhower administration officials with personal ties to UFCO were Secretary of State John Foster Dulles, CIA director Allen Dulles, Assistant Secretary of State (and former CIA director) Walter Bedell Smith, Special White House Assistant for National Security Affairs Robert Cutler, Assistant Secretary of State for Inter-American Affairs John Moors Cabot, U.S. Ambassador to the United Nations Henry Cabot Lodge, and Eisenhower's personal White House secretary, Ann Whitman. Influential "outsiders" with UFCO connections included World Bank President John J. McCloy and former Assistant Secretary of State for Inter-American Affairs Spruille Braden. See Schlesinger and Kinzer, *Bitter Fruit*, 106–107; Immerman, *CIA in Guatemala*, 124–128.

42. Cullather, *Secret History*, 19, 37; *FRUS, 1952–1954*, 4: 191–196. The NSC hypothesized additional repercussions: "Institution of the action would provide a propaganda weapon generally to Communists and leftists in Central America. Moreover, to the degree that it would promote governmental seizure, it would assure the placement of extremists in charge of the former Company properties, and would thus increase the power of elements opposed to the United States in Central America, possibly including Panama, and make uncertain the cooperation of the governments of the area with the United States. Finally, it might contribute to the spread of the Guatemalan example and to the eventual overthrow of four Central American governments now friendly to the United States, which would transform our present security in the Caribbean into a dangerous threat at our backdoor. . . . In Latin America generally, nationalization of the United Fruit Company properties would further stimulate the already serious movement for similar action against U.S. companies, which have properties with an established value of $5 billion in Latin America, including strategic industries in the fields of mining and petroleum. . . . Action by one branch of the U.S. Government against one private company, as a monopoly, would make most difficult the successful defense of that company's legitimate interests by the Department of State, and weaken very seriously the ability of that Department to oppose the tide of nationalization of other American properties in the entire area and elsewhere. Increased nationalization of U.S. properties would not only deprive the United States and U.S. nationals of a degree of control of strategic resources, but would be contrary to the policy . . . of encouraging Latin American countries to take measures to attract private investment" (*FRUS, 1952–1954*, 4: 193).

43. Cullather, *Secret History*, 37; Dulles quoted in Immerman, *CIA in Guatemala*, 82; Fortuny quoted in Gleijeses, *Shattered Hope*, 366 (also see 362–363); *FRUS, 1952–1954*, 4: 1059.

44. Allen Dulles quoted in Rabe, *Eisenhower and Latin America*, 31; Cabot quoted in Wood, *Dismantling of the Good Neighbor Policy*, 161; Milton Eisenhower quoted in Gleijeses, *Shattered Hope*, 268–269, and in Immerman, *CIA in Guatemala*, 133; *FRUS, 1952–1954*, 4: 1061–1064, 1070, 1083. "The Army," the May NIE noted presciently, "is the only organized element in Guatemala capable of rapidly and decisively altering the political situation" (*FRUS, 1952–1954*, 4: 1062).

45. John Prados, *Safe for Democracy: The Secret Wars of the CIA* (Chicago: Ivan R. Dee, 2006), 108.

46. Ibid., 26–27; Immerman, *CIA in Guatemala*, 82, 232n8; *FRUS, 1952–1954*, 4:

1095n1, 1106, 1109–1110. CIA officials "assumed the existence of links between the PGT and Moscow." They believed that "all Communist Parties, acting under the direction of the Soviet Union, followed the same general pattern in seeking to capture free social institutions and democratic governments. Some operate openly and others clandestinely, but all are integral parts of the world wide Communist effort" (Cullather, *Secret History*, 26, 47n27). Eisenhower's ambassador to Guatemala, John Peurifoy, was more colorful in his assessment: "Communism is directed by the Kremlin all over the world," he told a congressional committee in 1954, "and anyone who thinks differently doesn't know what he is talking about" (ibid., 26). After Arbenz's overthrow, U.S. agents combed through the ousted government's records but found "nothing conclusive" linking the PGT with the Soviets (Rabe, *Eisenhower and Latin America*, 57).

47. *FRUS, 1952–1954*, 4: 1078–1079, 1083–1084.

48. Ibid., 1145–1148; Cullather, *Secret History*, 33; Gaddis Smith, *The Last Years of the Monroe Doctrine, 1945–1993* (New York: Hill & Wang, 1994), 85. "Communist penetration in Guatemala was the most striking example of the Kremlin's strategy in Latin America," U.S. Ambassador Peurifoy told a congressional committee three months after the 1954 intervention. "Busy with power expansion in Europe and Asia, the Red rulers of Russia have long pushed their conspiracy in Latin America as a diversionary tactic which, while showing no immediate gain of territory under their domination, would at least weaken and harass our defenses" (Peurifoy testimony, U.S. House of Representatives, Select Committee on Communist Aggression, Subcommittee on Latin America, *Hearings on Guatemala*, 83rd Cong., 2nd sess., 27 September 1954, 116).

49. U.S. Department of State, *Foreign Relations of the United States, 1948*, vol. 9: *Western Hemisphere* (Washington, DC: Government Printing Office, 1972), 132; *FRUS, 1952–1954*, 4: 7, 468; Rabe, *Eisenhower and Latin America*, 30. "If we did not have the Latins with us in the voting processes in the UN," Eisenhower's ambassador to the United Nations, Henry Cabot Lodge, told Vice President Richard Nixon, "the United States would simply have to get out of the United Nations" (*FRUS, 1955–1957*, vol. 7: *American Republics: Central and South America* [Washington, DC: Government Printing Office, 1987], 615).

50. *FRUS, 1952–1954*, 4: 1065, 1068, 1074–1075, 1147; Cullather, *Secret History*, 24; U.S. Department of State, Office of Intelligence Research, "Guatemalan Support for Subversion and Communist Objectives (1950–1953)," Intelligence Report no. 6185, 30 April 1953, 16, in Kesaris, ed., *OSS/State Department Intelligence*, microfilm, reel 9, frame 0220. "The immediate Communist objective," U.S. ambassador Rudolf Schoenfeld reported in February 1953, was "the neutralizing of Guatemala as a Western nation" (*FRUS, 1952–1954: Guatemala Supplement*, 68–69).

51. *FRUS, 1952–1954*, 4: 1083, 1147–1149.

52. Quoted in Blanche Wiesen Cook, *The Declassified Eisenhower: A Divided Legacy* (Garden City, NY: Doubleday, 1981), 269–270.

53. *FRUS, 1952–1954*, 4: 1107.

54. Robert R. Bowie and Richard H. Immerman, *Waging Peace: How Eisenhower Shaped an Enduring Cold War Strategy* (New York: Oxford University Press, 1998), 124.

55. Ibid., 135.

56. Ibid., 75–80; Robert A. Divine, *Eisenhower and the Cold War* (New York: Oxford University Press, 1981), 12–19; Melvin Small, *Democracy & Diplomacy: The Impact of Domestic Politics on U.S. Foreign Policy, 1789–1994* (Baltimore: Johns Hopkins University Press, 1996), 95; Rabe, *Eisenhower and Latin America*, 29; Gleijeses, *Shattered Hope*, 234; Stephen G. Rabe, "Dulles, Latin America, and Cold War Anticommunism," in *John Foster*

Dulles and the Diplomacy of the Cold War, ed. Richard H. Immerman (Princeton, NJ: Princeton University Press, 1990), 160; Cole Blasier, *The Hovering Giant: U.S. Responses to Revolutionary Change in Latin America, 1910–1985,* rev. ed. (Pittsburgh: University of Pittsburgh Press, 1985), 229; Cullather, *Secret History,* 32.

57. Scott, "Dismantling the Good Neighbor," 19.

58. Edward L. Bernays, *Biography of an Idea: Memoirs of Public Relations Counsel Edward L. Bernays* (New York: Simon & Schuster, 1965), 758–762, 767; Cook, *Declassified Eisenhower,* 226; Immerman, *CIA in Guatemala,* 111–114, 125; Schlesinger and Kinzer, *Bitter Fruit,* 79–89; Gleijeses, *Shattered Hope,* 232–234. For a useful overview of Bernays' Guatemalan campaign, see Larry Tye, *The Father of Spin: Edward L. Bernays and the Birth of Public Relations* (New York: Crown, 1998), 166–182.

59. Schlesinger and Kinzer, *Bitter Fruit,* 80–81, 89–90, 94–97; Immerman, *CIA in Guatemala,* 126–128.

60. Quoted in *Time* magazine, 11 January 1954, 27.

61. Schlesinger and Kinzer, *Bitter Fruit,* 90–96; Immerman, *CIA in Guatemala,* 116; Gleijeses, *Shattered Hope,* 90, 129; David McKean, *Tommy the Cork: Washington's Ultimate Insider from Roosevelt to Reagan* (South Royalton, VT: Steerforth, 2004), 214–216, 219–224; Peter Grose, *Gentleman Spy: The Life of Allen Dulles* (Boston: Houghton Mifflin, 1994), 371; Cullather, *Secret History,* 16–18.

62. E. Howard Hunt, *Undercover: Memoirs of an American Secret Agent* (New York: Berkley Publishing Corp., 1974), 84, 97; Cook, *Declassified Eisenhower,* 227–228.

63. Robert J. Donovan, *Eisenhower: The Inside Story* (New York: Harper & Brothers, 1956), 10, 86, 125, 142–143, 148–151, 222; David W. Reinhard, *The Republican Right since 1945* (Lexington: University Press of Kentucky, 1983), 100–101, 104–108, 115, 121; Bowie and Immerman, *Waging Peace,* 76, 80; Gary W. Reichard, *Politics as Usual: The Age of Truman and Eisenhower* (Arlington Heights, IL: Harlan Davidson, 1988), 91; Chester J. Pach and Elmo Richardson, *The Presidency of Dwight D. Eisenhower* (Lawrence: University Press of Kansas, 1991), 59–62; Ronald J. Caridi, *The Korean War and American Politics: The Republican Party as a Case Study* (Philadelphia: University of Pennsylvania Press, 1968), 274–275; Immerman, *CIA in Guatemala,* 115; *New York Times,* 17 October 1953, 13; Harold A. Scott, "Covert Operations as an Instrument of Foreign Policy: U.S. Intervention in Iran and Guatemala" (Ph.D. diss., Carnegie Mellon University, 1999), 66–79, 142. Donovan reports that Eisenhower's "vexation with the powerful right wing reached such extremes in the summer of 1953 that for a time he gave prolonged thought to the idea of forming a new political party in America" (Donovan, *Eisenhower: The Inside Story,* 142). According to Harold Scott, Eisenhower chose "covert operations in Iran and Guatemala in this political context." The two interventions "helped the . . . administration ward off charges of appeasement from the Republican right." The conservative Republicans' "challenge . . . ranked as the administration's most pressing domestic concern" during its first two years in office. Eisenhower "needed demonstrable victories against Communism to quiet charges of appeasement. This required taking decisive actions that would play as dramatic victories before home audiences but did not risk increasing American commitments." Both interventions "achieved domestic political objectives," Scott concludes ("Covert Operations as an Instrument of Foreign Policy," 78, 142).

64. Pach and Richardson, *Presidency of Dwight D. Eisenhower,* 16–20, 50, 75–82, 88–89; Bowie and Immerman, *Waging Peace,* 43, 70–71, 75, 78–79.

65. Cullather, *Secret History,* 35–37.

66. There were tactical benefits as well. In contrast to Eastern Europe or Asia, a U.S.

rollback of communism in the United States' Central American sphere of influence was a "safe" intervention in the sense that it was unlikely to provoke a Soviet military response that might trigger a general war. If carried out covertly, utilizing Central American proxies, a U.S. intervention would also enable Eisenhower to "plausibly deny" U.S. involvement, shielding the administration from outraged protests by its Latin American allies (Bowie and Immerman, *Waging Peace*, 220; Scott, "Dismantling the Good Neighbor," 5, 12–13, 28).

67. *FRUS, 1952–1954*, 4: 1091–1093; Gleijeses, *Shattered Hope*, 363–364.

68. Gleijeses, *Shattered Hope*, 280, 295–304; Cullather, *Secret History*, 80–82; Immerman, *CIA in Guatemala*, 156, 158.

69. Immerman, *CIA in Guatemala*, 179; Scott, "Covert Operations as an Instrument of Foreign Policy," 132–133; John Foster Dulles, "International Communism in Guatemala," *Department of State Bulletin* 31, no. 785 (12 July 1954): 43–45.

70. Blasier, *Hovering Giant*, 229; Scott, "Dismantling the Good Neighbor," 29–30.

71. Immerman, *CIA in Guatemala*, 152–153; Gleijeses, *Shattered Hope*, 303; *Public Papers of the Presidents of the United States: Dwight D. Eisenhower, 1954* (Washington, DC: Government Printing Office, 1960), 731, 780, 981, 989, 998, 1004; *Public Papers of the Presidents of the United States: Dwight D. Eisenhower, 1955* (Washington, DC: Government Printing Office, 1959), 191–192; Scott, "Dismantling the Good Neighbor," 31; Stephen E. Ambrose, *Eisenhower*, vol. 2, *The President* (New York: Simon & Schuster, 1983), 196; Rabe, *Eisenhower and Latin America*, 4.

72. Scott, "Covert Operations as an Instrument of Foreign Policy," 134–135; Richard Harkness and Gladys Harkness, "The Mysterious Doings of the CIA," *Saturday Evening Post*, 30 October–13 November 1954; Thomas, *Very Best Men*, 124. Meanwhile, at lower echelons of the CIA, the intelligence officers who carried out the intervention were basking in the confident assurance "that their careers would take off." "After Guatemala," the wife of one CIA operative recalled, "it was, 'You can have any job you want! You can own the world!'" (Thomas, *Very Best Men*, 126).

Chapter Two. Cuba, 1961

1. Richard Reeves, *President Kennedy: Profile of Power* (New York: Simon & Schuster, 1993), 106; Peter Wyden, *Bay of Pigs: The Untold Story* (New York: Simon & Schuster, 1979), 272, 289, 306, 310; Richard E. Welch Jr., *Response to Revolution: The United States and the Cuban Revolution, 1959–1961* (Chapel Hill: University of North Carolina Press, 1985), 87, 91; Theodore C. Sorensen, *Kennedy* (New York: Harper & Row, 1965), 308; Peter Kornbluh, ed., *Bay of Pigs Declassified: The Secret CIA Report on the Invasion of Cuba* (New York: Free Press, 1998), 38, 55; Vladislav Zubok and Constantine Pleshakov, *Inside the Kremlin's Cold War: From Stalin to Khrushchev* (Cambridge, MA: Harvard University Press, 1996), 236, 241–242; W. W. Rostow, *The Diffusion of Power: An Essay in Recent History* (New York: Macmillan, 1972), 210–211. Casualty figures from Thomas G. Paterson, "Fixation with Cuba: The Bay of Pigs, Missile Crisis, and Covert War Against Fidel Castro," in *Kennedy's Quest for Victory: American Foreign Policy, 1961–1963*, ed. Thomas G. Paterson (New York: Oxford University Press, 1989), 132. Undersecretary of State Chester Bowles described Kennedy as "quite shattered" in the immediate aftermath of the invasion. Robert Dallek, *An Unfinished Life: John F. Kennedy, 1917–1963* (Boston: Little, Brown, 2003), 367.

2. Welch, *Response to Revolution*, 87–88; *Public Papers of the Presidents of the United States: John F. Kennedy, 1961* (Washington, DC: Government Printing Office, 1962), 304–

306; Michael R. Beschloss, *The Crisis Years: Kennedy and Khrushchev, 1960–1961* (New York: HarperCollins, 1991), 129; Lloyd C. Gardner, *Pay Any Price: Lyndon Johnson and the Wars for Vietnam* (Chicago: Ivan R. Dee, 1995), 44. As Richard J. Walton noted, Kennedy's denial of U.S. military involvement in the Bay of Pigs invasion was "quite an extraordinary statement. Not only was the invasion planned by the United States, but the United States recruited, paid, and trained the exile force. . . . The exiles used American military equipment. They were trained by American military men. . . . The warplanes were American, flown by Americans. The frogmen who were the first on the beach were American. American ships carried the invaders, and American naval units accompanied them. Americans were killed in the operation. To claim that America did not intervene was to lie and be caught in the lie" (*Cold War and Counterrevolution: The Foreign Policy of John F. Kennedy* [New York: Viking, 1972], 49–50).

3. Louis A. Pérez Jr., *Cuba: Between Reform and Revolution* (New York: Oxford University Press, 1988), 295–303; Marífeli Pérez-Stable, *The Cuban Revolution: Origins, Course, and Legacy*, 2nd ed. (New York: Oxford University Press, 1999), 27–31; James O'Connor, *The Origins of Socialism in Cuba* (Ithaca, NY: Cornell University Press, 1970), 58.

4. Louis A. Pérez Jr., *Cuba and the United States: Ties of Singular Intimacy* (Athens: University of Georgia Press, 1997), 218–225; Thomas G. Paterson, *Contesting Castro: The United States and the Triumph of the Cuban Revolution* (New York: Oxford University Press, 1994), 35, 41–43; Morris H. Morley, *Imperial State and Revolution: The United States and Cuba, 1952–1986* (New York: Cambridge University Press, 1987), 51; Sebastian Balfour, *Castro*, 2nd ed. (London: Longman, 1995), 8.

5. Pérez, *Cuba and the United States*, 113–117, 138–139, 152–159; Whitney Perkins, *Constraint of Empire: The United States and Caribbean Interventions* (Westport, CT: Greenwood, 1981), chap. 1; Paterson, *Contesting Castro*, chap. 3; Morley, *Imperial State and Revolution*, chap. 2; U.S. Department of State, *Foreign Relations of the United States* (hereafter cited as *FRUS*), *1958–1960*, vol. 6: *Cuba* (Washington, DC: Government Printing Office, 1991), 190; Balfour, *Castro*, 9.

6. Castro, quoted in Tad Szulc, *Fidel: A Critical Portrait* (New York: Avon, 1986), 164, 240.

7. Mario Llerena, *The Unsuspected Revolution: The Birth and Rise of Castroism* (Ithaca, NY: Cornell University Press, 1978), 60–61. Also see Marta Harnecker, *Fidel Castro's Political Strategy: From Moncada to Victory* (New York: Pathfinder, 1987), 24–25.

8. Fidel Castro speeches, Havana, 23 March 1959 and 15 December 1959, Foreign Broadcast Information Service, available through the *Castro Speech Data Base: Speeches, Interviews, Articles*, Latin American Network Information Center, http://www1.lanic.utexas.edu/la/cb/cuba/castro.html; J. P. Morray, *The Second Revolution in Cuba* (New York: Monthly Review Press, 1962), 31.

9. Szulc, *Fidel*, 38, 145–146, 166, 173–176, 355; Rolando Bonachea and Nelson Valdes, eds., *Selected Works of Fidel Castro*, vol. 1: *Revolutionary Struggle, 1947–1958* (Cambridge, MA: MIT Press, 1972), 272; Balfour, *Castro*, 64; Carlos Franqui, *Diary of the Cuban Revolution* (New York: Viking, 1980), 338.

10. Jules R. Benjamin, *The United States and the Origins of the Cuban Revolution: An Empire of Liberty in the Age of National Liberation* (Princeton, NJ: Princeton University Press, 1990), 215; Fidel Castro speech, Havana, 17 January 1959, *Castro Speech Data Base*; Robert E. Quirk, *Fidel Castro* (New York: Norton, 1993), 224; Hugh Thomas, *The Cuban Revolution* (New York: Harper & Row, 1977), 294, 296; *New York Times*, 16 January 1959, 1, and 21 February 1959, 8; Morray, *Second Revolution in Cuba*, 30.

11. Morray, *Second Revolution in Cuba*, 31; Fidel Castro speech, Havana, 21 January 1959, *Castro Speech Data Base; New York Times*, 22 January 1959, 1, and 21 February 1959, 8.

12. Boris Goldenberg, *The Cuban Revolution and Latin America* (New York: Praeger, 1965), 179; *New York Times*, 21 February 1959, 8, and 23 March 1959, 1; Fidel Castro speeches, Caracas, 25 January 1959, and Havana, 1 March 1959, *Castro Speech Data Base;* Jorge I. Domínguez, *To Make a World Safe for Revolution: Cuba's Foreign Policy* (Cambridge, MA: Harvard University Press, 1989), 26–27.

13. Fidel Castro speech, Havana, 21 January 1959, *Castro Speech Data Base;* Benjamin, *The United States and the Origins of the Cuban Revolution*, 170–171; Thomas, *The Cuban Revolution*, 308; Andrés Suárez, *Cuba: Castroism and Communism, 1959–1966* (Cambridge, MA: MIT Press, 1967), 48n36. "At the beginning of the first revolutionary government," Castro's first treasury minister writes, "Castro believed that the U.S. would eventually invade Cuba. Most of his moves were made with this idea in mind. . . . He had a psychopathic suspicion of everything American." Rufo López-Fresquet, *My Fourteen Months with Castro* (Cleveland: World Publishing, 1966), 164–165. Also see Philip W. Bonsal, *Cuba, Castro, and the United States* (Pittsburgh: University of Pittsburgh Press, 1971), 67.

14. Szulc, *Fidel*, 364; Wayne S. Smith, "Castro's Cuba: Soviet Partner or Nonaligned?" Latin American Program working paper (Washington, DC: Woodrow Wilson International Center for Scholars, 1984), 6, 9. During his January 1959 trip to Venezuela, Castro proclaimed that his "dream" was to see Latin America "entirely united in a single force." He hoped, he said, "to sow the seeds of unity in the countries of Latin America in defense of their common interests," and he envisioned the day when Latin Americans would be united by a common market and a common passport, a day when "the U.S. will have to adapt itself to Latin American politics [and] will not always be defending the interests of monopolies" or helping to "install and maintain Latin American dictators" (Thomas, *The Cuban Revolution*, 304, 307–308; Fidel Castro speech, Caracas, 25 January 1959, *Castro Speech Data Base*).

15. Welch, *Response to Revolution*, 11; Smith, "Castro's Cuba," 7; Thomas, *The Cuban Revolution*, 450; Bonsal, *Castro, Cuba, and the United States*, 66, 76.

16. Domínguez, *To Make a World Safe for Revolution*, 18, 32; Szulc, *Fidel*, 512–513, 531, 536–539; Balfour, *Castro*, 65, 68; Wyden, *Bay of Pigs*, 26–27; *New York Times*, 18 April 1959, 1, and 20 April 1959, 1; Jeffrey J. Safford, "The Nixon-Castro Meeting of 19 April 1959," *Diplomatic History* 4, no. 4 (Fall 1980): 425–431; Thomas, *Cuban Revolution*, 431; López-Fresquet, *My Fourteen Months with Castro*, 114.

17. Pérez, *Cuba: Between Reform and Revolution*, 320; Pérez-Stable, *Cuban Revolution*, 64; Benjamin, *The United States and the Origins of the Cuban Revolution*, 181; Szulc, *Fidel*, 543–545; Pérez, *Cuba and the United States*, 240; Morley, *Imperial State and Revolution*, 83. In Castro's words, the May 1959 agrarian reform "truly established a rupture between the Revolution and the richest and most privileged sectors of the country, and a rupture with the United States [and] transnational corporations" (quoted in Szulc, *Fidel*, 543).

18. Aleksandr Fursenko and Timothy Naftali, *"One Hell of a Gamble": Khrushchev, Castro, and Kennedy, 1958–1964* (New York: Norton, 1997), 21–22; Szulc, *Fidel*, 523–525; Thomas, *The Cuban Revolution*, 435.

19. Balfour, *Castro*, 55–56, 65; Szulc, *Fidel*, 214, 230–231, 264, 360–361, 363, 512–514; Smith, "Castro's Cuba," 3.

20. I am indebted to Professor Carlos Alzugaray, a Cuban diplomat and scholar at the Instituto Superior de Relaciones Internacionales in Havana, for defining the ideological

and geopolitical views of the 26th of July Movement's moderate and radical factions. See Alzugaray's July–August 1998 Internet dialogue with U.S. subscribers to H-DIPLO, the H-NET List for Diplomatic History (h-diplo@h-net.msu.edu), especially his postings of 25 July, 26 July, and 28 July, at the H-NET archives, which can be accessed through the H-DIPLO subscription page at http://www.lsoft.com/scripts/wl.exe?SL1=H-DIPLO &H=H-NET.MSU.EDU.

21. Jacques Levesque, *The USSR and the Cuban Revolution: Soviet Ideological and Strategical Perspectives, 1959–1977* (New York: Praeger, 1978), xix; López-Fresquet, *My Fourteen Months with Castro*, 163; Balfour, *Castro*, 54–55, 65–66; Szulc, *Fidel*, 311, 465, 518–522; Thomas, *The Cuban Revolution*, 220–221.

22. Szulc, *Fidel*, 63, 513, 524, 544, 554–558, 575; Balfour, *Castro*, 66–67; Fursenko and Naftali, *"One Hell of a Gamble,"* 21–22, 31; Thomas, *The Cuban Revolution*, 473; Quirk, *Fidel Castro*, 274–275.

23. Quirk, *Fidel Castro*, 162; López-Fresquet, *My Fourteen Months with Castro*, 148, 163; Smith, "Castro's Cuba," 9–11; Fursenko and Naftali, *"One Hell of a Gamble,"* 11–12, 20–29, 36, 38.

24. Domínguez, *To Make a World Safe for Revolution*, 16, 21–22; Nicola Miller, *Soviet Relations with Latin America, 1959–1987* (Cambridge, UK: Cambridge University Press, 1989), 73; Suárez, *Cuba: Castroism and Communism*, 84–85; Fursenko and Naftali, *"One Hell of a Gamble,"* 38–39. "By the end of 1959," Szulc writes, "Castro had the Russians pretty much where he wanted them—as an antidote to the Americans" (*Fidel*, 559). In his memoirs, Nikita Khrushchev acknowledged that it was the Cubans who initiated proposals for collaboration with the USSR. See *Khrushchev Remembers*, ed. and trans. Strobe Talbott (Boston: Little, Brown, 1970), 489, 491.

25. *FRUS, 1958–1960*, 6: 190–191, 264, 302–307, 732; *Operation ZAPATA: The "Ultrasensitive" Report and Testimony of the Board of Inquiry on the Bay of Pigs* (Frederick, MD: University Publications of America, 1981), 55–56; Levesque, *The USSR and the Cuban Revolution*, xx; Morley, *Imperial State and Revolution*, 63–64; Paterson, *Contesting Castro*, 225 and chaps. 17–19.

26. *FRUS, 1958–1960*, 6: 1000–1001.

27. Ibid., 635–639, 651–652, 656–658, 732–733, 733n6, 742–743, 850–851, 861–863, 955; David J. Ulbrich, "Research Note: 'A Program for Covert Action against the Castro Regime, 16 March 1960,'" *Newsletter of the Society for Historians of American Foreign Relations* 33, no. 3 (September 2002): 1–19; Kornbluh, ed., *Bay of Pigs Declassified*, 24.

28. Paterson, *Containing Castro*, 183–187; *FRUS, 1958–1960*, vol. 5: *American Republics* (Washington, DC: Government Printing Office, 1991), 393, 412; *FRUS, 1958–1960*, 6: 187, 190, 459, 506, 636.

29. Morley, *Imperial State and Revolution*, 400n114; *FRUS, 1958–1960*, 6: 305, 331, 653, 870–871; Paterson, *Contesting Castro*, 221; U.S. Senate, Committee on Foreign Relations, *Executive Sessions of the Senate Foreign Relations Committee (Historical Series)*, vol. 11, 86th Cong., 1st sess., 1959, 125; Bonsal, *Castro, Cuba, and the United States*, 40; Safford, "The Nixon-Castro Meeting of 19 April 1959," 431; U.S. Senate, Committee on the Judiciary, *Communist Threat to the United States through the Caribbean: Hearings before the Subcommittee to Investigate the Administration of the Internal Security Act and Other Internal Security Laws* (pt. 3), 86th Cong., 1st sess., 5 November 1959, 162–164.

30. *FRUS, 1958–1960*, 6: 513–516, 539–542, 552, 605–611, 1001.

31. Alzugaray, H-DIPLO posting, 22 July 1998; *FRUS, 1958–1960*, 6: 742–743, 1000–1001; *FRUS, 1958–1960*, 5: 429.

32. *FRUS, 1958–1960*, 6: 539–542, 552–553, 732; Pérez, *Cuba and the United States*, 240; Morley, *Imperial State and Revolution*, 99–102, 127.

33. *FRUS, 1958–1960*, 6: 519, 722; Stephen G. Rabe, *Eisenhower and Latin America: The Foreign Policy of Anticommunism* (Chapel Hill: University of North Carolina Press, 1988), 92–96, 131.

34. Dwight D. Eisenhower, *Mandate for Change, 1953–1956* (Garden City, NJ: Doubleday, 1963), 420; Rabe, *Eisenhower and Latin America*, 64–65; *FRUS, 1958–1960*, 5: 429.

35. Benjamin, *The United States and the Origins of the Cuban Revolution*, 181; Morley, *Imperial State and Revolution*, 84; *FRUS, 1958–1960*, 5: 398.

36. CIA, "Sino-Soviet Activity in Latin America," intelligence précis, 14 March 1960, Annex A of National Security Council, "Operations Coordinating Board Report on U.S. Policy toward Latin America," NSC 5902/1, 6 April 1960, 11, in *Documents of the National Security Council—Second Supplement* (Washington, DC: University Publications of America, 1983), microfilm, reel 2, frame 848.

37. *FRUS, 1958–1960*, 5: 91–92 (emphasis added).

38. *FRUS, 1958–1960*, 6: 455, 460, 482, 636, 760, 1001; Dwight D. Eisenhower, *Waging Peace, 1956–1961* (Garden City, NJ: Doubleday, 1965), 522; Paterson, *Contesting Castro*, 256; Welch, *Response to Revolution*, 35.

39. *FRUS, 1958–1960*, 5: 372, 383–384; *FRUS, 1958–1960*, 6: 502, 542, 562, 636, 742, 760. It was during June–July 1959—at the height of U.S. concern over the Cuban agrarian-reform program—that U.S. officials began to seriously contemplate Castro's overthrow. Nevertheless, discussion of Cuban matters in National Security Council meetings of 25 June and 9 July focused almost entirely on the issue of Cuban support for revolutionary activity in the Caribbean; the expropriation of U.S. investments was scarcely mentioned. See ibid., 541–555. For a detailed U.S. intelligence analysis of Castro's efforts to promote revolution in neighboring countries, see Department of State, Bureau of Intelligence and Research, "Castro's Revolution and Subversive Plotting in the Western Hemisphere (February–April 1959)," Intelligence Report no. 7956.1, 18 May 1959, in *OSS/State Department Intelligence and Research Reports: Latin America, 1941–1961*, ed. Paul Kesaris (Washington, D.C.: University Publications of America, 1979), microfilm, reel 8, frame 0427.

40. Speech by Raúl Roa, in *Official Records of the United Nations General Assembly*, Fourteenth Session, 806th Plenary Meeting, 24 September 1959 (New York: United Nations, 1959), 145–146; *New York Times*, 20 December 1959, 19; Bonsal, *Cuba, Castro, and the United States*, 97; *FRUS, 1958–1960*, 6: 740–741, 765, 926. Also see Smith, "Castro's Cuba," 7–9. U.S. officials had been expressing concern over Castro's "Nasser-like ambition" and the danger that the Cuban leader would go off "on a Nasserist or neutralist tangent" after the early weeks of 1959. See, e.g., *FRUS, 1958–1960*, 6: 387, 405.

41. Bonsal, *Cuba, Castro, and the United States*, 104, 108, 133–135; *FRUS, 1958–1960*, 6: 628, 639, 642, 823–825; *New York Times*, 27 October 1959, 1; Quirk, *Fidel Castro*, 269–270, 301–302; Thomas, *The Cuban Revolution*, 468; Castro speeches, Havana, 27 October 1959 and 7 March 1960, *Castro Speech Data Base*.

42. "Communist Influence in Cuba," Special National Intelligence Estimate no. 85-60, 22 March 1960, 1, in *Declassified Documents Reference System* (Washington, DC: Carrollton, 1984), microfiche no. 1513; CIA, "Sino-Soviet Activity in Latin America," intelligence précis, 14 March 1960; Zachary Karabell, *Architects of Intervention: The United States, the Third World, and the Cold War, 1946–1962* (Baton Rouge: Louisiana State University Press, 1999), 183.

43. John Lewis Gaddis, *Strategies of Containment: A Critical Appraisal of Postwar American National Security Policy* (New York: Oxford University Press, 1982), 154; H. W. Brands, *The Spectre of Neutralism: The United States and the Emergence of the Third World, 1947–1960* (New York: Columbia University Press, 1989), 305; *FRUS, 1958–1960*, 6: 858.

44. *FRUS, 1958–1960*, 6: 830 (emphasis added).

45. Despatch no. 789, Bonsal to Department of State, 27 November 1959, decimal file 611.37/11–2759, Record Group 59, General Records of the Department of State, U.S. National Archives, College Park, MD.

46. Quirk, *Fidel Castro*, 291–292; Chester J. Pach and Elmo Richardson, *The Presidency of Dwight D. Eisenhower* (Lawrence: University Press of Kansas, 1991), 170–171; Robert A. Divine, *Foreign Policy and U.S. Presidential Elections, 1952–1960* (New York: New Viewpoints, 1974), 184–185, 187–188.

47. *FRUS, 1958–1960*, 6: 656–658 (emphasis added).

48. Ibid., 519, 605–610, 831 (emphasis added).

49. Welch, *Response to Revolution*, 105–107; Pamela K. Starr and Abraham F. Lowenthal, "The United States and the Cuban Revolution, 1958–1960," *Pew Case Studies in International Affairs*, no. 328 (Washington, DC: Georgetown University Institute for the Study of Diplomacy, 1988), 33.

50. Welch, *Response to Revolution*, 60, 110–112; Bonsal, *Cuba, Castro, and the United States*, 134; *National Review*, 13 February 1960, 95, and 23 April 1960, 253–254.

51. Rabe, *Eisenhower and Latin America*, 58, 97–98; Stephen G. Rabe, *The Most Dangerous Area in the World: John F. Kennedy Confronts Communist Revolution in Latin America* (Chapel Hill: University of North Carolina Press, 1999), 12; *FRUS, 1958–1960*, 6: 90; Lee Riley Powell, *J. William Fulbright and His Time: A Political Biography* (Memphis, TN: Guild Bindery Press, 1996), 71–72; Eugene Brown, *J. William Fulbright: Advice and Dissent* (Iowa City: University of Iowa Press, 1985), 34–35; *New York Times*, 9 September 1959, 11.

52. Welch, *Response to Revolution*, 112–113.

53. Ibid., 48; Richard M. Nixon, "Cuba, Castro and John F. Kennedy: Reflections on U.S. Foreign Policy," *Reader's Digest*, November 1964, 288; Trumbull Higgins, *The Perfect Failure: Kennedy, Eisenhower, and the CIA at the Bay of Pigs* (New York: Norton, 1989), 44.

54. *FRUS, 1958–1960*, 6: 705; Rabe, *Eisenhower and Latin America*, 128.

55. Richard M. Nixon, *Six Crises* (Garden City, NY: Doubleday, 1962), 352.

56. Quirk, *Fidel Castro*, 349; U.S. Senate, Committee on Commerce, *Freedom of Communications*, pt. 1, *The Speeches, Remarks, Press Conferences, and Statements of Senator John F. Kennedy, August 1 through November 7, 1960*, 87th Cong., 1st sess., 1961, S. Rept. 994, 510; Kent M. Beck, "Necessary Lies, Hidden Truths: Cuba in the 1960 Campaign," *Diplomatic History* 8, no. 1 (Winter 1984): 45; Bonsal, *Cuba, Castro, and the United States*, 171; James N. Giglio, *The Presidency of John F. Kennedy*, 2nd rev. ed. (Lawrence: University Press of Kansas, 2006), 51; Divine, *Foreign Policy and U.S. Presidential Elections*, 235.

57. Melvin Small, *Democracy & Diplomacy: The Impact of Domestic Politics on U.S. Foreign Policy, 1789–1994* (Baltimore: Johns Hopkins University Press, 1996), 105; U.S. Senate, Committee on Commerce, *Freedom of Communications*, pt. 1, 515; Bonsal, *Cuba, Castro, and the United States*, 172–173; Beck, "Necessary Lies, Hidden Truths," 46.

58. Bonsal, *Cuba, Castro, and the United States*, 174; Beck, "Necessary Lies, Hidden Truths," 38, 40–42, 47.

59. Beck, "Necessary Lies, Hidden Truths," 40; Wyden, *Bay of Pigs*, 29–30.

60. *FRUS, 1958–1960*, 6: 1089; Beck, "Necessary Lies, Hidden Truths," 40; Wyden,

Bay of Pigs, 30, 66. According to Wyden, Nixon's press secretary, Herbert Klein, "had been briefed by the Vice President about the Cuban operation" and was hopeful that Castro would be overthrown in October. Klein "was deeply involved in the difficult presidential campaign" and knew that "[a] successful Cuba operation would have been 'a major plus,' indeed 'a real trump card.' He knew that Nixon kept urging Eisenhower on. He worried that no move might come until November. If it had to be November, he would have been grateful if it were to be November 1 rather than closer to the election on the eighth" (8).

61. Stephen E. Ambrose, *Nixon: The Education of a Politician, 1913–1962* (New York: Simon & Schuster, 1987), 590–591; Beck, "Necessary Lies, Hidden Truths," 49n35; Bonsal, *Cuba, Castro, and the United States*, 170–171.

62. Beck, "Necessary Lies, Hidden Truths," 50; Quirk, *Fidel Castro*, 349. Nixon strongly suspected that his Democratic rival had been briefed on the CIA's secret preparations for a Cuban intervention by agency director Allen Dulles and that Kennedy was deliberately using that knowledge to gain political advantage in the campaign. By advocating a militant interventionist policy, knowing all the while that Nixon would need to protect the secrecy of the planned intervention, Kennedy would attract the support of voters who favored strong action against Castro. As Nixon later wrote, "I thought that Kennedy, with full knowledge of the facts, was jeopardizing the security of a United States foreign policy operation. And my rage was greater because I could do nothing about it. I was faced with what was probably the most difficult decision of the campaign. Kennedy had me at a terrible disadvantage. He knew, as I did, that public sentiment in the United States was overwhelmingly in favor of a tougher line against Castro. I had long favored and fought for this line within the Administration, and the covert training of Cuban exiles as well as the new overt quarantine policy were programs due, in substantial part at least, to my efforts. Kennedy was now publicly advocating what was already the policy of the American government—covertly—and Kennedy had been so informed. But by stating such a position publicly, he obviously stood to gain the support of all those who wanted a stronger policy against Castro but who, of course, could not know of our covert programs already under way. What could I do? One course would be simply to state that what Kennedy was advocating as a new policy was already being done, had been adopted as a policy as a result of my direct support, and that Kennedy was endangering the security of the whole operation in his public statement. But this would be, for me, an utterly irresponsible act: it would disclose a secret operation and completely destroy its effectiveness. There was only one thing I could do. The covert operation had to be protected at all costs. I must not even suggest by implication that the United States was rendering aid to rebel forces in and out of Cuba. In fact, I must go to the other extreme: I must attack the Kennedy proposal to provide such aid as wrong and irresponsible because it would violate our treaty commitments" (Nixon, *Six Crises*, 354–355). In the end, Nixon concluded, "The position I had to take on Cuba hurt rather than helped me. . . . The general 'image' to the end of the campaign was to be one of Kennedy stronger and tougher than I against Castro and Communism" (ibid., 356–357). For additional evidence supporting Nixon's contention that Kennedy learned about the planned intervention during the campaign and used it for political gain, see Seymour Hersh, *The Dark Side of Camelot* (Boston: Little, Brown, 1997), chap. 12; Beschloss, *The Crisis Years*, 28–30n; and the reminiscences of John Patterson, Democratic governor of Alabama in 1960, in Deborah Hart Strober and Gerald S. Strober, comps., *The Kennedy Presidency: An Oral History of the Era*, rev. ed. (Washington, DC: Brassey's, 2003), 325–327.

63. Beck, "Necessary Lies, Hidden Truths," 57; Quirk, *Fidel Castro*, 351. As the campaign neared its end, Castro worried that political considerations might prompt Eisenhower

to invade Cuba. According to the U.S. Embassy in Havana, Castro told Cuban army cadets in a 29 October 1960 graduation address "that since Cuba had become a matter of contention in [the] U.S. presidential campaign, there was danger [that the] present administration would attack Cuba to satisfy interests which support it and to outdo [the] other political party" (*FRUS, 1958–1960*, 6: 1112). During the campaign's final two weeks, Kennedy's staff was also worried that Eisenhower would provoke a Cuban crisis in order to boost Nixon's campaign (Hersh, *The Dark Side of Camelot*, 182).

64. Quirk, *Fidel Castro*, 350; Dallek, *An Unfinished Life*, 356. Nixon later wrote that "most observers agree that our positions on the Cuban issue could well have been the decisive factor" in the election and that the appearance of being "softer" on Cuba than Kennedy cost him the presidency (Nixon, "Cuba, Castro and John F. Kennedy," 288). See also Fawn M. Brodie, *Richard Nixon: The Shaping of His Character* (New York: Norton, 1981), 412. According to Gleijeses, Kennedy's "inflammatory language" during the campaign "came back to haunt him" as president. "It limited his options by raising the political cost of scuttling the operation once he was in office" (Piero Gleijeses, "Ships in the Night: The CIA, the White House and the Bay of Pigs," *Journal of Latin American Studies* 27, no. 1 [February 1995]: 25). During the campaign, former secretary of state Dean Acheson warned Kennedy that his campaign rhetoric was locking him into an untenable position on Cuba (Higgins, *The Perfect Failure*, 60). The political pressures on President Kennedy to approve the Bay of Pigs invasion are discussed more fully below.

65. Karabell, *Architects of Intervention*, 174, 195–197; Bonsal, quoted in Pérez, *Cuba and the United States*, 248. Alfredo Durán, a member of the exile brigade that landed at the Bay of Pigs, offers additional evidence that the Cuban exiles were consciously manipulating U.S. policy for their own purposes. According to Durán, "The Cuban government and some others have said that we worked for the CIA—that the CIA used us. I think that the feeling among the people in the brigade was that we were using the CIA, not the CIA using us." See James G. Blight and Peter Kornbluh, eds., *Politics of Illusion: The Bay of Pigs Invasion Reexamined* (Boulder, CO: Lynne Rienner, 1998), 71.

66. Karabell, *Architects of Intervention*, 195; Dallek, *An Unfinished Life*, 361.

67. Karabell, *Architects of Intervention*, 173.

68. Benjamin, *The United States and the Origins of the Cuban Revolution*, 195; Pérez, *Cuba and the United States*, 242–243; Szulc, *Fidel*, 562, 571–572; Bonsal, *Cuba, Castro, and the United States*, 145–153, 158–161, 165–166.

69. Theodore Draper, *Castro's Revolution: Myths and Realities* (New York: Praeger, 1962), 81; Szulc, *Fidel*, 577, 586–587.

70. Fursenko and Naftali, *"One Hell of a Gamble,"* 42, 52–55, 60–61, 71; Szulc, *Fidel*, 573, 582–583, 595; Quirk, *Fidel Castro*, 332.

71. *FRUS, 1958–1960*, 6: 962, 1124–1125; Bohlen, quoted in Fursenko and Naftali, *"One Hell of a Gamble,"* 52; Mann statement, in *FRUS, 1961–1963*, vol. 10: *Cuba, 1961–1962* (Washington, DC: Government Printing Office, 1997), 97. In February 1961, Bohlen also "assured Kennedy that 'Khrushchev would not go to war over as strategically unimportant an area as Cuba'" (Beschloss, *The Crisis Years*, 90).

72. Beschloss, *The Crisis Years*, 57; U.S. Department of State, Bureau of Intelligence and Research, "The Situation in Cuba," Intelligence Report no. 8385, 27 December 1960, 4, in Kesaris, ed., *OSS/State Department Intelligence*, microfilm, reel 8, frame 0464; U.S. Department of State, "Cuba," Department of State Publication no. 7171, Inter-American Series 66, April 1961, 33; *FRUS, 1958–1960*, 6: 1005, 1142, 1174. Two days after Kennedy's inauguration, CIA director Dulles warned the new administration's top national-security

advisers that "the Castro regime had plans to export Castro's communism" and that "they already have power among the people in the Caribbean countries and elsewhere, particularly in Venezuela and Colombia" (*FRUS, 1961–1963*, 10: 50). Three days later, Chairman of the Joint Chiefs of Staff Gen. Lyman Lemnitzer personally warned Kennedy that Castro was "sending agents and arms into other countries of Latin America" (ibid., 54). A 17 February 1961 CIA study concluded that "Cuba will, of course, never present a direct military threat to the United States and it is unlikely that Cuba would attempt open invasion of any other Latin American country since the U.S. could and almost certainly would enter the conflict on the side of the invaded country. Nevertheless, as Castro further stabilizes his regime, obtains more sophisticated weapons, and further trains the militia, Cuba will provide an effective and solidly defended base for Soviet operations and expansion of influence in the Western Hemisphere. Arms, money, organizational and other support can be provided from Cuba to dissident leaders and groups throughout Latin America in order to create political instability, encourage Communism, weaken the prestige of the U.S., and foster the inevitable popular support that Castro's continuance of power will engender. A National Estimate states: 'For the Communist powers, Cuba represents an opportunity of incalculable value. More importantly, the advent of Castro has provided the Communists with a friendly base for propaganda and agitation throughout the rest of Latin America and with a highly exploitable example of revolutionary achievement and successful defiance of the United States'" (ibid., 101). In April 1961, Llewellyn Thompson, the U.S. ambassador to the Soviet Union, informed Khrushchev that "what bothered us particularly about Cuba was its use as a base for attempts on overthrow of other Latin American govts" (ibid., 183). "Cuba alone was not regarded as a threat," President Kennedy told Khrushchev at the June 1961 Vienna summit. "It was Castro's announced intentions to subvert the hemisphere that could be dangerous" (Sorensen, *Kennedy*, 547).

73. Welch, *Response to Revolution*, 64, 67–68; *Public Papers of the Presidents of the United States: John F. Kennedy, 1961*, 1; I. M. Destler, Leslie H. Gelb, and Anthony Lake, *Our Own Worst Enemy: The Unmaking of American Foreign Policy* (New York: Simon & Schuster, 1984), 52–53; Quirk, *Fidel Castro*, 363.

74. Blight and Kornbluh, eds., *Politics of Illusion*, 63–64, 271–272; Fursenko and Naftali, *"One Hell of a Gamble,"* 73, 78, 79; Castro, quoted in Quirk, *Fidel Castro*, 342; Kennedy, quoted in U.S. Senate, Committee on Commerce, *Freedom of Communications*, pt. 1, 434, and *Public Papers of the Presidents of the United States: John F. Kennedy, 1961*, 564; Paterson, "Fixation with Cuba," 127. "If Castro can spread his influence throughout all of Latin America," candidate Kennedy told a St. Paul audience on 2 October 1960, "then the balance of power will begin to move in the direction of the Communist world, and his future and the Communist future is assured" (U.S. Senate, Committee on Commerce, *Freedom of Communications*, pt. 1, 434).

75. Paterson, "Fixation with Castro," 126; Gleijeses, "Ships in the Night," 25–26; O'Donnell, quoted in Dallek, *An Unfinished Life*, 358; Rostow, *The Diffusion of Power*, 214; Walt W. Rostow oral history interview, 59–60, in *The John F. Kennedy Presidential Oral History Collection*, pt. 1, *The White House and Executive Departments* (Frederick, MD: University Publications of America, 1988), microfiche no. 161. CIA Deputy Director of Planning Richard Bissell, the principal architect of the Bay of Pigs invasion, later recalled that "there was nothing that the president wanted less than to seem, at the beginning of his term, to be soft in the face of a threat; to be unwilling to use strong measures if they held some promise of success. I'm sure he had visions of being told in the press that he had lost Cuba in the first few weeks of his administration by throwing away a plan to retrieve Cuba

from Castro" (quoted in Strober and Strober, comps., *The Kennedy Presidency*, 335). During a 1996 scholarly conference on the Bay of Pigs invasion, historian James G. Hershberg suggested that "what happened at the Bay of Pigs can be read as deriving mainly from the fear of looking soft on communism. Obviously, for Democrats there was the possibility of this being exacerbated by the fear of attack from the right wing, the fear that they would be accused of not living up to campaign promises—in this case, to unseat Castro." In reply, Arthur Schlesinger Jr., who served as special assistant in the Kennedy White House, agreed that "the fear of sounding soft on communism was a very strong one. A liberal Democrat like Kennedy had to be constantly concerned with this issue" (Blight and Kornbluh, eds., *Politics of Illusion*, 62, 65).

76. Quirk, *Fidel Castro*, 359, 362–363; Wyden, *Bay of Pigs*, 308; Arthur M. Schlesinger Jr., *A Thousand Days: John F. Kennedy in the White House* (Boston: Houghton Mifflin, 1965), 242; Bundy, quoted in Higgins, *The Perfect Failure*, 88, and in Blight and Kornbluh, eds., *Politics of Illusion*, 268; Dallek, *An Unfinished Life*, 357, 359; Sorensen, *Kennedy*, 296–297; *Operation ZAPATA*, 18. Wyden writes that on 11 March 1961 "the president agreed it might be best to let the exiles go to the destination of their choice: Cuba. After all, Ike had urged him to go ahead and the retired President was more than a revered general. He and his party commanded powerful political support. If Kennedy cancelled the project, the Cuban exiles would be loudly furious. The Republicans would call him chicken. The political repercussions would be nasty" (Wyden, *Bay of Pigs*, 100). According to Higgins, "It would have been difficult—even secretly—for Kennedy to repudiate Dulles' program . . . so soon after the President's closely contested election victory. In fact, the President-Elect was deeply concerned over both his marginal electoral victory and Republican criticism of him" (Higgins, *The Perfect Failure*, 67–68). Also see Welch, *Response to Revolution*, 160; Rabe, *Eisenhower and Latin America*, 171; Paterson, "Fixation with Cuba," 132.

77. Blight and Kornbluh, eds., *Politics of Illusion*, 64.

78. Sorensen, *Kennedy*, 399, 534; Welch, *Response to Revolution*, 77, 79, 80; Kornbluh, ed., *Bay of Pigs Declassified*, 2; Higgins, *The Perfect Failure*, 112.

79. Gleijeses, "Ships in the Night," 17, 22, 23; Kornbluh, ed., *Bay of Pigs Declassified*, 291; Schlesinger, *A Thousand Days*, 249–250.

80. Kornbluh, ed., *Bay of Pigs Declassified*, 2, 13, 265; John Ranelagh, *The Agency: The Rise and Decline of the CIA* (New York: Simon & Schuster, 1986), 364–372; Richard Bissell, *Reflections of a Cold Warrior: From Yalta to the Bay of Pigs* (New Haven, CT: Yale University Press, 1996), 169; Schlesinger, *A Thousand Days*, 242–243; *FRUS, 1961–1963*, 10: 143; Gleijeses, "Ships in the Night," 22, 34, 37–39; Blight and Kornbluh, eds., *Politics of Illusion*, 2, 65; Beschloss, *The Crisis Years*, 105, 128, 144; Wyden, *Bay of Pigs*, 100, 102, 308; Higgins, *The Perfect Failure*, 145, 151; Sorensen, *Kennedy*, 297.

81. Wyden's *Bay of Pigs: The Untold Story* remains the best narrative account of the invasion. For contrasting White House and CIA perspectives, see Schlesinger, *A Thousand Days*, chaps. 10–11; and Bissell, *Reflections of a Cold Warrior*, chap. 7.

82. Blight and Kornbluh, eds., *Politics of Illusion*, 2–3, 108, 139, 150; Higgins, *The Perfect Failure*, 161, 163–164; Wyden, *Bay of Pigs*, 310–311; Sorensen, *Kennedy*, 309.

83. CIA, "Consequences for the U.S. of the Abortive Rebellion in Cuba: Some Preliminary Thoughts," 28 April 1961, *Declassified Documents Reference System*, 1976, microfiche 10B; *FRUS, 1961–1963*, 10: 61–63, 327, 329. Europeans were "incredulous . . . that the U.S. Government had been quite so incompetent, irresponsible and stupid," a White House aide informed Kennedy in early May (Blight and Kornbluh, eds., *Politics of Illusion*, 271).

84. Haynes Johnson, *The Bay of Pigs: The Leaders' Story of Brigade 2506* (New York: Norton, 1964), 237; Gardner, *Pay Any Price*, 40; Welch, *Response to Revolution*, 107–108; Paterson, "Fixation with Cuba," 136; Sorensen, *Kennedy*, 669, 670. "Barry Goldwater declared that Kennedy's Cuban fiasco should fill every American with 'apprehension and shame'" (Beschloss, *The Crisis Years*, 129).

85. See *Operation ZAPATA;* the CIA inspector general's critical assessment, published in Kornbluh, ed., *Bay of Pigs Declassified;* and McGeorge Bundy, "Some Preliminary Administrative Lessons of the Cuba Expedition," in Blight and Kornbluh, eds., *Politics of Illusion*, 266–269.

Chapter Three. British Guiana, 1963

1. Thomas J. Spinner Jr., *A Political and Social History of Guyana, 1945–1983* (Boulder, CO: Westview, 1984), 17–37; Jane L. Sillery, "Salvaging Democracy? The United States and Britain in British Guiana, 1961–1964" (Ph.D. diss., Oxford University, 1996), 10–26, 71. Also see Cheddi Jagan, *The West on Trial: The Fight for Guyana's Freedom*, rev. ed. (New York: International Publishers, 1972), chaps. 1–6.

2. Sillery, "Salvaging Democracy?" 26–31, 34–35; Spinner, *A Political and Social History of Guyana*, 37–46, 59–60; Jagan, *The West on Trial*, chaps. 6–8.

3. Sillery, "Salvaging Democracy?" 18, 22, 23, 29, 30, 35; Robert Waters and Gordon Daniels, "The World's Longest General Strike: The AFL-CIO, the CIA, and British Guiana," *Diplomatic History* 29, no. 2 (April 2005): 285–286; Spinner, *A Political and Social History of Guyana*, 35; Jagan, *The West on Trial*, 106, 123.

4. Sillery, "Salvaging Democracy?" 25, 45, 48–49; Cary Fraser, *Ambivalent Anti-colonialism: The United States and the Genesis of West Indian Independence, 1940–1964* (Westport, CT: Greenwood, 1994), 169, 174, 197n46; Spinner, *A Political and Social History of Guyana*, 72–74, 80.

5. Spinner, *A Political and Social History of Guyana*, 68; Sillery, "Salvaging Democracy?" 41–42.

6. *New York Times*, 1 September 1957, 24, and 16 September 1957, 11; Jagan, *The West on Trial*, 189–192, 198; Fraser, *Ambivalent Anti-colonialism*, 179–180; Sillery, "Salvaging Democracy?" 93–95; Spinner, *A Political and Social History of Guyana*, 73–74.

7. Fraser, *Ambivalent Anti-colonialism*, 181–182; Sillery, "Salvaging Democracy?" 48, 49, 56; Spinner, *A Political and Social History of Guyana*, 76, 82.

8. Sillery, "Salvaging Democracy?" 78, 80; Fraser, *Ambivalent Anti-colonialism*, 184, 185; Spinner, *A Political and Social History of Guyana*, 81–82.

9. U.S. Department of State, Office of Intelligence Research, "Communist-Led Party Sweeps British Guiana General Election," Intelligence Report no. 6292, 27 May 1953, 1, 2, 4, 8, in *OSS/State Department Intelligence and Research Reports: Latin America, 1941–1961*, ed. Paul Kesaris (Washington, DC: University Publications of America, 1979), microfilm, reel 9, frame 318; Fraser, *Ambivalent Anti-colonialism*, 129; Sillery, "Salvaging Democracy?" 32–33; Jagan, *The West on Trial*, 138.

10. Sillery, "Salvaging Democracy?" 47, 49, 56, 68, 70, 73.

11. Ibid., 68, 76; U.S. Department of State, *Foreign Relations of the United States* (hereafter cited as *FRUS*), *1961–1963*, vol. 12: *American Republics* (Washington, DC: Government Printing Office, 1996), 519–520. For a useful overview of U.S.-British tensions over British Guiana, see Nigel Ashton, *Kennedy, Macmillan and the Cold War: The Irony of Interdependence* (New York: Palgrave Macmillan, 2002), 67–71.

12. *FRUS, 1961–1963*, 12: 521–522; Sillery, "Salvaging Democracy?" 69, 73, 76–77.

13. Sillery, "Salvaging Democracy?" 73–74, 81, 84–86, 88–89, 103–104; *FRUS, 1961–1963*, 12: 524, 530, 533–534.

14. Spinner, *A Political and Social History of Guyana*, 83–84; Arthur M. Schlesinger Jr., *A Thousand Days: John F. Kennedy in the White House* (Boston: Houghton Mifflin, 1965), 775; Sillery, "Salvaging Democracy?" 110, 116. Stephen G. Rabe, *U.S. Intervention in British Guiana: A Cold War Story* (Chapel Hill: University of North Carolina Press, 2005), 87. According to Schlesinger, Jagan's refusal "to say anything critical of the Soviet Union" during his *Meet the Press* appearance "left an impression of either wooliness or fellow-traveling. This appearance instantly diminished the enthusiasm for helping his government. The President, who caught the last half of the show, called for a re-examination of all aspects of the problem, saying he wanted no commitments made until he had seen Jagan himself" (Schlesinger, *A Thousand Days*, 775).

15. *FRUS, 1961–1963*, 12: 537; Spinner, *A Political and Social History of Guyana*, 84; Schlesinger, *A Thousand Days*, 775–777.

16. *FRUS, 1961–1963*, 12: 537.

17. Schlesinger, *A Thousand Days*, 776–777; *FRUS, 1961–1963*, 12: 539; Jagan, *The West on Trial*, 353; Sillery, "Salvaging Democracy?" 111–114; Fowler Hamilton interview, 18 August 1964, 26, in *John F. Kennedy Oral History Collection*, pt. 1: *The White House and Executive Departments* (Frederick, MD: University Publications of America, 1988), microfiche no. 80. Following his unsatisfactory meeting with AID's Hamilton, Jagan "demanded another meeting with Kennedy, 'to let him know exactly what he thought about being given the run around in this way'" (Sillery, "Salvaging Democracy?" 113). Kennedy responded with "a personal note . . . regretting his inability to accede to a request . . . for a further meeting" due to "his crowded schedule" (*FRUS, 1961–1963*, 12: 539).

18. *FRUS, 1961–1963*, 12: 542, 544–545 (emphasis added); Fowler Hamilton interview, *John F. Kennedy Oral History Collection*, 26; Sillery, "Salvaging Democracy?" 126, 155, 158.

19. Sillery, "Salvaging Democracy?" 163–164; letter, Thomas J. Dodd to President Kennedy, 17 May 1962, President's Office Files, Countries: British Guiana, Security, 1961–1963, box 112A, John F. Kennedy Library, Boston, MA.

20. Schlesinger, *A Thousand Days*, 778–779; telegram, U.S. State Department to U.S. embassy, London, and U.S. consulate, Georgetown, British Guiana, 11 August 1961, in *John F. Kennedy National Security Files: Latin America, 1961–1963*, ed. George C. Herring (Frederick, MD: University Publications of America, 1987), microfilm, reel 3, frame 0834; Sillery, "Salvaging Democracy?" 164; *FRUS, 1961–1963*, 12: 572–573. Also see Rabe, *U.S. Intervention in British Guiana*, 99–100. In 1959, the British governor of British Guiana described Burnham as "cynical, superficial, unreliable, prejudiced and irrational" (quoted in Sillery, "Salvaging Democracy?" 50).

21. Sillery, "Salvaging Democracy?" 133, 141, 184; Philip Reno, *The Ordeal of British Guiana* (New York: Monthly Review Press, 1964), 52; Spinner, *A Political and Social History of Guyana*, 78, 91; Ronald Radosh, *American Labor and United States Foreign Policy* (New York: Random House, 1969), 394, 398, 402; telegram, U.S. State Department to U.S. consulate, Georgetown, British Guiana, and U.S. embassy, London, 10 September 1961, in Herring, ed., *John F. Kennedy National Security Files*, microfilm, reel 3, frame 940. In addition, Peter D'Aguiar, a conservative Guianese businessman and leader of the right-wing United Front party, was warning administration officials that Jagan would deliver British Guiana "lock, stock, and barrel to the Communist camp." Rabe, *U.S. Intervention in British Guiana*, 83.

22. Sillery, "Salvaging Democracy?" 138–140, 149–154, 159–161, 172, 180; *FRUS, 1961–1963*, 12: 550, 553, 556, 558–564, 571.

23. Waters and Daniels, "The World's Longest General Strike," 290–307; Sillery, "Salvaging Democracy?" 180, 184–197; Rabe, *U.S. Intervention in British Guiana*, 85–86, 91–92, 99–101, 110–113. Spinner, *A Political and Social History of Guyana*, 100–102; Richard J. Barnet, *Intervention and Revolution: America's Confrontation with Insurgent Movements around the World*, rev. ed. (New York: Meridian, 1980), 281–283; Jagan, *The West on Trial*, 249; Radosh, *American Labor and United States Foreign Policy*, 399–404; Fraser, *Ambivalent Anti-colonialism*, 191. John Prados draws on recently declassified U.S. government documents to provide an informative up-to-date survey of the intervention in *Safe for Democracy: The Secret Wars of the CIA* (Chicago: Ivan R. Dee, 2006), 3–19.

24. Waters and Daniels, "The World's Longest General Strike," 290–307; Spinner, *A Political and Social History of Guyana*, 101–102; Sillery, "Salvaging Democracy?" 190–191, 193, 198; Barnet, *Intervention and Revolution*, 283; Reno, *The Ordeal of British Guiana*, 54–56. Jagan offers his perspective on the strike in chap. 11 of *The West on Trial*.

25. Waters and Daniels, "The World's Longest General Strike," 290–307; Spinner, *A Political and Social History of Guyana*, 93, 102; Sillery, "Salvaging Democracy?" 199, 204–208; William Blum, *The CIA: A Forgotten History* (London: Zed, 1986), 122; *FRUS, 1961–1963*, 12: 608.

26. Nigel Fisher, *Harold Macmillan: A Biography* (New York: St. Martin's, 1982), 293; Sillery, "Salvaging Democracy?" 211–212; Spinner, *A Political and Social History of Guyana*, 103–104. "At the time of Kennedy's death in November 1963," Sillery writes, "Jagan remained in office, but the . . . machinery for his removal had been put in place." British officials "had called for an election under an electoral system rigged to ensure Jagan's defeat in an ostensibly democratic manner" (Sillery, "Salvaging Democracy?" 220).

27. Fraser, *Ambivalent Anti-colonialism*, 194; Sillery, "Salvaging Democracy?" 243–247; Jagan, *The West on Trial*, 324–326; Spinner, *A Political and Social History of Guyana*, 114, 116, and chaps. 7–10; Rabe, *U.S. Intervention in British Guiana*, 105–107, 118–138.

28. Sillery, "Salvaging Democracy?" 202–203; Arthur M. Schlesinger Jr., *Robert Kennedy and His Times* (Boston: Houghton Mifflin, 1978), 2: 606n; *FRUS, 1961–1963*, 12: 548, 559, 604; George W. Ball, *Diplomacy for a Crowded World: An American Foreign Policy* (Boston: Little, Brown, 1976), 222–223.

29. Jagan, *The West on Trial*, 361, 380, 417; Schlesinger, *A Thousand Days*, 776; Rabe, *U.S. Intervention in British Guiana*, 181–182.

30. Sillery, "Salvaging Democracy?" 67, 149, 157.

31. Ibid., 60–61. British Guiana represented "a notable opportunity for Castro/Communist penetration," a 1961 national intelligence estimate reported ("Latin American Reactions and Developments in and With Respect to Cuba," National Intelligence Estimate no. 80/90–61, 18 July 1961, 8, in *Declassified Documents Reference System* (Washington, DC: Carrollton, 1984), microfiche no. 1515.

32. *FRUS, 1961–1963*, 12: 516–517.

33. Ibid., 565.

34. Ibid., 555.

35. Ibid., 515, 562.

36. Ibid., 572.

37. Ibid., 544, 559 (emphasis added).

38. Sillery, "Salvaging Democracy?" ii–iii, 258; For a competing interpretation that underemphasizes the influence of U.S. domestic politics on Kennedy's decision to intervene,

see Rabe, *U.S. Intervention in British Guiana*. Rabe attributes causation to a security-driven U.S. fear of communism, and to Kennedy's "feverish anticommunism" (113–114).

39. Sillery, "Salvaging Democracy?" 64; Theodore C. Sorensen, *Kennedy* (New York: Harper & Row, 1965), 293; Lawrence W. Bassett and Stephen E. Pelz, "The Failed Search for Victory: Vietnam and the Politics of War," in *Kennedy's Quest for Victory: American Foreign Policy, 1961–1963*, ed. Thomas G. Paterson (New York: Oxford University Press, 1989), 228–231; Robert H. Johnson, *Improbable Dangers: U.S. Conceptions of Threat in the Cold War and After* (New York: St. Martin's, 1994), 158; Richard E. Welch Jr., *Response to Revolution: The United States and the Cuban Revolution, 1959–1961* (Chapel Hill: University of North Carolina Press, 1985), 90–91; Tad Szulc, *Fidel: A Critical Portrait* (New York: Avon, 1986), 616; Richard Reeves, *President Kennedy: Profile of Power* (New York: Simon & Schuster, 1993), 261.

40. Johnson, *Improbable Dangers*, 158; Reeves, *President Kennedy*, 257; I. M. Destler, Leslie H. Gelb, and Anthony Lake, *Our Own Worst Enemy: The Unmaking of American Foreign Policy* (New York: Simon & Schuster, 1984), 54; Welch, *Response to Revolution*, 107–109; Barry M. Goldwater, *Why Not Victory? A Fresh Look at American Foreign Policy* (New York: McGraw-Hill, 1962), 83–88, 93.

41. Peter Wyden, *Bay of Pigs: The Untold Story* (New York: Simon & Schuster, 1979), 305.

42. Halpern, quoted in Seymour Hersh, *The Dark Side of Camelot* (Boston: Little, Brown, 1997), 268–270. Also see James G. Blight and Peter Kornbluh, eds., *Politics of Illusion: The Bay of Pigs Invasion Reexamined* (Boulder, CO: Lynne Rienner, 1998), 115.

43. Schlesinger, quoted in Blight and Kornbluh, eds., *Politics of Illusion*, 125.

44. Sillery, "Salvaging Democracy?" 75. Also see *Congressional Record*, 87th Cong., 1st sess., 1961, 107, pt. 10, 12630–12631.

45. *Congressional Record*, 87th Cong., 1st sess., 1961, 107, pt. 12, 16647–16648. Also see Rabe, *U.S. Intervention in British Guiana*, 85.

46. Letter, Thomas Dodd and Ernest Gruening to President Kennedy, 6 September 1961, White House Central Subject Files, C0 39, British Guiana (Executive), box 43, John F. Kennedy Library; Fraser, *Ambivalent Anti-colonialism*, 188.

47. *U.S. News & World Report*, 7 August 1961, 74, and 4 September 1961, 59; *Time*, 1 September 1961, 29; *Saturday Evening Post*, 30 September 1961, 114; Sillery, "Salvaging Democracy?" 110.

48. *FRUS, 1961–1963*, 12: 555.

49. Sillery, "Salvaging Democracy?" 110.

50. *FRUS, 1961–1963*, 12: 575.

51. Ibid., 544, 563, 609.

52. Sillery, "Salvaging Democracy?" 208.

53. Ibid., 159.

54. Jagan, *The West on Trial*, 354.

55. *FRUS, 1961–1963*, 12: 538–540, 549–551, 558–563, 572.

56. "Tale of Two Books," *Nation*, 4 June 1990, 763–764.

57. Victor Kaufman, "Domestic Politics as a Catalyst for United States Intervention in the Caribbean: The Case of British Guiana," *Journal of Caribbean History* 30 (1996): 125; letter, Schlesinger to Victor Kaufman, 22 March 1994. I am greatly indebted to Professor Kaufman for sharing Schlesinger's letter with me.

58. Jagan, *The West on Trial*, 321; memorandum and enclosure, Gordon Chase to McGeorge Bundy, 14 September 1964, National Security File, Intelligence File, "British Guiana," box 5, Lyndon Baines Johnson Library, Austin, Texas; memorandum, Rusk to

President Johnson, 24 October 1964, National Security File, Country File, "United Kingdom: Walker Talks with President and Others," box 213, Lyndon Baines Johnson Library; memorandum, George Ball to President Johnson, [early December 1964], National Security File, Country File, "United Kingdom: PM Wilson Visit (I), December 7–8, 1964," box 214, Lyndon Baines Johnson Library. The National Security Council paper advised the administration to warn Wilson that any attempt to set "an early date for [British Guiana's] independence prior to the outcome of the elections" would "severely damage UK-U.S. relations . . . and adversely influence our continuing cooperation in other areas."

Chapter Four: Dominican Republic, 1965

1. Robert Dallek, *Flawed Giant: Lyndon Johnson and His Times, 1961–1973* (New York: Oxford University Press, 1998), 60–61, 82–83, 86; Brian VanDeMark, *Into the Quagmire: Lyndon Johnson and the Escalation of the Vietnam War* (New York: Oxford University Press, 1991), xv, 54, 213.

2. Dallek, *Flawed Giant*, 100–101.

3. Michael R. Beschloss, ed., *Taking Charge: The Johnson White House Tapes, 1963–1964* (New York: Simon & Schuster, 1997), 401n4; Robert J. McMahon, "Credibility and World Power: Exploring the Psychological Dimension in Postwar American Diplomacy," *Diplomatic History* 15, no. 4 (Fall 1991): 446. According to McMahon, "The Vietnam War provides the most dramatic case of how America's fixation with its credibility could overshadow most other policy considerations. American leaders explained, justified, and defended the U.S. commitment to South Vietnam so frequently in terms of the need to prove U.S. credibility that their statements resemble ritualistic incantations. . . . Indeed, it is difficult to avoid the conclusion that for Presidents Dwight D. Eisenhower, John F. Kennedy, Lyndon B. Johnson, and Richard M. Nixon, Vietnam's importance derived primarily from the meanings that others would ascribe to American actions there" (ibid.).

4. VanDeMark, *Into the Quagmire*, xiv–xv, 106, 112–113; Dallek, *Flawed Giant*, 106, 269.

5. Robert H. Johnson, *Improbable Dangers: U.S. Conceptions of Threat in the Cold War and After* (New York: St. Martin's, 1994), 143; Dallek, *Flawed Giant*, 100; Beschloss, ed., *Taking Charge*, 135.

6. VanDeMark, *Into the Quagmire*, xiv, 25, 216, 220.

7. Quoted in Doris Kearns, *Lyndon Johnson and the American Dream* (New York: Harper & Row, 1976), 252–253. According to VanDeMark, "LBJ seemed determined, even obsessed, with avoiding Truman's ordeal. This dread of a conservative backlash—much more than personal pride or fear of another 'Munich'—conditioned Johnson's basic attitude toward Vietnam. As he had remarked in private shortly after assuming the presidency: 'I am not going to lose Vietnam. I am not going to be the President who saw Southeast Asia go the way China went'" (VanDeMark, *Into the Quagmire*, 25).

8. Beschloss, ed., *Taking Charge*, 213nn6, 7; Dallek, *Flawed Giant*, 106; VanDeMark, *Into the Quagmire*, xv.

9. VanDeMark, *Into the Quagmire*, 47, 60, 140; H. W. Brands, *The Wages of Globalism: Lyndon Johnson and the Limits of American Power* (New York: Oxford University Press, 1995), 28, 231; Dallek, *Flawed Giant*, 244.

10. Quoted in David Halberstam, *The Best and the Brightest* (New York: Random House, 1972), 530.

11. Lyndon Baines Johnson, *The Vantage Point: Perspectives of the Presidency, 1963–*

1969 (New York: Holt, Rinehart & Winston, 1971), 180–184; Michael L. Conniff, *Panama and the United States: The Forced Alliance* (Athens: University of Georgia Press, 1992), 120.

12. Thomas Skidmore, *Politics in Brazil, 1930–1964: An Experiment in Democracy* (New York: Oxford University Press, 1967), 113–115, 214, 253–286; Skidmore, *The Politics of Military Rule in Brazil, 1964–85* (New York: Oxford University Press, 1988), 15; Peter Flynn, *Brazil: A Political Analysis* (Boulder, CO: Westview, 1978), 230–237, 266–276.

13. Skidmore, *Politics in Brazil*, 286–292; John W. F. Dulles, *Unrest in Brazil: Political-Military Crises, 1955–1964* (Austin: University of Texas Press, 1970), 267–272; Ruth Leacock, *Requiem for Revolution: The United States and Brazil, 1961–1969* (Kent, OH: Kent State University Press, 1990), 174–176; Jorge G. Castañeda, *Utopia Unarmed: The Latin American Left after the Cold War* (New York: Vintage, 1993), 34n21.

14. Vernon A. Walters, *Silent Missions* (Garden City, NJ: Doubleday, 1978), 377.

15. Brands, *Wages of Globalism*, 48.

16. U.S. Department of State, *Foreign Relations of the United States* (hereafter cited as *FRUS*), *1964–1968*, vol. 31: *South and Central America; Mexico* (Washington, DC: Government Printing Office, 2004), 412–413.

17. Brands, *Wages of Globalism*, 47; Philip Geyelin, *Lyndon B. Johnson and the World* (New York: Frederick A. Praeger, 1966), 78; Walters, *Silent Missions*, 386.

18. Walters, *Silent Missions*, 381–383, 388; Brands, *Wages of Globalism*, 47–48, 261; Phyllis R. Parker, *Brazil and the Quiet Intervention, 1964* (Austin: University of Texas Press, 1979), 75–76, 86–87, 104; Leacock, *Requiem for Revolution*, 214; Gaddis Smith, *The Last Years of the Monroe Doctrine, 1945–1993* (New York: Hill & Wang, 1994), 121.

19. Piero Gleijeses, *The Dominican Crisis: The 1965 Constitutionalist Revolt and American Intervention* (Baltimore: Johns Hopkins University Press, 1978), chaps. 5–9; Abraham F. Lowenthal, *The Dominican Intervention* (Cambridge, MA: Harvard University Press, 1972), chap. 3 (the "bloodiest single battle in Dominican history," 93).

20. Telegram, Connett to Rusk, 25 April 1965, in *Crises in Panama and the Dominican Republic: National Security Files and NSC Histories (1963–1969)*, ed. Paul Kesaris (Frederick, MD: University Publications of America, 1982), microfilm, reel 5, frame 0022. "We believe there is serious threat of Communist takeover in country and that very little time remains in which to act," the embassy reported the following day (telegram, Connett to Rusk, 26 April 1965, in ibid., reel 5, frame 0047).

21. Lowenthal, *Dominican Intervention*, 72–73, 78–79, 88, 215–216n42; John Bartlow Martin, *Overtaken by Events: The Dominican Crisis—From the Fall of Trujillo to the Civil War* (Garden City, NJ: Doubleday, 1966), 647–651, 654–655; Gleijeses, *Dominican Crisis*, 226; *FRUS, 1964–1968*, vol. 32: *Dominican Republic; Cuba; Haiti; Guyana* (Washington, DC: Government Printing Office, 2005), 69. Also see Johnson's account in his memoir *The Vantage Point*, 193–194. An April 29 embassy report described the rebel forces as "mad dogs" (*FRUS, 1964–1968*, 32: 99).

22. *FRUS, 1964–1968*, 32: 71, 73–74, 76–77, 85; Lowenthal, *Dominican Intervention*, 101, 109–110; Peter Felten, "The 1965–1966 United States Intervention in the Dominican Republic" (Ph.D. diss., University of Texas at Austin, 1995), 116; Gleijeses, *Dominican Crisis*, 253.

23. Felten, "The 1965–1966 United States Intervention in the Dominican Republic," 120, 132–133, 135–141, 162; Lowenthal, *Dominican Intervention*, 108–110, 115; Gleijeses, *Dominican Crisis*, 256–258. On 29 April, Ambassador Bennett complained to Washington that loyalist military commanders "feel . . . that they can sit back now and let us do an efficient job for them" (*FRUS, 1964–1968*, 32: 96).

24. Gleijeses, *Dominican Crisis*, chap. 10; Felten, "The 1965–1966 United States Intervention in the Dominican Republic," chaps. 5–7. For a detailed account of the intervention by the commander of U.S. military forces in the Dominican Republic, see General Bruce Palmer Jr., *Intervention in the Caribbean: The Dominican Crisis of 1965* (Lexington: University of Kentucky Press, 1989).

25. Felten, "The 1965–1966 United States Intervention in the Dominican Republic," 52–55, 74, 111–112, 174; Gleijeses, *Dominican Crisis*, 133–145, 228–230, 251; Lowenthal, *Dominican Intervention*, 154–155, 215–217n42; Jerome Slater, *Intervention and Negotiation: The United States and the Dominican Revolution* (New York: Harper & Row, 1970), 36–42; Juan Bosch, "A Tale of Two Nations," *New Leader*, 21 June 1965, 5.

26. Geyelin, *Lyndon B. Johnson and the World*, 69–70; Lowenthal, *Dominican Intervention*, 154–155; Felten, "The 1965–1966 United States Intervention in the Dominican Republic," 74.

27. Howard J. Wiarda, interview with author, 11 December 1997; Wiarda, *Universities, Think Tanks and War Colleges: The Main Institutions of American Educational Life—A Memoir* (Philadelphia: Xlibris, 1999), 113–114.

28. Martin, *Overtaken by Events*, 451. As Senate Foreign Relations Committee Chairman J. William Fulbright observed in September 1965: "The specter of a second Communist state in the hemisphere—and its probable repercussions within the United States and possible effects on the careers of those who might be held responsible—seems to have been the most important single factor in distorting the judgment of otherwise sensible and competent men" (*Congressional Record*, 89th Cong., 1st sess., 1965, 111, pt. 18, 23859; also quoted in Slater, *Intervention and Negotiation*, 32n).

29. George W. Ball, *The Past Has Another Pattern: Memoirs* (New York: Norton, 1982), 327–328; Slater, *Intervention and Negotiation*, 25. According to journalist Tad Szulc, who covered the intervention for the *New York Times*, Bennett privately referred to the Constitutionalists as "Communist scum" (Slater, *Intervention and Negotiation*, 230n17).

30. Felten, "The 1965–1966 United States Intervention in the Dominican Republic," 71–73, 79, 81, 96–97, 137, 167; Slater, *Intervention and Negotiation*, 41; Lowenthal, *Dominican Intervention*, 69, 87, 109; Martin, *Overtaken by Events*, 651, 708. Felten concludes that "the conservative, anti-communist bias of its Dominican contacts colored the embassy's reporting from the beginning of the crisis" (Felten, "The 1965–1966 United States Intervention in the Dominican Republic," 72). Slater recounts a "story told by a wealthy oligarch sympathetic to the constitutionalists. On the first day of the revolution he received a telephone call suggesting that he contact all his friends and ask each to tell the American Embassy that the revolutionaries were 'Communists'" (Slater, *Intervention and Negotiation*, 41). According to Felten, the loyalists also endeavored to influence U.S. public opinion: "The loyalists intended to create a political climate in the United States which made accommodation with the rebels impossible. To this end, the loyalist military helped Jules Dubois, the rabidly anti-communist *Chicago Tribune* Latin America correspondent, enter the Dominican Republic before any other English-language reporter. Like nearly all involved, the coup caught the media by surprise, so no members of the U.S. press were in the country when the crisis broke. The subsequent chaos kept foreign reporters out, despite a large number clambering to get the story. Dubois, however, had unparalleled access to the loyalists, interviewing by telephone General Wessin on April 27 and arriving at a loyalist airport early the next morning, the first foreign reporter to enter the country since hostilities began. Dubois served as a mouthpiece for the loyalists, whom he called the 'anti-communist forces.'

He repeated Wessin's claims that 'Bosch is a communist sympathizer' and that 'this country came within 12 hours of a communist takeover' on April 26. By using journalists like Dubois, San Isidro conducted a propaganda offensive aimed at both official and public opinion in the United States" (Felten, "The 1965–1966 United States Intervention in the Dominican Republic," 96–97).

31. Lowenthal, *Dominican Intervention*, 79, 100–102; Felten, "The 1965–1966 United States Intervention in the Dominican Republic," 90, 114–115, 117, 135; Martin, *Overtaken by Events*, 656–657. Representatives of conservative governments elsewhere in Latin America reinforced the loyalists' warnings. Ambassador Bennett informed Washington on 30 April that the Colombian and Guatemalan ambassadors in Santo Domingo concurred with his assessment and believed that only a U.S. military intervention could prevent another Cuba (Felten, "The 1965–1966 United States Intervention in the Dominican Republic," 139).

32. Gleijeses, *Dominican Crisis*, 292–293; Slater, *Intervention and Negotiation*, 30.

33. Felten, "The 1965–1966 United States Intervention in the Dominican Republic," 143–145, 177, 181; *Public Papers of the Presidents of the United States: Lyndon B. Johnson, 1965* (Washington, DC: Government Printing Office, 1966), 465–466, 474. Invaluable insight into Johnson's views during the Dominican crisis can be found in the tapes of his telephone conversations. See *Lyndon Baines Johnson Library Recordings and Transcripts of Conversations and Meetings: Transcripts and Sound Recordings of Telephone Conversations—White House Series* (Austin, TX: Lyndon Baines Johnson Library, 1996–). Many of the recorded conversations are reproduced in Michael Beschloss, *Reaching for Glory: Lyndon Johnson's Secret White House Tapes, 1964–1965* (New York: Simon & Schuster, 2001).

34. See, e.g., Theodore Draper, *The Dominican Revolt: A Case Study in American Policy* (New York: Commentary, 1968); Lowenthal, *The Dominican Intervention*; Alan McPherson, "Misled by Himself: What the Johnson Tapes Reveal about the Dominican Intervention of 1965," *Latin American Research Review* 38, no. 2 (2003), 127–146.

35. Felten, "The 1965–1966 United States Intervention in the Dominican Republic," 129, 175–176, 235; *FRUS, 1964–1968*, 32: 109–111; Palmer, *Intervention in the Caribbean*, 5, 8. Even ambassador Bennett admitted, on 9 May, that the embassy did not have enough evidence to prove "in court" that communists actually controlled the rebel movement (Tad Szulc, *Dominican Diary* [New York: Delacorte, 1965], 170).

36. Gleijeses, *Dominican Crisis*, 43; Martin, *Overtaken by Events*, 631; Smith, *Last Days of the Monroe Doctrine*, 128. Ambassador Bennett referred to the Castro analogy in a 30 April television interview: "I don't think it's so important the actual number [of communists on the rebel side] when one recalls that Fidel Castro first took to the hills with only twelve men. I think it's a question of training, of determined objectives and of being able to influence others who, for very legitimate motives, may be in the fight" (quoted in Draper, *The Dominican Revolt*, 160). Secretary of State Rusk's analogies extended farther back in time. On 26 May, he stated that he was "not impressed by the remark that there were [only] several dozen known Communist leaders and that therefore this was not a very serious matter. There was a time when Hitler sat in a beer hall in Munich with seven people. And I don't believe that one underestimates what can be done in chaos, in a situation of violence and chaos, by a few highly organized, highly trained people who know what they are about and know what they want to bring about" (quoted in ibid., 160).

37. Geyelin, *Lyndon B. Johnson and the World*, 253–254 (emphasis in original).

38. Gleijeses, *Dominican Crisis*, 293, 413n18; Dallek, *Flawed Giant*, 265–266; VanDeMark, *Into the Quagmire*, 133; Martin, *Overtaken by Events*, 661.

39. *FRUS, 1964–1968*, 32: 101; Beschloss, *Reaching for Glory*, 300–301; McPherson, "Misled by Himself," 137.

40. Felten, "The 1965–1966 United States Intervention in the Dominican Republic," 173–174.

41. Palmer, *Intervention in the Caribbean*, 19.

42. Martin, *Overtaken by Events*, 739. Martin admitted that his interpretation of the president's motives was a "guess." Experience had convinced him, however, that "the makers of foreign policy must take into account domestic public opinion, that is, domestic politics" (ibid.).

43. Ball, quoted in Lloyd C. Gardner, *Pay Any Price: Lyndon Johnson and the Wars for Vietnam* (Chicago: Ivan R. Dee, 1995), 210.

44. Felten, "The 1965–1966 United States Intervention in the Dominican Republic," iv, 34, 132, 173, 231; Dallek, *Flawed Giant*, chap. 4.

45. Felten, "The 1965–1966 United States Intervention in the Dominican Republic," 125–129, 132, 231; Lowenthal, *Dominican Intervention*, 104–105.

46. Howard J. Wiarda, "The United States and the Dominican Republic: Intervention, Dependency, and Tyrannicide," *Journal of Interamerican Studies and World Affairs* 22, no. 2 (May 1980): 247.

47. Felten, "The 1965–1966 United States Intervention in the Dominican Republic," iv, 413.

48. VanDeMark, *Into the Quagmire*, chaps. 4–6; Dallek, *Flawed Giant*, chap. 5.

49. Ball, *The Past Has Another Pattern*, 330–331.

50. Palmer, *Intervention in the Caribbean*, 5, 19, 154–155.

51. Wiarda, "The United States and the Dominican Republic," 253; Christopher Andrew, *For the President's Eyes Only: Secret Intelligence and the American Presidency from Washington to Bush* (New York: HarperCollins, 1995), 327; Kai P. Schoenhals and Richard A. Melanson, *Revolution and Intervention in Grenada: The New Jewel Movement, the United States, and the Caribbean* (Boulder, CO: Westview, 1985), 92; Geyelin, *Lyndon B. Johnson and the World*, 254; Walter LaFeber, "Latin American Policy," in *Exploring the Johnson Years*, ed. Robert A. Divine (Austin: University of Texas Press, 1981), 76; Martin, *Overtaken by Events*, 661. According to Wiarda and Kryzanek, Johnson in 1965 "was in the midst of preparing for the massive buildup of U.S. forces in Viet Nam. His intervention in Santo Domingo was meant to send a message to the North Vietnamese of U.S. strength and a willingness to use it." See Howard J. Wiarda and Michael J. Kryzanek, *The Dominican Republic: A Caribbean Crucible* (Boulder, CO: Westview, 1982), 44.

52. Johnson, *Vantage Point*, 152. In March 1965, national security adviser McGeorge Bundy had informed Johnson that the "cardinal" objective of U.S. policy in Vietnam was "not to be a Paper Tiger." Quoted in VanDeMark, *Into the Quagmire*, 101. "The international prestige of the United States, and a substantial part of our influence, are directly at risk in Vietnam," Bundy advised the president (ibid., 66). That same month, a Defense Department study concluded that the predominant U.S. goal in Vietnam was "To avoid a humiliating US defeat (to our reputation as guarantor) [of South Vietnam's security]." It was "essential," the Defense Department study continued, that the United States be seen as having "kept promises, been tough, taken risks, gotten bloodied, and hurt the enemy very badly. We must avoid harmful appearances which will affect judgments by, and provide pretexts to, other nations regarding how the US will behave in future cases of particular interest to those nations—regarding US policy, power, resolve and competence to deal with

their problems" (*The Pentagon Papers: The Defense Department History of United States De-cisionmaking on Vietnam* [Boston: Beacon, 1971], 3: 695, 700).

53. Dallek, *Flawed Giant*, 100, 244–246; VanDeMark, *Into the Quagmire*, 47, 60, 96–97, 106, 213. National security adviser McGeorge Bundy had played heavily on Johnson's political fears in lobbying for a major U.S. military involvement in Vietnam. Arguing in February 1965 for a U.S. bombing campaign against North Vietnam, Bundy advised Johnson that even if the bombing failed, "the policy will be worth it. . . . At a minimum, it will damp down the charge that we did not do all that we could have done, and this charge will be important in many countries, *including our own*" (ibid., 67; emphasis added). The following month, Bundy advocated the deployment of U.S. ground forces to South Vietnam, asking Johnson, "In terms of domestic politics, which is better: to 'lose' now or to 'lose' after committing 100,000 men? Tentative answer: the latter"—because, according to Bundy's reasoning, "if we visibly do enough in the South, any failure will be, in that moment, beyond our control" (quoted in ibid., 101, and in Dallek, *Flawed Giant*, 255).

54. Johnson, *Vantage Point*, 324.

55. Ball, *The Past Has Another Pattern*, 330.

56. Johnson, *Vantage Point*, 187.

57. Quoted in Dallek, *Flawed Giant*, 100.

58. Beschloss, ed., *Taking Charge*, 401–402.

59. Felten, "The 1965–1966 United States Intervention in the Dominican Republic," 178, 230–232.

60. VanDeMark, *Into the Quagmire*, 133–134; Gardner, *Pay Any Price*, 209, 211–212.

61. VanDeMark, *Into the Quagmire*, 132, 134. VanDeMark drew the quote "sheared away the left wing of Lyndon Johnson's Great Society consensus" from Rowland Evans and Robert Novak, *Lyndon B. Johnson: The Exercise of Power* (New York: New American Library, 1966), 511.

62. Felten, "The 1965–1966 United States Intervention in the Dominican Republic," 131, 173, 182, 232–233, 301–302.

Chapter Five. Chile, 1970

1. Thomas Powers, *The Man Who Kept the Secrets: Richard Helms and the CIA* (New York: Pocket, 1979), 294.

2. Paul E. Sigmund, *The Overthrow of Allende and the Politics of Chile, 1964–1976* (Pittsburgh: University of Pittsburgh Press, 1977), 131, 147; Robert J. Alexander, *The Tragedy of Chile* (Westport, CT: Greenwood, 1978), 137–143.

3. Sigmund, *Overthrow of Allende*, 24; Mark Falcoff, *Modern Chile, 1970–1989: A Critical History* (New Brunswick, NJ: Transaction, 1989), 44.

4. Sigmund, *Overthrow of Allende*, 88–89; Falcoff, *Modern Chile, 1970–1989*, 26–30; Julio Faúndez, *Marxism and Democracy in Chile: From 1932 to the Fall of Allende* (New Haven, CT: Yale University Press, 1988), 165, 167–169, 171, 191–192, 194–195; Alexander, *The Tragedy of Chile*, 133–137.

5. Falcoff, *Modern Chile, 1970–1989*, 31; Robert Moss, *Chile's Marxist Experiment* (Newton Abbot, UK: David & Charles, 1973), 49; Faúndez, *Marxism and Democracy in Chile*, 164–171, 196–197; Paul E. Sigmund, *The United States and Democracy in Chile* (Baltimore: Johns Hopkins University Press, 1993), 33; Sigmund, *The Overthrow of Allende*, 140. Also see the revealing assessment of former Allende supporter Roberto Ampuero,

"Thirty Years On, a Chilean Laments 'We All Killed Allende,'" *Washington Post*, 7 September 2003.

6. Sigmund, *The Overthrow of Allende*, 63, 84, 93.

7. Ibid., 112, 118–120; Faúndez, *Marxism and Democracy in Chile*, 188–189. Specifically, the "statute of democratic guarantees" guaranteed "the free functioning of political parties, trade unions, private education, and the mass media and the independence of the armed forces from political control" (Sigmund, *The United States and Democracy in Chile*, 49).

8. Sigmund, *The Overthrow of Allende*, 111; Faúndez, *Marxism and Democracy in Chile*, 193.

9. "The Programme of Unidad Popular," in *Chile's Road to Socialism*, ed. Joan E. Garces, trans. J. Darling, introduction by Richard Gott (Harmondsworth, UK, and Baltimore: Penguin, 1973), 23–24, 27, 29–30.

10. Moss, *Chile's Marxist Experiment*, 59.

11. Sigmund, *The United States and Democracy in Chile*, 58; Allende, "The Programme of Unidad Popular," 25.

12. U.S. House of Representatives, *United States and Chile during the Allende Years, 1970–1973: Hearings before the Subcommittee on Inter-American Affairs of the Committee on Foreign Affairs, July 1, 1971–September 18, 1974*, 92nd Cong., 1st sess. (Washington, DC: Government Printing Office, 1975), 375, 405, 408, 546; address by Salvador Allende, *Official Records of the United Nations General Assembly*, Twenty-Seventh Session, 2,096th Plenary Meeting, 4 December 1972, 2; Armando Uribe, *The Black Book of American Intervention in Chile* (Boston: Beacon, 1975), 21; "The Programme of Unidad Popular," 25; Jacques Zylberberg and Miguel Monterichard, "An Abortive Attempt to Change Foreign Policy: Chile, 1970–3," in *Why Nations Realign: Foreign Policy Restructuring in the Postwar World*, ed. K. J. Holsti (London: Allen & Unwin, 1982), 191. As president, Allende quickly nationalized the U.S. copper companies and arrived at a compensation figure that, after "excess profits" had been deducted from the book value of the companies' Chilean holdings, left the copper companies owing the Chilean government nearly $400 million. Sigmund, *The United States and Democracy in Chile*, 61–62.

13. Sigmund, *The Overthrow of Allende*, 131; F. Parkinson, *Latin America, the Cold War, and the World Powers, 1945–1973* (Beverly Hills and London: Sage, 1974), 239; "The Programme of Unidad Popular," 49; Uribe, *The Black Book of American Intervention in Chile*, 74, 76, 78; James Petras and Morris Morley, *The United States and Chile: Imperialism and the Overthrow of the Allende Government* (New York: Monthly Review Press, 1975), 178n13; Zylberberg and Monterichard, "An Abortive Attempt to Change Foreign Policy: Chile, 1970–3," 180.

14. Parkinson, *Latin America, the Cold War*, 64n69, 196; Jan Knippers Black, *United States Penetration of Brazil* (Philadelphia: University of Pennsylvania Press, 1977), 7; U.S. Senate, Select Committee on Intelligence Activities, *Intelligence Activities: Hearings before the Select Committee to Study Governmental Operations with Respect to Intelligence Activities*, vol. 7: *Covert Action*, 94th Cong., 1st sess. (Washington, DC: Government Printing Office, 1976), 33, 116 (hereafter cited as Senate Hearings, *Intelligence Activities*); Sigmund, *The Overthrow of Allende*, 131; "The Programme of Unidad Popular," 49–50.

15. Falcoff, *Modern Chile, 1970–1989*, 46; Brian Loveman and Thomas M. Davies Jr., eds., *The Politics of Antipolitics: The Military in Latin America*, 3rd rev. ed. (Wilmington, DE: Scholarly Resources, 1997), 129; William Sater, *Chile and the United States: Empires in Conflict* (Athens: University of Georgia Press, 1990), 133 (also quoted in Stephen G.

Rabe, *The Most Dangerous Area in the World: John F. Kennedy Confronts Communist Revolution in Latin America* [Chapel Hill: University of North Carolina Press, 1999], 111); Faúndez, *Marxism and Democracy in Chile*, 170; Alexander, *The Tragedy of Chile*, 140–141.

16. Christopher Andrew and Vasili Mitrokhin, *The World Was Going Our Way: The KGB and the Battle for the Third World* (New York: Basic, 2005), 69–70, 72, 75.

17. Sigmund, *The Overthrow of Allende*, 24–25, 44, 53; Edward Korry, "The Sell-Out of Chile and the American Taxpayer," *Penthouse*, March 1978, 72; U.S. Senate, Select Committee on Intelligence Activities, *Covert Action in Chile 1963–1973: Staff Report*, 94th Cong., 1st sess. (Washington, DC: Government Printing Office, 1975), 14–17 (hereafter cited as Senate, *Covert Action in Chile, 1963–1973*); Powers, *The Man Who Kept the Secrets*, 285.

18. Senate, *Covert Action in Chile, 1963–1973*, 20–22; Henry Kissinger, *White House Years* (Boston: Little, Brown, 1979), 662–669; Powers, *The Man Who Kept the Secrets*, 291; Seymour M. Hersh, *The Price of Power: Kissinger in the Nixon White House* (New York: Summit, 1983), 266. Also see Christopher Andrew, *For the President's Eyes Only: Secret Intelligence and the American Presidency from Washington to Bush* (New York: HarperCollins, 1995), 370–371; and Falcoff, *Modern Chile, 1970–1989*, 204–207.

19. Peter Kornbluh, *The Pinochet File: A Declassified Dossier on Atrocity and Accountability* (New York: New Press, 2003), chap. 1; Kissinger, *White House Years*, 670–672; Senate, *Covert Action in Chile, 1963–1973*, 23–26; U.S. Senate, Select Committee to Study Governmental Operations with Respect to Intelligence Activities, *Alleged Assassination Plots Involving Foreign Leaders: An Interim Report* (Washington, DC: Government Printing Office, 1975), 231–234 (hereafter cited as Senate, *Alleged Assassination Plots*); Gregory F. Treverton, *Covert Action: The Limits of Intervention in the Postwar World* (New York: Basic, 1987), 104.

20. Kornbluh, *The Pinochet File*, chap. 1; Senate, *Alleged Assassination Plots*, 225–229, 231–235; Senate, *Covert Action in Chile, 1963–1973*, 23, 25–26. One U.S. official present at the September 15 meeting described Nixon as "frantic." Stephen Kinzer, *Overthrow: America's Century of Regime Change from Hawaii to Iraq* (New York: Henry Holt, 2005), 172. A special CIA task force was created to carry out Track II. Its assignment consisted of a "three-part program": "a. Collect intelligence on coup-minded officers; b. Create a coup climate by propaganda, disinformation, and terrorist activities intended to provoke the left to give a pretext for a coup; [and] c. Inform those coup-minded officers that the U.S. Government would give them full support in a coup short of direct U.S. military intervention" (Senate, *Alleged Assassination Plots*, 234).

21. Hersh, *The Price of Power*, 277; Senate, *Covert Action in Chile, 1963–1973*, 26; Kornbluh, *The Pinochet File*, 29.

22. Kornbluh, *The Pinochet File*, chap. 2; Senate, *Covert Action in Chile, 1963–1973*, 26–28; Mark Falcoff, "Kissinger and Chile: The Myth That Will Not Die," *Commentary*, November 2003, 41–49.

23. Hersh, *The Price of Power*, 270, 296.

24. Petras and Morley, *The United States and Chile*, viii–ix.

25. Address by Salvador Allende, *Official Records of the United Nations General Assembly*, 4 December 1972, 3; Uribe, *The Black Book of American Intervention in Chile*, 144–145.

26. Treverton, *Covert Action*, 161–162; Hersh, *The Price of Power*, 266–268, 276; Senate, *Covert Action in Chile, 1963–1973*, 12; U.S. Senate, Committee on Foreign Relations, Subcommittee on Multinational Corporations, *Multinational Corporations and United States Foreign Policy: Hearings on the International Telephone and Telegraph Company and Chile, 1970–71*, 93rd Cong., 1st sess., March 20–April 2, 1973, pt. 1, 21–22 (hereafter cited as Senate, *ITT Hearings*).

27. Senate, *Covert Action in Chile, 1963–1973*, 45; Senate, *Alleged Assassination Plots*, 229.

28. *New York Times*, 26 May 1977, B6.

29. Henry Kissinger, *White House Years*, 656; Kissinger, *Years of Upheaval* (Boston: Little, Brown, 1982), 376; Hersh, *The Price of Power*, 270; Roger Morris, *Uncertain Greatness: Henry Kissinger and American Foreign Policy* (New York: Harper & Row, 1977), 241.

30. Hersh, *The Price of Power*, 266, 268, 276; Senate, *Covert Action in Chile, 1963–1973*, 12. Although it turned down ITT funds for anti-Allende operations, the CIA advised the company on how to pass money to Allende's opponent Alessandri and his National Party. According to a subsequent Senate investigation, "Eventually at least $350,000 was passed by ITT to [Alessandri's] campaign. A roughly equal amount was passed by other U.S. companies; the CIA learned of this funding but did not assist in it" (Senate, *Covert Action in Chile 1963–1973*, 13). Danish historian Poul Jensen offers an economic interpretation of a different stripe. Jensen places Nixon's Chilean intervention within the context of a severe balance-of-payments crisis that was threatening to deplete U.S. gold reserves in 1969–1970. Because U.S. foreign-exchange earnings were heavily dependent on "remitted income . . . from direct US overseas investments," Jensen writes, Allende's determination to nationalize foreign capital would—by eliminating the $100 million in income that U.S. corporations in Chile remitted each year to the U.S. domestic economy—have made a bad situation considerably worse. Nixon responded to the growing balance-of-payments deficits by establishing the Overseas Private Investment Corporation (OPIC), a new "government insurance company" that provided U.S. foreign investors with insurance coverage to protect their investments in the event of expropriation. By late 1970, according to Jensen, more than $310 million of U.S. investment capital in Chile was protected by OPIC expropriation insurance, even though the corporation had available less than $70 million in financial reserves to meet its expropriation-insurance commitments worldwide. Administrators were openly warning that a series of large-scale nationalizations in Chile would be "catastrophic" for their corporation. And if successful expropriations in Chile stimulated a wave of nationalizations throughout Latin America and the Third World, Jensen concludes, the "harmful economic effects" on the United States would obviously be "even greater." Nevertheless, even Jensen is forced to admit that there is no actual evidence that the White House officials who ordered the Chilean intervention had any "awareness of" or "interest in . . . the particular consequences of the expected Chilean nationalizations for OPIC." See Poul Jensen, *The Garotte: The United States and Chile, 1970–1973* (Aarhus, Denmark: Aarhus University Press, 1988), 450–460, 464–466, 474, 484–485, 487, 495.

31. Kissinger, *White House Years*, 656.

32. *New York Times*, 25 May 1977, B6.

33. Ibid. Nixon repeated his "Italian businessman" anecdote in *RN: The Memoirs of Richard Nixon* (New York: Grosset & Dunlap, 1978), 490.

34. Kissinger, *Years of Upheaval*, 376.

35. Edward M. Korry, "Contingency Paper ('Fidelism without Fidel')," August 1970, 23, reproduced in "Chile in the Archives of the USA (1970): Documents from the Former U.S. Ambassador to Chile Edward M. Korry (1967–1971)," *Estudios Públicos* (Centro de Estudios Públicos, Santiago, Chile), no. 72 (1998), www.cepchile.cl/dms/archivo_1147_316/rev72_korrydocing.pdf; Senate, *Alleged Assassination Plots*, 229; Kornbluh, *The Pinochet File*, 8, 11.

36. Senate, *Covert Action in Chile, 1963–1973*, 44.

37. Ibid., 47.

38. Korry to Rogers, 5 September 1970, 4, in *Chile and the United States: Declassified Documents Relating to the Military Coup, 1970–1976*, National Security Archive Electronic Briefing Book no. 8, http://www.gwu.edu/~nsarchiv/NSAEBB/NSAEBB8/nsaebb8.htm.

39. Paul E. Sigmund, "Crisis Management: Chile and Marxism," in *United States Policy in Latin America: A Quarter Century of Crisis and Challenge, 1961–1986*, ed. John D. Martz (Lincoln: University of Nebraska Press, 1988), 158; Treverton, *Covert Action*, 173.

40. Melvin Small, *The Presidency of Richard Nixon* (Lawrence: University Press of Kansas, 1999), 59–60.

41. Ibid., 60–65, 97; John Lewis Gaddis, *Strategies of Containment: A Critical Appraisal of Postwar American National Security Policy* (New York: Oxford University Press, 1982), chaps. 9–10; Kissinger, *White House Years*, 124–130, 135–136, 163–165, 191–192; Nixon, *RN*, 341–349.

42. Nixon, *RN*, 380, 406; Kissinger, *White House Years*, 143–147, 159–161, 278, 283, 313; Michael A. Genovese, *The Nixon Presidency: Power and Politics in Turbulent Times* (Westport, CT: Greenwood, 1990), 116; Jeffrey Kimball, *Nixon's Vietnam War* (Lawrence: University Press of Kansas, 1998), 116, 118, 171.

43. Kissinger, *White House Years*, chaps. 14–15; Nixon, *RN*, 483.

44. Kissinger, *White House Years*, chap. 16; Stephen E. Ambrose, *Nixon: The Triumph of a Politician, 1962–1972* (New York: Simon & Schuster, 1989), 381. Also see Nixon, *RN*, 485–486.

45. Kissinger, *White House Years*, 118–119, 162, 316, 570, 594; Walter Isaacson, *Kissinger: A Biography* (New York: Simon & Schuster, 1992), 292; Nixon, *RN*, 485, 490; Hersh, *The Price of Power*, 251.

46. Small, *The Presidency of Richard Nixon*, 65; Kimball, *Nixon's Vietnam*, 38, 62, 72; Isaacson, *Kissinger*, 120. Also see H. R. Haldeman, *The Ends of Power* (New York: Times Books, 1978), 98–99.

47. Kissinger, *White House Years*, 228.

48. Kimball, *Nixon's Vietnam*, 225.

49. Nixon, *RN*, 380; Kimball, *Nixon's Vietnam*, 136.

50. *Public Papers of the Presidents of the United States: Richard Nixon, 1970* (Washington, DC: Government Printing Office, 1971), 408–409.

51. Nixon, *RN*, 490; Kissinger, *White House Years*, 593 (emphasis added). According to Kissinger, "The Nixon Administration had told Moscow many times that we were prepared for a period of mutual restraint and conciliation. In the autumn of 1970 Moscow chose to test whether this willingness reflected indecision, domestic weakness due to Vietnam, or the strategy of a serious government" (ibid., 652).

52. Kissinger, *White House Years*, 654.

53. Nixon, *RN*, 490. In Kissinger's view, "None" of the "three major crises" that "descended upon the Administration" in September 1970—Jordan, Cienfuegos, or Chile—"could have succeeded without Communist impetus or encouragement" (Kissinger, *White House Years*, 594).

54. Kissinger, *White House Years*, 656; Petras and Morley, *The United States and Chile*, 39.

55. Kimball, *Nixon's Vietnam*, 173, 182–183, 230; William Buckley, "U.S. Policies in Chile under the Allende Government: An Interview with Former Ambassador Edward Korry," in *Chile: The Balanced View*, ed. Francisco Orrego Vicuña (Santiago: University of Chile Institute of International Studies, 1975), 294.

56. Korry to Senator Frank Church, 23 October 1975, in Senate Hearings, *Intelligence Activities*, 118–119.

57. Buckley, "U.S. Policies in Chile under the Allende Government," 294; Kissinger, *White House Years*, 102–103, 388, 657, 920–922; Gerry Argyris Andrianopoulos, *Kissinger and Brzezinski: The NSC and the Struggle for Control of US National Security Policy* (New York: St. Martin's, 1991), 21–22; Robert H. Johnson, *Improbable Dangers: U.S. Conceptions of Threat in the Cold War and Beyond* (New York: St. Martin's, 1994), 66; Ricardo Israel, *Politics and Ideology in Allende's Chile* (Tempe: Arizona State University Center for Latin American Studies, 1989), 157. Kissinger's concern about the link between the "Chilean model" and Eurocommunism may have been well founded. Robert Alexander writes that "European Communists, especially those of Italy and France, were keeping a close eye on the Unidad Popular experiment. . . . In both Italy and France, the Communist parties ha[d] for some time been seeking an alliance with Socialists—and in Italy's case, even with Christian Democrats—which would permit them to return to the government of those countries, at least as junior partners" (Alexander, *The Tragedy of Chile*, 136). Mark Falcoff reports that "a group of Italian sympathizers told Allende shortly after his election, 'If you can show in Chile that a second road to socialism is possible . . . , then the next country to advance along that road will be Italy, and very soon others in Latin America, and later, in one or two generations, half the world"(Falcoff, *Modern Chile, 1970–1989*, 2). Allende's foreign minister, Clodomiro Almeyda, later recalled that "the victory of a clearly anti-imperialist, socialist political force in an important Latin American country changed the balance of power on the continent, and was inevitably linked to the general political process in Latin America and the hemisphere. This in turn had ramifications, at least to some extent, in the world political arena where the East-West conflict overshadowed . . . every event. Indeed, important actors in the *Unidad Popular* had participated in that world conflict and saw the Chilean experience in a larger context" (Clodomiro Almeyda Medina, "The Foreign Policy of the Unidad Popular Government," in *Chile at the Turning Point: Lessons of the Socialist Years, 1970–1973*, ed. Federico G. Gil, Ricardo Lagos E., and Henry A. Landsberger (Philadelphia: Institute for the Study of Human Issues, 1979), 76.

58. Korry to Church, Senate Hearings, *Intelligence Activities*, 118.

59. Hersh, *The Price of Power*, 270.

60. Morris, *Uncertain Greatness*, 241 (emphasis in original).

61. Senate, *Alleged Assassination Plots*, 229n3; Kornbluh, *The Pinochet File*, 8.

62. Quoted in Kornbluh, *The Pinochet File*, 79, 119.

63. Kissinger, *White House Years*, 129, 664, 668n678. Kissinger later observed that "the *appearance* of inferiority—whatever its actual significance—can have serious political consequences" (Gaddis, *Strategies of Containment*, 288; emphasis in original).

64. Small, *The Presidency of Richard Nixon*, 67; Kissinger, *Years of Upheaval*, 1187.

65. George C. Herring, *America's Longest War: The United States and Vietnam, 1950–1975*, 3rd ed. (New York: McGraw-Hill, 1996), 245; Kimball, *Nixon's Vietnam*, 118, 216–217, 229–230; Small, *The Presidency of Richard Nixon*, 67; Isaacson, *Kissinger: A Biography*, 287; Kissinger, *White House Years*, 969. That Nixon had inherited the domestic political turmoil over U.S. involvement in Vietnam that had driven Johnson from the presidency became evident during his 1969 inaugural parade when the incoming president's limousine was pelted by "a barrage of sticks, stones, beer cans, and what looked like firecrackers" by crowds of antiwar demonstrators (Nixon, *RN*, 366).

66. H. R. Haldeman, *The Haldeman Diaries: Inside the Nixon White House* (New York: Putnam's, 1994), 192–194. "Richard Nixon was a full-time politician," White House domestic affairs counsel John Ehrlichman later wrote. "At home and abroad, every day of the

week and whatever the occasion, he (and we) looked after the politics" (John Ehrlichman, *Witness to Power: The Nixon Years* [New York: Pocket, 1982], 288).

67. Kissinger, *White House Years*, 126, 634; Ambrose, *Nixon: The Triumph of a Politician*, 19–20.

68. Ambrose, *Nixon: The Triumph of a Politician*, 378. One of Kissinger's National Security Council aides said of the administration's interventionist motives: "It was the 'who-lost-Chile' syndrome" (Morris, *Uncertain Greatness*, 241).

69. Kissinger, *White House Years*, 671 (emphasis in original).

70. National Security Council, "Options Paper on Chile (NSSM97)," 3 November 1970, 3, 5, in *Chile and the United States: Declassified Documents Relating to the Military Coup, 1970–1976*.

71. Memorandum, Chapin to H. R. Haldeman, 4 November 1970, in File 66-6, "National Security Council, 9-1-70 to 11-4-70," White House Central Files, Subject Files, Confidential Files, 1969–1974, box 14, Nixon Presidential Materials Project, U.S. National Archives, College Park, MD. Also quoted in Kornbluh, *The Pinochet File*, 80.

72. Kissinger, *White House Years*, 653. The full text of Korry's cable can be found in *Chile and the United States: Declassified Documents Relating to the Military Coup, 1970–1976*.

73. Peter Kornbluh, "The *El Mercurio* File: Secret Documents Shine New Light on How the CIA Used a Newspaper to Foment a Coup," *Columbia Journalism Review*, September–October 2003, 14, 16–17; Kinzer, *Overthrow*, 170–172, 177; Israel, *Politics and Ideology in Allende's Chile*, 171; Hersh, *The Price of Power*, 266; Sigmund, *The United States and Democracy in Chile*, 50, 55, 83; Korry, "The Sell-Out of Chile and the American Taxpayer," 88; *Washington Post*, 28 November 1975, A4; Powers, *The Man Who Kept the Secrets*, 291–292, 299; Ambrose, *Nixon: The Triumph of a Politician*, 378; Jensen, *The Garotte*, 244; Senate, *Alleged Assassination Plots*, 228n1; Kissinger, *White House Years*, 673. For Edwards' extensive ties to the CIA, see Hersh, *The Price of Power*, 260; Senate, *Covert Action in Chile 1963–1973*, 19, 22, 29; Korry, "The Sell-Out of Chile and the American Taxpayer," 114.

74. Senate Hearings, *Intelligence Activities*, 29; Senate, *ITT Hearings*, 292, 305.

75. Jensen, *The Garotte*, 491, 596n151.

76. National Security Council, "Options Paper on Chile (NSSM 97)," 3 November 1970, 17, in *Chile and the United States: Declassified Documents Relating to the Military Coup, 1970–1976*.

Chapter Six. Nicaragua, 1981

1. Robert Kagan, *A Twilight Struggle: American Power and Nicaragua, 1977–1990* (New York: Free Press, 1996), 200–203, 225–226; Peter H. Smith, *Talons of the Eagle: Dynamics of U.S.-Latin American Relations*, 2nd ed. (New York: Oxford University Press, 2000), 188; Ariel C. Armony, *Argentina, the United States, and the Anti-communist Crusade in Central America, 1977–1884*, Monographs in International Studies no. 26 (Athens: Ohio University Center for International Studies, 1997), 115.

2. E. Bradford Burns, *At War in Nicaragua: The Reagan Doctrine and the Politics of Nostalgia* (New York: Harper & Row, 1987), 22–23; Ronnie Dugger, *On Reagan: The Man and His Presidency* (New York: McGraw-Hill, 1983), 353, 518.

3. Matilde Zimmermann, *Sandinista: Carlos Fonseca and the Nicaraguan Revolution* (Durham, NC: Duke University Press, 2000), chaps. 2–5 (1968 Fonseca quote, 108); Dennis Gilbert, *Sandinistas: The Party and the Revolution* (New York: Basil Blackwell, 1988), 4,

19–20, 22, 25; "The Historic Program of the FSLN (1969)," in *Conflict in Nicaragua: A Multidimensional Perspective,* ed. Jiri Valenta and Esperanza Duran (Boston: Allen & Unwin, 1987), a B, 321; David Nolan, *The Ideology of the Sandinistas and the Nicaraguan Revolution* (Coral Gables, FL: University of Miami Institute of Interamerican Studies, 1984), 17. Victor Tirado, a member of the Sandinista national directorate, later recalled that "we, the founders and builders of the FSLN, prepared our strategy, our tactics and our program, on the basis of Marx's teachings" (quoted in Gilbert, *Sandinistas,* 22).

4. Zimmermann, *Sandinista,* 79, 173; "Historic Program of the FSLN (1969)," 319; Borge, quoted in Jorge Castañeda, *Utopia Unarmed: The Latin American Left after the Cold War* (New York: Vintage, 1993), 105n33.

5. Zimmermann, *Sandinista,* 162–169, 206; Nolan, *Ideology of the Sandinistas,* chaps. 3–4; Gilbert, *Sandinistas,* 8; Holly Sklar, *Washington's War on Nicaragua* (Boston: South End Press, 1988), 14; Lawrence Pezzullo and Ralph Pezzullo, *At the Fall of Somoza* (Pittsburgh: University of Pittsburgh Press, 1993), 50. For a descriptive overview of the 1978–1979 insurrection that drove Somoza from power, see Thomas W. Walker, *Nicaragua: The Land of Sandino* (Boulder, CO: Westview, 1981), 34–40.

6. Nolan, *Ideology of the Sandinistas,* 61–67, 76; "General Political-Military Platform of the FSLN for the Triumph of the Popular Sandinista Revolution (May 1977)," in Valenta and Duran, eds., *Conflict in Nicaragua,* a A, 302–303, 305, 309; Gilbert, *Sandinistas,* 30. The "General Political-Military Platform" identified capitalism as "the major obstacle to social progress"—a system that "subjects the majority of the people—from laborers and semiproletarians, to farmers and other sectors of the population—to the cruelest oppression and exploitation." According to the document, "The dialectical development of human society" led ultimately to a transformation "from capitalism to socialism" (301).

7. Nolan, *Ideology of the Sandinistas,* 67–68.

8. Kagan, *Twilight Struggle,* chap. 13; "The Seventy-two Hour Document," in *The Continuing Crisis: U.S. Policy in Central America and the Caribbean,* ed. Mark Falcoff and Robert Royal (Lanham, MD: Ethics and Public Policy Center, 1987), a C, 497, 500, 504; Christopher Andrew and Vasili Mitrokhin, *The World Was Going Our Way: The KGB and the Battle for the Third World* (New York: Basic, 2005), 120–121.

9. Zimmermann, *Sandinista,* 45–47; Nolan, *Ideology of the Sandinistas,* 20–21; Andrew and Mitrokhin, *The World Was Going Our Way,* 41–42.

10. "General Political-Military Platform of the FSLN," 293, 301.

11. Kagan, *Twilight Struggle,* 195–196. According to Arturo Cruz, a prominent Nicaraguan economist who served in the Sandinistas' initial Government of National Reconstruction, "During the first months after the victory, some of the *comandantes* adopted the extreme view that the United States had not intervened in Nicaragua in 1979 . . .because of the shift in the world balance of power between the United States and the Soviet Union. They even claimed that the United States actually had been constrained by fear of Cuba. . . . At the beginning of the revolution," he continued, "there was a pro-Soviet consensus among the *comandantes*" (Arturo Cruz Sequiera, "The Origins of Sandinista Foreign Policy," in *Central America: Anatomy of Conflict,* ed. Robert S. Leiken (New York: Pergamon, 1984), 102, 106. Jaime Wheelock, leader of the FSLN's "Proletarian" faction and Nicaraguan minister of agriculture in the Sandinista government, recalls that "we thought there was a great potential and vast resources in the socialist countries and the USSR. We underestimated the extent of the crisis of socialism" (quoted in Castañeda, *Utopia Unarmed,* 108n38).

12. Andrew and Mitrokhin, *The World Was Going Our Way*, 121; Kagan, *Twilight Struggle*, 130, 194–196; Nolan, *Ideology of the Sandinistas*, 116–117; Gilbert, *Sandinistas*, 162; Jiri Valenta, "Nicaragua: Soviet-Cuban Pawn or Non-aligned Country?" *Journal of Interamerican Studies and World Affairs* 27 no. 3 (Fall 1985): 168; Mary Vanderlaan, *Revolution and Foreign Policy in Nicaragua* (Boulder, CO: Westview, 1986), 315.

13. Kagan, *Twilight Struggle*, 195; Gilbert, *Sandinistas*, 162; Nolan, *Ideology of the Sandinistas*, 117, 125–126; Vanderlaan, *Revolution and Foreign Policy in Nicaragua*, 257, 277, 293.

14. Zimmermann, *Sandinista*, chaps. 3–4; Robert A. Pastor, *Condemned to Repetition: The United States and Nicaragua* (Princeton, NJ: Princeton University Press, 1988), 35; Roger Miranda and William Ratliff, *The Civil War in Nicaragua: Inside the Sandinistas* (New Brunswick, NJ: Transaction, 1993), 97. For Tomás Borge, a founding member of the Sandinistas, "The Victory of the armed struggle in Cuba, more than a joy, was the lifting of innumerable curtains, a flash of light that shone beyond the simple and boring dogmas of the time" (quoted in Nolan, *Ideology of the Sandinistas*, 22).

15. Pezzullo, *At the Fall of Somoza*, 50, 78, 123; Kagan, *Twilight Struggle*, 159–160; Castañeda, *Utopia Unarmed*, 59; Miranda and Ratliff, *The Civil War in Nicaragua*, 98–99.

16. Castañeda, *Utopia Unarmed*, 59n9; Pastor, *Condemned to Repetition*, 143.

17. Castañeda, *Utopia Unarmed*, 32, 110–111; Dario Moreno, *U.S. Policy in Central America: The Endless Debate* (Miami: Florida International University Press, 1990), 63–66; Morris H. Morley, *Washington, Somoza, and the Sandinistas: State and Regime in U.S. Policy toward Nicaragua, 1969–1981* (New York: Cambridge University Press, 1994), 298–300; Humberto Ortega, quoted in Kagan, *Twilight Struggle*, 122. Once Somoza had been overthrown, Ortega recalled, "We radicalized our model to look more like Cuba. Whether *Terceristas* or not, we wanted to copy in a mechanical way the model that we knew—which was Cuba—and we identified with it. . . . We didn't want to follow the other models" (quoted in Kagan, *Twilight Struggle*, 122).

18. Vanderlaan, *Revolution and Foreign Policy in Nicaragua*, 252; "General Political-Military Platform of the FSLN," 291, 305; Gilbert, *Sandinistas*, 28–29.

19. "General Political-Military Platform of the FSLN," 294; Fonseca, quoted in Zimmermann, *Sandinista*, 78 (emphasis in original).

20. "General Political-Military Platform of the FSLN," 301–302 (emphasis in original).

21. Miranda and Ratliff, *The Civil War in Nicaragua*, 73; Ortega, quoted in telegram 1552, U.S. Embassy Managua to State Department, 2 April 1981, 1, in National Security Archive, *Nicaragua: The Making of U.S. Policy* (Alexandria, VA: Chadwyck-Healey, 1991), microfiche, document no. 01304.

22. Fonseca quoted in Pastor, *Condemned to Repetition*, 40; Karl Bermann, *Under the Big Stick: Nicaragua and the United States since 1848* (Boston: South End Press, 1986), chaps. 8–10; Nolan, *Ideology of the Sandinistas*, 45; Carlos Fonseca Amador, "Nicaragua: Zero Hour," in *Sandinistas Speak*, by Tomás Borge et al. (New York: Pathfinder, 1982), 23; Ortega, quoted in telegram 1552, U.S. Embassy Managua to State Department, 2 April 1981, 2, in National Security Archive, *Nicaragua: The Making of U.S. Policy*, microfiche, document 01304. The historical record suggests that U.S. support for the senior Somoza's regime fluctuated over time. During World War II and the early Cold War period, faced with security threats from European totalitarian enemies, the United States government welcomed Somoza as a reliable ally. From 1945 to 1947, however, the State Department actively promoted democratic change in Nicaragua, pressuring Somoza to step down as president, suspending U.S. military assistance, and even threatening to break relations. See Paul

Coe Clark, *The United States and Somoza: A Revisionist Look* (Westport, CT: Praeger, 1992), chaps. 8–9; and Richard E. Clinton Jr., "The United States and the Caribbean Legion: Democracy, Dictatorship, and the Origins of the Cold War in Latin America, 1945–1950" (Ph.D. diss., Ohio University Department of History, 2001), chap. 4.

23. Telegram 1552, U.S. Embassy Managua to State Department, 2 April 1981, 2–3, in National Security Archive, *Nicaragua: The Making of U.S. Policy*, microfiche, document 01304; Fonseca, "Nicaragua: Zero Hour," in Borge et al., *Sandinistas Speak*, 23. It was the Somoza family, not U.S. firms, that controlled Nicaragua's economy. According to Thomas W. Walker: "By the time the dynasty was overthrown the [Somoza] family had acquired a portfolio worth well in excess of $500 million (U.S.)—perhaps as much as one or one-and-a-half billion dollars. The Somozas owned about one-fifth of the nation's arable land and produced export products such as cotton, sugar, coffee, cattle, and bananas. They were involved in the processing of agricultural exports. They held vital export-import franchises and had extensive investments in urban real estate. They owned or had controlling interests in two seaports, a maritime line, the national airline, the concrete industry, a paving-block company, construction firms, a metal extruding plant, and various other businesses including *Plasmaféresis de Nicaragua*, which exported plasma extracted from whole blood purchased from impoverished Nicaraguans" (Walker, *Nicaragua: The Land of Sandino*, 58). As late as 1978, direct U.S. investments in Nicaragua totaled a relatively insignificant $90 million (Bermann, *Under the Big Stick*, 295–296).

24. Fonseca, "Nicaragua: Zero Hour," 42; "The Historic Program of the FSLN (1969)," 328; "The Seventy-two Hour Document," 504; Pastor, *Condemned to Repetition*, 202; "Literacy Campaign Textbooks (August 1980): The FSLN Anthem," in *The Central American Crisis Reader*, ed. Robert S. Leiken and Barry Rubin (New York: Summit, 1987), 235.

25. Kagan, *Twilight Struggle*, 51; Pastor, *Condemned to Repetition*, 49; Moreno, *U.S. Policy in Central America*, 5, 30–35.

26. Kagan, *Twilight Struggle*, 30–31; Moreno, *U.S. Policy in Central America*, 5–6.

27. Morley, *Washington, Somoza, and the Sandinistas*, 114–115, 166, 175–176; Anthony Lake, *Somoza Falling* (Boston: Houghton Mifflin, 1989), 193, 199; Pastor, *Condemned to Repetition*, 53–54; Kagan, *Twilight Struggle*, 74–75. Another conservative Democrat, Congressman Charles Wilson of Texas, a member of the House Appropriations Committee, warned the White House that he would block the administration's entire foreign-aid bill if any further cuts were made in U.S. economic assistance to Nicaragua (Lake, *Somoza Falling*, 165; Morley, *Washington, Somoza, and the Sandinistas*, 114).

28. Morley, *Washington, Somoza, and the Sandinistas*, 166–167, 175–176; Sklar, *Washington's War on Nicaragua*, 24.

29. Pastor, *Condemned to Repetition*, 142, 148; Lake, *Somoza Falling*, 220–221, 226; Kagan, *Twilight Struggle*, 92.

30. Moreno, *U.S. Policy in Central America*, 59; Morley, *Washington, Somoza, and the Sandinistas*, 188; Bermann, *Under the Big Stick*, 270; Pastor, *Condemned to Repetition*, 147; Lake, *Somoza Falling*, 220–221, 226.

31. Pastor, *Condemned to Repetition*, 148; Lake, *Somoza Falling*, 226, 275; Moreno, *U.S. Policy in Central America*, 59–60.

32. Sklar, *Washington's War on Nicaragua*, 25.

33. Morley, *Washington, Somoza, and the Sandinistas*, 227–228, 305; Kagan, *Twilight Struggle*, 92; Pastor, *Condemned to Repetition*, 192–195, 206–207; Moreno, *U.S. Policy in Central America*, 61–62; Lars Schoultz, *National Security and United States Policy toward Latin America* (Princeton, NJ: Princeton University Press, 1987), 46–47.

34. Pastor, *Condemned to Repetition*, 193–194.

35. Quoted in Moreno, *U.S Policy in Central America*, 65–66.

36. Pastor, *Condemned to Repetition*, 194.

37. Moreno, *U.S. Policy in Central America*, 63–69; Kagan, *Twilight Struggle*, 157.

38. Robert D. Schulzinger, *U.S. Diplomacy since 1900*, 4th ed. (New York: Oxford University Press, 1998), 326–331; I. M. Destler, Leslie H. Gelb, and Anthony Lake, *Our Own Worst Enemy: The Unmaking of American Foreign Policy* (New York: Simon & Schuster, 1984), 73–78.

39. Moreno, *U.S. Policy in Central America*, 30, 44–48, 76–77.

40. Morley, *Washington, Somoza, and the Sandinistas*, 293, 307; Moreno, *U.S. Policy in Central America*, 102–103; Peter Kornbluh, *Nicaragua: The Price of Intervention* (Washington, DC: Institute for Policy Studies, 1987), 19.

41. Moreno, *U.S. Policy in Central America*, 47–48, 77, 79–81; Pastor, *Condemned to Repetition*, 225–228.

42. Dinesh D'Souza, *Ronald Reagan: How an Ordinary Man Became an Extraordinary Leader* (New York: Free Press, 1997), 85; William E. Pemberton, *Exit with Honor: The Life and Presidency of Ronald Reagan* (Armonk, NY: M. E. Sharpe, 1997), 85, 95, 97; Lou Cannon, *President Reagan: The Role of a Lifetime* (New York: Simon & Schuster, 1991), 188, 338; Martin Anderson, *Revolution* (New York: Harcourt Brace Jovanovich, 1988), 92; Alexander M. Haig Jr., *Caveat: Realism, Reagan, and Foreign Policy* (New York: Macmillan, 1984), 81.

43. Ronald Reagan, *An American Life* (New York: Simon & Schuster, 1990), 205; Pemberton, *Exit with Honor*, 109; Kai Schoenhals and Richard A. Melanson, *Revolution and Intervention in Grenada: The New Jewel Movement, the United States, and the Caribbean* (Boulder, CO: Westview, 1985), 122; Peter Schweizer, *Victory: The Reagan Administration's Secret Strategy That Hastened the Collapse of the Soviet Union* (New York: Atlantic Monthly Press, 1994), 10, 22; Haig, *Caveat*, 26–27, 30–31, 123; James M. Scott, *Deciding to Intervene: The Reagan Doctrine and American Foreign Policy* (Durham, NC: Duke University Press, 1996), 16–17, 28. Haig recalled that "We confronted a situation where strategic passivity during the Ford Administration and the excessive piety of the Carter Administration's human rights crusade had sapped the will of authoritarian anti-communist governments, eroded the confidence of Western allies, and encouraged risk-taking by the Soviet Union and by Soviet-manipulated totalitarian regimes. Since 1978, this bi-partisan policy of failure had permitted the Soviet Union to inflict disastrous defeats on the United States at regular six month intervals" (quoted in Moreno, *U.S. Policy in Central America*, 85).

44. Reagan, *An American Life*, 266–267.

45. Quoted in Pemberton, *Exit with Honor*, 133.

46. *Public Papers of the Presidents of the United States: Ronald Reagan, 1982* (Washington, DC: Government Printing Office, 1983), 360.

47. Haig, *Caveat*, 95–96.

48. Ibid., 96.

49. Ibid., 30–31.

50. Ibid., 96–97. In his January 1981 Senate confirmation hearing, Haig stated that "over the last decade, America's confidence in itself was shaken, and America's leadership faltered. The United States seemed unable or unwilling to act when our strategic interests were threatened. We earned a reputation for 'strategic passivity,' and that reputation still weighs heavily upon us and cannot be wished away by rhetoric. What we once took for granted abroad—confidence in the United States—must be reestablished through a steady

accumulation of prudent and successful actions" (quoted in Schoenhals and Melanson, *Revolution and Intervention in Grenada*, 124).

51. Piero Gleijeses, *Tilting at Windmills: Reagan in Central America*, Occasional Papers in International Affairs (Washington, DC: Johns Hopkins University School of Advanced International Studies, Foreign Policy Institute, April 1982), 4; Haig, *Caveat*, 30; Raymond L. Garthoff, *The Great Transition: American-Soviet Relations and the End of the Cold War* (Washington, DC: Brookings Institution, 1994), 26; Laurence I. Barrett, *Gambling with History: Ronald Reagan in the White House* (Garden City, NJ: Doubleday, 1983), 207; Cynthia J. Arnson, *Crossroads: Congress, the Reagan Administration, and Central America* (New York: Pantheon, 1989), 52–53.

52. William M. LeoGrande, "A Splendid Little War: Drawing the Line in El Salvador," *International Security* 6, no. 1 (Summer 1981): 45.

53. U.S. House of Representatives, Committee on Foreign Affairs, *Foreign Assistance Legislation for Fiscal Year 1982 (Part 1): Hearings before the Committee on Foreign Affairs*, 97th Cong., 1st sess., 18 March 1981, 194; Sklar, *Washington's War on Nicaragua*, 71–72.

54. *New York Times*, 28 April 1983, A12; Reagan, *An American Life*, 473.

55. Schoultz, *National Security and United States Policy toward Latin America*, 259; Bob Woodward, *Veil: The Secret Wars of the CIA, 1981–1987* (New York: Pocket, 1987), 331.

56. Moreno, *U.S. Policy in Central America*, 85.

57. Quoted in Barbara Epstein, "Reagan Administration Policymakers," in *Vital Interests: The Soviet Issue in U.S. Central American Policy*, ed. Bruce D. Larkin (Boulder, CO: Lynne Rienner, 1988), 195–196.

58. Haig, *Caveat*, 129.

59. *Public Papers of the Presidents of the United States: Ronald Reagan, 1983* (Washington, DC: Government Printing Office, 1984), 605, 607.

60. Kagan, *Twilight Struggle*, 170.

61. Cannon, *President Reagan*, 344. According to William LeoGrande, "In the midst of the [1980] presidential campaign, a skeptical reporter asked one of Ronald Reagan's foreign policy advisers whether he and his candidate really believed their own rhetoric about the communist menace in El Salvador. 'El Salvador itself doesn't really matter,' the adviser replied, 'we have to establish credibility because we're in very serious trouble'" (LeoGrande, "A Splendid Little War," 27).

62. Moreno, *U.S. Policy in Central America*, 89.

63. Ibid., 186; Reagan, *An American Life*, 238; Haig, quoted in Moreno, *U.S. Policy in Central America*, 97; Viron Vaky, "Reagan's Central American Policy: An Isthmus Restored," in Leiken, ed., *Central America: Anatomy of Conflict*, 240. As Eldon Kenworthy writes, "In an important sense, Reagan policy toward Nicaragua was only marginally about Nicaragua" (Kenworthy, "Selling the Policy," in *Reagan versus the Sandinistas: The Undeclared War on Nicaragua*, ed. Thomas W. Walker [Boulder, CO: Westview, 1987], 162).

64. Roy Gutman, *Banana Diplomacy: The Making of American Policy in Nicaragua, 1981–1987* (New York: Simon & Schuster, 1988), 28–29; I. M. Destler, "The Evolution of Reagan Foreign Policy," in *The Reagan Presidency: An Early Assessment*, ed. Fred I. Greenstein (Baltimore: Johns Hopkins University Press, 1983), 135–136; Alex Roberto Hybel, *How Leaders Reason: US Intervention in the Caribbean Basin and Latin America* (Oxford, UK, and Cambridge, MA: Basil Blackwell, 1990), 265–266; Cannon, *President Reagan*, 196, 345; Moreno, *U.S. Policy in Central America*, 101. In November 1980, during the presidential transition, Reagan's designate as national security adviser, Richard Allen, promised that the new administration would take "quick action against Fidel Castro's Soviet directed,

armed, and financed marauders in Central America, specifically Nicaragua, El Salvador, and Guatemala" (quoted in LeoGrande, "A Splendid Little War," 43n30). In a December 1980 preinaugural meeting of Reagan and his key national security officials, Haig stated that "it was quite clear we would have to invade Cuba and, one way or another, put an end to the Castro regime" (Caspar W. Weinberger, *Fighting for Peace: Seven Critical Years in the Pentagon* [New York: Warner, 1990], 31).

65. Moreno, *U.S. Policy in Central America*, 101; Hybel, *How Leaders Reason*, 266; Hedrick Smith, *The Power Game: How Washington Works* (New York: Random House, 1988), 349–350; Destler, "The Evolution of Reagan Foreign Policy," 137; Haig, *Caveat*, 99–100; I. M. Destler, "The Elusive Consensus: Congress and Central America," in Leiken, ed., *Central America: Anatomy of Conflict*, 321.

66. Moreno, *U.S. Policy in Central America*, 101–102; Barry Rubin, "Reagan Administration Policymaking and Central America," in Leiken, ed., *Central America: Anatomy of Conflict*, 305.

67. Cannon, *President Reagan*, 196, 355, 382; Smith, *The Power Game*, 350; Rubin, "Reagan Administration Policymaking and Central America," 302, 304, 306–307; Destler, "The Elusive Consensus," 321. Deaver later recalled that "Baker was convinced from day one that the hard-right people—Casey, Clark, and Haig—would try to move the president into some kind of military action in Central America and destroy his presidency" (Deborah Hart Strober and Gerald S. Strober, comps., *The Reagan Presidency: An Oral History of the Era* [Washington, DC: Brassey's, 2003], 165–166).

68. Destler, "The Elusive Consensus," 321; Cannon, *President Reagan*, 344.

69. Gergen, quoted in Smith, *The Power Game*, 350–351.

70. Ibid., 351.

71. Kagan, *Twilight Struggle*, 176–177, 187–188; Woodward, *Veil*, 174; Arnson, *Crossroads*, 76; Moreno, *U.S. Policy in Central America*, 96.

72. Kagan, *Twilight Struggle*, 190–192; Gutman, *Banana Diplomacy*, 67, 73, 77; Christopher Dickey, *With the Contras: A Reporter in the Wilds of Nicaragua* (New York: Simon & Schuster, 1985), 110; Moreno, *U.S. Policy in Central America*, 99; Rubin, "Reagan Administration Policymaking and Central America," 307; William M. LeoGrande, *Our Own Backyard: The United States in Central America, 1977–1992* (Chapel Hill: University of North Carolina Press, 1998), 119; Woodward, *Veil*, 175. Enders' strategy was to see if he could "use the threat of confrontation rather than confrontation itself" to stop the Sandinistas from continuing their assistance to the Salvadoran guerrillas (Kagan, *Twilight Struggle*, 190).

73. Ortega, quoted in Kagan, *Twilight Struggle*, 194.

74. Ibid., 192; Pastor, *Condemned to Repetition*, 235; Woodward, *Veil*, 175.

75. Kagan, *Twilight Struggle*, 192; Gutman, *Banana Diplomacy*, 70.

76. Kagan, *Twilight Struggle*, 192; Gutman, *Banana Diplomacy*, 67.

77. Gutman, *Banana Diplomacy*, 66–67.

78. Kagan, *Twilight Struggle*, 193; Hybel, *How Leaders Reason*, 266. A U.S. military officer described the military maneuvers as "a deliberate attempt to stick it in their eye" (Gutman, *Banana Diplomacy*, 73).

79. Kagan, *Twilight Struggle*, 193–194, 197. For a different interpretation, which places the blame for the collapse of negotiations on the unreasonable demands imposed by Reagan administration hard-liners seeking to "sabotage" Enders' initiative in favor of a paramilitary option, see LeoGrande, *Our Own Backyard*, 118–123.

80. Gutman, *Banana Diplomacy*, 66; Scott, *Deciding to Intervene*, 159.

81. *Washington Post*, 8 May 1983, A10; Gutman, *Banana Diplomacy*, 64, 84–85; Scott,

Deciding to Intervene, 160; Duane R. Clarridge (with Digby Diehl), *A Spy for All Seasons: My Life in the CIA* (New York: Scribner, 1997), 199.

82. Schweizer, *Victory*, 10, 22–23; Scott, *Deciding to Intervene*, 15, 19–20, 160.

83. Cannon, *President Reagan*, 355–356; Woodward, *Veil*, 186; Robert M. Gates, *From the Shadows: The Ultimate Insider's Story of Five Presidents and How They Won the Cold War* (New York: Simon & Schuster, 1996), 243; Kagan, *Twilight Struggle*, 188, 200; Moreno, *U.S. Policy in Central America*, 96–97; Gutman, *Banana Diplomacy*, 80–81; D'Souza, *Ronald Reagan*, 89, 102.

84. Kagan, *Twilight Struggle*, 203; Gutman, *Banana Diplomacy*, 83. For a useful chronology of U.S. policy decisions between November 16 and December 1, see LeoGrande, *Our Own Backyard*, 143–146.

85. Kagan, *Twilight Struggle*, 204–205.

86. Gutman, *Banana Diplomacy*, 39–44; Dickey, *With the Contras*, 46; Armony, *Argentina, the United States, and the Anti-communist Crusade in Central America*, 114; Clarridge, *A Spy for All Seasons*, 200–201.

87. Dickey, *With the Contras*, 80, 90, 118–119; Kagan, *Twilight Struggle*, 151, 185, 200–201; Gutman, *Banana Diplomacy*, 52–55; LeoGrande, *Our Own Backyard*, 115–116; Armony, *Argentina, the United States, and the Anti-communist Crusade in Central America*, 125–126; Clarridge, *A Spy for All Seasons*, 200–201, 208. Argentines had been actively involved on both sides in the Nicaraguan revolution. Members of Argentina's leftist revolutionary movements—the Montoneros and the Ejército Revolucionario del Pueblo (ERP)—fought alongside the Sandinistas during the 1979 insurrection and subsequently remained in Nicaragua, assisting the FSLN in running its intelligence and security organizations. See Armony, *Argentina, the United States, and the Anti-communist Crusade in Central America*, 79–80; Dickey, *With the Contras*, 30. Meanwhile, the military regime in Buenos Aires provided covert support to Somoza's government in an effort to prevent its overthrow. According to Ariel Armony, Argentine military operatives arrived in Nicaragua in 1978 "to identify Argentine guerrillas fighting in the Sandinista ranks." At least one guerrilla was captured in Nicaragua and sent back to Buenos Aires where he was executed in the infamous Navy Mechanics School torture center (Armony, *Argentina, the United States, and the Anti-communist Crusade in Central America*, 82–83). During the 1979 revolution, Argentine military officers assisted Somoza's National Guard and secret police; three of the officers were captured by the Sandinistas when they seized control of Managua in July 1979 (ibid., 82–83). Also see Dickey, *With the Contras*, 54. The Argentine dictatorship's subsequent support of the Contras was the logical extension of this involvement. Indeed, according to Armony, the military regime in Buenos Aires began to provide money to Nicaragua's counterrevolutionaries as soon as they began organizing following the fall of Somoza, and by the end of 1980 Argentine operatives were organizing and training bands of former National Guardsmen in exile in Guatemala (Armony, *Argentina, the United States, and the Anti-communist Crusade in Central America*, 93–94). Contra leader Enrique Bermúdez later stated that "the Argentines were the ones who gave us the necessary sponsorship to begin our military struggle against the Sandinistas." The U.S. government, Bermúdez said, "wanted to do something but at that time they didn't know how to do it. And the Argentines eased the way for United States involvement" (ibid., 130–132).

88. Clarridge, *A Spy for All Seasons*, 200–201; Gutman, *Banana Diplomacy*, 45–47; LeoGrande, *Our Own Backyard*, 116.

89. Gutman, *Banana Diplomacy*, 48–49; LeoGrande, *Our Own Backyard*, 116–118; Kagan, *Twilight Struggle*, 201; Armony, *Argentina, the United States, and the Anti-communist*

Crusade in Central America, 119, 130–131. Also see Duane Clarridge's recollections in Strober and Strober, *The Reagan Presidency*, 165.

90. Kagan, *Twilight Struggle*, 202; *Washington Post*, 8 May 1983, A10. According to Duane Clarridge, the CIA "did not 'invent' the Nicaraguan guerrillas, freedom fighters, or contras, whatever you want to call them. The truth is that anti-Sandinista forces, both political and military, were in Honduras *before* we got there. We simply capitalized on the disenchantment of a sizable Nicaraguan population with the anti-Catholic Church, agricultural-collectivization, single-political-party, and generally dictatorial policies of the Sandinistas themselves to create the single largest guerrilla force in Latin American history" (Clarridge, *A Spy for All Seasons*, 198–199; emphasis in original).

91. Kornbluh, *Nicaragua: The Price of Intervention*, 22–23; Sklar, *Washington's War on Nicaragua*, 100; Gutman, *Banana Diplomacy*, 84–85.

92. Scott, *Deciding to Intervene*, 160–161; LeoGrande, *Our Own Backyard*, 111, 144, 285–286, 299–300; Gutman, *Banana Diplomacy*, 80, 85; Kagan, *Twilight Struggle*, 202, 204–206; Woodward, *Veil*, 185; Cannon, *President Reagan*, 355–356. "The proposal for covert action 'was presented to [Reagan] as pressure rather than conquest,' Enders recalls, 'a lowball option, a small operation not intended to overthrow'" (Kagan, *Twilight Struggle*, 202).

93. LeoGrande, *Our Own Backyard*, 111, 141–142, 306–309; Scott, *Deciding to Intervene*, 160; Clarridge, *A Spy for All Seasons*, 209; Cannon, *President Reagan*, 355; Sklar, *Washington's War on Nicaragua*, 98–99, 131; Arnson, *Crossroads*, 102.

94. Kagan, *Twilight Struggle*, 172; Howard J. Wiarda, *American Foreign Policy in the 80s and 90s: Issues and Controversies from Reagan to Bush* (New York: New York University Press, 1992), 8. In his autobiography *An American Life*, Reagan writes that "in late 1981, I authorized Bill Casey to undertake a program of covert operations aimed at cutting the flow of arms to Nicaragua and other Central American countries" (474). For additional evidence that interdiction was Reagan's initial goal, see Douglas Brinkley, ed., *The Reagan Diaries* (New York: HarperCollins, 2007), 50, 52. William LeoGrande, however, concludes that "Reagan was one of the least enthusiastic supporters of the covert action proposal at first—not because it appeared overly ambitious, but because it was not ambitious enough. 'It took some persuading' to get Reagan interested in the contra program, according to a senior administration official. Plans for a small force to harass the Sandinistas or interdict arms did not interest him. He was only convinced the plan had merit when it was presented as a way to roll back the Nicaraguan revolution. The contra army would be Washington's answer to Soviet support for wars of national liberation" (LeoGrande, *Our Own Backyard*, 145).

95. LeoGrande, *Our Own Backyard*, 299–322; Kagan, *Twilight Struggle*, chaps. 22, 25, 27–29; Arnson, *Crossroads*, 76–78, 100–110, 117–129; Gutman, *Banana Diplomacy*, 84–86, 116–117, 192–193, 199–200.

Chapter Seven. Grenada, 1983

1. Lou Cannon, *President Reagan: The Role of a Lifetime* (New York: Simon & Schuster, 1991), 232–233; Dinesh D'Souza, *Ronald Reagan: How an Ordinary Man Became an Extraordinary Leader* (New York: Free Press, 1997), 104–105; Peter Goldman and Tony Fuller, *The Quest for the Presidency: 1984* (New York: Bantam, 1985), 20; Jack W. Germond and Jules Witcover, *Wake Us When It's Over: Presidential Politics of 1984* (New York: Macmillan, 1985), 34–35; William E. Pemberton, *Exit with Honor: The Life and Presidency of Ronald Reagan* (Armonk, NY: M. E. Sharpe, 1997), 85.

2. D'Souza, *Ronald Reagan*, 104; Pemberton, *Exit with Honor*, 125–126, 128; Goldman and Fuller, *Quest for the Presidency: 1984*, 10.

3. Melvin Small, *Democracy & Diplomacy: The Impact of Domestic Politics on U.S. Foreign Policy, 1789–1994* (Baltimore: Johns Hopkins University Press, 1996), 138; Pemberton, *Exit with Honor*, 85.

4. I. M. Destler, Leslie H. Gelb, and Anthony Lake, *Our Own Worst Enemy: The Unmaking of American Foreign Policy* (New York: Simon & Schuster, 1984), 79–80; Pemberton, *Exit with Honor*, 130, 133, 149, 162; Cannon, *President Reagan*, 313.

5. Destler et al., *Our Own Worst Enemy*, 80.

6. Goldman and Fuller, *Quest for the Presidency: 1984*, 20–21; Cannon, *President Reagan*, 233; D'Souza, *Ronald Reagan*, 106–107; Germond and Witcover, *Wake Us When It's Over*, 35, 86–87, 89; Beth Fischel, *The Reagan Reversal: Foreign Policy and the End of the Cold War* (Columbia: University of Missouri Press, 1997), 54, 56, 61–62; Pemberton, *Exit with Honor*, 126.

7. William M. LeoGrande, *Our Own Backyard: The United States in Central America, 1977–1992* (Chapel Hill: University of North Carolina Press, 1998), 216–217, 314; Eldon Kenworthy, "Central America: Beyond the Credibility Trap," in *The Central American Crisis: Sources of Conflict and the Failure of U. S. Policy*, ed. Kenneth M. Coleman and George C. Herring (Wilmington, DE: Scholarly Resources, 1985), 132. Also see Holly Sklar, *Washington's War on Nicaragua* (Boston: South End Press, 1988), 191–192.

8. Fischel, *The Reagan Reversal*, 53, 55–57, 62–63.

9. Germond and Witcover, *Wake Us When It's Over*, 91–94; Cannon, *President Reagan*, 390, 441–445.

10. On the New Jewel Movement's political background and ideological orientation, see Kai P. Schoenhals and Richard Melanson, *Revolution and Intervention in Grenada: The New Jewel Movement, the United States, and the Caribbean* (Boulder, CO: Westview, 1985), chap. 2 and 81–82; Tony Thorndike, *Grenada: Politics, Economics and Society* (London: Frances Pinter, 1985), chap. 4 and 186–187; Gordon K. Lewis, *Grenada: The Jewel Despoiled* (Baltimore: Johns Hopkins University Press, 1987), chap. 5; Reynold A. Burrowes, *Revolution and Rescue in Grenada: An Account of the U.S.-Caribbean Invasion* (Westport, CT: Greenwood, 1988), chap. 1; Gregory Sandford and Richard Vigilante, *Grenada: The Untold Story* (Lanham, MD: Madison Books, 1984), chap. 2; and Maurice Bishop's revealing "Line of March" speech of September 1982, reprinted in *Grenada Documents: An Overview and Selection*, ed. Michael Ledeen and Herbert Romerstein (Washington, DC: U.S. Department of State and U.S. Department of Defense, 1984), document 1. The New Jewel Movement membership figure is drawn from Frederic L. Pryor, *Revolutionary Grenada: A Study in Political Economy* (New York: Praeger, 1986), 168.

11. The following interpretation of the New Jewel Movement's record in power is based on Schoenhals and Melanson, *Revolution and Intervention in Grenada*, chaps. 3–4 and 138; Thorndike, *Grenada: Politics, Economics and Society*, chaps. 5–7 and 188–189; Sandford and Vigilante, *Grenada: The Untold Story*, chaps. 3–5; Lewis, *Grenada: The Jewel Despoiled*, chap. 7; Burrowes, *Revolution and Rescue in Grenada*, chap. 2; Anthony Payne, Paul Sutton, and Tony Thorndike, *Grenada: Revolution and Invasion* (New York: St. Martin's, 1984), chap. 2; and Courtney Glass, "The Setting," in *American Intervention in Grenada: The Implications of Operation "Urgent Fury,"* eds. Peter M. Dunn and Bruce W. Watson (Boulder, CO: Westview, 1985), 6–9.

12. Sandford and Vigilante, *Grenada: The Untold Story*, 72. Also see Burrowes, *Revo-*

lution and Rescue in Grenada, 44; Michael Massing, "Grenada Before and After," *Atlantic Monthly,* February 1984, 79–80.

13. Quoted in Schoenhals and Melanson, *Revolution and Intervention in Grenada,* 61.

14. Thorndike, *Grenada: Politics, Economics and Society,* 118–119; Pryor, *Revolutionary Grenada,* 49; Sandford and Vigilante, *Grenada: The Untold Story,* 49–50.

15. Sandford and Vigilante, *Grenada: The Untold Story,* 43, 52–55, 89; Payne et al., *Grenada: Revolution and Invasion,* 81–85; Schoenhals and Melanson, *Revolution and Intervention in Grenada,* 37.

16. Quoted in Anthony P. Maingot, "Grenada and the Caribbean: Mutual Linkages and Influences," in *Grenada and Soviet/Cuban Policy: Internal Crisis and U.S./OECS Intervention,* eds. Jiri Valenta and Herbert J. Ellison (Boulder, CO: Westview, 1986), 132.

17. Anthony Payne, "The Foreign Policy of the People's Revolutionary Government," in *A Revolution Aborted: The Lessons of Grenada,* ed. Jorge Heine (Pittsburgh: University of Pittsburgh Press, 1991), 133; Sandford and Vigilante, *Grenada: The Untold Story,* 89.

18. Sandford and Vigilante, *Grenada: The Untold Story,* 89.

19. Payne, "Foreign Policy of the People's Revolutionary Government," 133–134; Sandford and Vigilante, *Grenada: The Untold Story,* 91, 94. According to Caspar Weinberger, "In 1982, ninety-two percent of Grenada's votes were cast with the Soviet bloc in the UN General Assembly" (Caspar W. Weinberger, *Fighting for Peace: Seven Critical Years in the Pentagon* [New York: Warner, 1990], 102).

20. Thorndike, *Grenada: Politics, Economics and Society,* 128; Nicholas Dujmovic, *The Grenada Documents: Window on Totalitarianism* (Cambridge, MA: Institute for Foreign Policy Analysis, 1988), 74.

21. Sandford and Vigilante, *Grenada: The Untold Story,* 92–93; Fredric L. Pryor, "Socialism via Foreign Aid: The PRG's Economic Policies with the Soviet Bloc," in Heine, ed., *A Revolution Aborted,* 163; Ledeen and Romerstein, eds., *Grenada Documents,* documents 13, 14, 20.

22. Payne, "The Foreign Policy of the People's Revolutionary Government," 136–137; Sandford and Vigilante, *Grenada: The Untold Story,* 93–94.

23. Ledeen and Romerstein, eds., *Grenada Documents,* document 26.

24. Bruce Marcus and Michael Taber, eds., *Maurice Bishop Speaks: The Grenada Revolution, 1979–83* (New York: Pathfinder, 1984), 118; Sandford and Vigilante, *Grenada: The Untold Story,* 54; Payne, "The Foreign Policy of the People's Revolutionary Government," 127–128.

25. Thorndike, *Grenada: Politics, Economics and Society,* 63; Robert M. Gates, *From the Shadows: The Ultimate Insider's Story of Five Presidents and How They Won the Cold War* (New York: Simon & Schuster, 1996), 125; Robert Pastor, "The United States and the Grenada Revolution: Who Pushed First and Why?" in Heine, ed., *A Revolution Aborted,* 188. According to a U.S. diplomat who was actively involved in early U.S.-PRG (People's Revolutionary Government) relations, the U.S. embassy in Barbados "had had contact" with Bishop "for many years" (Frank Ortiz, letter to the editor, *Atlantic,* June 1984, 7).

26. Ortiz, letter in *Atlantic,* June 1984; Pastor, "The United States and the Grenada Revolution: Who Pushed First and Why?" 189–192; Sandford and Vigilante, *Grenada: The Untold Story,* 51–55.

27. For the full text of Bishop's 13 April 1979 speech, see Chris Searle, ed., *In Nobody's Backyard: Maurice Bishop's Speeches, 1979–1983* (London: Zed Books, 1984), 9–14. Bishop and his colleagues later claimed that Ortiz was an "arrogant racist" who had lectured them

in a condescending and threatening manner. According to Bishop, "Ortiz did everything possible to arouse a black man" (Pastor, "The United States and the Grenada Revolution: Who Pushed First and Why?" 193–194). Ortiz characterized his talks with the Grenadian revolutionaries as "low-key and at least superficially cordial" (Ortiz, letter in *Atlantic*, June 1984, 9).

28. Gates, *From the Shadows*, 143.

29. Pastor, "The United States and the Grenada Revolution: Who Pushed First and Why?" 193–197.

30. Ibid., 198; *Washington Post*, 27 February 1983, A1; Schoenhals and Melanson, *Revolution and Intervention in Grenada*, 57, 127, 130–131; Pryor, *Revolutionary Grenada*, 349–351; Payne et al., *Grenada: Revolution and Invasion*, 62–63.

31. *Washington Post*, 27 February 1983, A11; Pastor, "The United States and the Grenada Revolution: Who Pushed First and Why?" 200.

32. Pastor, "The United States and the Grenada Revolution: Who Pushed First and Why?" 199; Robert J. Beck, *The Grenada Invasion: Politics, Law, and Foreign-Policy Decisionmaking* (Boulder, CO: Westview, 1993), 28.

33. Beck, *The Grenada Invasion*, 28; Thorndike, *Grenada: Politics, Economics and Society*, 129; Pryor, *Revolutionary Grenada*, 352.

34. Payne, "The Foreign Policy of the People's Revolutionary Government," 131; Payne et al., *Grenada: Revolution and Invasion*, 66; Schoenhals and Melanson, *Revolution and Intervention in Grenada*, 55–56; Thorndike, *Grenada: Politics, Economics and Society*, 124–127.

35. Thorndike, *Grenada: Politics, Economics and Society*, 128; "Cuba's Renewed Support for Violence in Latin America," report, 14 December 1981, in *American Foreign Policy Current Documents: 1981*, U.S. Department of State (Washington, DC: Government Printing Office, 1984), document 663, 1220; "The Role of Cuba in International Terrorism and Subversion" (testimony by Undersecretary of Defense Fred Iklé before the Subcommittee on Security and Terrorism of the Senate Judiciary Committee, 11 March 1982), in *American Foreign Policy Current Documents: 1982*, U.S. Department of State (Washington, DC: Government Printing Office, 1985), document 677, 1407; Bosworth, quoted in Schoenhals and Melanson, *Revolution and Intervention in Grenada*, 132.

36. Pastor, "The United States and the Grenada Revolution: Who Pushed First and Why?" 201; Sanchez, quoted in Schoenhals and Melanson, *Revolution and Intervention in Grenada*, 135.

37. Schoenhals and Melanson, *Revolution and Intervention in Grenada*, 133–134.

38. Ibid., 58–59, 134–135. In response to the U.S. charges, Grenadian officials emphatically denied that the airport had a military capability. They pointed out (1) that the facility lacked the antiaircraft batteries, underground fuel-storage tanks, and other features essential for military use, (2) that many other commercial airports in the eastern Caribbean had runways of at least 10,000 feet, and (3) that several Western companies—including two U.S. firms, England's Plessey Airport, Ltd., and firms from several member states of the European Economic Union—were participating in the construction project under People's Revolutionary Government contracts. On the other hand, as Anthony Payne writes: "This is not to say that, if asked, the PRG would have denied Cuba military use of the airport once it was complete. Airports can accommodate all types of aircraft" (Payne, "The Foreign Policy of the People's Revolutionary Government," 132). The only "evidence" that U.S. officials ever found to support their claims that the airport was to be used for military purposes consisted of "a single phrase in the rough notes made by Liam James [deputy commander

of the People's Revolutionary Army] of a party meeting held in March 1980 . . . : 'The Revo has been able to crush Counter-Revolution internationally, airport will be used for Cuban and Soviet military.'" Nevertheless, as Payne points out, given the shorthand nature of the note and "the casual way in which party minutes and government documents were prepared in Grenada," the passage in question may actually have meant "the revolution has been able to crush [the claim of] counterrevolution internationally [that the] airport will be used for the Cuban and Soviet military" (ibid., 132).

39. Searle, ed., *In Nobody's Backyard*, 30, 220; Massing, "Grenada Before and After," 82; Pastor, "The United States and the Grenada Revolution: Who Pushed First and Why?" 201; Payne et al., *Grenada: Revolution and Invasion*, 67.

40. Pastor, "The United States and the Grenada Revolution: Who Pushed First and Why?" 202–203; Payne, "The Foreign Policy of the People's Revolutionary Government," 141–142; Thorndike, *Grenada: Politics, Economics and Society*, 131–132; U.S. Senate, Committee on Foreign Relations, *The Situation in Grenada: Hearing before the Committee on Foreign Relations*, 98th Cong., 1st sess., 27 October 1983, 12.

41. Payne, "The Foreign Policy of the People's Revolutionary Government," 142; Payne et al., *Grenada: Revolution and Invasion*, 115–117; Thorndike, *Grenada: Politics, Economics and Society*, 131–132, 141; Glass, "The Setting," 10. Dam later speculated that it was Bishop's "desire for a better relationship with the United States . . . which led to his downfall. . . . When he went back to Grenada he did not have the support. He obviously had a serious problem from people who were more radical than he was" (U.S. Senate, *The Situation in Grenada*, 12, 26).

42. Thorndike, *Grenada: Politics, Economics and Society*, 139, 143–144; Payne et al., *Grenada: Revolution and Invasion*, 111; Gary Williams, "Prelude to an Intervention: Grenada 1983," *Journal of Latin American Studies* 29, no. 1 (February 1997): 138–140; Sandford and Vigilante, *Grenada: The Untold Story*, 152–153. "The loss of state power" was "only a few months away," Coard predicted in a 17 September 1983 party Central Committee meeting (Schoenhals and Melanson, *Revolution and Intervention in Grenada*, 69).

43. Thorndike, *Grenada: Politics, Economics and Society*, 142, 144–145; Williams, "Prelude to an Intervention: Grenada 1983," 139–140, 142; Sandford and Vigilante, *Grenada: The Untold Story*, 146–154; Schoenhals and Melanson, *Revolution and Intervention in Grenada*, 64–66; Jay R. Mandle, *Big Revolution, Small Country: The Rise and Fall of the Grenada Revolution* (Lanham, MD: North-South, 1985), 84.

44. Thorndike, *Grenada: Politics, Economics and Society*, 145–56; Payne et al., *Grenada: Revolution and Invasion*, 120–130; Williams, "Prelude to an Intervention: Grenada 1983," 141–144; Schoenhals and Melanson, *Revolution and Intervention in Grenada*, 66–74.

45. Williams, "Prelude to an Intervention: Grenada 1983," 158–162; Payne et al., *Grenada: Revolution and Invasion*, 131–136; Thorndike, *Grenada: Politics, Economics and Society*, 156–163; Schoenhals and Melanson, *Revolution and Intervention in Grenada*, 74–78. Fidel Castro later characterized the Coard faction as "a group of extremists drunk on political theory." Laurence Whitehead, "Democracy and Socialism: Reflections on the Grenada Experience," in Heine, ed., *A Revolution Aborted*, 319.

46. Thorndike, *Grenada: Politics, Economics and Society*, 163–164. An early public communiqué issued by the Revolutionary Military Council proudly proclaimed that "the friends of imperialism" had been "crushed" (Williams, "Prelude to an Intervention: Grenada 1983," 163).

47. Thorndike, *Grenada: Politics, Economics and Society*, 172–175; Payne et al., *Grenada: Revolution and Invasion*, 160.

48. *Public Papers of the Presidents of the United States: Ronald Reagan, 1983* (Washington, DC: Government Printing Office, 1985), 2:1505–1506; Payne et al., *Grenada: Revolution and Invasion*, 154–155.

49. Payne et al., *Grenada: Revolution and Invasion*, 91–94; Thorndike, *Grenada: Politics, Economics and Society*, 14, 58–63, 127–128, 179–180. Also see Lewis, *Grenada: The Jewel Despoiled*, 141–145.

50. Beck, *The Grenada Invasion*, 97–101, 108–109; Williams, "Prelude to an Intervention: Grenada 1983," 151–152, 156–157; Payne et al., *Grenada: Revolution and Invasion*, 94; Bob Woodward, *Veil: The Secret Wars of the CIA, 1981–1987* (New York: Pocket, 1987), 325. The State Department's director of Central American affairs, Craig Johnstone, recalls that Charles "and the other leaders in the area . . .were pushing [for U.S. intervention] harder and faster than we were prepared to respond" (quoted in Deborah Hart Strober and Gerald S. Strober, comps., *The Reagan Presidency: An Oral History of the Era* [Washington, DC: Brassey's, 2003], 265).

51. Beck, *The Grenada Invasion*, 99, 106–107, 110.

52. Ibid., 110, 151–153, 204.

53. Ibid., 153–154. In her remarks at Reagan's 25 October press conference, Charles stated: "It is not a matter of opinion. It is a matter of preventing this thing from spreading to all the islands" (Woodward, *Veil*, 327).

54. Beck, *The Grenada Invasion*, 154, 156.

55. Williams, "Prelude to an Intervention: Grenada 1983," 168; Beck, *The Grenada Invasion*, 199–200; Robert D. Schulzinger, *U.S. Diplomacy since 1900*, 4th ed. (New York: Oxford University Press, 1998), 328–331; Small, *Democracy & Diplomacy*, 139.

56. Small, *Democracy & Diplomacy*, 139; Williams, "Prelude to an Intervention: Grenada 1983," 168; Schulzinger, *U.S. Diplomacy since 1900*, 332.

57. Williams, "Prelude to an Intervention: Grenada 1983," 150, 168; Burrowes, *Revolution and Rescue in Grenada*, 73.

58. Beck, *The Grenada Invasion*, 93–98; Williams, "Prelude to an Intervention: Grenada 1983," 147, 151.

59. Beck, *The Grenada Invasion*, 102–103, 110; George P. Shultz, *Turmoil and Triumph: My Years as Secretary of State* (New York: Charles Scribner's Sons, 1993), 328.

60. Beck, *The Grenada Invasion*, 104–108; Payne et al., *Grenada: Revolution and Invasion*, 148–149.

61. Beck, *The Grenada Invasion*, 115, 146–151; D'Souza, *Ronald Reagan*, 156. Also see Cannon, *President Reagan*, 445–447.

62. Beck, *The Grenada Invasion*, 151–152, 156, 157, 161–162. In a 1987 interview with journalist Seymour Hersh, Langhorne Motley said: "I think that, absolutely, the potential for taking a large number of hostages and the inability to get assurances that that would not happen, in my mind, was the driving force for the President's final decision" (Public Broadcasting System [PBS], *Frontline* documentary, "Operation Urgent Fury," 1987).

63. Williams, "Prelude to an Intervention: Grenada 1983," 154, 164; Beck, *The Grenada Invasion*, 142–143, 145; Schoenhals and Melanson, *Revolution and Intervention in Grenada*, 80, 144–145.

64. Duane R. Clarridge, *A Spy for All Seasons: My Life in the CIA* (New York: Scribner, 1997), 254; Schoenhals and Melanson, *Revolution and Intervention in Grenada*, 145.

65. Beck, *The Grenada Invasion*, 201; Austin, quoted in Strober and Strober, comps., *The Reagan Presidency*, 288.

66. Cannon, *President Reagan*, 446.

67. Woodward, *Veil*, 329–330.

68. Payne et al., *Grenada: Revolution and Invasion*, 161; Russell Burgos, Internet posting on the H-NET List for Diplomatic History (H-Diplo@h-net.msu.edu), 5 November 2003, at the H-NET archives, which can be accessed through the H-DIPLO subscription page at http://www.lsoft.com/scripts/wl.exe?SL1=H-DIPLO&H=H-NET.MSU.EDU.

69. Williams, "Prelude to an Intervention: Grenada 1983," 144–145, 153; Constantine C. Menges, *Inside the National Security Council: The True Story of the Making and Unmaking of Reagan's Foreign Policy* (New York: Simon & Schuster, 1988), 60–64; Payne et al., *Grenada: Revolution and Invasion*, 150.

70. Eldon Kenworthy, "Grenada as Theater," *World Policy Journal* 1, no. 3 (1984): 649; Shultz, *Turmoil and Triumph*, 340; Strober and Strober, comps., *The Reagan Presidency*, 290; PBS *Frontline* documentary, "Operation Urgent Fury"; Germond and Witcover, *Wake Us When It's Over*, 99.

71. Burrowes, *Revolution and Rescue in Grenada*, 73; Beck, *The Grenada Invasion*, 225–226; Woodward, *Veil*, 326; Payne et al., *Grenada: Revolution and Invasion*, 150–151 (emphasis in original).

72. Strober and Strober, comps., *The Reagan Presidency*, 290; Payne et al., *Grenada: Revolution and Invasion*, 150; Pastor, "The United States and the Grenada Revolution: Who Pushed First and Why?" 206; Shultz, *Turmoil and Triumph*, 344.

73. Woodward, *Veil*, 331; Strober and Strober, comps., *The Reagan Presidency*, 271, 290; Burrowes, *Revolution and Rescue in Grenada*, 72–73; Menges, *Inside the National Security Council*, 63–64; *Time*, 7 November 1983, 28. Also see Robert C. McFarlane, *Special Trust* (New York: Cadell & Davies, 1994), 261–262.

74. *New York Times*, 9 January 1983, 22E; Michael J. Kryzanek, "The Grenada Invasion: Approaches to Understanding," in *United States Policy in Latin America: A Decade of Crisis and Challenge*, ed. John D. Martz (Lincoln: University of Nebraska Press, 1995), 75; Kenworthy, "Grenada as Theater," 636, 647; Cannon, *President Reagan*, 415. British Army Major Mark Adkin, who was stationed in neighboring Barbados during the invasion, writes that the real motive of the intervention was "the intense desire of the President and his advisers to improve U.S. prestige. . . . With Bishop's execution, a fleeting opportunity presented itself in the United States to act dramatically in the Caribbean. . . . The United States needed a success, something to be proud of. . . . Although announced repeatedly as the primary reason for launching Urgent Fury, the safety of U.S. citizens was really one of several pretexts for grabbing an unprecedented opportunity to halt communist expansion in the U.S. backyard. . . . The decision to intervene in Grenada was made on the basis of seizing a fleeting strategic-political advantage, which had the added merit that inevitable military success would raise flagging U.S. morale" (Mark Adkin, *Urgent Fury: The Battle for Grenada* [Lexington, MA: Lexington Books, 1989]), 106–109, 115, quoted in Stephen Kinzer, *Overthrow: America's Century of Regime Change from Hawaii to Iraq* [New York: Henry Holt, 2005], 233).

75. Steven Emerson, *Secret Warriors: Inside the Covert Military Operations of the Reagan Era* (New York: Putnam's, 1988), 190–191.

76. Burrowes, *Revolution and Rescue in Grenada*, 72, 140.

77. Cannon, *President Reagan*, 390; Elizabeth Drew, *On the Edge: The Clinton Presidency* (New York: Simon & Schuster, 1994), 326. After a White House briefing of Congressional leaders on 24 October, Speaker of the House Tip O'Neill, one of Reagan's most partisan political adversaries, remarked that "they're invading Grenada so people will forget what happened yesterday in Beirut." In his memoirs, O'Neill wrote that "the students were never

in danger," nor were "any of the American residents on the island" harmed. "As far as I can see, it was all because the White House wanted the country to forget about the tragedy in Beirut." (Tip O'Neill, *Man of the House: The Life and Political Memoirs of Speaker Tip O'Neill* [New York: Random House, 1987], 365–367).

78. *Public Papers of the Presidents of the United States: Ronald Reagan, 1983*, 2:1521.

79. Ibid., 1520.

80. *Public Papers of the Presidents of the United States: Ronald Reagan, 1984* (Washington, DC: Government Printing Office, 1987), 2:1419, 1589.

81. Shultz, *Turmoil and Triumph*, 344.

82. *Public Papers of the Presidents of the United States: Ronald Reagan, 1984*, 2:1638.

83. Woodward, *Veil*, 336; Cannon, *President Reagan*, 448; *Public Papers of the Presidents of the United States: Ronald Reagan, 1984*, 2:1186.

84. *Public Papers of the Presidents of the United States: Ronald Reagan, 1984*, 2:1416.

85. Ibid., 2:1637.

86. Kryzanek, "The Grenada Invasion," 58; Kenworthy, "Grenada as Theater," 647; Goldman and Fuller, *Quest for the Presidency: 1984*, 23.

87. Payne et al., *Grenada: Revolution and Invasion*, 165; Goldman and Fuller, *Quest for the Presidency: 1984*, 21.

88. Goldman and Fuller, *Quest for the Presidency: 1984*, 21; Kenworthy, "Grenada as Theater," 647.

Chapter Eight. Panama, 1989

1. *Public Papers of the Presidents of the United States: George Bush, 1989* (Washington, DC: Government Printing Office, 1990), 1:1722–1723.

2. Thomas Carothers, *In the Name of Democracy: U.S. Policy toward Latin America in the Reagan Years* (Berkeley: University of California Press, 1991), 181–182; Karin von Hippel, *Democracy by Force: US Military Intervention in the Post–Cold War World* (Cambridge, UK: Cambridge University Press, 2000), 53. According to von Hippel, "In Panama there was no threat. Only one American had been killed prior to the intervention. This was the worst U.S.-Panamanian incident in twenty-five years, despite the large U.S. presence. This low incidence rate could be replicated in only a handful of very small American towns, and was completely out of kilter with most American cities" (ibid., 47).

3. Margaret E. Scranton, *The Noriega Years: U.S.-Panamanian Relations, 1981–1990* (Boulder, CO: Lynne Rienner, 1991), 7; Peter H. Smith, *Talons of the Eagle: Dynamics of U.S.-Latin American Relations*, 1st ed. (New York: Oxford University Press, 1996), 275; *New York Times*, 10 April 1992, A1; Frederick Kempe, *Divorcing the Dictator: America's Bungled Affair with Noriega* (New York: Putnam's, 1990), chap. 12; John Dinges, *Our Man in Panama: The Shrewd Rise and Brutal Fall of Manuel Noriega* (New York: Random House, 1990), xxi, 316; Carothers, *In the Name of Democracy*, 182.

4. Smith, *Talons of the Eagle*, 1st ed., 290; Scranton, *The Noriega Years*, 2, 67, 75–76, 89, 91, 164–166; Kempe, *Divorcing the Dictator*, chap. 10; Dinges, *Our Man in Panama*, chaps. 8–9; Kevin Buckley, *Panama: The Whole Story* (New York: Simon & Schuster, 1991), chaps. 1, 10; *Newsweek*, 8 January 1990, 26. As Thomas Carothers writes, "The notion that a burning desire to bring democracy to Panama pushed the Bush administration to military action is groundless. The U.S. government managed to live with a nondemocratic government in Panama for decades before it turned against Noriega. . . . And the Bush administration was obviously able to live with nondemocratic governments in other countries of

importance to the United States. . . . Restoring democracy was not a major motivation in and of itself" (*In the Name of Democracy*, 182).

5. Von Hippel, *Democracy by Force*, 49, 53–54; Carothers, *In the Name of Democracy*, 181; *Newsweek*, 1 January 1990, 21.

6. Except where otherwise noted, the following overview of Noriega's rise to power is drawn from Kempe, *Divorcing the Dictator*, chaps. 3–8, 12, and Dinges, *Our Man in Panama*, chaps. 2–7.

7. Quoted in Haynes Johnson, *Sleepwalking through History: America in the Reagan Years* (New York: Norton, 1991), 265.

8. Kempe, *Divorcing the Dictator*, 194–195; Joseph E. Persico, *Casey: From the OSS to the CIA* (New York: Viking, 1990), 480; Luis E. Murillo, *The Noriega Mess: The Drugs, the Canal, and Why America Invaded* (Berkeley, CA: Video-Books, 1995), 648.

9. Kempe, *Divorcing the Dictator*, 28, 48, 50–51, 58, 80–82, 90–91, 95; John Weeks and Phil Gunson, *Panama: Made in the USA* (London: Latin America Bureau, 1991), 47; Mark Perry, *Eclipse: The Last Days of the CIA* (New York: William Morrow, 1992), 110–112.

10. Kempe, *Divorcing the Dictator*, 157–167; Guillermo de St. Malo Arias and Godfrey Harris, *The Panamanian Problem: How the Reagan and Bush Administrations Dealt with the Noriega Regime* (Los Angeles: Americas Group, 1993), 93; Stephen Rosskamm Shalom, *Imperial Alibis: Rationalizing U.S. Intervention after the Cold War* (Boston: South End Press, 1993), 180–181; Scranton, *The Noriega Years*, 80, 91; Perry, *Eclipse*, 114.

11. Kempe, *Divorcing the Dictator*, 87, 95–98, 108–109, 120–121, 158, 243; *Christian Science Monitor*, 5 January 1990, 18, and 9 November 1990, 7. Kempe, drawing on U.S. intelligence sources, reported that Noriega received payments from at least ten foreign intelligence services, including those of the United States, England, France, Cuba, Nicaragua, Libya, Israel, and Taiwan (Kempe, *Divorcing the Dictator*, 119, 281). According to former U.S. ambassador to Costa Rica Frank McNeil, Noriega "never met an intelligence service he couldn't con" (Frank McNeil, *War and Peace in Central America* [New York: Scribner's, 1988], 226).

12. Buckley, *Panama*, 147–148; Weeks and Gunson, *Panama: Made in the USA*, 48; Perry, *Eclipse*, 110.

13. Kempe, *Divorcing the Dictator*, chap. 12; Dinges, *Our Man in Panama*, 203–204; Colin Powell (with Joseph E. Persico), *My American Journey* (New York: Random House, 1995), 628. According to Weeks and Gunson, Noriega appointed as Panama's chief liaison officer to the U.S. Drug Enforcement Agency a man who "also acted as an intermediary between the general and the Medellín cartel" (*Panama: Made in the USA*, 52).

14. Kempe, *Divorcing the Dictator*, 112, 122, 158; Powell, *My American Journey*, 628; Persico, *Casey*, 479; Dinges, *Our Man in Panama*, 234; Thomas Donnelly, Margaret Roth, and Caleb Baker, *Operation Just Cause: The Storming of Panama* (New York: Lexington Books, 1991), 8; Scranton, *The Noriega Years*, 12, 84; McNeil, *War and Peace in Central America*, 237; Johnson, *Sleepwalking through History*, 273.

15. Janet Westrick, "Empire by Invitation: Operation 'Just Cause' and Panamanian Manipulation of U.S. Foreign Policy" (master's thesis, Ohio University, Department of History, 1997), chaps. 2–3; Dinges, *Our Man in Panama*, 319; Richard L. Millett, "The Failure of Panama's Internal Opposition, 1987–1989," in *Conflict Resolution and Democratization in Panama: Implications for U.S. Policy*, ed. Eva Loser (Washington, DC: Center for Strategic and International Studies, 1991), 31; *New York Times*, 19 February 1989, I15.

16. Dinges, *Our Man in Panama*, 138, 145, 158; Westrick, "Empire by Invitation," 57–61.

17. Buckley, *Panama*, 110; Westrick, "Empire by Invitation," 64, 69–77; Dinges, *Our Man in Panama*, 241. Early in 1985, Eisenmann began circulating copies of *La Prensa Digest*, a condensed English-language version of *La Prensa*, to some 350 U.S. lawmakers, journalists, and think tanks in the hope that accurate information about the Panamanians' plight under Noriega would stimulate a U.S. policy shift (Westrick, "Empire by Invitation," 66–68).

18. Frederick Kempe, *Divorcing the Dictator*, 126–139, 176–177, "The Panama Debacle," in Loser, ed., *Conflict Resolution and Democratization in Panama*, 9; Dinges, *Our Man in Panama*, 134–136, 174–184, 190–195, 210–222, 237–238, 240–241; Buckley, *Panama*, 21–28, 42–43, 47–48; Scranton, *The Noriega Years*, 85–86, 96–97.

19. Buckley, *Panama*, 53; Kempe, *Divorcing the Dictator*, 177–178.

20. *New York Times*, 12 June 1986, 1; Buckley, *Panama*, 54; Kempe, *Divorcing the Dictator*, 177–178; Scranton, *The Noriega Years*, 92–93.

21. Dinges, *Our Man in Panama*, 242; Carothers, *In the Name of Democracy*, 170; Scranton, *The Noriega Years*, 92.

22. Dinges, *Our Man in Panama*, 254–255, 276–279; Kempe, *Divorcing the Dictator*, 175, 179–180; Scranton, *The Noriega Years*, 97; George Kourous, "Bush v. Noriega: The Noriega Challenge to George Bush's Credibility and the 1989 Invasion of Panama" (master's thesis, Ohio University, Center for International Studies, 2000), 154, 160.

23. Dinges, *Our Man in Panama*, 259–266; Scranton, *The Noriega Years*, 106–109; Buckley, *Panama*, 68–77, 80–85; Kempe, *Divorcing the Dictator*, 207–214; Michael L. Conniff, *Panama and the United States: The Forced Alliance* (Athens: University of Georgia Press, 1992), 156–157; Westrick, "Empire by Invitation," 79–80; Public Broadcasting System (PBS), *MacNeil-Lehrer NewsHour*, "Panama," 18 June 1987.

24. Kempe, *Divorcing the Dictator*, 214–220; Scranton, *The Noriega Years*, 111; Dinges, *Our Man in Panama*, 269–270; Buckley, *Panama*, 85–88; letter, Roberto Eisenmann to Janet Westrick, 21 June 1997, copy in possession of author. Of Lewis, Robert Pastor writes: "No Latin American has understood the U.S. political process better or has used his influence more effectively in Washington" (Robert Pastor, *Whirlpool: U.S. Foreign Policy toward Latin America and the Caribbean* [Princeton, NJ: Princeton University Press, 1992], 10).

25. Scranton, *The Noriega Years*, 118–119, 127–128; Buckley, *Panama*, 99–108, 110–111, 114–117; Dinges, *Our Man in Panama*, 290–292; Murillo, *The Noriega Mess*, 647–648.

26. Scranton, *The Noriega Years*, 95.

27. Kempe, *Divorcing the Dictator*, 179, 224; Martha L. Cottam, *Images & Intervention: U.S. Policies in Latin America* (Pittsburgh: University of Pittsburgh Press, 1994), 162; Dinges, *Our Man in Panama*, 244.

28. Scranton, *The Noriega Years*, 105. So appreciative were Casey and North of Noriega's services that in the summer of 1986 they went so far as to put the Panamanian dictator in contact with the U.S. public-relations firm International Business Communications "to help him improve his image in the United States and at home" (Kempe, "The Panama Debacle," 7; Dinges, *Our Man in Panama*, 254).

29. Kempe, *Divorcing the Dictator*, 222–223; Dinges, *Our Man in Panama*, 270; Buckley, *Panama*, 88–89; Scranton, *The Noriega Years*, 112; Carothers, *In the Name of Democracy*, 171.

30. Kempe, *Divorcing the Dictator*, 224; Scranton, *The Noriega Years*, 114, 126–127; *Washington Post*, 14 January 1990, A1; Dinges, *Our Man in Panama*, 288.

31. Kempe, *Divorcing the Dictator*, chap. 14; Carothers, *In the Name of Democracy*, 172–173, 177.

32. Murillo, *The Noriega Mess*, 643; Kempe, *Divorcing the Dictator*, 296; Scranton, *The Noriega Years*, 147; *New York Times*, 25 March 1988, I8; George P. Shultz, *Turmoil and Triumph: My Years as Secretary of State* (New York: Scribner's, 1993), 1057.

33. Scranton, *The Noriega Years*, 137–140, 147; Kempe, *Divorcing the Dictator*, 306–308; Buckley, *Panama*, 135–136.

34. Kempe, *Divorcing the Dictator*, chap. 18; Scranton, *The Noriega Years*, 149–152; Buckley, *Panama*, 140–145; Carothers, *In the Name of Democracy*, 174–175.

35. Kempe, *Divorcing the Dictator*, 333, 335; Perry, *Eclipse*, 113; Murillo, *The Noriega Mess*, 708; Buckley, *Panama*, 147.

36. Murillo, *The Noriega Mess*, 708, 710; Steve C. Ropp, "The Bush Administration and the Invasion of Panama: Explaining the Choice and Timing of the Military Option," in *United States Policy in Latin America: A Decade of Crisis and Challenge*, ed. John D. Martz (Lincoln: University of Nebraska Press, 1995), 92; Kempe, *Divorcing the Dictator*, 313, 336.

37. Kempe, *Divorcing the Dictator*, 336; Buckley, *Panama*, 152–154; Perry, *Eclipse*, 131; Murillo, *The Noriega Mess*, 709 (emphasis in original sources). Perry writes that "in order for Bush not to have known of Noriega's drug ties, [he would] have had to be nearly comatose during the ten years that preceded Noriega's . . .indictment."

38. Buckley, *Panama*, 117; Anthony King and Giles Alston, "Good Government and the Politics of High Exposure," in *The Bush Presidency: First Appraisals*, ed. Colin Campbell and Bert A. Rockman (Chatham, NJ: Chatham House, 1991), 269; Kourous, "Bush v. Noriega," 169–170; *New York Times*, 20 May 1988, A1; Weeks and Gunson, *Panama: Made in the USA*, 78; Ropp, "The Bush Administration and the Invasion of Panama," 92.

39. Shultz, *Turmoil and Triumph*, 1051–1052, 1062–1066, 1071; Kempe, *Divorcing the Dictator*, 309–310, 312–313; Kempe, "The Panama Debacle," 14; Buckley, *Panama*, 154–156; James A. Baker, *The Politics of Diplomacy: Revolution, War, and Peace, 1989–1992* (New York: Putnam, 1995), 179; *New York Times*, 20 May 1988, A1.

40. Shultz, *Turmoil and Triumph*, 1062, 1067, 1072, 1074.

41. Buckley, *Panama*, 156; Kempe, *Divorcing the Dictator*, 337; Shultz, *Turmoil and Triumph*, 1070–1071; Murillo, *The Noriega Mess*, 708.

42. Buckley, *Panama*, 155–156; Kempe, *Divorcing the Dictator*, 313–314, 337; Carothers, *In the Name of Democracy*, 175.

43. Buckley, *Panama*, 169; Bob Woodward, *The Commanders* (New York: Simon & Shuster, 1991), 56.

44. Donnelly et al., *Operation Just Cause*, 35–36; Kempe, *Divorcing the Dictator*, 333, 335; Buckley, *Panama*, 156, 162–163. According to one Reagan administration official, "When negotiations broke down, there was a conscious decision by the political staff of the White House to remove Panama from the agenda" (quoted in Cottam, *Images & Intervention*, 155).

45. Scranton, *The Noriega Years*, 156; Kourous, "Bush v. Noriega," 177; Murillo, *The Noriega Mess*, 719; *New York Times*, 26 December 1989, A11.

46. Baker, *The Politics of Diplomacy*, 180; Buckley, *Panama*, 168.

47. Buckley, *Panama*, 169–170; *Public Papers of the Presidents of the United States, George Bush, 1989*, 1:506; Kourous, "Bush v. Noriega," 204; *Washington Post*, 30 April 1989, A32, quoted in Kourous, "Bush v. Noriega," 205.

48. Buckley, *Panama*, chap. 10; Kempe, *Divorcing the Dictator*, 350–362; Scranton, *The Noriega Years*, 158–164; Kourous, "Bush v. Noriega," 206–210.

49. Carothers, *In the Name of Democracy*, 180; *Public Papers of the Presidents of the United States: George Bush, 1989*, 1:533, 547–548; Buckley, *Panama*, 183–184; Kempe, *Di-*

vorcing the Dictator, 362, 365; Scranton, *The Noriega Years*, 166. The Chaney quote is from PBS, *MacNeil-Lehrer NewsHour*, 11 May 1989.

50. Michael Duffy and Dan Goodgame, *Marching in Place: The Status Quo Presidency of George Bush* (New York: Simon & Schuster, 1992), 71.

51. *Public Papers of the Presidents of the United States, George Bush, 1989*, 1:533–534, 547–548, 701–702, 2:1031; Carothers, *In the Name of Democracy*, 178.

52. Duffy and Goodgame, *Marching in Place*, 133; Herbert S. Parmet, *George Bush: The Life of a Lone Star Yankee* (New York: Scribner, 1997), 238, 309; Carothers, *In the Name of Democracy*, 178; Conniff, *Panama and the United States*, 162; Westrick, "Empire by Invitation," 100.

53. Robert D. Schulzinger, *U.S. Diplomacy since 1900*, 4th ed. (New York: Oxford University Press, 1998), 352–357; St. Malo and Harris, *The Panamanian Problem*, 227–231; Kourous, "Bush v. Noriega," 183–202; Conniff, *Panama and the United States*, 162–163; *Time*, 15 May 1989, 22–23; *New York Times*, 21 May 1989, sec. 4, 1; George Bush and Brent Scowcroft, *A World Transformed* (New York: Knopf, 1998), 81.

54. Kourous, "Bush v. Noriega," 190–191; Conniff, *Panama and the United States*, 163; von Hippel, *Democracy by Force*, 35.

55. Kempe, *Divorcing the Dictator*, chap. 21; Buckley, *Panama*, chaps. 12–13; Scranton, *The Noriega Years*, 185–191; Woodward, *The Commanders*, chap. 11; Murillo, *The Noriega Mess*, chap. 41.

56. Scranton, *The Noriega Years*, 192; Buckley, *Panama*, 206, 209; Woodward, *The Commanders*, 97; Westrick, "Empire by Invitation," 104; Harold Molineu, *U.S. Policy toward Latin America: From Regionalism to Globalism*, 2nd ed. (Boulder, CO: Westview, 1990), 247. In the aftermath of the October coup attempt, Noriega announced "a catchy new slogan": "Bullets for my enemies, beatings for the indecisive, and money for my friends" (Buckley, *Panama*, 210; Scranton, *The Noriega Years*, 192).

57. Parmet, *George Bush*, 413; Buckley, *Panama*, 212; Murillo, *The Noriega Mess*, 751; Scranton, *The Noriega Years*, 189; Kempe, *Divorcing the Dictator*, 386; Woodward, *The Commanders*, 100; *New York Times*, 8 October 1989, 16.

58. Woodward, *The Commanders*, 100; Baker, *The Politics of Diplomacy*, 186–187.

59. *New York Times*, 8 October 1989, sec. 4, 20; St. Malo and Harris, *The Panamanian Problem*, 241; *Newsweek*, 16 October 1989, 26; Ropp, "The Bush Administration and the Invasion of Panama," 100–101 (citing *Human Events*, 14 October 1989, 3). "Sir, how about Panama?" a reporter asked the president three days after the failed coup. "Simply put, a lot of critics say you blew it. Your administration blew it on Panama" (*Public Papers of the Presidents of the United States, George Bush, 1989*, 2:1315).

60. St. Malo and Harris, *The Panamanian Problem*, 241; *Washington Post*, 6 October 1989, A31; Woodward, *The Commanders*, 100, 102–103; *New York Times*, 9 October 1989, A17.

61. *Washington Post*, 22 October 1989, C4; Scranton, *The Noriega Years*, 191.

62. Kourous, "Bush v. Noriega," 224–225, quoting the *Washington Post*, 6 October 1989, A33, and the *New York Times*, 6 October 1989, A1, A11. In *The Politics of Diplomacy*, former Secretary of State Baker writes: "It is an understatement to say that administration decision making was less than crisp" (186).

63. *Washington Post*, 11 October 1989, A23, as quoted in Kourous, "Bush v. Noriega," 225.

64. Baker, *The Politics of Diplomacy*, 187; Scranton, *The Noriega Years*, 185; *Newsweek*, 16 October 1989, 30; St. Malo and Harris, *The Panamanian Problem*, 226; Howard J.

Wiarda, "From Reagan to Bush: Continuity and Change in U.S. Latin American Policy," in Martz, ed., *United States Policy in Latin America*, 39; Woodward, *The Commanders*, 102. Susan G. Horwitz writes that "the political backlash" that followed the coup "was one of the most difficult moments of Bush's presidency" (Susan G. Horwitz, "Indications and Warning Factors," in *Operation Just Cause: The U.S. Intervention in Panama*, ed. Bruce W. Watson and Peter G. Tsouras [Boulder, CO: Westview, 1990], 55).

65. St. Malo and Harris, *The Panamanian Problem*, 226–227.

66. Dan Quayle, *Standing Firm: A Vice-Presidential Memoir* (New York: HarperCollins, 1994), 142; Kempe, *Divorcing the Dictator*, 11; Carothers, *In the Name of Democracy*, 181; Buckley, *Panama*, 220, 222; Peter H. Smith, *Talons of the Eagle: Dynamics of U.S.-Latin American Relations*, 2nd ed. (New York: Oxford University Press, 2000), 316; Woodward, *The Commanders*, 100–101. Vice President Quayle admits that "the administration . . .often paid too much attention to the press," and that "late in the first year of the administration," Noriega was the "specific nagging issue driving The Wimp Factor" (141). In *Marching in Place*, Michael Duffy and Dan Goodgame write that "contrary to their public rhetoric, Bush and his top aides were keenly sensitive to opinion surveys and news coverage. . . . Bush and [White House chief of staff John] Sununu frequently consulted a chart entitled 'Comparative Presidential Job Approval,' which showed Bush's poll ratings month by month on a line, alongside lines that tracked the ratings of Presidents Reagan, Carter, Ford, and Nixon." National Security Adviser Brent Scowcroft told Duffy and Goodgame that Bush was "constantly popping into Press Secretary [Marlin] Fitzwater's office after a major presidential speech or action or (more likely) reaction to ask 'How are the overnights, Marlin?'—meaning 'How is it playing?'" (75, 77). In the aftermath of the coup embarrassment, Admiral William Crowe, the outgoing chairman of the Joint Chiefs of Staff, concluded that a U.S. invasion was a question of "when" rather than "if" (von Hippel, *Democracy by Force*, 33).

67. Quayle, *Standing Firm*, 142; Stiner quoted in Donnelly et al., *Operation Just Cause*, 61; Baker, *The Politics of Diplomacy*, 187. One administration official later characterized Bush's postcoup determination to launch an invasion "a decision in search of an excuse" (Smith, *Talons of the Eagle*, 1st ed., 273).

68. Buckley, *Panama*, 223; Weeks and Gunson, *Panama: Made in the USA*, 15; Kempe, "The Panama Debacle," 17; Independent Commission of Inquiry on the U.S. Invasion of Panama, *The U.S. Invasion of Panama: The Truth Behind Operation "Just Cause"* (Boston: South End Press, 1991), 24; Council on Hemispheric Affairs (COHA) report, quoted in Eldon Kenworthy, "Panama as Media Event," *LASA Forum* (newsletter of the Latin American Studies Association), 21, no. 2 (Summer 1990): 15; Donnelly et al., *Operation Just Cause*, 49–50; Woodward, *The Commanders*, 111, 116; Scranton, *The Noriega Years*, 38–39, 196, 200.

69. Duffy and Goodgame, *Marching in Place*, 189; Kourous, "Bush v. Noriega," 188–190; Pfaff quoted in St. Malo and Harris, *The Panamanian Problem*, 243; Gephardt quoted in David Mervin, *George Bush and the Guardianship Presidency* (New York: St. Martin's, 1996), 172.

70. Robert W. Tucker and David C. Hendrickson, *The Imperial Temptation: The New World Order and America's Purpose* (New York: Council on Foreign Relations, 1992), 4–8, 24–27, 40–41, 87.

71. Kempe, *Divorcing the Dictator*, 34; Kourous, "Bush v. Noriega," 190–194, 254–256; Charles William Maynes, "Coping With the '90s," *Foreign Policy* 74 (Spring 1989): 42–43, as quoted in Kourous, "Bush v. Noriega," 193–194; Perry, *Eclipse*, 273–274; Powell, *My*

American Journey, 644; *New York Times*, 21 December 1989, A31; Donnelly et al., *Operation Just Cause*, 96–97. According to Bush presidential historian John Robert Greene, James Baker later stated "that one of the most important results of the Panama invasion was to show the world that the United States was not afraid to act unilaterally ('the surest test of a great power')" (John Robert Greene, *The Presidency of George Bush* [Lawrence: University Press of Kansas, 2000], 106).

72. Buckley, *Panama*, 225–226; St. Malo and Harris, *The Panamanian Problem*, 245–246; Scranton, *The Noriega Years*, 197. The Bush administration subsequently justified the U.S. invasion in part by using these Panamanian pronouncements as evidence that Noriega's government had declared war on the United States (Buckley, *Panama*, 231). Noriega tells a different story. In *America's Prisoner: The Memoirs of Manuel Noriega* (New York: Random House, 1997), he writes that on December 15, 1989, "I said that a state of war existed because we were under siege, but it was not a declaration of war. . . . We were living in a state of war—with constant provocation by the Americans, constant threats. . . . My words were twisted by the Bush administration, which was looking for as much justification as it could find to invade Panama. . . . The speech was seized upon by the United States, which made the absurd claim that I was declaring war" (167).

73. Buckley, *Panama*, 226–229; Scranton, *The Noriega Years*, 198–200; Kempe, *Divorcing the Dictator*, 8–10; St. Malo and Harris, *The Panamanian Problem*, 246–248; John G. Roos, "Did President Bush Jump the Gun in Ordering the Invasion of Panama?" *Armed Forces Journal International*, September 1992, 10–14; Murillo, *The Noriega Mess*, 771–772; Weeks and Gunson, *Panama: Made in the USA*, 16. According to Bob Woodward, the JCS staff at the Pentagon knew "that the Paz incident wasn't a clear-cut incident of unprovoked PDF aggression—the car had sped away from a legitimate roadblock, lending an element of ambiguity" (Woodward, *The Commanders*, 132). Brent Scowcroft also later characterized the Paz killing and abuse of the Navy couple as "the excuse" for the invasion (Greene, *The Presidency of George Bush*, 105).

74. Kempe, *Divorcing the Dictator*, 10–24, 398–417; Buckley, *Panama*, 229–232, 238–254; Dinges, *Our Man in Panama*, 300–314; *New York Times*, 10 April 1992, A1, 11 July 1992, A1.

75. Westrick, "Empire by Invitation," 106–107; Scranton, *The Noriega Years*, 203; Buckley, *Panama*, 234.

76. Buckley, *Panama*, 230; Kempe, *Divorcing the Dictator*, 11–12; Dinges, *Our Man in Panama*, 308; Scranton, *The Noriega Years*, 202–203; *New York Times*, 21 December 1989, A31; Independent Commission of Inquiry on the U.S. Invasion of Panama, *The U.S. Invasion of Panama*, 26, 28; Weeks and Gunson, *Panama: Made in the USA*, 9–10; Woodward, *The Commanders*, 152.

77. Scranton, *The Noriega Years*, 208, 223–224; Kempe, *Divorcing the Dictator*, xxvi–xxviii; Weeks and Gunson, *Panama: Made in the USA*, 104; *Wall Street Journal*, 3 August 1994, A1.

78. Kourous, "Bush v. Noriega," 269.

79. Ibid., 10, 230, 235, 269; Conniff, *Panama and the United States*, 162; Perry, *Eclipse*, 294; Parmet, *George Bush*, 419; *Wall Street Journal*, 21 December 1989, A20; Powell, *An American Journey*, 658; *New York Times*, 21 December 1989, A1, as quoted in Kourous, "Bush v. Noriega," 251; Jack Germond and Jules Witcover, "After Panama, Goodbye to the Bush Wimp Image," *Boston Globe*, 6 January 1990, 19, quoted in Parmet, *George Bush*, 419.

80. *Boston Globe*, 22 December 1989, 3.

Conclusion

1. Fredrick Pike, "Corporatism and Latin American–United States Relations," in *The New Corporatism: Social-Political Structures in the Iberian World,* ed. Fredrick Pike and Thomas Stritch (Notre Dame, IN, and London: University of Notre Dame Press, 1974), 139.

2. WGBH (Boston), "The Yankee Years," Public Broadcasting System (PBS) documentary, *Crisis in Central America,* pt. 1, produced in association with the Blackwell Corporation (Wilmette, IL: Films Incorporated, 1985), videorecording.

3. Christopher Andrew and Vasili Mitrokhin, *The World Was Going Our Way: The KGB and the Battle for the Third World* (New York: Basic, 2005), 72; Robert Alexander, *The Tragedy of Chile* (Westport, CT: Greenwood, 1978), 212.

4. Andrew and Mitrokhin, *The World Was Going Our Way,* 121.

5. Alan McPherson, "Misled by Himself: What the Johnson Tapes Reveal about the Dominican Intervention of 1965," *Latin American Research Review* 38, no. 2 (2003): 127–128.

6. Several of the leftist leaders who became targets of U.S. intervention traveled to Washington, DC, in ostensible efforts to reduce discord or—more likely—to neutralize U.S. suspicions while they consolidated their revolutions at home. Fidel Castro visited the U.S. capital in April 1959 to offer assurances to U.S. officials and the U.S. public that he was not a communist. Cheddi Jagan arrived in October 1961 to solicit large-scale U.S. economic assistance for British Guiana. A high-level Sandinista delegation headed by Daniel Ortega requested, and received, a White House meeting with President Carter in September 1979 to discuss future relations between the two countries. Maurice Bishop traveled to DC in June 1983 in an attempt to reduce the rapidly escalating tensions in U.S.-Grenadian relations. None of these visits, however, allayed U.S. doubts about the ideological and international leanings of the visitors or prevented eventual intervention. At the time of Castro's visit, the Eisenhower administration was prepared to co-opt the Cuban revolutionary with U.S. foreign aid, but Fidel chose to maintain his international independence during the trip by refusing to make any aid requests. The announcement a month later of the revolution's agrarian-reform program, together with the anti-U.S. invective that continued to pervade Castro's public rhetoric, effectively derailed any subsequent prospects for harmonious relations. (See Richard E. Welch, *Response to Revolution: The United States and the Cuban Revolution, 1959–1961* [Chapel Hill: University of North Carolina Press, 1985], 34–36; and Chapter 2 above.) Jagan's U.S. visit ended disastrously when the Guianese leader's suspicion-raising comments about Marxism led President Kennedy to conclude that intervention was warranted. (See Chapter 3 above.) In response to Daniel Ortega's blunt demands for "unconditional" U.S. economic assistance, Carter expressed a willingness to increase U.S. aid to Nicaragua in return for the Sandinistas' commitment to democracy, human rights, international nonalignment, and noninterference in the internal affairs of their Central American neighbors. Subsequent U.S. aid disbursements—and prospects for a civil relationship—ended when the Sandinistas proved unwilling to terminate their covert support for the Farabundo Martí National Liberation Front in neighboring El Salvador (Robert Pastor, *Condemned to Repetition: The United States and Nicaragua* [Princeton, NJ: Princeton University Press, 1987], 206–207, 223–228). Reagan administration representatives responded to Bishop's assurances that Grenada posed no threat to U.S. national security by informing him that actions spoke louder than words and that improved relations would come only after Grenada had distanced itself from the Soviet Union and Cuba. In

the end, Bishop's attempted rapprochement proved doubly disastrous for him: it not only failed to reduce the Reagan administration's hostility but at the same time also fueled growing opposition to Bishop within the New Jewel Movement's hardline Leninist faction, which sharply criticized him for compromising the Grenadian revolution's international integrity. (See Chapter 7 above.)

7. Stephen Van Evera, "The United States and the Third World: When to Intervene," in *Eagle in a New World: American Grand Strategy in the Post–Cold War Era*, ed. Kenneth A. Oye, Robert J. Lieber, and Donald Rothchild (New York: HarperCollins, 1992), 114; Robert J. McMahon, "Credibility and World Power: Exploring the Psychological Dimension in Postwar American Diplomacy," *Diplomatic History* 15, no. 4 (Fall 1991): 455–457, 465–466; Robert H. Johnson, *Improbable Dangers: U.S. Conceptions of Threat in the Cold War and After* (New York: St. Martin's, 1994), 142–143; Lars Schoultz, *National Security and United States Policy toward Latin America* (Princeton, NJ: Princeton University Press, 1987), 270–278.

8. McMahon, "Credibility and World Power," 456, 466, 471; Richard J. Barnet, *Intervention and Revolution*, rev. ed. (New York: New American Library, 1972), 254–255.

9. Robert C. McFarlane (with Zofia Smardz), *Special Trust* (New York: Cadell & Davies, 1994), 261–262.

10. McMahon, "Credibility and World Power," 460.

11. Johnson, *Improbable Dangers*, 132.

12. The presence of Fidel Castro had a powerful influence on every U.S. intervention after Guatemala. Following the failure of the 1961 intervention in Cuba, it was the politics-and-credibility-driven fear of a "second Cuba in the hemisphere" that propelled U.S. presidents into action in the next five cases (British Guiana, the Dominican Republic, Chile, Nicaragua, and Grenada). For Kennedy, Johnson, and Nixon, the electoral consequences of allowing a second Cuba to materialize "on their watch" exercised a predominant influence, while for Reagan the principal goal was to strengthen U.S. credibility by preventing the "Moscow-Havana Axis" from transforming Nicaragua, El Salvador, or Grenada into new Cuban-style bases of hemispheric subversion. Even in Panama—hardly a second Cuba in formation—Bush's initial hesitancy to attack Noriega stemmed from his reluctance to risk a repeat of Kennedy's Bay of Pigs humiliation early in his presidency.

13. Kennedy campaign adviser Pat Frank quoted in Steven M. George, "Anatomy of Fiasco: How President Kennedy Let Politics Provoke the Bay of Pigs Disaster" (master's thesis, Ohio University, Department of History, 2005), 33.

14. Piero Gleijeses, "Ships in the Night: The CIA, the White House and the Bay of Pigs," *Journal of Latin American Studies* 27, no. 1 (February 1995): 25.

15. Dan Quayle, *Standing Firm: A Vice-Presidential Memoir* (New York: HarperCollins, 1994), 141.

16. *New York Times*, 18 September 1994, E4–E5. After resigning as Reagan's secretary of state, Alexander Haig publicly criticized the "impulse" within the administration "to view the Presidency as a public relations opportunity and to regard Government as a campaign for re-election" (*Time*, 9 April 1984, 67). Admiral William Crowe Jr., the chairman of the Joint Chiefs of Staff in the Bush administration, later told Bob Woodward that he had been appalled at how "much of the discussion at [Bush's] National Security Council meetings was political. Decisions were made based on their likely impact on the Congress, the media and public opinion, and the focus was on managing the reaction. Crowe had serious doubts that these should be the main criteria for military and foreign-policy decisions" (Woodward, *The Commanders* [New York: Pocket, 1991], 50).

17. Alexander Butterfield, quoted in Stanley I. Kutler, *The Wars of Watergate: The Last Crisis of Richard Nixon* (New York: Knopf, 1990), 87.

18. Lyndon Baines Johnson, *The Vantage Point: Perspectives of the Presidency, 1963–1969* (New York: Holt, Rinehart & Winston, 1971), 22.

19. Johnson, *Improbable Dangers*, 194.

20. Karabell, *Architects of Intervention: The United States, the Third World, and the Cold War, 1946–1962* (Baton Rouge: Louisiana State University Press, 1999), 123.

21. Stephen Schlesinger and Stephen Kinzer, *Bitter Fruit: The Untold Story of the American Coup in Guatemala* (New York: Doubleday, 1982), 31, 42, 122–123.

22. Karabell, *Architects of Intervention*, 7–8.

Essential Sources

U.S. International Credibility (General/Conceptual)

Johnson, Robert H. *Improbable Dangers: U.S. Conceptions of Threat in the Cold War and After.* New York: St. Martin's, 1994.

McMahon, Robert J. "Credibility and World Power: Exploring the Psychological Dimension in Postwar American Diplomacy." *Diplomatic History* 15, no. 4 (Fall 1991): 455–471.

Schoultz, Lars. *National Security and United States Policy toward Latin America.* Princeton, NJ: Princeton University Press, 1987.

Domestic Politics and U.S. Foreign Policy (General/Conceptual)

Destler, I. M., Leslie H. Gelb, and Anthony Lake. "Presidents: The Triumph of Politics." In *Our Own Worst Enemy: The Unmaking of American Foreign Policy.* New York: Simon & Schuster, 1984: 33–87.

Levering, Ralph B. "Is Domestic Politics Being Slighted as an Interpretive Framework?" *Newsletter of the Society for Historians of American Foreign Relations (SHAFR)*, March 1994, 17–35.

Logevall, Fredrik. "Party Politics." In *Encyclopedia of American Foreign Policy*, edited by Alexander DeConde, Richard Dean Burns, and Fredrik Logevall. 2nd ed. New York: Charles Scribner's Sons, 2002: 99–111.

Small, Melvin. *Democracy & Diplomacy: The Impact of Domestic Politics on U.S. Foreign Policy, 1789–1994.* Baltimore: Johns Hopkins University Press, 1996.

Latin American Influence on U.S. Foreign Policy (General/Conceptual)

Friedman, Max Paul. "Retiring the Puppets, Bringing Latin America Back In: Recent Scholarship on United States–Latin American Relations." *Diplomatic History* 27, no. 5 (November 2003): 621–636.

Karabell, Zachary. *Architects of Intervention: The United States, the Third World, and the Cold War, 1946–1962.* Baton Rouge: Louisiana State University Press, 1999.

Pike, Fredrick. "Corporatism and Latin American–United States Relations." In *The New Corporatism: Social-Political Structures in the Iberian World*, edited by Fredrick Pike and Thomas Stritch. Notre Dame, IN: University of Notre Dame Press, 1974: 132–170.

Smith, Tony. "New Bottles for New Wine: A Pericentric Framework for the Study of the Cold War." *Diplomatic History* 24, no. 4 (Fall 2000): 567–591.

Guatemala, 1954

Cook, Blanche Wiesen. *The Declassified Eisenhower: A Divided Legacy.* Garden City, NY: Doubleday, 1981.

Cullather, Nick. *Secret History: The CIA's Classified Account of Its Operations in Guatemala, 1952–1954.* Stanford, CA: Stanford University Press, 1999.

Gleijeses, Piero. *Shattered Hope: The Guatemalan Revolution and the United States, 1944–1954.* Princeton, NJ: Princeton University Press, 1991.

Immerman, Richard H. *The CIA in Guatemala: The Foreign Policy of Intervention.* Austin: University of Texas Press, 1982.

Rabe, Stephen G. *Eisenhower and Latin America: The Foreign Policy of Anticommunism.* Chapel Hill: University of North Carolina Press, 1988.

Schlesinger, Stephen, and Stephen Kinzer. *Bitter Fruit: The Untold Story of the American Coup in Guatemala.* New York: Doubleday, 1984.

Scott, Harold A. "Dismantling the Good Neighbor: Domestic Politics and the Overthrow of the Guatemalan Revolution." University of Pittsburgh, Graduate School of Public and International Affairs, 1998. Photocopy.

———. "Covert Operations as an Instrument of Foreign Policy: U.S. Intervention in Iran and Guatemala." Ph.D. diss., Carnegie Mellon University, 1999.

U.S. Department of State. *Foreign Relations of the United States, 1952–1954.* Vol. 4, *The American Republics.* Washington, DC: Government Printing Office, 1976.`

———. *Foreign Relations of the United States, 1952–1954: Guatemala Supplement.* Washington, DC: Government Printing Office, 2003.

Cuba, 1961

Beck, Kent M. "Necessary Lies, Hidden Truths: Cuba in the 1960 Campaign." *Diplomatic History* 8, no. 1 (Winter 1984): 37–59.

Benjamin, Jules R. *The United States and the Origins of the Cuban Revolution: An Empire of Liberty in the Age of National Liberation.* Princeton, NJ: Princeton University Press, 1990.

Blight, James G., and Peter Kornbluh, eds. *Politics of Illusion: The Bay of Pigs Invasion Reexamined.* Boulder, CO: Lynne Rienner, 1998.

Bonsal, Philip W. *Cuba, Castro, and the United States.* Pittsburgh, PA: University of Pittsburgh Press, 1971.

Fursenko, Aleksandr, and Timothy Naftali. *"One Hell of a Gamble": Khrushchev, Kennedy, and Castro.* New York: W. W. Norton, 1997.

Gleijeses, Piero. "Ships in the Night: The CIA, the White House and the Bay of Pigs." *Journal of Latin American Studies* 27, no. 1 (February 1995): 1–42.

Higgins, Trumbell. *The Perfect Failure: Kennedy, Eisenhower, and the CIA at the Bay of Pigs.* New York: W. W. Norton, 1989.

Kornbluh, Peter, ed. *Bay of Pigs Declassified: The Secret CIA Report on the Invasion of Cuba.* New York: Free Press, 1998.

Morley, Morris H. *Imperial State and Revolution: The United States and Cuba, 1952–1986.* New York: Cambridge, 1987.

Paterson, Thomas C. "Fixation with Cuba: The Bay of Pigs, Missile Crisis, and Covert War against Fidel Castro." In *Kennedy's Quest for Victory: American Foreign Policy, 1961–1963,* edited by Thomas C. Paterson. New York: Oxford, 1989.

———. *Contesting Castro: The United States and the Triumph of the Cuban Revolution.* New York: Oxford, 1994.

Smith, Wayne S. "Castro's Cuba: Soviet Partner or Nonaligned?" Latin American Program Working Paper. Washington, DC: Woodrow Wilson International Center for Scholars, 1984.

U.S. Department of State. *Foreign Relations of the United States, 1958–1960.* Vol. 6, *Cuba.* Washington, DC: Government Printing Office, 1991.

————. *Foreign Relations of the United States, 1961–1963.* Vol. 10, *Cuba, 1961–1962.* Washington, DC: Government Printing Office, 1997.

Welch, Richard E. *Response to Revolution: The United States and the Cuban Revolution, 1959–1961.* Chapel Hill: University of North Carolina Press, 1985.

Wyden, Peter. *Bay of Pigs: The Untold Story.* New York: Simon & Schuster, 1979.

British Guiana, 1963

Ashton, Nigel. *Kennedy, Macmillan and the Cold War: The Irony of Interdependence.* New York: Palgrave Macmillan, 2002.

Fraser, Cary. *Ambivalent Anti-colonialism: The United States and the Genesis of West Indian Independence, 1940–1964.* Westport, CT: Greenwood, 1994.

Jagan, Cheddi. *The West on Trial: The Fight for Guyana's Freedom.* New York: International, 1972.

Kaufman, Victor. "Domestic Politics as a Catalyst for United States Intervention in the Caribbean: The Case of British Guiana." *Journal of Caribbean History* 30 (1996): 107–131.

Prados, John. *Safe for Democracy: The Secret Wars of the CIA,* chap. 1. Chicago: Ivan R. Dee, 2006.

Rabe, Stephen G. *U.S. Intervention in British Guiana: A Cold War Story.* Chapel Hill: University of North Carolina Press, 2005.

Radosh, Ronald. *American Labor and United States Foreign Policy.* New York: Random House, 1969.

Reno, Philip. *The Ordeal of British Guiana.* New York: Monthly Review Press, 1964.

Schlesinger, Arthur M., Jr. *A Thousand Days: John F. Kennedy in the White House.* Boston: Houghton Mifflin, 1965.

Sillery, Jane L. "Salvaging Democracy? The United States and Britain in British Guiana, 1961–1964." Ph.D. diss., Oxford University, 1996.

Spinner, Thomas J., Jr. *A Political and Social History of Guyana, 1945–1983.* Boulder, CO: Westview, 1984.

"Tale of Two Books." *Nation,* 4 June 1990, 763–764.

U.S. Department of State. *Foreign Relations of the United States, 1961–1963.* Vol. 12, *American Republics.* Washington, DC: Government Printing Office, 1996.

Waters, Robert, and Gordon Daniels. "The World's Longest General Strike: The AFL-CIO, the CIA, and British Guiana." *Diplomatic History* 29, no. 2 (April 2005): 279–307.

Dominican Republic, 1965

Beschloss, Michael. *Reaching for Glory: Lyndon Johnson's Secret White House Tapes, 1964–1965.* New York: Simon & Schuster, 2001.

Bosch, Juan. "A Tale of Two Nations." *New Leader,* 21 June 1965: 3–7.

Draper, Theodore. *The Dominican Revolt: A Case Study in American Foreign Policy.* New York: Commentary, 1968.

Felten, Peter. "The 1965–1966 United States Intervention in the Dominican Republic." Ph.D. diss., University of Texas at Austin, 1995.

Geyelin, Philip. *Lyndon B. Johnson and the World*. New York: Frederick A. Praeger, 1966.

Gleijeses, Piero. *The Dominican Crisis: The 1965 Constitutionalist Revolt and American Intervention*. Baltimore: Johns Hopkins University Press, 1978.

Lowenthal, Abraham F. *The Dominican Intervention*. Cambridge, MA: Harvard University Press, 1972.

Lyndon Baines Johnson Library Recordings and Transcripts of Conversations and Meetings: Transcripts and Sound Recordings of Telephone Conversations—White House Series. Austin, TX: Lyndon Baines Johnson Library, 1996–.

Martin, John Bartlow. *Overtaken by Events: The Dominican Crisis—From the Fall of Trujillo to the Civil War*. Garden City, NJ: Doubleday, 1966.

McPherson, Alan. "Misled by Himself: What the Johnson Tapes Reveal about the Dominican Intervention of 1965." *Latin American Research Review* 38, no. 2 (2003): 127–146.

Palmer, Bruce, Jr. *Intervention in the Caribbean: The Dominican Crisis of 1965*. Lexington: University of Kentucky Press, 1989.

Slater, Jerome. *Intervention and Negotiation: The United States and the Dominican Revolution*. New York: Harper & Row, 1970.

Szulc, Tad. *Dominican Diary*. New York: Delacourt, 1965.

U.S. Department of State. *Foreign Relations of the United States, 1964–1968*. Vol. 32: *Dominican Republic; Cuba; Haiti; Guyana*. Washington, DC: Government Printing Office, 2005.

Chile, 1970

Buckley, William F. "U.S. Policies in Chile under the Allende Government: An Interview with Former Ambassador Edward Korry." In *Chile: The Balanced View*, edited by Francisco Orrego Vicuña. Santiago, Chile: University of Chile, Institute of International Studies, 1975.

Gustafson, Kristian C. "CIA Machinations in Chile in 1970." *Studies in Intelligence* 47, no. 1, 2003, 35–50.

Hersh, Seymour M. *The Price of Power: Kissinger in the Nixon White House*. New York: Summit, 1983.

Jensen, Poul. *The Garotte: The United States and Chile, 1970–1973*. Aarhus, Denmark: Aarhus University Press, 1988.

Kissinger, Henry. *White House Years*. Boston: Little, Brown, 1979.

Kornbluh, Peter. *The Pinochet File: A Declassified Dossier on Atrocity and Accountability*. New York: New Press, 2003.

———. "The *El Mercurio* File: Secret Documents Shine New Light on How the CIA Used a Newspaper to Foment a Coup." *Columbia Journalism Review*, September–October 2003, 14–19.

Korry, Edward M. "The Sell-Out of Chile and the American Taxpayer." *Penthouse*, March 1978.

———. "The USA-in-Chile and Chile-in-USA: A Full Retrospective Political and Economic View (1963–1975)." *Estudios Públicos* (Centro de Estudios Públicos, Santiago, Chile), vol. 72 (1998). www.cepchile.cl/dms/archivo_1145_314/rev72_korryconf_ing.pdf.

———. "Chile in the Archives of the USA (1970): Documents from the Archives of Former U.S. Ambassador to Chile Edward M. Korry (1967–1971)." *Estudios Públicos* (Centro de Estudios Públicos, Santiago, Chile), no. 72 (1998). www.cepchile.cl/dms/archivo_1147_316/rev72_korrydocing.pdf.

National Security Archive Electronic Briefing Book, no. 8. *Chile and the United States: Declassified Documents Relating to the Military Coup, 1970–1976.* www.gwu.edu/~nsarchiv/NSAEBB/NSAEBB8/nsaebb8.html.

Petras, James, and Morris Morley. *The United States and Chile: Imperialism and the Overthrow of the Allende Government.* New York: Monthly Review Press, 1975.

Sigmund, Paul E. *The Overthrow of Allende and the Politics of Chile, 1964–1976.* Pittsburgh, PA: University of Pittsburgh Press, 1977.

———. *The United States and Democracy in Chile.* Baltimore: Johns Hopkins University Press, 1993.

Uribe, Armando. *The Black Book of American Intervention in Chile.* Boston: Beacon, 1975.

U.S. House of Representatives. *United States and Chile during the Allende Years, 1970–1973: Hearings before the Subcommittee on Inter-American Affairs of the Committee on Foreign Affairs, July 1, 1971–September 18, 1974,* 94th Cong., 1st sess. Washington, DC: Government Printing Office, 1976.

U.S. Senate, Committee on Foreign Relations, Subcommittee on Multinational Corporations. *Multinational Corporations and United States Foreign Policy: Hearings on the International Telephone and Telegraph Company and Chile, 1970–71.* 93rd Cong., 1st sess., March 20–April 2, 1973.

U.S. Senate, Select Committee on Intelligence Activities. *Covert Action in Chile, 1963–1973: Staff Report.* 94th Cong., 1st sess. Washington, DC: Government Printing Office, 1975.

———. *Intelligence Activities: Hearings before the Select Committee to Study Governmental Operations with Respect to Intelligence Activities.* Vol. 7: *Covert Action.* 94th Cong., 1st sess. Washington, DC: Government Printing Office, 1976.

U.S. Senate, Select Committee to Study Governmental Operations with Respect to Intelligence Activities. *Alleged Assassination Plots Involving Foreign Leaders: An Interim Report.* Washington, DC: Government Printing Office, 1975.

Nicaragua, 1981

Armony, Ariel C. *Argentina, the United States, and the Anti-communist Crusade in Central America, 1977–1984.* Athens: Ohio University, Center for International Studies, 1997.

Gutman, Roy. *Banana Diplomacy: The Making of American Policy in Nicaragua, 1981–1987.* New York: Simon & Schuster, 1988.

Haig, Alexander, Jr. *Caveat: Realism, Reagan, and Foreign Policy.* New York: Macmillan, 1984.

Kagan, Robert. *A Twilight Struggle: American Power and Nicaragua, 1977–1990.* New York: Free Press, 1996.

Kornbluh, Peter. *Nicaragua: The Price of Intervention.* Washington, DC: Institute for Policy Studies, 1987.

LeoGrande, William M. *Our Own Backyard: The United States in Central America, 1977–1992.* Chapel Hill: University of North Carolina Press, 1998.

Moreno, Dario. *U.S. Policy in Central America: The Endless Debate.* Miami: Florida International University Press, 1990.

Morley, Morris H. *Washington, Somoza, and the Sandinistas: State and Regime in U.S. Policy toward Nicaragua, 1969–1981.* New York: Cambridge University Press, 1994.

Pastor, Robert. *Condemned to Repetition: The United States and Nicaragua.* Princeton, NJ: Princeton University Press, 1988.

National Security Archive. *Nicaragua: The Making of U.S. Policy.* Alexandria, VA: Chadwyck-Healey, 1991. Microfiche.

Sklar, Holly. *Washington's War on Nicaragua.* Boston: South End Press, 1988.

Woodward, Bob. *Veil: The Secret Wars of the CIA, 1981–1987.* New York: Pocket Books, 1987.

Grenada, 1983

Beck, Robert J. *The Grenada Invasion: Politics, Law, and Foreign Policy Decisionmaking.* Boulder, CO: Westview, 1993.

Burrowes, Reynold A. *Revolution and Rescue in Grenada: An Account of the U.S.-Caribbean Invasion.* Westport, CT: Greenwood, 1988.

Dunn, Peter M., and Bruce W. Watson, eds. *American Intervention in Grenada: The Implications of Operation "Urgent Fury."* Boulder, CO: Westview, 1985.

Kenworthy, Eldon. "Grenada as Theater." *World Policy Journal* 1, no. 3 (1984): 635–651.

Kryzanek, Michael J. "The Grenada Invasion: Approaches to Understanding." In *United States Policy in Latin America: A Decade of Crisis and Challenge,* edited by John D. Martz. Lincoln: University of Nebraska Press, 1995: 58–79.

Ortiz, Frank V. "Letter to the Editor." *Atlantic* 253, no. 6 (June 1984): 7, 9, 12.

Pastor, Robert. "The United States and the Grenada Revolution: Who Pushed First and Why?" In *A Revolution Aborted: The Lessons of Grenada,* edited by Jorge Heine. Pittsburgh, PA: University of Pittsburgh Press, 1991: 181–214.

Payne, Anthony, Paul Sutton, and Tony Thorndike. *Grenada: Revolution and Invasion.* New York: St. Martin's Press, 1984.

Sandford, Gregory, and Richard Vigilante. *Grenada: The Untold Story.* Lanham, MD: Madison Books, 1984.

Schoenhals, Kai P., and Richard Melanson. *Revolution and Intervention in Grenada: The New Jewel Movement, the United States, and the Caribbean.* Boulder, CO: Westview, 1985.

Thorndike, Tony. *Grenada: Politics, Economics and Society.* London: Frances Pinter, 1985.

Valenta, Jiri, and Herbert J. Ellison, eds. *Grenada and Soviet/Cuban Policy: Internal Crisis and U.S./OECS Intervention.* Boulder, CO: Westview, 1986.

Williams, Gary. "Prelude to an Intervention: Grenada 1983." *Journal of Latin American Studies* 29, no. 1 (February 1997): 131–169.

Panama, 1989

Buckley, Kevin. *Panama: The Whole Story.* New York: Simon & Schuster, 1991.

Carothers, Thomas. *In the Name of Democracy: U.S. Policy toward Latin America in the Reagan Years.* Berkeley: University of California Press, 1991.

Conniff, Michael. *Panama and the United States: The Forced Alliance.* Athens: University of Georgia Press, 1992.

Dinges, John. *Our Man in Panama: The Shrewd Rise and Brutal Fall of Manuel Noriega.* New York: Random House, 1990.

Donnelly, Thomas, Margaret Roth, and Caleb Baker. *Operation Just Cause: The Storming of Panama.* New York: Lexington Books, 1991.

Independent Commission of Inquiry on the U.S. Invasion of Panama. *The U.S. Invasion of Panama: The Truth behind Operation "Just Cause."* Boston: South End Press, 1991.

Kempe, Frederick. *Divorcing the Dictator: America's Bungled Affair with Noriega.* New York: G. P. Putnam's Sons, 1990.

Kourous, George. "Bush v. Noriega: The Noriega Challenge to George Bush's Credibility and the 1989 Invasion of Panama." Master's thesis, Ohio University, Center for International Studies, 2000.

Loser, Eva, ed. *Conflict Resolution and Democratization in Panama: Implications for U.S. Policy.* Washington, DC: Center for Strategic and International Studies, 1991.

Murillo, Luis E. *The Noriega Mess: The Drugs, The Canal, and Why America Invaded.* Berkeley, CA: Video-Books, 1995.

Noriega, Manuel. *America's Prisoner: The Memoirs of Manuel Noriega.* New York: Random House, 1997.

Roos, John G. "Did President Bush Jump the Gun in Ordering the Invasion of Panama?" *Armed Forces Journal International,* September 1992, 10–14.

Ropp, Steve C. "The Bush Administration and the Invasion of Panama: Explaining the Choice and Timing of the Military Option." In *United States Policy in Latin America: A Decade of Crisis and Challenge,* edited by John D. Martz. Lincoln: University of Nebraska Press, 1995: 80–109.

Scranton, Margaret E. *The Noriega Years: U.S.-Panamanian Relations, 1981–1990.* Boulder, CO: Lynne Rienner, 1991.

St. Malo Arias, Guillermo de, and Godfrey Harris. *The Panamanian Problem: How the Reagan and Bush Administrations Dealt with the Noriega Regime.* Los Angeles: Americas Group, 1993.

Watson, Bruce W., and Peter G. Tsouras, eds. *Operation* Just Cause*: The U.S. Intervention in Panama.* Boulder, CO: Westview, 1990.

Weeks, John, and Phil Gunson. *Panama: Made in the USA.* London: Latin America Bureau, 1991.

Westrick, Janet. "Empire by Invitation: Operation 'Just Cause' and Panamanian Manipulation of U.S. Foreign Policy." Master's thesis, Ohio University, Department of History, 1997.

Woodward, Bob. *The Commanders.* New York: Simon & Schuster, 1991.